As one of the world's longest e
and best-known tra
Thomas Cook are the exper

For more than 1
guidebooks have unlocked
of destinations around the world,
sharing with travellers a wealth of
experience and a passion for travel.

**Rely on Thomas Cook as your
travelling companion on your next trip
and benefit from our unique heritage.**

Thomas Cook **driving** guides

WASHINGTON DC
VIRGINIA, MARYLAND & DELAWARE

**Tom Bross, Patricia Harris, David Lyon, Tim Nollen,
Barbara Radcliffe Rogers and Stillman D Rogers**

Your travelling companion since 1873

Thomas
Cook

Written and updated by Tom Bross, Patricia Harris, David Lyon, Tim Nollen, Barbara Radcliffe Rogers and Stillman D Rogers
Original photography by Ethel Davies

Published by Thomas Cook Publishing
A division of Thomas Cook Tour Operations Limited
Company registration no. 3772199 England
The Thomas Cook Business Park, Unit 9, Coningsby Road,
Peterborough PE3 8SB, United Kingdom
Email: books@thomascook.com, Tel: + 44 (0) 1733 416477
www.thomascookpublishing.com

Produced by Cambridge Publishing Management Limited
Burr Elm Court, Main Street, Caldecote CB23 7NU

ISBN: 978-1-84848-210-4

© 2006, 2008 Thomas Cook Publishing
This third edition © 2009
Text © Thomas Cook Publishing
Maps © Thomas Cook Publishing/PCGraphics (UK) Limited

Series Editor: Adam Royal
Production/DTP: Steven Collins

Printed and bound in India by Ajanta Offset & Packaging Ltd

Cover photography: © Blakeley/Alamy

All rights reserved. No part of this publication may be reproduced, stored in a retrieval system or transmitted, in any form or by any means: electronic, mechanical, recording or otherwise, in any part of the world, without the prior permission of the publisher. Requests for permission should be made to the publisher at the above address.

Although every care has been taken in compiling this publication, and the contents are believed to be correct at the time of printing, Thomas Cook Tour Operations Limited cannot accept responsibility for errors or omissions, however caused, or for changes in details given in the guidebook, or for the consequences of any reliance on the information provided. Descriptions and assessments are based on the authors' views and experiences when writing and do not necessarily represent those of Thomas Cook Tour Operations Limited.

About the authors and acknowledgements

Tim Nollen, who contributed the chapters on Washington DC and on northern and western Virginia to this book, is a Washingtonian by upbringing and schooling, with two degrees from Georgetown University and dozens of jaunts into the Shenandoah. He lived in Prague for much of the 1990s, where he worked in real estate and wrote three guidebooks about the vibrant towns and peoples of the Czech Republic, including *Culture Shock! Czech Republic*. This work expanded into full-time guidebook and newspaper writing on European destinations from Spain to Lithuania. Now back in the US (though living in New York), he has traded in his wanderlust for a more sedentary day job, and he writes on a part-time basis for Thomas Cook, contributing primarily to guides on East Coast destinations. Tim would like to thank the exceedingly helpful tourist offices throughout Virginia for their wealth of information, as well as Josh and Katie Nickerson and, as always, Andela Mala.

Barbara Radcliffe Rogers and **Stillman D Rogers** are the authors of more than a dozen books about places from New England to South Africa. Among their recent volumes are *The Adventure Guide to Maryland and the Chesapeake Bay* and *Baltimore & the Chesapeake Bay Alive!* For this book, they contributed the Maryland chapters. They wish to express their thanks to Larry Noto, Anne Mannix, Connie Yingling, Charles and Shirley Radcliffe and Corinna Metcalf.

Tom Bross contributed Canadian and New England chapters to previous Thomas Cook guidebooks. For this Drive Around volume, he covered central and eastern Virginia. He'd like to thank Julia Scott (Virginia Tourism Corp), Doretha Vaughan (Metro Richmond CVB), Patricia MacDonald (Williamsburg Area CVB), Debby Padgett (Jamestown-Yorktown Foundation), Susan Tipton (Northern Neck Tourism Council), Karen Hedelt (Fredericksburg Office of Economic Development and Tourism), Kelly Larkin (Norfolk CVB), Hester Waterfield (Virginia Beach Dept of Convention and Visitor Development), Rebecca Cutchins (Portsmouth CVB), Sam Martinette (Hampton CVB) and Suzanne Pearson (Newport News Tourism Development Office) for their help.

Patricia Harris and **David Lyon** are authors and contributors to several Thomas Cook guides on Canada, New England and Spain and write extensively on art, food and travel for a range of print and online media. For this volume, Pat and David contributed the introductory chapters as well as chapters on Pennsylvania and Delaware. They would like to thank Ellen Kornfield of the Philadelphia Convention and Visitors Bureau for her sage advice.

Contents

About driving guides — 6

Washington DC, Virginia, Maryland and Delaware at a glance — 8

Introduction — 10

Travel facts — 12

Driver's guide — 22

Getting to Washington DC, Virginia, Maryland and Delaware — 28

Setting the scene — 30

Highlights and touring itineraries — 38

● **Washington DC** — 40
The political powerhouse of the USA

● **Arlington and Alexandria** — 60
Colonial gentility and historic buildings

● **Northern Virginia** — 68
Civil War battlefields, rolling hills and fine inns

● **Shenandoah** — 76
The sublime beauty of the Blue Ridge Mountains and the fertile
Shenandoah Valley

● **The Piedmont** — 88
Small cities full of cultural delights

● **Richmond** — 100
The state capital with a rich and turbulent history

● **Richmond battlefields** — 112
Visit the site of battles that tore the emerging American nation
apart

● **Fredericksburg area** — 120
Prosperous former tobacco-trading port and George
Washington's childhood home

● **Tidewater** — 128
The tidal creeks, inlets, bays and coves of Virginia's coastal plain

● **Virginia's historic triangle** — 136
History preserved and brought to life at Jamestown, Yorktown
and Williamsburg

● **Hampton Roads** _____ 146
Surf-washed beaches and oceanside boardwalks

● **Baltimore** _____ 156
Transformed docks filled with museums, shops and places to
have fun

● **Annapolis** _____ 170
The home of the US Naval Academy

● **Eastern Shore** _____ 180
Barrier islands with beaches, dunes and wild horses

● **Rockville to Frederick** _____ 190
The historic C&O canal and the Great Falls of the Potomac

● **Western Maryland and borderlands** _____ 198
Battlefield sites and rolling mountain roads

● **Southern Maryland** _____ 208
Escape from the crowds in this land of fishermen and shoreside
parks

● **North Chesapeake Bay** _____ 218
Tidal estuaries and pleasure boats

● **Ocean City and Delaware Shore** _____ 226
Barrier islands, boardwalks, birds and seaside fun

● **Wilmington** _____ 236
A city rich in art, museums and history

● **Brandywine Valley** _____ 244
Colonial towns, antiques and lush countryside

● **Philadelphia** _____ 252
The bustling, artistic 'City of Brotherly Love'

● **Valley Forge to Gettysburg** _____ 266
Venerated sites associated with America's traumatic wars

Capital speak   280
Index   281
Notes   285
Feedback form   287

About driving guides

Thomas Cook's driving guides are designed to provide you with a comprehensive but flexible reference source to guide you as you tour a country or region by car. This guide divides Washington DC, Virginia, Maryland and Delaware into touring areas – one per chapter. Major cultural centres or cities form chapters in their own right. Each chapter contains enough attractions to provide at least a day's worth of activities – often more.

Star ratings

To make it easier for you to plan your time and decide what to see, every sight and attraction is given a star rating. A three-star rating indicates a major attraction, worth at least half a day of your time. A two-star attraction is worth an hour or so of your time, and a one-star attraction indicates a site that is worth visiting, but often of specialist interest. To help you further, individual attractions within towns or theme parks are also graded, so that travellers with limited time can quickly find the most rewarding sights.

Chapter contents

Every chapter has an introduction summing up the main attractions of the area or town, and a ratings box, which will highlight its appeal – some places may be more attractive to families travelling with children, others to wine-lovers visiting vineyards, and others to people interested in finding castles, churches, nature reserves or good beaches.

Each chapter is then divided into an alphabetical gazetteer, and a suggested tour or walk. You can select whether you just want to visit a particular sight or attraction, choosing from those described in the gazetteer, or whether you want to tour the area comprehensively. If the latter, you can construct your own itinerary, or follow the author's suggested tour, which comes at the end of every area chapter.

The gazetteer

The gazetteer section describes all the major attractions in the area – the villages, towns, historic sites, nature reserves, parks or museums that you are most likely to want to see. Maps of the area highlight all the places mentioned in the text. Using this comprehensive overview of the area, you may choose just to visit one or two sights.

One way to use the guide is simply to find individual sights that interest you, using the index, overview map or star ratings, and read what our authors have to say about them. This will help you decide

Symbol Key

- **Tourist Information Centre**
- **Advice on arriving or departing**
- **Parking locations**
- **Advice on getting around**
- **Directions**
- **Sights and attractions**
- **Accommodation**
- **Eating**
- **Shopping**
- **Sport**
- **Entertainment**

Practical information

The practical information in the page margins, or sidebar, will help you locate the services you need as an independent traveller – including the tourist information centre, car parks and public transport facilities. You will also find the opening times of sights, museums, churches and other attractions, as well as useful tips on shopping, market days, cultural events, entertainment, festivals and sports facilities.

whether to visit the sight. If you do, you will find plenty of practical information, such as the street address, the telephone number for enquiries and opening times.

Alternatively, you can choose a hotel, with the help of the accommodation recommendations contained in this guide. You can then turn to the overall map on pages 10–11 to help you work out which chapters in the book describe the cities and regions closest to your touring base.

Driving tours

The suggested tour is just that – a suggestion, with plenty of optional detours and one or two ideas for making your own discoveries, under the heading *Also worth exploring*. The routes are designed to link the attractions described in the gazetteer section, and to cover outstandingly scenic coastal, mountain and rural landscapes. The total distance is given for each tour, and the time it will take you to drive the complete route, but bear in mind that this indication is just for driving time: you will need to add on extra time for visiting attractions along the way.

Many of the routes are circular, so that you can join them at any point. Where the nature of the terrain dictates that the route has to be linear, the route can either be followed out and back, or you can use it as a link route, to get from one area in the book to another.

As you follow the route descriptions, you will find names picked out in bold capital letters – this means that the place is described fully in the gazetteer. Other names picked out in bold indicate additional villages or attractions worth a brief stop along the route.

Accommodation and food

In every chapter you will find lodging and eating recommendations for individual towns, or for the area as a whole. These are designed to cover a range of price brackets and concentrate on more characterful small or individualistic hotels and restaurants. In addition, you will find information in the *Travel Facts* chapter on chain hotels, with an address to which you can write for a guide, map or directory.

The price indications used in the guide have the following meanings:

$ budget level
$$ typical/average prices
$$$ de luxe

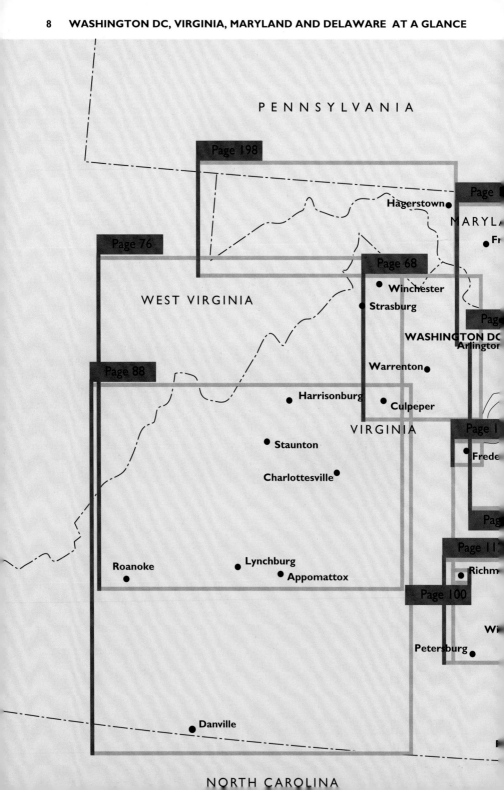

PENNSYLVANIA

Page 198

Hagerstown

MARYLA

Fr

Page 76

Page 68

WEST VIRGINIA

Winchester

Strasburg

Page

WASHINGTON DC

Arlington

Page 88

Warrenton

Harrisonburg

Culpeper

VIRGINIA

Page

Staunton

Frede

Charlottesville

Pag

Page 11

Roanoke

Lynchburg

Richm

Appomattox

Page 100

Wi

Petersburg

Danville

NORTH CAROLINA

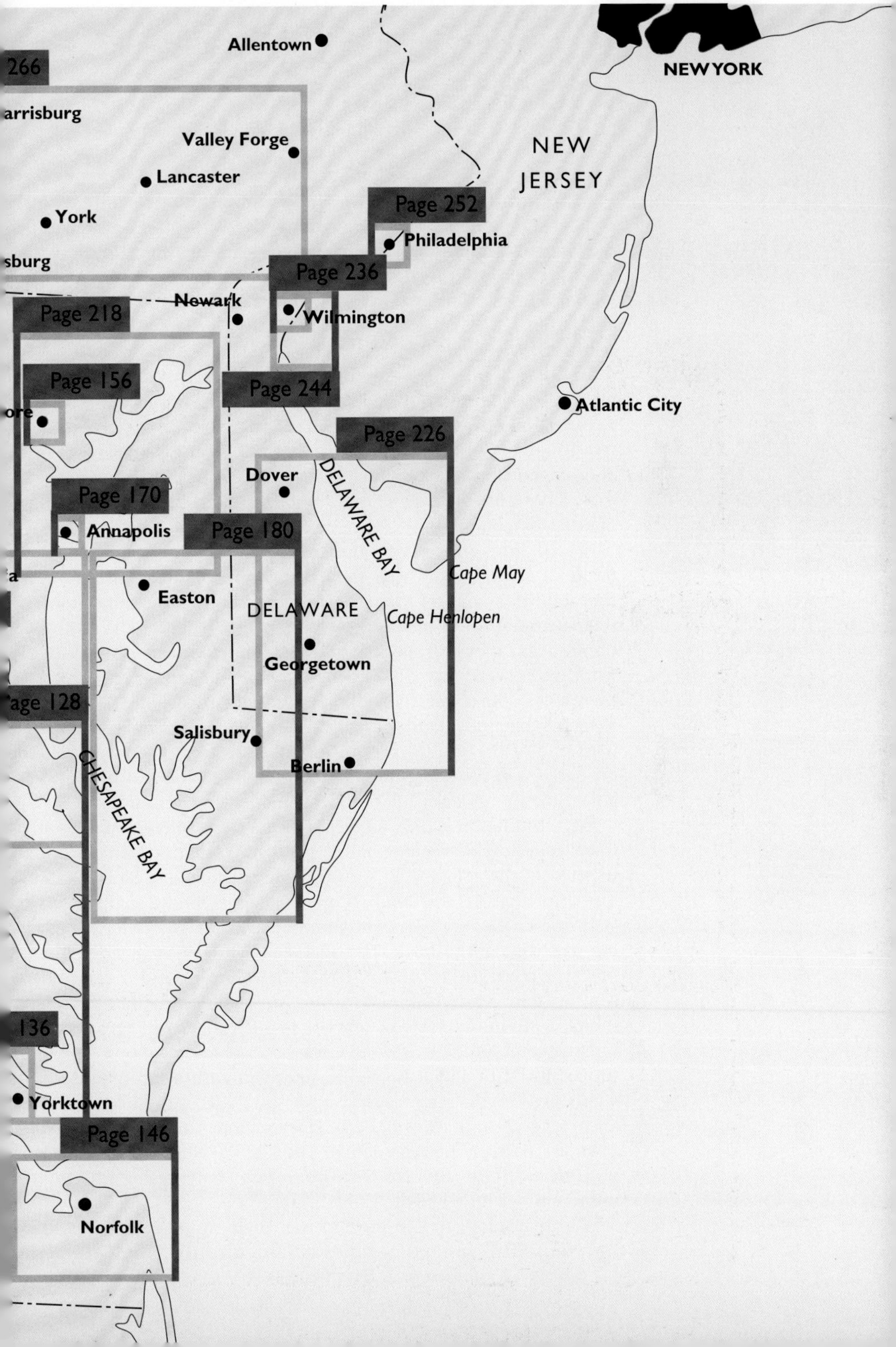

Allentown

266

NEW YORK

Harrisburg

Valley Forge

NEW
JERSEY

Lancaster

Page 252

York

Philadelphia

sburg

Page 236

Newark

Page 218

Wilmington

Page 156

Page 244

ore

Atlantic City

Page 226

Dover

DELAWARE BAY

Page 170

Annapolis

Page 180

a

Cape May

Easton

DELAWARE

Cape Henlopen

Georgetown

age 128

Salisbury

CHESAPEAKE BAY

Berlin

136

Yorktown

Page 146

Norfolk

Above
Washington State Capitol

Introduction

Washington DC is a rarity in the world: a planned, intentional, dedicated capital. Philadelphia (and, briefly, other places) served as the seat of government in the formative years of the republic when Washington was little more than muddy farmland on the banks of the Potomac River. The creation of a splendid marble city full of grandeur and pomp was an act of political will – and some would say that wilful politics has been its lot ever since.

As proud as Americans are of their representative democracy, they make a national sport of deriding officials elected from other districts or representing the 'other' party. In this context, the word 'Washington' is a pejorative. Yet roughly 20 million people come from around the world to Washington DC each year, not so much to see the US government at work, but to marvel at the power and the glory of official Washington.

For all their protests to the contrary, Americans *do* love their national capital. Ask them about the Smithsonian Institution, and they will beam and tell you that it is the nation's attic, full of some of their people's finest memories. Mention the White House or the US Capitol, and they will speak with awe – not necessarily of the officials who live or work there, but of the symbolic majesty of the structures themselves. Ask about 'the Wall', as they persist in calling the Vietnam Veterans' Memorial, and they grow inarticulate with choked-back tears over one of the most powerful pieces of abstract sculpture ever set on public soil. Washington is much more than the seat of American government; it is a city full of touchstones of American life.

Yet Washington is only a place to begin, especially for the fly-drive traveller, whose best plan of attack is to see Washington first or last, to be shed of the responsibility and inconvenience of a car in the city. The term used in this book, 'Capital Region', traditionally refers to Washington DC and the contiguous areas of Maryland and Virginia, but the scope of this book is broader, embracing all of Maryland, most of eastern Virginia, the tiny state of Delaware and a crescent of southeastern Pennsylvania. With so many rich destinations so close, it seems a shame to restrict oneself to official Washington and its satellite communities within the Beltway. The marble monuments and processional boulevards of the American capital are wonderfully augmented by the country roads, tidewater villages, rolling farmlands and craggy mountains of the broader region. City and countryside alike are part of the experience. The Capital Region found in this volume is richly diverse in topography, culture, activities and attractions – a little like the United States itself.

Washingtonians like to pretend that their city is neither Northern nor Southern, invoking diplomatic neutrality. They are being disingenuous. The entire Capital Region is stamped with some of the South's finest hallmarks. Washington is a Southern city, and its ways were set in the era before air conditioning made the South fully habitable in the summer and capable of year-round industriousness. In those days a certain manner evolved: the famous Southern hospitality, the languid Southern approach to time and even the drawn-out enunciation of the Southern accent.

Like much of the wider USA, the Capital Region has a sometimes troubled, always colourful past. The inhabitants of Williamsburg, Virginia, play their 18th-century roles to perfection in a community where time has been truly stopped. At the same time, the 21st-century folk of Annapolis, Maryland, and New Castle, Delaware, see nothing anachronistic about walking down their cobbled streets past Georgian houses. The past has a way of rebounding in Virginia's Tidewater, where grand old plantations bear mute testament to a feudal agriculture based on slave labour. Old ways of life drift into view in tiny villages along Maryland's eastern shore, where fishermen harvest oysters from sailing boats using long hand tongs. It is a case of picturesque traditions persisting in the name of scientific conservation and sound resource management. On the Amish farms of southeastern Pennsylvania, field hands still walk behind horse- or ox-drawn ploughs and ride into town on horse-drawn buggies with large reflective safety triangles mounted on the back. Perhaps no segment of the past so occupies the Capital Region as the Civil War. The horrors of those four difficult years between 1861 and 1865 resound down the generations, and the war's battlefields and cemeteries still mark the face of the region as indelibly as a tattoo.

Below
Elfreth's Alley, Philadelphia

Be careful, traveller, not to become lost in the Capital Region's past and overlook the timeless beauty of the countryside, from the gentle peaks of the Blue Ridge Mountains to the coves and inlets of the eastern shore. Long rolling plains of rich farmland seem to embody the American promise of the New World, while the Atlantic beaches of Maryland and Virginia suggest another kind of Promised Land, where frolic is never done. Follow the narrow paths into Delaware's marshes at dawn to see thousands of waterfowl gathered in a feathery peaceable kingdom. Take the ferry out to see the wild ponies of Assateague Island galloping down the beach. Pull off the Skyline Drive to sit with binoculars and watch a bald eagle, America's national bird, ride the thermal lifts from the sunny side of the hills.

Travel facts

Before you go

Ensure that you have the full address (including zip code) of where you are staying on your first night in the US – the Visa Waiver Program requires this information to be entered on the ESTA form, which you must complete online before travelling (https://esta.cbp.dhs.gov).

Room bookings

It is most difficult to find a room in tourist destinations from Memorial Day (end of May) to Labor Day (early September) or during special events. September and October are becoming increasingly popular with travellers. Thomas Cook or any good travel agent can handle room bookings, air tickets and local transportation. Advance bookings require a voucher or credit card number. Ask for discounts if you are a senior citizen, belong to a motoring club or are travelling off-season.

Local or state taxes on accommodation range from 5 to 14.5 per cent.

Above
Washington National Airport

Accommodation

Tourist offices can provide information about lodgings in every style and price, but cannot usually make bookings.

Most major chain hotels can be found in urban centres, along with more distinctive historic properties. At chain hotels and motels of every price, expect a clean, comfortable, relatively spacious room with one or two double- or queen-sized beds and a private bathroom. Some independent hotels and motels provide a lower standard, but many are well maintained, and have more character. Motels often line major auto routes and display 'vacancy' signs if rooms are available. Most chains have free phone reservation telephone numbers.

Bed and breakfasts can be more personal than hotels and offer an opportunity to meet other travellers. Enquire whether bath facilities are shared or private and whether a 'full' or 'continental' breakfast is served.

Country inns bridge the gap between hotels and bed and breakfasts – more charm and personal attention than a hotel; more services and amenities than a bed and breakfast.

Camping facilities for tents and recreational vehicles (RVs) are plentiful. Those in state or national parks and forests are the quietest and most primitive – facilities may be limited to pit toilets and cold showers. Private sites usually offer more amenities, but may be crowded with RVs.

Airports

Four major airports serve the Capital Region: Washington/Dulles International Airport; Ronald Reagan Washington National Airport; Baltimore/Washington International Airport; and Philadelphia International Airport. All have foreign exchange and banking services, car-hire facilities and public transport to the nearest city. Information booths help travellers with transport, lodging or touring, but cannot make bookings and usually have limited hours.

Children

The Capital Region's beaches and natural areas and some museums will appeal to children. For museums and transport, check for children's rates, often segmented by age, eg, under 3 free, 6–12 years $3, 12–18 years $4. Some attractions offer family rates.

Electricity

The USA uses 110v 60hz current. Two- or three-pin electrical plugs are standard. Electrical appliances from outside North America require plug and power converters, best purchased at home. Beware of buying electrical appliances in the USA since most cannot run on 220v 50hz power. Exceptions are battery-operated or dual-voltage equipment.

Entry formalities

Citizens of Australia, New Zealand, Ireland, Canada, Mexico, the Caribbean and the UK (as well as citizens of most western European countries and Japan) need only a valid machine-readable passport (valid for at least 6 months) to enter the USA if their stay is less than 90 days, they have a return ticket and have arrived on an airline participating in the visa-waiver programme (most major carriers). They must also complete an ESTA form online before travelling at https://esta.cbp.dhs.gov. There is also an extra check when you arrive at a US airport – a photo plus fingerprinting. Citizens of South Africa and most other countries must present a passport and tourist visa, obtained from a US consulate or embassy in their home country.

Right
Hotel Roanoke, Roanoke

Except for some luxury inns, most lodgings welcome children and are equipped to meet needs such as nappies, rollaway beds, cribs, video games and in some places (expensive) babysitters. Most chains allow children under 12, 14 and sometimes 18, to stay free in their parents' rooms.

Climate

The region's mountains are rather cooler and drier than the coast. Spring arrives in March with profuse fruit tree blossom and remains balmy into May when summer arrives. July and August temperatures frequently reach the mid-90s°F (35°C). The hurricane and tropical storm season in September can mean the evacuation of low-lying coastal areas, but autumn weather is pleasant between storms, with colourful foliage, especially in the mountains. In December, most of the region endures brief periods of sub-freezing temperatures and occasional snowfalls, heavier in the colder mountains and southeastern Pennsylvania.

Currency

US dollars are the only currency, available as notes (bills) – $1, $2, $5, $10, $20, $50, $100 – and coins – the 1-cent penny, 5-cent nickel, 10-cent dime, 25-cent quarter and, more rarely, 50-cent and dollar pieces.

Dollar traveller's cheques from well-known issuers such as Thomas Cook can be used like cash or changed easily almost everywhere. Major banks will usually exchange foreign currency. Rates of exchange and commission charges are often less favourable in hotel receptions.

K 98a
HOTEL ROANOKE

The Hotel Roanoke was built in 1882 by the Norfolk and Western Railroad. Over the next century, despite fire and depression, it became the city's social center. The Tudor Revival building became a beloved landmark for thousands of visitors. Its original 34 rooms had grown to 384 rooms when, in 1989, the N&W donated it to Virginia Polytechnic Institute and State University. After a major renovation and the addition of a conference center, it reopened in 1995. The Hotel Roanoke was listed on the Virginia Landmarks Register in 1995 and the National Register of Historic Places in 1996.

DEPARTMENT OF HISTORIC RESOURCES, 1998

Information Address requests for information well in advance.

Delaware Tourism Office 99 Kings Hwy, Dover, DE 19901; tel: (866) 284-7483 or (302) 739-4271; www.visitdelaware.com

Maryland Office of Tourism 401E Pratt St, 14th Floor, Baltimore, MD 21202; tel: (866) 639-3526; http://visitmaryland.org

Pennsylvania Tourism Office 400 North St, 4th Floor, Harrisburg, PA 17120; tel: (800) 237-4363 or (717) 787-5453; www.visitpa.com

Virginia Division of Tourism 901 E Byrd St, Richmond, VA 23219; tel: (800) VISIT-VA; www.virginia.org

Washington DC Convention and Visitors Association 901 7th St NW, 4th Floor, Washington DC 20001; tel: (800) 422-8644 or (202) 789-7000; www.washington.org

Cash withdrawals and advances can be made with debit and credit cards from the ubiquitous cash machines (ATMs or MACs – Money Access Centers), but check terms and availability with the card issuer before leaving home.

Credit cards are necessary to secure car hire and most lodging reservations, and sometimes as security for incidental lodging expenses.

Customs regulations

Personal duty-free allowances for visitors entering the USA are 1 litre of spirits or wine; 200 cigarettes or 100 (non-Cuban) cigars or 2kg of smoking tobacco or any proportionate combination of tobacco products; gifts valued up to $100 total. On your return home you will be allowed to take:

- **Australia:** AU$900 in goods (AU$450 under age 18). Travellers over 18: 2250ml of alcoholic liquor; 250 cigarettes or 250g of tobacco products.
- **Canada:** C$750 in goods (provided you have been away a week or more) per year: 200 cigarettes, 50 cigars or cigarillos, 200 tobacco sticks plus 200g tobacco; 1.5 litres of wine or 1.14 litres of liquor or 8.5 litres of beer or ale.
- **Ireland:** Goods purchased outside the EU and/or in EU duty-free shops by travellers aged 17 and older are subject to the following restrictons: 200 cigarettes or 100 cigarillos or 50 cigars or 250g tobacco; 1 litre of spirits or 2 litres of other alcoholic beverages plus 2 litres of table wine; 50g of perfume and 250ml of toilet water.
- **New Zealand:** NZ$700 in goods. Travellers over 17 are allowed 200 cigarettes or 250g tobacco; three 1125ml bottles of spirits, liqueur or other spirituous beverages; 4.5 litres of beer or 4.5 litres of wine.
- **South Africa:** Gifts valued up to R1250 per traveller (20 per cent duty on gifts valued R1251–10,000). Travellers over 18 can take in 400 cigarettes or 50 cigars or 250g tobacco; 1 litre of spirits; 2 litres of wine; 50ml of perfume; 250ml of toilet water.
- **UK:** Goods purchased outside the EU and/or in EU duty-free shops are subject to the following restrictions: £145 goods; 200 cigarettes or 50 cigars or 100 cigarillos or 250g tobacco; 2 litres of wine; 1 litre of spirits or 2 litres fortified or sparkling wine; 50ml of perfume; 250ml of eau de toilette.

Drinking

Tap water is safe, and fruit juices, carbonated and spring water and soft drinks are readily available. People drink far more (weak) coffee than tea, which is usually imbibed cold and sweetened with meals. Pennsylvania, Maryland and Virginia have a few small wineries, but their products are not broadly distributed. Microbreweries and brew-pubs are found throughout the region.

Insurance

Experienced travellers carry insurance that covers their belongings, holiday investment (including provision for cancelled or delayed flights and weather problems) and health (including evacuation home in a medical emergency). Many hospitals refuse treatment without proof of insurance. Thomas Cook and other travel agencies offer comprehensive policies. Medical coverage should be high – at least $1 million.

National Park Service

National Capital Region, 1100 Ohio Dr. SW, Washington DC 20242; tel: (202) 619-7222; www.nps.gov

National holidays

1 Jan New Year's Day
Third Mon in Jan Martin Luther King Jr Day
Third Mon in Feb Presidents' Day
Last Mon in May Memorial Day
4 Jul Independence Day
First Mon in Sept Labor Day
Second Mon in Oct Columbus Day
11 Nov Veterans' Day
Fourth Thur in Nov Thanksgiving
25 Dec Christmas

The drinking age for all alcoholic beverages is 21. Pennsylvania permits beer and wine sales in retail stores but limits spirits to state-controlled Wine and Spirits Shoppes. Delaware and Maryland's Montgomery County (adjacent to DC) exercise similar control. Elsewhere in the Capital Region, alcoholic beverages are sold in wine shops, package stores and retail liquor stores. Prices are often as good or better than those in duty-free stores, especially on American products such as Bourbon whiskey.

Eating out

Breakfasts tend to be hearty, lunches casual and light and dinners large. 'Southern home cooking' means hefty portions of meat, large helpings of potato or rice and vegetables cooked very soft with salt and butter or bacon fat.

Delightful exceptions are found in the cities and in coastal regions, where fresh fish and shellfish are plentiful and delicious and the variety of ethnic cuisines can boggle even a seasoned world traveller.

Fast-food dining offers convenience and relative thrift. McDonald's, Burger King, Wendy's, KFC and Popeye's Chicken are ubiquitous. One rung higher in price and variety are chain restaurants such as Applebee's.

Expect to pay $4–$10 for breakfast (more at hotels), $8–$20 for lunch and $20 and up per person for dinner before tax or tip.

Festivals

Washington DC's Cherry Blossom Festival begins in late March. Washington DC and Philadelphia stage extensive Independence Day (Fourth of July) festivities, while even small towns celebrate with parades and fireworks.

Above
Michie Tavern, Charlottesville

Spectator sports

Washington DC:

The Verizon Center: the Wizards (basketball), Mystics (women's basketball) and Capitals (hockey);

FedEx Field, Landover, MD: the Redskins (American football);

RFK Stadium: DC United (soccer), Washington Nationals (baseball).

Baltimore:

Oriole Park at Camden Yards; the Baltimore Orioles (baseball);

M & T Bank Stadium: the Baltimore Ravens (American football).

Philadelphia:

Citizens Bank Park: the Philadelphia Phillies (baseball);

Wachovia Complex: the Flyers (hockey), the 76ers (basketball), the Kicks (soccer);

Lincoln Financial Field: Philadelphia Eagles (American football).

Re-enactments and commemorative events occur throughout the year at historic sites and battlefields. In rural areas, agricultural fairs take place from late August into October.

See route chapters for local festivals.

Food

The 'Pennsylvania Dutch' cuisine of southeastern Pennsylvania features meals suitable for hard-working farmhands. Among the specialities are relishes, fruit pies and a sugar pie called 'shoo-fly pie'. The Philadelphia cheese steak is a sandwich of thinly sliced beef, grilled onions and melted cheese on long Italian rolls.

Both sides of the Chesapeake Bay claim the best oysters and crabs, while Tidewater Virginia mussels are noted for their sweetness. Crab cakes and fried oysters are found throughout the region, and fried soft-shell crabs are a favoured local delicacy.

Health

Hospital emergency rooms handle life-threatening medical problems. Treatment will be swift and top-notch, with payment problems sorted out later. For mundane problems, doctors' offices or health clinics can provide care.

Non-USA national health plans are not accepted by USA medical providers, so some form of health insurance coverage is mandatory - at least $1 million of coverage is essential.

Bring enough prescription medicine for the trip and carry a copy of all prescriptions. No inoculations are required, and the Capital Region is basically a healthy place to visit. When visiting state and national parks or other natural areas, check for posted warnings about rabies, Lyme disease, West Nile Virus or other local health risks.

Maps

State, regional and city maps are produced by the American Automobile Association, known as AAA ('Triple A'), and distributed free to members at AAA offices. Most automobile clubs world-wide have reciprocal agreements with AAA to provide maps and other member services. Be prepared to show a membership card. State tourism offices also provide excellent touring maps.

Museums

Many major museums open seven days a week all year. Others close Mondays, and all close New Year's Day, Christmas and Thanksgiving. Hours are generally 0900 or 1000 to 1700 or 1800. Some museums have longer summer hours and stay open one evening. Some offer

Useful telephone codes

911 – emergency calls to fire, police or ambulance;
0 – operator;
411 – information: charged;
011 – international dialling: followed by the country code (omitting the first zero if there is one) then the local number;
800/877/888 – freephone codes;
900 – information or other services, often premium-rate.

Country codes

Australia – 61
New Zealand – 64
Republic of Ireland – 353
South Africa – 27
United Kingdom – 44

Security measures

Due to heightened security measures since the 9/11 terrorist attacks, certain government buildings and other sites may be closed to visitors if security levels are raised. Changes to traffic patterns may be implemented in the event of severe concern. Although the frequency of such alerts has subsided, they can be cumbersome to visitors. In addition, visitors should be aware that some common items such as nail scissors and other potential weapons may not be allowed into government buildings or museums; it is best to leave them at your hotel.

reduced or free admission on one day. Smaller museums, particularly outside tourist areas, may be open limited days or hours and may close in winter.

National parks

National parks abound in the Capital Region, apart from Delaware – *see the individual chapters.*

Opening times

Office hours are generally Monday to Friday 0900 to 1700. Some tourist offices also open on Saturday morning all year and on weekends in summer. Many banks open from 0900 or 1000 to 1500 or 1600; some may open one evening and on Saturday morning. Petrol stations open from early till late; some open 24 hours on major routes. Large stores and shopping centres open at 0900 or 1000 Monday to Saturday and usually close between 1900 and 2100, with shorter hours on Sunday.

Packing

Everything you could ever need is available, so don't pack too much. In fact, USA prices on many goods may seem low. Do pack all medicines, glasses and contraceptives and keep duplicate prescriptions to verify your need for medication. You can buy whatever you forget, but useful items include mini-binoculars, a magnifying torch for reading maps and examining marks on antiques, and a Swiss Army knife (packed in checked airline luggage).

Postal services

Post offices are open from Monday to Friday morning and afternoon, although hours may vary. Major USA Postal Service branches are open Saturday and a few on Sunday. Stamps may be purchased from machines in some pharmacies and convenience stores and from some ATMs. Letters and cards with correct postage may be dropped in blue boxes outside postal branches or on street corners; parcels over 1lb must be handled by a postal clerk. All USA mail must include the 5-digit zip, and the 4-digit suffix speeds delivery. Mail everything going overseas as air mail (surface mail takes weeks).

Public holidays

On national holidays, post offices and government offices close, as do many businesses and shops. Large department stores usually stay open and often have sales. Convenience stores, supermarkets, liquor stores

and petrol stations generally remain open (sometimes with curtailed hours). Workers often take short holidays, so tourist destinations can be crowded.

Nearly everything closes at New Year, Thanksgiving and Christmas.

Public transport

Amtrak (*tel: (800) 872-7245 or (202) 484-7540; www.amtrak.com*) provides passenger rail services linking New York to Washington via Philadelphia and Baltimore, with some trains continuing south through Virginia. **Greyhound Bus Lines** (*tel: (800) 231-2222 or (202) 289-5160; www.greyhound.com*) and **Peter Pan/Trailways** (*tel: (800) 343-9999; www.peterpanbus.com*) provide long-distance, and in some cases, local bus services to major cities and smaller towns. Ask your travel agent to enquire about discount passes for non-US residents. The bi-monthly *Thomas Cook Overseas Timetable* contains timetables for trains and buses, plus some ferry services, and much additional travel information; buy online at *www.thomascookpublishing.com* or *tel: 01733 416477 (UK number)*.

Smoking

All states in this guide have legal bans on indoor smoking in public places, although some communities may make exceptions for bars and casinos. As non-smoking becomes the norm in the USA, many hotels and almost all B&Bs ban smoking in their rooms.

Tipping

Most people performing services expect a tip. As a general guide:

restaurant bills – 15–20 per cent;
airport and hotel porters – $1 per bag;
valet parking attendants – $2;
bartenders – 50 cents to $1 per drink;
hairdressers/taxi drivers – 10 per cent;
restroom attendants – 25–50 cents.

Reading

Most museums and National Park visitor centres have substantial book selections in their stores. Useful outdoors guides include the appropriate Appalachian Mountain Club trail guides for Virginia and Maryland. A broad variety of materials can be found at **Borders Books and Music** *1800 L St NW, Washington DC; tel: (202) 466-4999.*

Shopping

Clothing can be a bargain, particularly at discount stores or factory outlets, and photo equipment is generally less expensive in the USA than in Europe. Prices on alcohol, tobacco and perfume are often lower in retail stores than in duty-free shops. Do your homework on prices before you go, and shop around.

Capital Region souvenirs include folk art and crafts (particularly quilts) from the Pennsylvania Dutch region, antiques and small collectibles (notably 20th-century American pottery), and reproductions of objects in the collections of Colonial Williamsburg, Winterthur and similar domestic life museums.

The USA has no VAT. Each state (except Delaware) imposes its own tax on sales of products and meals, ranging up to 7 per cent. In some jurisdictions, groceries are exempt from sales tax but ready-to-eat foods are not. Pennsylvania exempts clothing.

Above
Rossetti's *La Bella Mano* in the Delaware Art Museum

Toilets

The most common terms are 'restroom' or 'bathroom', though 'toilet' or 'washroom' are also used. Few people recognise 'WC'.

Most businesses, including bars and restaurants, reserve restrooms for clients. Petrol stations provide keys to customers to access restrooms. Public toilets are not common along city streets. The larger tourist information centres and roadside rest stops often have them. Hotels, museums and other tourist attractions are the most dependable.

Stores

Neiman Marcus and Hecht Co. are the major department stores in Washington DC. All cities in the region have numerous shopping malls, often in restored historic buildings. Most have food courts for inexpensive dining.

Outlet malls are common in the Capital Region. Individual stores are owned by the manufacturer and offer discounts of 20–70 per cent off retail prices for clothing (including Calvin Klein, Donna Karan, Tommy Hilfiger, J. Crew) and housewares (Lenox, Dansk, Waterford/Wedgwood). Most merchandise is first quality although often last season's stock, a discontinued line or a line made for outlet sale. Examine irregular merchandise carefully.

Telephones

Dialling instructions are in the white pages telephone directory. Phone numbers are seven digits, preceded by a three-digit area code when calling outside the local area. (The area code must always be dialled in Maryland and Philadelphia.) For long-distance calls in the USA and Canada, dial 1, then the area code, followed by the local number.

Pay phones are located at petrol stations, on street corners or inside restaurants, hotels and public buildings. Local calls usually cost 50 cents; a computer voice will announce when additional coins are needed. Prepaid phone cards are available at pharmacies, news stands, convenience stores and post offices. Lodgings often surcharge the cost of calls from rooms.

Right
Apples, honey and cider at a roadside stall

Information for travellers with a disability

SATH (Society for Accessible Travel and Hospitality) www.sath.org

RADAR 12 City Forum, 250 City Rd, London EC1V 8AF; tel: (020) 7250 3222; www.radar.org.uk

Safety

Violent crime throughout the Capital Region is on the decline. Safety is a matter of exercising common sense. Never publicly discuss travel plans, money or valuables you are carrying; keep to well-lit and well-travelled areas; do not wear expensive jewellery or carry expensive cameras or large sums of cash; do not make cash withdrawals from ATMs in deserted areas. Use a hidden money-belt for valuables and travel documents. In the unlikely event you are mugged, do not resist.

If you encounter trouble, dial 911 on any telephone for police, fire and medical assistance.

Time

Capital Region clocks are set to GMT minus 5 hours, Eastern Standard Time (EST). From the second Sunday in March until the first Sunday in November, clocks go forward 1 hour to Eastern Daylight Time (EDT).

Travellers with disabilities

State and federal laws require that all public businesses, buildings and services be accessible by people with disabilities, ie, the buildings must have access ramps and toilets designed for wheelchair users. Most cities and towns have ramps built into street crossings, and most city buses have provisions for wheelchair users. Outside Washington DC, many older facilities and historic sites don't yet comply with the standards.

Some theatres offer assisted listening devices and some attractions provide large print information materials.

Special controls for drivers with disabilities are seldom an option on hired vehicles.

For information about accessible attractions and restaurants inthe Washington DC metro area, call *(800) 949-4232; www.disabilityguide.org*

Right
Society Hill bookshop, Philadelphia

Opposite
Skyline Drive, Virginia

Driver's guide

Automobile clubs

Many non-North American auto clubs have reciprocal privileges with the AAA, including touring books, road maps, discounts at hotels and motels and some roadside assistance. Emergency towing is not always included. For information on services, ask your own club or request *Office to Serve You Abroad*, American Automobile Association, *1000 AAA Drive, Heathrow, FL 32756-5063; tel: (407) 444-8402; www.aaa.com*

Documents

A valid driver's licence from your home country should be on your person at all times. Vehicle registration and, where applicable, a valid car-hire contract must be in the vehicle when it is underway. Proof of liability insurance must also be supplied in the event of an accident.

Accidents

In the event of a collision, always stop. (Penalties for failing to stop can include imprisonment.) If either vehicle is damaged or any person injured, immediately report the accident to state police if it occurred on a state or interstate road, or to local police. Everyone involved should exchange the numbers of drivers' licences, car registration, insurance coverage information and address and telephone number for further contact. The police will also require this information. Collisions with property or personal damage must also be reported to your car-hire company.

Breakdowns

Should a breakdown occur, pull to the side of the road where you will be visible but out of the way of traffic. Switch on hazard lights and, if it is safe to do so, raise the bonnet and boot (trunk) lids. Change a tyre only if you're out of the flow of traffic.

Dial 911 from any telephone to summon emergency medical or police assistance. Report your telephone number, problem, location and any need for medical assistance. Emergency phone boxes are usually placed at frequent intervals along interstate highways. If one is not visible, stay with the vehicle and wait for a patrol car to stop to render assistance.

Caravans and camper vans (Trailers and RVs)

Convenient as it may be to drive around in one's own lodging, caravans and camper vans can also pose some difficulties. Most communities require that they be parked in a proper campground before using them as a place to sleep, and some communities prohibit all roadside parking, especially after dark. Some urban car parks lack the overhead clearance to accommodate caravans. Very large caravans must follow posted road regulations for trucks, which generally ban them from travelling at high-speed or from passing lanes. Walmart stores permit free overnight parking of RVs.

Car hire

Hiring a vehicle provides you with freedom to travel as you please with a vehicle you can leave behind when you depart. Whether

Above
Buggy sign in Amish country

Drinking and driving laws

Driving under the influence of alcohol or other drugs is illegal throughout the USA. Intoxication is defined as 0.08 per cent blood alcohol in most states. If a police officer stops you and suspects you may be impaired, you may be asked to take an instant 'breathalyser' test. You are permitted to refuse the test, but doing so means automatic suspension of your driver's licence.

booking a fly-drive package or making independent arrangements, plan well in advance to ensure getting the type and size of vehicle you desire. Unlimited mileage is standard on most auto-rental contracts, but not on RVs.

Subcompact cars are very small, rarely available and make poor long-distance touring vehicles under USA driving conditions. Compact or economy cars are usually the least expensive, with small price increases for intermediate cars. Full-size and luxury vehicles are more expensive to hire and operate. Most USA rental cars come with either two or four doors, an automatic transmission and air conditioning. Intermediate and larger vehicles are often equipped with cruise control, allowing constant-speed long distance travel. Some vehicles may be equipped with four-wheel-drive (4WD), a necessity for traversing some unpaved roads in the mountains or along seashores where permitted.

Most rental companies require that the driver be at least 21 years of age (some specify 25), hold a valid driver's licence and use a credit card to secure the value of the vehicle. Before leaving the hire agency, be certain that you have the car registration and all rental documentation. Also be sure you know how to operate the vehicle (there's nothing more maddening than running low on petrol and being unable to find the fuel tank lid). If possible, ask for a vehicle without obvious rental company identifiers, as thieves often target such cars.

Driving in Washington

The worst driving conditions in the region involve winter snow, or heavy rain and high winds during the autumn storm season. Drive with low-beam headlights at all times as a safety precaution. Avoid using main beam in snow, rain or fog as it can blind other drivers (or yourself with reflected glare). If visibility is poor, pull over and wait for the storm to pass. The danger of hydroplaning arises during sudden heavy rain, particularly at speeds above 35 mph.

Driving on snow takes skill, and if you are unfamiliar with stopping, turning and negotiating skids on snow, practise in a vacant car park before venturing out on the road. Apply brakes lightly but repeatedly to stop on snow. Hired cars are generally equipped with all-season tyres, which do not grip well in more than 1 inch of snow. During winter, keep the petrol tank topped up in case you become stuck. If you are stranded, stay in the vehicle, place a red flag on the antenna or door handle, try to keep warm with blankets, and do not run the engine any more than necessary. Make sure the exhaust pipe is not clogged with snow. Useful winter driving gear includes a blanket, a windscreen ice scraper, a small shovel and a bucket or bag of sand. Serious snowstorms are infrequent in the region; as a result, municipalities are often poorly equipped to clear the roads.

Fuel

Petrol ('gas' or 'gasoline') is sold by the gallon (3.82 litres) at prices posted in cents and tenths of a cent – ranging from 200.9 cents to 399.9 cents, with a great deal of volatility based on season, location and Middle Eastern politics. All gasoline sold in the Capital Region is unleaded and most also contains various additives to decrease emissions of sulphur and nitrogen oxides. Diesel fuel is sold at separate pumps. Most fuel pumps are self-service, and many accept credit and bank cards for payment. 'Full-service' pumps sometimes charge as much as 20 cents more per gallon.

Information

In addition to automobile clubs, drivers will find the roadside tourist centres of each state useful sources of maps and road condition updates.

Below
Annapolis, Maryland

Right
Historic gas station

Insurance

Third-party liability insurance is required throughout the region. In practice, coverage far in excess of the minimum is desirable. Visitors from outside the USA are wise to take out supplemental liability coverage – check with your travel agent or hire car agent – which covers liability up to $1 million. Car hire agencies also ask drivers to take out collision damage waiver (CDW) or loss damage waiver (LDW). Declining makes the driver personally responsible for damage to the vehicle. CDW is often included as part of a fly-drive package. USA and Canadian drivers may be covered by their own insurance. Some premium credit cards also provide CDW as a free benefit when using the card for car hire.

Parking

Public car parks are generally indicated with a blue sign carrying the letter 'P' and a directional arrow. Rates are posted at the entrance. Urban garages are often expensive but may give discounts to shoppers or theatregoers who have their timecards stamped with a validation sticker. Coin-operated parking meters are in effect in most areas, with rates ranging from $2 per hour in urban areas to as little as 25 cents per hour in small towns. Parking is forbidden near a fire hydrant, a red or yellow kerb or in front of a wheelchair access ramp. In urban areas, kerbside parking may be banned during morning and evening commuting hours. If you violate parking regulations or let a meter expire, expect to be issued a citation. If you do not pay it, the car hire company may charge the fine to your credit card along with a substantial penalty.

Seat belts

All jurisdictions in the Capital Region require drivers and passengers to use seat belts whenever a vehicle is in motion.

Tolls

Toll roads, bridges and tunnels are a fact of life throughout the Capital Region. On short toll roads, bridges and tunnels, drivers are expected to pay cash at the toll booths. (A good supply of quarters, also useful for parking meters, comes in handy.) On longer toll roads, drivers pick up a toll card when entering the highway and pay a variable rate based on mileage when exiting.

Security

Lock your car. Lock it when you are inside, particularly in towns and cities, and when you leave it. Do not leave maps, guidebooks and other tourist paraphernalia in clear view. Try always to park in well-lit areas.

Police

Police cars signal drivers with flashing blue or blue-and-red lights and sometimes with a siren. While most police vehicles are marked, some highways are patrolled by unmarked cars. When signalled, pull over to the side and have your driver's licence and vehicle registration ready for inspection. Roll down the window but do not leave the vehicle unless requested. You have the right to ask an officer for identification.

Speed limits

Official highway speed limits are 65 mph in rural areas, 55 mph in urban areas. Many Capital Region drivers take these as suggestions rather than law. You are safest when moving with the flow of traffic, neither faster nor significantly slower. Note that most interstate highways also have minimum speed limits. Expect to be overtaken and passed on both sides if you are moving slower than the rest of the traffic. This can be disconcerting but is perfectly legal in most states. On secondary roads, speed limits are much lower. When not posted, assume the limit is 30 mph in residential areas, 20 mph near schools and hospitals.

Road signs

International symbols are used for many road signs but sometimes differ from European symbols. All language signs are in English. Signs may be white, yellow, green, brown or blue. Stop, Yield, Do Not Enter and Wrong Way signs are usually *red and white*. Warning or direction indicators are generally *yellow*. Roadwork and temporary detour signs are generally reflective orange. Green indicates highway directions, blue denotes non-driving information (parking, informational radio frequencies). Brown signs are usually reserved to indicate parks, campsites and outdoor activities.

Traffic lights are red (stop), green (go) and yellow (caution). Simultaneous red and yellow lights indicate a pedestrian crossing. Unless otherwise posted, it is legal to make a right-hand turn at a red light if there is no traffic and no pedestrian-crossing light is lit. Motorists are expected to yield the right of way to pedestrians at all zebra crossings or 'crosswalks', although the law is more observed in the breach than the practice.

Typical road signs in Washington DC

INSTRUCTIONS

Stop

Give way

Wrong way - often together
with 'No entry' sign

No right turn

No U-turn

One-way
traffic

Two-way left
turn lanes

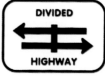

Divided highway
(dual carriageway)
at junction ahead

Speed limit
signs: maximum
and maximum/
minimum limits

WARNINGS

Crossroads

Junction

Curve (bend)

Winding road

Stop ahead

Two-way traffic

Divided highway
(dual carriageway)

Road narrows
on right

Roadworks
ahead

Railway
crossing

No-overtaking
zone

Getting to Washington DC, Virginia, Maryland and Delaware

Using your car

Consider going without a car during your stay in downtown Washington, as public transit is a reasonably priced and efficient way to see the major sights, and parking in DC can be very difficult and expensive. Driving is even worse than parking, often confusing even the residents. If you must pick up your car at the airport, arrange parking in advance with your Washington hotel. However, if you choose to stay outside Washington in the suburbs, a car is an absolute necessity.

Reservations

It is always a good idea to book your first night's room in advance, especially from April to November in Washington and anywhere in the region during July and August. If you are arriving on a weekend and plan to stay outside of Washington, be sure to reserve your room in advance, as weekend getaway accommodation often fills up.

By air

International travellers to the Capital Region generally arrive at Washington's Dulles Airport (IAD), about 26 miles west of Washington in Virginia; Baltimore-Washington Airport (BWI), about 25 miles north of Washington in Maryland, or sometimes Philadelphia International Airport (PHL) in Pennsylvania. After clearing Customs and Immigration and rechecking baggage, passengers transfer for flights into Richmond or Newport News (both in Virginia) or smaller cities. If a particularly good fare is available, it is also feasible to enter the USA through New York's John F Kennedy Airport (JFK) or Newark (New Jersey) Airport (NWK), then transfer to a connecting flight.

It is also possible to travel by train from JFK or Newark airports by transferring to Amtrak's terminal at Grand Central Station in Manhattan. (Newark is closer to Manhattan and the transfer takes less time.)

Travellers from other parts of North America might also arrive at the older and smaller Ronald Reagan National Airport (NAT), 4 miles from Washington, where transfer downtown is easy on the metro.

Most international carriers service either Dulles or Baltimore-Washington international airports, with frequent daily service to the UK offered by British Air, Virgin Atlantic, United, Continental and American. Philadelphia also has direct UK flights through US Airways and British Airways, often priced slightly lower than the Washington service. Many UK and European charter flights to the Capital Region use Baltimore-Washington International.

Domestic USA air service is extensive but often expensive. There are shuttle flights into Washington hourly from Boston and every half hour from New York. Virtually every major airport in North America offers regular Washington flights, often several per day.

Car-hire facilities are found at every airport (be sure to reserve in advance) and public transport (train, bus, limousine and, at Ronald Reagan National Airport only, metro) is available into the nearest city. Travellers hiring a car will do well to look for an off-airport agency, as the airport tax on car hire can hike rates as much as 20 per cent. Agencies generally provide shuttle bus services to and from the airport.

By train or bus

Amtrak, the USA passenger rail system, offers frequent services to Washington, with more than 50 trains arriving per day at the historic and beautifully refurbished Union Station. Washington is the southern terminus of Amtrak's Northeast Corridor Metroliner service (between Boston and Washington via New York, Philadelphia and Baltimore). A premium-priced high speed service was inaugurated between New York and Washington in late 1999. Washington also serves as the eastern terminus of several east–west train lines and the northern hub of trains from Florida and Georgia. Amtrak is also a viable way to reach downtown Washington from Baltimore-Washington Airport by picking up the connector shuttle bus at the arrivals area.

Bus service to Washington is usually through Greyhound Bus Lines or Peter Pan, with connections to all major cities and many small towns. It is usually the least expensive way to reach Washington and is comparable in time to the train. Although coach services have been upgraded in recent years, bus travel remains the least comfortable and most confining.

Interstate highways

Interstate highways are always the fastest way to drive anywhere within the Capital Region but are usually the least scenic. They are convenient for travellers, as services (fuel, restaurants and motels) are found clustered at many exits. Away from the major cities, rest stops between exits offer picnic spots and some also have toilet facilities. Rest stops on toll roads generally offer food and fuel as well.

By car

The USA East Coast is virtually paved with the multi-lane roadways known as the USA Interstate Highway System. Many of these highways converge on Washington, as the seat of government. DC is surrounded by the Capital Beltway, formed by interstates I-95 and I-495. I-95 joins the circle from the south from Richmond and leaves it heading north to Baltimore, Wilmington, Philadelphia and New York. Other major interstate spurs converging on Washington are I-270, which heads south from Frederick, Maryland, to join the Beltway's northwest corner, and I-66, which comes in from the west. Major state highways connecting to the Beltway include Rte 50 from Annapolis.

Just to confuse matters, the western half of the Beltway is signposted both I-495 and I-95 ('400' series highways are circumferential connectors in the Interstate system). To get into Washington from the south, drive I-95 to I-395 and cross the 14th St Bridge into DC. From the north, stay on I-95 south to Rte 50, also called the John Hanson Hwy, which becomes New York Ave in DC.

Above
Railroad train at the Virginia Museum of Transportation

Setting the scene

Land and water

The Capital Region begins in the west with the ancient rounded hills of the Appalachian Mountains. The landscape then sweeps down across rolling plains and farmland to the tidal edges of great rivers and commodious bays. It finally concludes on the eastern periphery with hundreds of miles of sandy barrier beaches facing the Atlantic Ocean.

Yet the Capital Region is also highly compact by North American standards. A determined driver can traverse it north to south or east to west in less than a full day, although no one except a fugitive would do so. Because it includes three of the major Eastern Seaboard cities – Philadelphia, Baltimore and Washington – the region is well served by major highways. Yet even the rural districts of the Capital Region support excellent road systems, making the area a prime region for fly-drive touring.

The most populous areas of the Capital Region lie on the water, and the rivers and bays have dictated much of the region's destiny. The great inland sea of the Chesapeake Bay is the central defining feature of the coasts of Maryland and Virginia. It divides Maryland between the heavily populated western side and the almost mythical water-world of the Eastern Shore, an area seemingly removed both in geography and chronology from the bustle of Baltimore, Annapolis and Washington. Virginia's portion of the Chesapeake, often called the Tidewater, is no less magical in its vast marshy tracks and swampy rivers that drain the interior highlands. Even the northern reaches of the Chesapeake, where the broad and deep Susquehanna River flows down through the black soil of eastern Pennsylvania's fertile farmland to empty into salt water, have an undeniable scenic appeal.

The Chesapeake was America's first great inland waterway. This bay of sandy shores and shoals quickly proved one of the New World's finest shellfish fisheries, and its protected waters encouraged a steady flow of local trade by sail. An abundance of safe harbours virtually guaranteed the emergence of great shipbuilding centres, some of which, such as Norfolk–Newport News, persist to this day.

The Chesapeake also proved essential to the opening of the continental United States because the only practical road to the interior of the continent began at Baltimore and followed the Susquehanna upriver, connecting across western Pennsylvania to the mighty Ohio Valley. When transportation technology matured, Baltimore became the eastern railhead to the west, linked by water to Philadelphia through a canal that connected the Delaware and Chesapeake bays.

Above
Swallow Falls, near Deep Creek in Western Maryland

The significance of the Chesapeake in the fledgling economy of the United States helped determine the siting of the District of Columbia as the new national capital. Safely sheltered from enemy warships on the Potomac River (or so the Founding Fathers thought), the District stood halfway down the coast of the new country, poised between the industrial and mechanical North and the agricultural South.

Overland travel by motorcar has changed all the circumstances that led to the initial heavy settlement of the western banks of the Chesapeake, for journeys to the interior that once took weeks by horse or mule now take only hours by automobile.

The Piedmont Plateau rises from the 'fall line' of the rivers flowing into the Chesapeake Bay (the point where waterfalls and rapids make them no longer navigable, even in small boats). Hardly as flat as the term 'plateau' implies, the Piedmont is a shelf of metamorphic rock that ranges from 400 to 1200 ft above sea level. The rolling country is broken by sharp ridges and deep hollows and punctuated with loaf-shaped hills. The Piedmont extends all the way from Virginia's southern border through Maryland, into southeastern Pennsylvania at Gettysburg and around to northern Delaware. It encompasses some of the Capital Region's richest farmland, from the tobacco country of Virginia to the truck farms of Maryland and the hard-working farms of the Pennsylvania Dutch country.

The Appalachian Mountain chain rises west of the Piedmont, walling off the Atlantic coast from the continental interior. The Capital Region's portion of this long mountain system, which extends from Georgia north into Maine, includes the Blue Ridge and Allegheny mountains, with the fertile valleys of Shenandoah (Virginia) and Cumberland (Maryland) between them. The South Mountains, which encircle Gettysburg in Pennsylvania, are a northerly extension of the Blue Ridge chain. Some of the most scenic motorways in eastern North America, including Virginia's Skyline Drive, cross the sparsely populated mountain country of the Capital Region.

Native Americans

Virtually the entire Capital Region was extensively inhabited by Native Americans when European settlers first arrived. Archaeologists group the diverse Native American peoples of the region as 'Eastern Woodlands tribes' because they shared a common cultural pattern, but they belonged to several distinct linguistic groups. The Chesapeake Bay was inhabited by about 10,000 Algonquian-speaking Chesapeakes under the general leadership of Chief Powhatan. To the north, the Lenni Lenape (called 'Delawares' by the English) and the Susquehannocks were also Algonquian peoples. The people of the Piedmont were Sioux of the Monacan and Monahoac tribes. Iroquois-speaking Nottoways inhabited southeastern coastal Virginia, while the

Below
Living history in Jamestown

Cherokee occupied the highlands in the southwestern sector of the Capital Region. The recreated Powhatan Village at Jamestown, Virginia, represents in broad strokes the semi-nomadic lifestyle of these hunter-gatherer-farmers at the time of European contact.

Disease and conflict with the colonists drastically reduced the number of Native Americans in the Capital Region, and the remaining groups were further decimated during the American Revolution, having allied themselves with the British. Only the Cherokee survived as a cohesive tribe at the end of the Revolution. Although the tribe was officially removed by force from the eastern states in the 19th century, many Cherokees remained behind and were assimilated into the general population.

While there is some evidence that early colonists in Virginia adopted crops and fishing techniques from the local tribes, the principal legacy of the first inhabitants of the Capital Region has been the semi-legendary figure of Pocahontas. She was the daughter of the powerful Chief Powhatan, and her affinity for the English helped the Jamestown colonists establish a toehold in the New World. According to adventurer-explorer John Smith's sometimes exaggerated accounts of his year and a half in Virginia, Pocahontas interceded with her father to save Smith's life when he was taken prisoner by a Powhatan hunting party. She visited the English settlers often and married John Rolfe, the man who introduced the mild West Indies tobacco to Virginia that would become the state's economic mainstay. Christened Lady Rebecca, Pocahontas visited the English court with her husband, where, by all accounts, she was captivating. Only 21 years old, she died at the outset of her return trip to Virginia. Some years later her son Thomas returned to Virginia and prospered as a planter. Her story, augmented in successive retellings, remains a touchstone in American cultural myth.

Exploration and settlement

One of the first European captains to explore the coast of the Capital Region was the Dutchman Henry Hudson, but the first detailed maps, particularly of the Chesapeake Bay, were drawn by John Smith to promote further settlement.

Unlike New England and Florida, the Capital Region was initially colonised by many nations. The first permanent English settlement in the

Below
Colonial Williamsburg, Virginia

Above
Historic quilt, Taubman
Museum of Art, Roanoke

New World was planted at Jamestown, Virginia, in 1607. Soon thereafter, Sweden and the Netherlands vied for hegemony in Delaware, with Wilmington becoming the Swedish town and New Castle the Dutch. When the Dutch got the upper hand, they let the Swedish settlers stay, and when the English gained control of the entire seaboard by 1664, they permitted both groups to remain. The community that would become Philadelphia saw the same succession, concluding with the grant to Quaker William Penn from the English king in 1681. Pennsylvania (literally 'Penn's Woods') was a great experiment in religious tolerance, and soon attracted many pacifist Mennonites of primarily German descent who later spread into other parts of the Capital Region.

Religious refugees formed a large portion of the early settlers. English Roman Catholics took refuge in Maryland beginning in 1634. Annapolis was settled in 1649 by Puritans fleeing intolerance in Virginia. The last frontiers of the region were settled in the early 18th century, when Scots-Irish immigrants flowed into the mountains of Appalachia. Even before the great waves of immigration that remade the USA in the mid-19th century, the Capital Region was already a diverse cultural stew.

Making a nation

By the time of the American Revolution, Penn's 'City of Brotherly Love', founded on the twin virtues of industriousness and tolerance, had grown into the largest, richest and most powerful city in the American colonies. It's not surprising that history tapped Philadelphia as the political as well as the economic capital of the evolving United States of America during the last quarter of the 18th century.

In 1774, representatives of the American colonies convened in Philadelphia as the First Continental Congress to air their grievances against the British Crown. When those grievances were rebuffed, the city became the first capital of a new nation in revolt. Fervour for independence ran high and fighting at last broke out in April 1775 in Massachusetts.

As relations between the colonies and the Crown deteriorated, Congress authorised a committee to draft a Declaration of Independence. Virginian Thomas Jefferson took the lead, transforming Enlightenment philosophy into a document of political action. Making some changes, Congress adopted the statement on 4 July 1776, commemorated ever since as Independence Day. (Philadelphia, predictably, pulls out all the stops to celebrate.) Soon thereafter, the representatives reconstituted themselves as the Second Continental Congress, which remained in Philadelphia (with brief refuges in York, Pennsylvania, and Annapolis, Maryland) as the national government until the Revolution was concluded with the Treaty of Paris in 1783. In 1787 delegates to the Continental Congress drafted the Constitution of the United States which was ratified first by Delaware and ultimately by all 13 states by 1789. Philadelphia's Independence National Historical Park is a compact area in the heart of the old city, dense with some of the country's most important touchstones of the Revolution, including Independence Hall, where both the Declaration of Independence and the Constitution were signed.

Below
Roanoke's History Museum

As the politics and ideology of the new nation were being forged in Philadelphia, war raged throughout the Capital Region. Many battle sites recall those difficult years with commemorative parks, but two that hold prominent places in USA history are Valley Forge, Pennsylvania, where the Continental Army endured desperate hardship over the winter of 1777–8 and emerged strengthened with resolve, and Yorktown, Virginia, where the largest of the British armies, under the command of Lieutenant General Charles, Earl of Cornwallis, surrendered to Washington's American forces, spelling the end of the war.

THEY (WHO) SEEK TO ESTABLISH
SYSTEMS OF GOVERNMENT BASED ON
THE REGIMENTATION OF ALL HUMAN
BEINGS BY A HANDFUL OF INDIVIDUAL
RULERS.. CALL THIS A NEW ORDER.
IT IS NOT NEW AND IT IS NOT ORDER.

Above
Franklin D Roosevelt
Memorial, Washington DC

Creating the capital

With the advent of peace, the US Congress set out to build a new capital worthy of a new nation. As a political compromise over payment of war debts, the district was to be situated in the South and Congress left it to President George Washington to select the spot. Washington settled on a diamond-shaped parcel near the mouth of the Potomac River close to his home, Mount Vernon, in Virginia. In 1791, Virginia and Maryland ceded land to create the District of Columbia, which Congress named in honour of Christopher Columbus. The capital city of Washington was named after the president. The initial grand plans drawn by Pierre Charles L'Enfant were slow in being realised. Congress moved into the half-finished Capitol and President John Adams into the President's House (as the White House was then called) in 1800.

Thomas Jefferson was the first president to be inaugurated in the new capital. Washington remained a muddy miasmal district in its early years, and in 1814 British forces burned both the Capitol and the White House during what Americans call the War of 1812. During that same war, a poetic-minded young man named Francis Scott Key observed the night-time bombardment of Fort McHenry in Baltimore. Seeing the American flag intact when the smoke cleared, he penned 'The Star-Spangled Banner', which became the national anthem. Washington was rebuilt from the ravages of the War of 1812, but did not take on the grandeur its original architects had envisioned until six decades later. Monuments and memorials, including those to the casualties of more recent wars, continue to be added even today.

Above
Turning back the clock in
Charlottesville

A house divided

The great watershed in the history and the psyche of the Capital
Region was not the creation of Washington, but rather the Civil War,
as it was called by the victorious Union, or the War Between the
States, as it was known in the vanquished Confederacy. Political
rationales for the Civil War differ. In no small part, it was fought over
the abolition of slavery, although equal rights unabridged by race did
not become the law of the land until 98 years after the Confederacy's
defeat. Other historians cast the war as the struggle for economic
hegemony between the agricultural South and the industrial North.
And a generation of Southern political leaders, some still in office,
insist it was fought over the rights of individual states to govern
themselves without interference by the federal government. At any
rate, the Civil War remains a sensitive subject throughout the region,
subject to much melodrama and mythology. In parts of Virginia, in
particular, 'the war' still refers to the Civil War.

The conflagration of 1861–65 literally pitted brother against brother
in the bloodiest war the world had seen to that point. No other part of
the country was so rent as the Capital Region where Virginia, with
some reluctance, joined the Confederacy and the other states, often by
the slimmest of political margins, remained with the Union.
Washington, capital of the Union, and Richmond, Virginia, capital of
the Confederacy, stood just 106 miles apart, virtually guaranteeing
that the lands between and around them would be laid waste by four
years of unrelenting warfare.

Virginia, it can be argued, suffered the most. In fact, the first battle
of the Civil War took place on 21 July 1861 in Manassas, Virginia,
near the creek called Bull Run, and the war came to an effective close
in Virginia when Confederate General Robert E Lee surrendered, on
9 April 1865, at Appomattox Court House. During the course of the
conflict, more Americans died than in both World Wars combined. At
Antietam near Sharpsburg, Maryland, 23,000 men were killed or
wounded in a single day in 1862 in the first attempt of the
Confederacy to invade the North. At Gettysburg, Pennsylvania, nearly
53,000 were killed, wounded or captured in three grim days of battle
in July 1863. National, state and local parks commemorate a trauma
that refuses to fade from memory. Many artefacts remain and
interpretation of battle strategy and the human toll is often excellent,
particularly at the larger sites. The ferocity of the fighting is still hard
to grasp, but travellers may get a sense of the scope of the battles at
the re-enactments staged by costumed history buffs.

A collage of cultures and styles

Although travellers often encounter a distinctly Southern flavour in
the pace, food, customs and spoken accent of the Capital Region, the

area has a startling diversity. At the heart, of course, is official Washington of the power brokers, where the film-set landscape of the Washington Mall, Pennsylvania Avenue and Capitol Hill provides the backdrop for the daily interactions of some of the most influential people in the world. But Washington is more than elected officials. It was the US's first city with a majority of African-American population, and issues of racial justice are always on the front burner. At the same time, the cosmopolitan clique of foreign embassy personnel guarantees an exotic tinge to Washington life, while an entire subculture of career government employees (many living in the city part-time, far from their families) ensures an active nightlife.

Baltimore and Philadelphia are vibrant metropolitan centres where extensive African-American and Italian-American populations influence the culinary and cultural traditions of city life. While nearby Wilmington, Delaware, has a similar ethnic composition, it is also strongly influenced by the glass-towered business district. Half the Fortune 500 companies (and one-third of those listed on the New York Stock Exchange) maintain their corporate headquarters in the small state. That industrial and financial power finds a genteel expression in the adjacent suburbs of northern Delaware and southeastern Pennsylvania, where some of the US's finest mansion gardens are open to the public.

The money is older along Virginia's Tidewater, where literally hundreds of plantations and grand country homes line the coastal plain from the mouth of the James River north to Richmond. Yet between the big houses of the Tidewater gentry are small villages and towns tied intimately to the ebb and flow of life along the edge of the Chesapeake. Maryland's Eastern Shore, on the far side of the Chesapeake Bay, offers a glimpse into a nearly vanished way of life, where time is measured in the shift of tides and a resident's worth is measured in his or her skill with a boat. Half fishing villages, half yacht harbours, the Eastern Shore is the Capital Region's most enduring water-world.

The title of pleasure-boat capital of the region, however, goes to Annapolis, where the traditions and contradictions of the Capital Region converge. From its 18th-century city centre, Annapolis spills down into one of the Chesapeake's busiest harbours, full of swift little day-sailors, private schooners and the no-nonsense military vessels of the US Naval Academy. In Annapolis, ancient skills of hauling canvas in the wind are augmented by the latest in satellite navigation.

No such technology is used by the region's most unusual cultural survival, the Amish and Old Order Mennonites, in the Pennsylvania Dutch Country west of Philadelphia. Less than two hours' drive from the hurly-burly of Washington, these devout farmers work their land without the aid of electricity or the internal combustion engine, a horse-and-buggy world just at the fringe of perhaps the world's most modern capital.

Above
Colonial house, Williamsburg

Highlights and touring itineraries

Spend at least four days, preferably a full week, in Washington, but don't stop there. Get out to the countryside and the other cities of the region to enjoy some of the greatest scenic and cultural variety available anywhere in the USA. These suggested routes are starting points for explorations that can last from one to three weeks each.

The northern history route

This route encompasses some of the major battlefields of the Civil War, several sites associated with the American Revolution and some of the prettiest farmland and gardens of the region. Drive northwest from Washington on I-270 to Frederick, Maryland, veering westward to visit the sombre Civil War battlefields of Antietam and Sharpsburg and the flashpoint of North–South hostilities, Harper's Ferry, just inside West Virginia (*pages 190–207*). Return through Frederick to drive north on Rte 15 to Gettysburg, Pennsylvania, to Gettysburg National Military Park for more Civil War history (*pages 266–79*). Continue on Rte 15 to Lancaster and tour the unusually anachronistic farming region known as Pennsylvania Dutch Country, ending at the Revolutionary War site of Valley Forge and the outlet shopping of King-of-Prussia. I-76 leads south a mere 12 miles to the US's first capital, Philadelphia (*pages 252–65*). Follow Rte 1 south from Philadelphia through small towns filled with gardens and mansions in the Brandywine Valley (*pages 244–51*), pausing to tour Wilmington, Delaware (*pages 236–43*). Follow Rte 40 south along the western shore of the Chesapeake Bay (*pages 218–25*), stopping to savour the coastal attractions. Continue south to the bustling city of Baltimore (*pages 156–69*). I-95 is the best return route to Washington.

High country

The mountains and broad valleys of the southwestern segment of the Capital Region have a wild and stunning beauty especially accentuated by colourful autumn foliage. The entire route follows the mountainous backbone of Virginia. Follow I-66 west from Washington to exit 57 (Rte 50) through picturesque horse farm country to Winchester for a taste of Civil War history and country music. Follow Rte 11 south to Strasburg (*pages 68–75*), one of the region's antiquing capitals. Drive east on Rte 55 to Front Royal and follow Rte 340 south to the magnificent geological wonder of Luray Caverns. Rte 211 east connects to the Skyline Drive (*pages 76–87*). Drive south through Shenandoah National Park to Waynesboro, detouring east to visit the university city of Charlottesville and Appomattox, where the largest Confederate Army surrendered to the largest Union force (*pages 88–99*). Double back and continue south on the Blue Ridge Parkway, an extension of the Skyline Drive to Roanoke. From Roanoke return north along Rte 11 through the Shenandoah Valley, stopping for such scenic marvels as Natural Bridge. At Staunton, consider the detour west along the designated 'scenic byways' to George Washington National Forest (*page 86*). At Strasburg, return to Washington via I-66 with a stop at the Manassas National Battlefield Park, site of two critical Civil War battles.

By the water

The Chesapeake Bay and the Atlantic Ocean have stamped portions of the Capital Region with a distinctly nautical lifestyle. This route traverses both the modern resort playgrounds and the venerable waterside settlements of Maryland and Virginia, crossing Chesapeake Bay through the twin engineering feats of a long bridge and even longer bridge-tunnel. Drive east from Washington on Rte 50 to the postcard-perfect city of Annapolis (*pages 170–79*), wandering its Georgian streets and touring the US Naval Academy. Continue east across the Chesapeake Bay Bridge to Maryland's fabled Eastern Shore (*pages 180–89*), where you should eat your fill of oysters and crabs. Explore the small villages of the region, eventually returning to Rte 50 through Cambridge and Salisbury and finally to the brazen seaside resort town of Ocean City on the Atlantic. Trace the Atlantic shore southward along Chincoteague Bay and follow Rte 13 south all the way to the Chesapeake Bay Bridge-Tunnel to cross into the Hampton Roads, Virginia, area (*pages 146–55*).

Below
Folk musicians

Consider the long detour to North Carolina's Outer Banks if you are transfixed by sea island life or enamoured of birdwatching. Otherwise, follow Rte 17 north to Yorktown, the beginning of the end of the American Revolution, and pick up the Colonial Parkway to Williamsburg (*pages 136–45*), the most extensive restoration of colonial-era life in the US. Drive Rte 5 north along the James River (*pages 128–35*) through plantation country to Richmond (*pages 100–19*), capital of the Confederacy. Rte 1 north leads through Fredericksburg and its historic Civil War battlefields (*pages 120–27*) back to Washington.

Washington DC

Ratings

Museums	●●●●●
Gastronomy	●●●●●
Children	●●●●○
History	●●●●○
Shopping	●●●●○
Entertainment	●●●○○
Nature and wildlife	●●●○○
Beaches	●○○○○

Visitors to Washington DC are often surprised both by its approachability and by its wealth of cultural attractions. Power is, of course, Washington's defining feature, and the city's architecture, characterised by stern monuments of dazzling white Greek- and Roman-inspired columns, is a statement of its eminence. Politics aside, Washington is host to a mind-boggling collection of museums and art galleries, many operated by the Smithsonian Institution, one of the finest museum complexes in the world. What's more, nearly all are free. Founded in 1791, Washington DC – or just DC to its residents (the DC stands for 'District of Columbia', referring to Christopher Columbus) – was constructed specifically as the nation's seat of government. Its highbrow status does lend the city a certain stuffiness, but with a decidedly international population, some lively neighbourhoods and good concert life, Washington cannot fail to impress for days on end.

Getting there and getting around

ⓘ Washington DC Convention and Visitors Association
901 7th St NW; tel: (202) 789-7000;
www.washington.org

White House Visitor Center
1450 Pennsylvania Ave NW; tel: (202) 456-7041; www.whitehouse.gov/history/ tours; open Tue–Sat 0730–1230. White House tours must be scheduled well in advance.

By air
Washington DC is served by three airports. **Dulles Airport** is the largest; Washington Flyer buses run every half an hour to several downtown locations and a bus connects to the Metro line into Washington. **Ronald Reagan National Airport** is practically in the centre of town, and handles shorter domestic routes; the easiest way into town is on the Metrorail subway system. **Baltimore/Washington International Airport,** on the southern fringes of Baltimore, is served by regional rail and Amtrak (catch a shuttle bus from the arrivals terminal) to Baltimore's Penn Station and Washington's Union Station.

By rail
Union Station has been gloriously reconstructed, and Amtrak serves many cities along the Eastern Seaboard as well as the Midwest. It is located at 1st St and Massachusetts Ave NE, just a few blocks from the

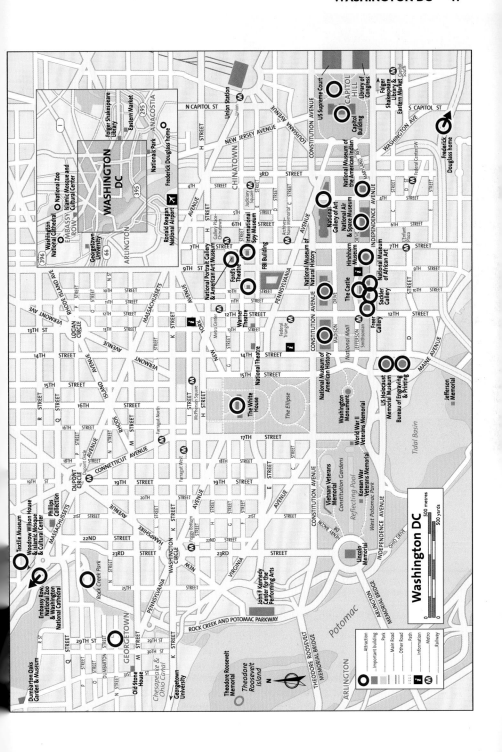

Above
Lincoln Memorial

Capitol, and is connected to the city by Metro. Greyhound and Peter Pan buses operate from a station a few blocks north, at 1st and L Sts NE.

By car

Washington's grid plan of streets is logically numbered and alphabetised, with broad avenues cutting across diagonally. The Beltway (I-495) rings the city; I-95 skirts the centre via I-495. From points north on I-95, follow signs to Downtown Washington via the Baltimore-Washington Parkway and Rte 50. From points south on I-95, follow I-395 to the National Mall. From points west, I-66 brings you across the Potomac to near the Lincoln Memorial.

Public transport

You may want to park your car at your hotel and use the excellent Metrorail subway system, one of the cleanest and safest you'll see anywhere. Fares vary according to distance travelled, and are the same anywhere in the District, except at rush hour; check the fare to your destination from well-lit signs in the station, and buy a farecard from machines. Be sure to hold on to it to exit the subway. A Metrorail One Day Pass costing $7.80 gives unlimited travel from 0930 to closing time (around midnight) on weekdays, and all day otherwise; a seven-day pass costs $39. Pick them up at Metro Center station. Metrobuses fill in where the subway does not; the only route you're likely to use is the 30 line (any of buses 30, 32, 34 or 36), which runs from the Capitol Building along Pennsylvania Ave to Foggy Bottom-GWU metro station, on through Georgetown and north to the National Cathedral.

Sights

Bureau of Engraving and Printing 14th and C Sts SW (metro: Smithsonian); tel: (202) 874-2330; www.moneyfactory.gov; tours Mon–Fri 0900–1045 and 1230–1400 (extended hours May–Aug 1400–1545 and 1700–1900); by ticket only. Free.

Bureau of Engraving and Printing

Jaws drop at the sight of millions of dollars a day being printed at the Bureau of Engraving and Printing. Some $100 billion is printed here annually, and tours lead you through glass-enclosed hallways past the engraving, cutting and printing rooms. Stacks of bills in uncut sheets line the walls – so near and yet so far – but you can buy shredded bills in canisters at the gift shop. Postage stamps are also printed here, but are not included in the tour. Tours are on a first come, first served basis – the ticket window on 15th St (Raoul Wallenberg Pl) opens at 0800 – arrive early for timed tickets (lines form as early as 0530).

Capitol Building
1st St between Independence and Constitution Aves (metro: Capitol South); tel: (202) 225-6827; www.aoc.gov; open Mon–Sat 0900–1630. The Capitol Visitor Center is open Mon–Sat 0830–1630; www.visitthecapitol.gov. Free.

Library of Congress
1st St and Independence Ave SE (metro: Capitol South); tel: (202) 707-8000; www.loc.gov; guided tours Mon–Fri 1030–1530, Sat 1030–1430; reading rooms open Mon–Sat varied hours. Free.

US Supreme Court
1st St and Maryland Ave NE (metro: Capitol South); tel: (202) 479-3211; www.supremecourtus.gov; open Mon–Fri 0900–1630. Lectures are given every hour on the half-hour Mon–Fri 0930–1530 when not in session. Free.

Folger Shakespeare Library *201 E Capitol St SE (metro: Capitol South); tel: (202) 544-4600; www.folger.edu; open Mon–Sat 1000–1600. Free*

Capitol Building

All four city districts converge on the Capitol Building, seat of the US government, and the nerve centre of all that is Washington. The building's physical beauty is one obvious attraction (its white dome is particularly striking at night); another is that you can witness Congress in session. Free tours are offered, taking in some of the magnificent art works and grand halls. Timed tickets are distributed on a first come, first served basis starting at 0900 from the Capitol Guide Service Kiosk in front of the Capitol near the intersection of Independence Ave and 1st St SW and are limited to one ticket per person. To get a congressional pass and watch the proceedings, Americans can apply to their senator or representative several weeks in advance, or if it's a slow day, find their relevant person and pick one up on the spot. Foreign visitors may obtain House passes at the gallery check-in desk on the south side of the building, and Senate passes at the Senate appointment desk on the north side, all subject to availability. *The Washington Post* records when Senators and Representatives are sitting.

Capitol Hill

Behind the Capitol are a number of other important buildings, and the neighbourhood itself is charming to stroll about. The **Library of Congress** is a research library created in 1800 to serve Congress, and now holds close to 100 million books and documents. A room in the James Madison building (there are three library buildings in the complex) contains the Gutenberg Bible and Martin Luther King's 'I Have a Dream' speech. The **US Supreme Court** building a block away has displays and a film outlining procedures in the nation's highest court. Court hearings may be watched on a first come, first served basis. Also in the area is the surprisingly good **Folger Shakespeare Library**, with a recreation of Shakespeare's original Elizabethan theatre and one of the world's greatest collections of Shakespeare and Renaissance material.

Right
The Capitol by night

The Castle: Smithsonian Institution Visitors Center *10th St and Jefferson Dr at the Mall SW (metro: Smithsonian); tel: (202) 633-1000; www.smithsonian.org; open daily 0830–1730.*

Woodrow Wilson House $$ *2340 S St NW (metro: Dupont Circle); tel: (202) 387-4062; www. woodrowwilsonhouse.org; open Tue–Sun 1000–1600.*

Islamic Mosque and Cultural Center *2551 Massachusetts Ave NW (metro: Dupont Circle); tel: (202) 332-8343; www.theislamiccenter.com; open daily 1000–2300. All limbs must be covered, women must cover their heads and shoes must be removed. Free.*

The Castle

Of all the distinctive architectural styles on the Mall, perhaps the most eye-grabbing is the original 1850s Smithsonian Institution museum, known simply as The Castle for its neo-Romanesque burgundy-brick design.

Embassy Row

Massachusetts Ave northwest of Dupont Circle has the highest concentration of embassies in the city, hence its nickname. Many of these are fine 19th-century mansions, while others are purpose-built in distinctive designs reflecting that country's style. The **Woodrow Wilson House**, just off Massachusetts Ave at 24th and S Sts, is the town house to which President Wilson retired in 1921. It is now a museum of personal memorabilia. Further to the northwest, the minaret and tiled courtyard of the beautiful **Islamic Mosque and Cultural Center** strongly evoke the Middle East. The edifice stands at a slight angle to face Mecca. Across Rock Creek Park, and beyond the British Embassy (notable for its statue of Winston Churchill saluting with a 'V') stands the Vice President's Mansion, part of the Naval Observatory, and formerly the Admiral's house. It is closed to the public.

Ford's Theatre *511 10th St NW (metro: Metro Center or Gallery Place-Chinatown); tel: (202) 426-5924; www.nps.gov/foth; open daily 0900–1700. Free.*

Frederick Douglass home $ *1411 W St SE (metro: Anacostia, then bus 82); tel: (202) 426-5960; www.nps.gov/frdo/freddoug. htm; open daily spring–summer 0900–1700, autumn–winter 0900–1600. This area is a little doubtful, but safe enough during the day; consider driving.*

The Freer Gallery *12th St and Jefferson Dr SW at the Mall (metro: Smithsonian); tel: (202) 633-4880; www.smithsonian.org; open daily 1000–1730. Free.*

Ford's Theatre

The pretty Ford's Theatre was the site of President Abraham Lincoln's assassination on 14 April 1865, just days after the end of the Civil War. His assassin, John Wilkes Booth, an actor at the theatre, conceived his act as a savage parting shot for the Confederacy. Lincoln died several hours later in **Petersen House** across the street, also open to the public (same hours), which contains the bed (and bloodstained pillowcase) on which Lincoln died. A museum underneath Ford's Theatre has more information on the assassination. The theatre is in active use, restored in the 1960s, with all the 19th-century trappings retained.

Frederick Douglass home

Worth the trip into southeast Washington is the home of the self-educated African-American who was one of the great figures in the emancipation of slavery. His home has been restored to its mid-19th-century appearance. A trip here is a history lesson in racial relations in America and also in DC history.

Left
Embassy Row

Right
The Islamic Mosque and Cultural Center

The Freer Gallery, The Sackler Gallery and The National Museum of African Art

African and Asian art is gathered in abundance at these three connected museums by the Castle on the Mall. The **Freer Gallery** is actually the Smithsonian's first art gallery, featuring the collection of 1920s industrialist James Freer. In addition to Chinese porcelain and Japanese calligraphy scrolls, the Freer contains one of the world's largest collections of paintings by the American James McNeil Whistler.

The Sackler Gallery *11th St and Independence Ave at the Mall (metro: Smithsonian); tel: (202) 633-4880; www.smithsonian.org; open daily 1000–1730. Free.*

The National Museum of African Art *10th St and Independence Ave at the Mall (metro: Smithsonian); tel: (202) 633-4600; www.smithsonian.org; open daily 1000–1730. Free.*

The **Sackler Gallery** features precious manuscripts and objects from ancient China and the Middle East, including jade and bronze from as far back as 3000 BC. The **National Museum of African Art** covers a broad range of sculptures, paintings and crafts from numerous African countries, and including several beautiful ivory carvings.

Georgetown

Georgetown dates from the 1750s, a city before Washington DC was even conceived, and amassed its wealth as a port handling tobacco and timber from Virginia and Maryland, and highly desired imports from Europe. There are many late 19th-century buildings, and Georgetown's urban mansions and cobblestone streets make a perfect backdrop for strolling, window-shopping and dining. The intersection of Wisconsin Ave and M St is its axis, and a prime commercial centre, but to appreciate the neighbourhood you'll want to explore the back streets and byways.

The **Chesapeake and Ohio (C&O) Canal**, built for inland trade in the mid-1800s, runs parallel to M St and the river; the towpath

Dumbarton Oaks $
*31st and R Sts NW (bus
30, 32, 34, 36 or D2); tel:
(202) 339-6410; museum
and shop open Tue–Sun
1400–1700 (free); gardens
$$ open mid-Mar–Oct
Tue–Sun 1400–1800,
Nov–mid-Mar Tue–Sun
1400–1700 (free in winter).*

**Hirshhorn Museum and
Sculpture Garden** *7th
St and Independence Ave
NW at the Mall (metro:
Smithsonian or L'Enfant
Plaza); tel: (202) 633-1000;
www.smithsonian.org; open
daily 1000–1730. Free.*

Above
Georgetown

Opposite
*The National Museum of
African Art*

between 29th and 31st Sts is particularly atmospheric, and from June to September you can take a short ride on a mule-drawn flat-bottomed canal barge ($$). North of M St, streets such as N and O Sts are lined with historic town houses and beautiful gardens and lead up to the pretty campus of **Georgetown University** at 37th and O Sts. This is the nation's first Catholic university, founded in 1789; its neo-Gothic Healy Hall dominates the local skyline.

Dumbarton Oaks, a lovely mansion and garden, was the setting for the 1944 Dumbarton Oaks Conference, where discussions between the US, UK, USSR and China eventually led to the formation of the United Nations. The mansion houses a superb collection of Byzantine coins and artefacts, as well as Mayan and Aztec figurines and gold carvings.

Hirshhorn Museum and Sculpture Garden
This cylindrical structure on the Mall holds some excellent 19th- and 20th-century works gathered by the financier Joseph Hirshhorn. Romantic- and Impressionist-era paintings and sculptures by Renoir, Degas and Rodin are complemented by works of such contemporary luminaries as Picasso, Matisse, Pollock, Bacon and O'Keeffe. The grounds of the museum, and a sunken garden across the street, form an open-air sculpture garden.

International Spy Museum $$$
800 F St NW (metro: Gallery Place-Chinatown); tel: (202) 393-7798 or (866) 779-6873; www.spymuseum.org; open daily 1000–2000; check for earlier opening hours during summer and other busy periods.

National Air and Space Museum
6th St and Independence Ave SW at the Mall (metro: Smithsonian or L'Enfant Plaza); tel: (202) 633-1000; www.smithsonian.org; open daily 1000–1730. Free.

Stephen F Udvar-Hazy Center
14390 Air & Space Museum Parkway, Chantilly, Virginia; tel: (202) 633-1000; www.smithsonian.org; open daily 1000–1730. Free.

International Spy Museum

A huge hit since its opening in 2002, the International Spy Museum presents an engrossing look at the world of espionage – tracing its history and focusing on the role of spies in the 20th century. Interactive exhibits and the collection of wacky gadgets let you act out your own spy fantasies. Last entrance is two hours before closing – a good indication of the amount of time you'll want to spend here.

National Air and Space Museum

The most popular Smithsonian museum stands at the southeastern corner of the Mall near the Capitol building, filled with its incredible array of real aircraft and spacecraft. Planes hang from the ceiling, while rockets stand along the walls. Notable are the first plane to fly solo trans-Atlantic (by Charles Lindbergh), the first glider plane to fly around the world non-stop, the original Saturn V rocket and several (decommissioned) American and Soviet nuclear warheads. The museum galleries chronicle the history of aviation from the Wright Brothers through to the Space Shuttle. Tickets for the IMAX cinema must be bought in advance.

The **Stephen F Udvar-Hazy Center**, located out near Dulles Airport in Chantilly, Virginia, is a huge new extension of the Air and Space Museum, housing the *Enola Gay* (which dropped the atomic bomb on Hiroshima), Concorde and the Space Shuttle *Enterprise*, among other aircraft and spacecraft in custom-built hangars. A shuttle bus ($) runs at irregular hours (call or check the website for schedules) to the Air and Space Museum on the Mall, taking about an hour.

The National Gallery of Art

Along the north side of the Mall, the first buildings west of the Capitol are the two wings of the marvellous National Gallery of Art, which exists thanks to the generosity of industrialist Andrew Mellon. The original west wing houses an excellent collection of paintings and sculptures from the Italian Renaissance, 17th–18th century Flanders and the Netherlands, and Romantic-era France, Spain, Britain and the USA, with renowned works by Raphael, Rembrandt, Rubens, Monet, Gauguin and Van Gogh. An underground walkway connects it to the east wing which focuses on contemporary

Above
The Hirshhorn Museum

Opposite
The National Air and Space Museum

The Mall and its monuments

The National Mall is the physical and cultural centre of Washington, a vast expanse of grass and footpaths lined on all sides by wonderful museums and many of the city's most recognisable monuments. Aside from spending hours, or even days upon end in the museums and galleries, the Mall is a wonderful place to relax, with a wintertime ice-skating rink by the National Museum of Natural History, and a children's funfair-type carousel ride by the Castle in the warm months. The chief monuments are covered below, while museums appear elsewhere in the text, with reference to their Mall location.

Unmissable wherever you stand, the 555ft Washington Monument is one of the city's most recognisable symbols. On clear days views from the top of the obelisk spread all the way to the Blue Ridge Mountains.

Behind the Washington Monument, the long, narrow Reflecting Pool stretches several hundred yards to the Lincoln Memorial, an impressive Grecian-style columned monument to one of the US's greatest presidents. A statue of a seated Abraham Lincoln lurks inside, and the steps have hosted countless national celebrations and demonstrations, most remarkable of which was Martin Luther King Jr's electrifying 'I Have a Dream' speech in 1963 – an appropriate setting at the feet of the man who risked the nation's unity in order to abolish slavery.

Lincoln's gaze falls kindly on the particularly moving Vietnam Veterans Memorial, just north of the Reflecting Pool. The black granite V-shaped memorial carries more than 58,000 names of those who died or remain missing in the Vietnam War, and is well visited by relatives of the dead. Across the Pool, the Korean War Veterans Memorial is made up of stainless steel sculptures of ground troops. At the eastern end of the Reflecting Pool stands the majestic new World War II Veterans Memorial.

South of the Reflecting Pool, the Tidal Basin is famous for its Japanese cherry blossom trees, especially enticing during early April when they explode in soft pink. You can rent paddleboats on the water in warm weather, or visit the graceful domed Jefferson Memorial along its southern edge. The design reflects Thomas Jefferson's fascination with classical architecture, and is similar to his home at Monticello, near Charlottesville, Virginia.

The National Gallery of Art *The Mall between 3rd and 7th Sts NW (metro: Smithsonian or Archives-Navy Memorial); tel: (202) 737-4215; www.nga.gov; open Mon–Sat 1000–1700, Sun 1100–1800. Free.*

The National Museum of American History *12th St and Constitution Ave NW at the Mall (metro: Smithsonian or Federal Triangle); tel: (202) 633-1000; www.smithsonian.org; open daily 1000–1730; check for later summer hours, which change yearly. Free.*

National Museum of the American Indian *Independence Ave and 4th St SW (metro: Federal Center SW or L'Enfant Plaza); tel: (202) 633-1000, www.smithsonian.org; open daily 1000–1730. Free.*

The National Museum of Natural History *10th St and Constitution Ave NW at the Mall (metro: Smithsonian or Federal Triangle); tel: (202) 633-1000; www.smithsonian.org; open daily 1000–1730; check for later summer hours, which change yearly. Free.*

National Portrait Gallery *8th and F Sts NW; tel: (202) 633-8300; www.npg.si.edu; open 1130–1900 daily. Free.*

American Art Museum *8th and F Sts NW; tel: (202) 633-1000; www.americanart.si.ed; open daily 1130–190. Free.*

art, including works by Picasso, Lichtenstein and Warhol, and a steady stream of visiting exhibitions. The building itself is something to marvel at.

The National Museum of American History

With a constantly changing gathering of important events in America's history, the museum's greatest strength is that it doesn't try to glamorise: exhibits include rich displays on, for example, the so-called Great Migration of African Americans northward after the Civil War. Exhibits are designed to be both visually appealing and educational, and any layman can learn from the displays on Thomas Edison's development of electricity or the building of the Hoover Dam. Exhibits range from turn-of-the-twentieth-century locomotives to the banquet gowns of recent First Ladies and the original Star-Spangled Banner flag.

National Museum of the American Indian

The American Indian Museum attempts to capture, in one facility, the lives of America's hundreds of Indian peoples, with much of the focus on present-day native Americans and their surviving artefacts and traditions, achieved largely with multi-media presentations. The organisation is somewhat confusing, although the building itself is impressive, designed as a traditional dwelling.

The National Museum of Natural History

The National Museum of Natural History is a wonderful array of the planet's physical being. Highlights include reconstructed skeletons of dinosaurs, precious gems, including the notorious Hope Diamond (largest in the world), displays on the lives of native American peoples, and the Insect Zoo, with live tarantulas, scorpions and lots more.

National Portrait Gallery and American Art Museum

Both of these outstanding art museums near the International Spy Museum have undergone extensive renovations, and are joined by a covered courtyard that is quite beautiful in itself. Don't expect walls of sombre paintings; the Portrait Gallery tells America's story through portraits, in all media, of the people who have shaped US culture, from George Washington and Chief Sequoyah to Marilyn Monroe and Bob Hope. The American Art Museum views the American experience through the eyes of its artists.

Rock Creek Park and the National Zoo

Rock Creek Park is a remarkable forest right in the city, extending from the Potomac River into suburban Maryland. Deer roam through the park and blue herons come to feed from the gurgling stream. The National Zoo, a local favourite, is carved into a slope in part of the park, and displays a wide range of species in commendably natural settings. The prime attraction is its two pandas. A century ago, the Rock Creek valley was filled with mills, but only Pierce Mill survives. It is not open to the public, but makes a nice setting for a picnic; by

National Zoo *3001 Connecticut Ave NW (metro: Woodley Park-Zoo or Cleveland Park); tel: (202) 673-4800; www.nationalzoo. si.edu; grounds open daily 0600–1800, buildings open daily 1000–1800 in summer, 1000–1630 in winter. Free.*

The Textile Museum *2320 S St NW; tel: (202) 667-0441; www.textilemuseum.org; open Tue–Sat 1000–1700, Sun 1300–1700. Free (donation suggested).*

US Holocaust Memorial Museum *100 Raoul Wallenberg Pl. SW, near 14th St and Independence Ave (metro: Smithsonian); tel: (202) 488-0400; open daily 1000–1730 except Yom Kippur and Christmas Day. Timed entry tickets must be purchased in advance, either online at www.tickets.com or at (800) 400-9373. Free.*

Washington National Cathedral *Wisconsin Ave and Massachusetts Ave NW (bus 30, 32, 34, 36 or N2); tel: (202) 364-6616; open daily 1000–1630 (extended in summer). Free.*

car, take Rock Creek Parkway to Beach Drive to the junction with Tilden St NW.

The Textile Museum

Displaying and interpreting textiles from Persian carpets to Amish quilts, this colourful collection is augmented by a learning centre and a stunning gift shop. Its permanent holdings include some of the finest collections in the world in early Islamic textiles, as well as those of India, Southeast and Central Asia, Turkey and Greece, and outstanding collections of pre-Columbian Peruvian work.

US Holocaust Memorial Museum

The harrowing story of the Nazi genocide is told at the US Holocaust Memorial Museum through photographs, artefacts, film, videotaped histories and memorial pieces. Particularly moving are the Tower of Faces, an actual barrack building from Auschwitz, and cases full of human hair, glasses and shoes of the victims.

Washington National Cathedral

Occupying one of the highest points in the city, the Washington National Cathedral bears a stunning similarity to many of Europe's finest cathedrals. Twentieth-century craftsmen used 14th- and 15th-century skills to build and adorn this Gothic house of worship for the Episcopal Church, which also honours events and personalities in US history. It was completed only in 1990 and is the world's sixth largest cathedral, noteworthy as much for its size as for its exceptional attention to the use of space, its smooth surfaces complementing the airy interior. The observation tower offers splendid views of the city,

Right
Washington National
Cathedral

The White House
1600 Pennsylvania Ave NW (metro: Farragut North, McPherson Sq or Metro Center).

White House Visitor Center *1450 Pennsylvania Ave NW; tel: (202) 456-7041; www.whitehouse.gov/history/tours*

and the lovely gardens on the south side make a soothing respite from the summer heat.

The White House

It is an undeniable thrill to stand inside perhaps the most famous house in the world, the home of all US presidents since John Adams (the second president, after George Washington, who served in Philadelphia). However, since 9/11 and until further notice, the White House is only open for groups of 10 or more who have arranged tickets in advance; call the White House Visitor Center for updates. A block away, it is worth seeing in its own right, with historical exhibits and displays of photographs about the White House through the years. Leafy Lafayette Square opposite the mansion is a gathering point for low-key protesters of all kinds.

Entertainment

🔺 **John F Kennedy Center for the Performing Arts** *Virginia and New Hampshire Aves NW (metro: Foggy Bottom-GWU); tel: (202) 467-4600; www.kennedy-center.org*

National Theatre *1321 Pennsylvania Ave NW (metro: Metro Center); tel: (202) 628-6161 or (800) 233-3123; www.nationaltheatre.org. Offers free performances regularly.*

Warner Theatre *513 13th St NW (metro: Metro Center); tel: (202) 783-4000; www.warnertheatre. com*

Ford's Theatre *511 10th St NW (metro: Metro Center or Gallery Place-Chinatown); tel: (202) 426-5924; www.fordstheatre.org*

Blues Alley *Rear of 1073 Wisconsin Ave NW; tel: (202) 337-4141; www.bluesalley.com*

The BricksKeller *1523 22nd St NW; tel: (202) 293-1885.*

Washington has a buzzing concert and theatre life. Listings of current shows, drama and concerts are given in *The Washington Post* and *Washington City Paper*. World-class orchestral, opera and dance performances take place at the **John F Kennedy Center for the Performing Arts**. The National Symphony Orchestra's season runs from September to May. There are also frequent concerts at the National Gallery of Art and at many of the Smithsonian museums.

There is no theatre district *per se*, but you can catch Broadway shows at the modern **National Theatre**, especially atmospheric is the reconstructed **Ford's Theatre** (*see page 45*). Other venues to try are the Shakespeare Theatre on 7th Street, the Folger Shakespeare Theatre in the Folger Library, the Warner Theatre and Studio Theatre on the revitalised 14th Street corridor.

Despite its rather stodgy image, DC can provide the needed excitement for a night at the pubs and clubs. Georgetown (particularly Wisconsin Ave and M St) and Adams Morgan (18th St between Columbia Rd and U St) are vigorous neighbourhoods with plenty of hotspots. DC has an unusually good collection of jazz and blues clubs, such as **Blues Alley**, a long-established, upscale jazz club in Georgetown. Anyone with a taste for good beer should head to **The BricksKeller**, a large but cosy pub near Dupont Circle with a menu of over 800 brews from around the world.

DC has rediscovered professional sports in recent years. The Washington Nationals baseball team draws huge crowds to its home stadium, **Nationals Park** (*metro: Navy Yard*). For tickets *tel: (202) 675-NATS*. Basketball and hockey are played at the MCI Center. For tickets *tel: (202) 397 SEAT*. Tickets to the football team Washington Redskins, however, are nearly impossible to obtain, being sold out years in advance.

Left
The White House

Right
Cherry blossom time at the Capitol

National Cherry Blossom Festival
A week-long exultation in early Apr of more than 6,000 Japanese cherry trees in bloom at various monuments.
www.nationalcherryblossom festival.org

Smithsonian Folklife Festival In late Jun/early Jul hundreds of thousands of people flock to the Mall for music, arts, crafts and cuisine from America's diverse ethnic groups.

Independence Day The biggest bash of the year is the 4th of July celebration on the Mall: day-long events culminate in a free evening concert by the National Symphony Orchestra on the west steps of the Capitol, and a glorious fireworks display at night.

Power in Washington

The US government is made up of three branches: the Executive, composed of the President and Vice President, along with their cabinet; the Legislative (Congress), a bicameral structure comprised of the Senate and the House of Representatives; and the Judicial, or the federal court system. This arrangement is intended to maintain a system of 'checks and balances' on the government.

The President and Vice President are the only elected officials of the Executive branch. He has the power to select ambassadors, judges and military leaders, and his role in the law-making process is significant in that he has the power to veto any law that Congress passes. The President chooses his Vice Presidential running mate, and elections are held every four years, with a maximum service of two terms.

The Legislative branch makes laws. The Senate has two Senators from each of the 50 states, while the House of Representatives is proportionate to the population of the state: thus California and New York have many representatives while Idaho and Alaska have few. Again, the structure is based upon the principle of checks and balances: House members represent their local constituencies, Senators represent an entire state. Senators are elected every six years, while House members are elected in their districts every two years. One irony of the federal government's location in Washington DC, is that the city itself, with nearly 600,000 residents, has no representation in Congress.

The top of the ladder in the Judicial system is the Supreme Court, with nine judges appointed by the President with the approval of Congress. Other federal courts include federal district courts and US courts of appeals. Federal courts handle cases that involve federal laws, cross state boundaries or are appealed from lower courts.

Apart from the power in these positions, Washington is loaded with lobbyists, who represent such organisations as Greenpeace or the American Medical Association, and whose purpose is to influence Members of Congress to vote on laws affecting their cause. In addition, the capital is home base for countless government-related organisations such as the World Bank and the International Monetary Fund, as well as influential national media such as *The Washington Post*.

Government is the city's chief industry, followed by tourism. Because of the frequent changes in government and related changes in government-related businesses and organisations, the Washington metropolitan area has a huge population turnover; this constant change of people has much to do with the city's lack of a clear personality.

Accommodation and food

ⓘ Reservation services

Capitol Reservations
Tel: (800) VISIT-DC or (202) 452-1270.

Washington DC Accommodation
Tel: (800) 554-2220 or (202) 289-2220.

Bed and Breakfast Accommodations Tel: (202) 328-3510.

ⓒ Willard InterContinental
$$$ 1401 Pennsylvania Ave NW; tel: (202) 628-9100; http://washington. intercontinental.com

Hay-Adams $$$
1 Lafayette Sq NW; tel: (202) 638-6600; www.hayadams.com

Latham Hotel $$
3000 M St NW; tel: (202) 726-5000; www. thelatham.com

Harrington Hotel $
11 00 E St NW; tel: (202) 528-8140 or (800) 424-8532; www.hotel-harrington.com

Tabard Inn $$ 1739 N St NW; tel: (202) 785-1277; www.tabardinn.com

Windsor Inn $–$$ 1842 16th St NW; tel: (202) 667-0300 or (800) 423-9111.

Kalorama Guest House
$ 1854 Mintwood Pl NW; tel: (202) 667-6369; and 2700 Cathedral Ave NW; tel: (202) 328-0860.

Washington's role as the centre of government and of tourism in the region means there are plenty of fine hotels, but it is still important to book as early as possible. For cheaper places and B&Bs, you really should book several weeks in advance. The better central hotels offer reduced rates at weekends and in July and August, when Congress is in recess.

The **Willard InterContinental** is a Washington institution, a lavish hotel near the White House. Its chief competition comes from the **Hay-Adams**, right opposite the White House and a frequent host of international politicos. The **Latham Hotel** is a comfortable hotel in Georgetown, with shopping, dining and entertainment on the doorstep.

There are at least a couple of cheaper options downtown. The **Allen Lee Hotel** is a decent budget hotel close to the monuments. The **Harrington Hotel** is a well-established basic standard near the White House and the Mall.

Washington has a nice selection of lower and mid-range B&Bs, which generally are situated in Victorian town houses, such as the **Tabard Inn**, with its own restaurant, on the cusp of Dupont Circle and Downtown. Also appealing, but a little cheaper, is the comfortable **Windsor Inn**, close to both Dupont Circle and Adams Morgan. **Kalorama Guest House** is a simple, popular B&B operating from two separate homes in Adams Morgan and Woodley Park, with the best rates in town. **Hotel Lombardy** is a well-located European-style hotel with a café.

As might be expected, Washington offers a culinary choice that sweeps across the international spectrum. Local culinary traditions centre on the Chesapeake Bay's abundance of fine seafood and on homey, southern-style cooking. Adams Morgan (*18th St between Columbia Rd and U St NW*) is the ethnic hotspot in town, with a rich selection of Ethiopian, Mexican, French and many others. Georgetown (*around Wisconsin Ave and M St NW*) is a long-established part of social life in DC, with everything from cheap diners to Irish pubs and fine Italian restaurants. Most of the Smithsonian museums have café/restaurants, which are good for a cheap lunch or snack; the one in the west wing of the National Gallery of Art is highly recommended.

Georgia Brown's is a well-established downtown restaurant offering gracious southern cooking such as gumbo and pork chops in a fanciful setting. **Old Ebbitt Grill**, close to the White House, is known for steak and oysters and famous for Washington hob-nobbing. To lunch among the Capitol Hill newsmakers, reserve a table at **The Monocle**, between the Capitol Building and Union Station. Sample the latest from a legendary American chef at Wolfgang Puck's **The Source**. Slightly less expensive, but tops for American contemporary and in a

Hotel Lombardy
$$ 2019 Pennsylvania
Ave NW; tel: (202) 828-
2600;
www.hotellombardy.com

Georgia Brown's $$$
950 15th St NW; tel: (202)
393-4499.

Old Ebbitt Grill $$–$$$
675 15th St NW; tel: (202)
347-4800.

The Monocle $$ 107 D
St NE; tel: (202) 546-4488;
www.themonocle.com

The Source $$$ 575
Pennsylvania Ave; tel: (202)
637-6100;
www.wolfgangpuck.com

1789 Restaurant
$$–$$$ 1226 36th St NW;
tel: (202) 965-1789;
www.1789restaurant.com

Martin's Tavern $$
1264 Wisconsin Ave NW;
tel: (202) 333-7370;
www.martins-tavern.com

Black Salt $$ 4883
MacArthur Blvd; tel: (202)
342-9101;
www.blacksaltrestaurant.com

Patisserie Poupon $
1645 Wisconsin Ave NW;
tel: (202) 342-3248.

Marvin's $–$$ 2007 14th
St NW; tel: (202) 797-7171;
www.marvindc.com

Cork $–$$ 1720 14th St
NW; tel: (202) 265-2675;
www.corkdc.com

Tabard Inn $$ 1739 N St
NW; tel: (202) 331-8528;
www.tabardinn.com

lovely old Georgetown building is **1789 Restaurant**. Also in Georgetown is **Martin's Tavern**, an old favourite with a history, and beyond Georgetown in the Palisades is **Black Salt**, a great fish restaurant. Locals agree that the best pastry in the city is found at **Patisserie Poupon**, a French bakery serving breakfast and lunch.

The U St/14th St/Logan Circle neighbourhood is the most recently renovated DC area and it's booming. Try **Marvin's** or **Cork**, both wine bars with good, inexpensive food, or **Tabard Inn**, which serves sustainable food in contemporary dishes. For the latest information on dining in Washington, visit *www.examiner.com/x-3652-DC-Culinary-Travel-Examiner*

Right
Georgetown

Suggested walking tour

Phillips Collection
$$ *1600 21st St NW;
tel: (202) 387-2151;
www.phillipscollection.org;
open Tue–Sat 1000–1700
(Thur until 2030),
Sun 1200–1600.*

**Corcoran Gallery of
Art** $ *17th St and New
York Ave NW; tel: (202)
639-1700; www.corcoran.org;
open Wed–Mon 1000–1700
(Thur until 2100).*

Total distance: 5 miles

Time: 3 hours for fit walkers, assuming no stops. Allow at least a full day with selected quick stops. This walk can easily be split into two separate walks: one from Dupont Circle to Georgetown (1 hour), the other from Georgetown across the Mall to the Capitol (2 hours).

Route: Hop on the metro and alight at Dupont Circle station. Take the Q St exit, then turn left down Q St to 21st St, where a burgundy-brick mansion houses the **Phillips Collection** ❶, an excellent private gallery of 19th- and 20th-century paintings, including a particularly acclaimed selection of works by Renoir. Continue a block further on Q St to Massachusetts Ave, the beginning of **EMBASSY ROW** ❷. Follow Massachusetts Ave to 22nd St for a taste of the opulence, or continue a few blocks up Massachusetts Ave for more, but be sure to double back to 22nd St. Walk south down 22nd St, turning right on to P St to cross the bridge over **ROCK CREEK PARK** ❸ and into **GEORGETOWN** ❹.

Detour: Wander along P St to 27th St, turn left, and then turn right on to either O St, **Dumbarton St** or N St to see some of Georgetown's finest town houses. To prolong your tour of Georgetown, take a detour to **Dumbarton Oaks** ❺ at 31st and R Sts. All of these streets empty out on to Wisconsin Ave, a prime centre of shopping and nightlife.

Turn left (south) on Wisconsin Ave to M St, and spend a little while poking into shops and cafés. Take note of the **Old Stone House** ❻ at 3051 M St, the oldest structure in Georgetown, dating from the 1760s, before heading down either 31st St or Thomas Jefferson St to the river. You could break the trip here by catching any No 30 bus downtown.

The Washington Harbour restaurant/office complex fronts the river, and a path from here follows along the banks of the Potomac past the **Watergate** ❼ (location of President Nixon's notorious campaign-meddling in the early 1970s) and the **John F Kennedy Center for Performing Arts** ❽. Cross the street at the **Lincoln Memorial** ❾ and continue on past the Reflecting Pool to the **Washington Monument** ❿.

Detour: From the base of the Washington Monument you get a good view of the **WHITE HOUSE** ⓫, and a quick walk north across the **Ellipse** ⓬ brings you closer to it. Once here, jog over to the corner of 17th St and New York Ave, where the **Corcoran Gallery of Art** ⓭ is filled with a wonderful collection of American paintings, including works by Cole, Eakins, Sargent and Cassat.

From the Washington Monument it's a leisurely walk along the **MALL** ⓮ to the **CAPITOL BUILDING** ⓯.

Shopping

Washington offers some fun opportunities to stock up on speciality gifts. The gift shops in many of the museums on the Mall have wonderful items for gift-giving or personal collections; try the **National Air and Space Museum** for children's toys, the **National Gallery of Art** for books and framed reproductions of artworks and the **National Museum of American History** for a wide assortment of quality American-themed knick-knacks.

For anything from fresh produce to flowers and oriental rugs, not to mention a lot of fun, head to the **Eastern Market** (*200 block of 7th St SE; metro: Eastern Market*) on Capitol Hill, on a weekend morning. Although the wonderful old market building was badly damaged by fire, the market continues in temporary quarters.

Below
The Capitol viewed from the
National Air and Space
Museum

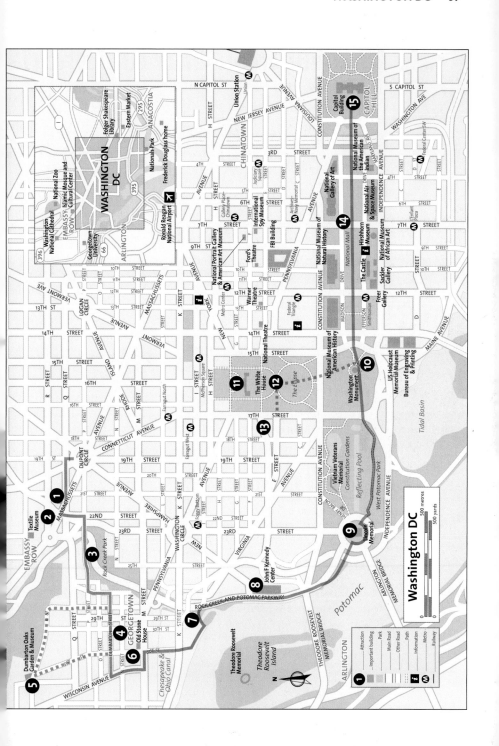

Arlington and Alexandria

Ratings

Art and museums	●●●●○
Gastronomy	●●●●○
History	●●●●○
Shopping	●●●○○
Children	●●○○○
Entertainment	●●○○○
Nature	●●○○○
Beaches	●○○○○

The northern Virginia suburbs of Arlington and Alexandria are really part of Washington DC, and as such have numerous important monuments that merit a visit. From 1789 to 1846, the two were in fact incorporated into the District of Columbia, and today both are served by the city's Metrorail system. Arlington County is a prosperous suburb, whose chief attraction, its famous cemetery, lies across the Potomac from the Lincoln Memorial. The city of Alexandria, further downstream, actually predates Washington, and retains its cobblestoned colonial gentility, with several historic buildings and some great restaurants to visit. Alexandria was a base of George Washington, and his beautiful home at Mount Vernon sits proudly on a bluff above the Potomac, downstream. In combination with a visit to Washington, a trip across the river gives a deeper impression of the growth of both the city and the nation.

ARLINGTON NATIONAL CEMETERY

Arlington National Cemetery $ *On the Virginia side of Memorial Bridge opposite the Lincoln Memorial (metro: Arlington Cemetery); tel: (703) 979-0690; www. arlingtoncemetery.org; open daily summer 0800–1900, winter 0800–1700. Fee is for parking.*

Rising on a gentle slope across the river from the Lincoln Memorial is the vast, perfectly manicured Arlington National Cemetery, final resting place of hundreds of thousands of US servicemen and women, and of President John F Kennedy. Tombs stretch in uniform rows over 200 acres, while Kennedy's grave is given special recognition with a serene eternal flame. Nearby, stern-columned Arlington House was the home of Robert E Lee, commander of the army of Virginia during the Civil War. His mansion is preserved in period furnishings, and offers a great view of Washington from its front steps. Elsewhere, the Tomb of the Unknowns symbolises unknown soldiers from America's involvement in the terrible wars of the 20th century. The tomb is watched over 24 hours a day; try to time your visit for the hourly changing of the guard. The cemetery is closed to vehicular traffic except for the disabled and relatives of those buried, so prepare for a long walk, or hop aboard the Tourmobile bus.

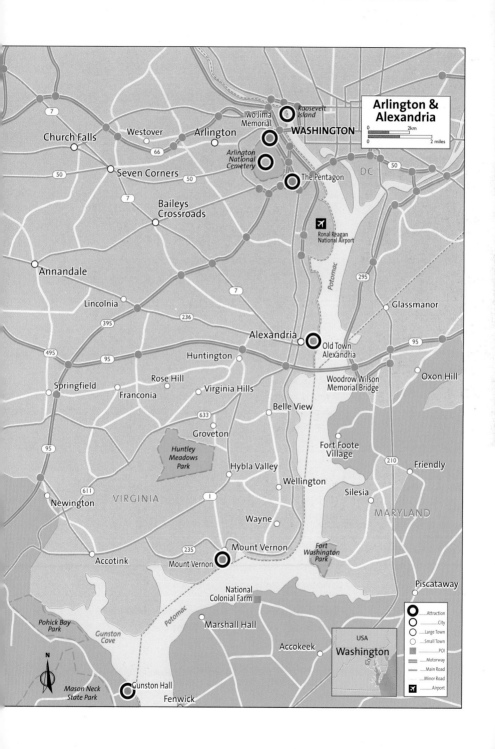

GUNSTON HALL

Gunston Hall $
Rte 242 (off Rte I near Lorton, about 15 miles southwest of Alexandria); tel: (703) 550-9220; www. gunstonhall.org; open daily 0930–1630.

A lifelong friend of George Washington, George Mason was one of the most important and yet least known of the Founding Fathers of the United States. He wrote the first ten amendments to the US Constitution, collectively known as the Bill of Rights. Although a member of the Constitutional Convention of 1787, Mason in fact refused to sign the Constitution because originally it had no declaration of basic human rights, such as those of freedom of speech and freedom of religion, and did not specifically outlaw slavery. Mason's Georgian-style home, Gunston Hall, a few miles downstream from Washington's Mount Vernon in Fairfax County, is distinguished by fine interior carved woodwork, beautiful 18th-century furnishings and lush formal gardens.

IWO JIMA MEMORIAL

Iwo Jima Memorial $ *(See Arlington National Cemetery for details.)*

Annexed to the northern edge of Arlington National Cemetery is the evocative Marine Corps War Memorial, better known as the Iwo Jima Memorial. The capture of the Japanese island of Iwo Jima in 1945 was critical to the Americans' strategic position during World War II, and the statue, sculpted from a Pulitzer Prize-winning photograph of six US Marines planting a flag in the ground, has become one of the most enduring images of America's involvement in the war. It can be reached on foot from either Arlington National Cemetery or Rosslyn metro stations.

MOUNT VERNON

Mount Vernon $$
George Washington Memorial Parkway; tel: (703) 780-2000; www. mountvernon.org; open daily Mar, Sept & Oct 0900–1700, Apr–Aug 0800–1700, Nov–Feb 0900–1600.

George Washington's home, Mount Vernon, is an enjoyable day trip from DC and essential for history buffs. Fairfax Connector bus No 101 runs every 30 minutes (rush hour) or every 60 minutes (non-rush hour and weekends) from Huntington metro station, or you can get there by boat from DC on Spirit Cruises, 6th and Water Sts SW (*metro Waterfront; tel: (866) 211-3811*). It is set on 500 rolling acres of riverfront Virginia countryside, 16 miles south of Washington. The house to which the great American general and first president retired retains its simple, gracious appearance, and among the furnishings you can see are a key to the Bastille presented by General Lafayette, and the bed in which Washington died in 1799. The grounds include slave quarters – ironically, many Founding Fathers owned slaves, despite proclamations that 'all men are created equal' – and George and Martha Washington's tombs, plus an innovative 16-sided threshing barn, built using hand-made bricks and hand-forged nails.

OLD TOWN ALEXANDRIA

Old Town Alexandria can be reached by Metrorail to King Street station (a 20-minute walk, or take Dash bus AT2 or AT5).

Ramsay House Visitor Center 221 King St; tel: (703) 838-4200; open daily 0900–1700.

Christ Church $ 118 N Washington St; tel: (703) 549-1450; www. historicchristchurch.org; open Mon–Sat 0900–1600, Sun 1400–1630.

Gadsby's Tavern Museum $ 134 N Royal St; tel: (703) 838-4242; open Apr–Oct Tue–Sat 1000–1700, Sun 1300–1700; Nov–Mar Tue–Sat 1000–1700, Sun & Mon 1300–1700.

Stabler-Leadbeater Apothecary Shop $ 105–107 S Fairfax St; tel: (703) 836-3713; open Mon–Sat 1000–1600, Sun 1300–1700.

Carlyle House $ 121 N Fairfax St; tel: (703) 549-2997; www.carlylehouse.org; open Tue–Sat 1000–1600, Sun 1200–1600.

Lee-Fendall House $ 614 Oronoco St; tel: (703) 548-1789; www. leefendallhouse.org; open Wed–Sat 1000–1600, Sun 1300–1600.

Scottish tobacco merchants established the colonial city of Alexandria in 1749. It grew as a port competing with Georgetown upstream, before Washington was built, but is now a prominent suburb south of downtown Washington. Alexandria's historic core is locally known as Old Town, and is one of the most charming sites in the entire metropolitan area. If you've got a few days to explore Washington, reserve an afternoon and evening for Alexandria.

Alexandria's prominent citizens include George Washington and Robert E Lee. Both attended services at the lovely dark brick **Christ Church**, a handsome structure with a simple whitewashed interior, with a quiet graveyard containing tombs of sailors and soldiers from both North and South. One intriguing Old Town site is **Gadsby's Tavern Museum**, a tavern dating from 1770, with an adjoining inn built in the Federal style in 1792. There is a restaurant and tours of the building, which is decorated with period furnishings and includes a graceful second-floor ballroom.

King Street, the Old Town's main street, swoops gently downhill to the river from Fairfax St, lined by wonderfully tidy brick and stone town houses, mostly converted into antique shops and restaurants. Stroll down to the riverfront, where sailboats are docked at the small pier, or poke into the Torpedo Factory, which indeed manufactured torpedoes during the two World Wars, and is now an acclaimed local art gallery complex. For a look at early Alexandria and the families who lived there, visit the **Stabler-Leadbeater Apothecary Shop**, a restored 18th-century pharmacy, **Carlyle House**, once the grandest manor home in the city, and the **Lee-Fendall House**, where Civil War Confederate General Robert E Lee lived as an infant. His boyhood home across the street is not open to the public.

Above
Alexandria

Sons of Alexandria: George Washington and Robert E Lee

Two of the most prominent Virginians in American history both lived parts of their lives in Alexandria, and both had a significant impact on the course of the country's two most defining wars. Washington commanded the Continental Army in its decisive victory over the British during the Revolutionary War in 1781, and later served as the nation's first president before retiring to his estate at Mount Vernon. Lee, one of the country's most brilliant military figures, was offered command of the Union troops by President Abraham Lincoln at the beginning of the Civil War, but although he believed in the Union, his true loyalties lay with the South. He spurned the offer, and left the capital to lead the Army of Virginia, which became the chief military position in the Confederacy. Lee ultimately surrendered to Ulysses S Grant's Union troops at Appomattox in April 1865.

Accommodation and food in Arlington and Alexandria

Although part of Washington DC, Alexandria has its own charm and, with its own metro station, makes an easy base from which to explore the entire city. There is a good reservations service for the area, charging upwards of $75 per night for B&B and rooms in private homes: **Alexandria and Arlington Bed & Breakfast Network** (*tel: (703) 549-3415 or (888) 549-3415; www.aabbn.com*). Old Town Alexandria is renowned for its many superb restaurants, especially their seafood.

The Fish Market $–$$ *105 King St, Alexandria; tel: (703) 836-5676, www.fishmarketoldtown.com.* A characterful place with excellent fish dishes, and not too dear.

Brabo $$ *1600 King St; tel: (703) 894-3440; www.braborestaurant.com.* Belgian chef/owner Robert Wiedmaier also owns the casual Brabo Tasting Room ($) next door, where they bake pizza and tarts in a wood oven.

Restaurant Eve $$–$$$ *110 S Pitt St; tel: (703) 706-0450, www.restauranteve.com.* Washington residents routinely cross the river to savour the Irish chef/owner's outstanding dinners.

Gadsby's Tavern $$$ *134 N Royal St, Alexandria; tel: (703) 548-1288, www.gadsbystavernrestaurant.com.* Soak up colonial tavern culture where George Washington himself used to dine.

Morrison House $$$ *116 S Alfred St, Alexandria; tel: (703) 838-8000, www.morrisonhouse.com.* This small Old Town hotel evoke Alexandria's luxurious heyday.

Le Refuge $$$ *127 N Washington Street; tel: (703) 548-4661, http://lerefugealexandria.com.* Owned by Chef Jean Francois o Beaugency, France, the bouillabaisse is just one of many dishes tha local epicures rave about.

THE PENTAGON

The Pentagon
*Washington Blvd and
I-395 (metro: Pentagon).
Tour information email:
tourschd.pa@osd.mil;
fax: (703) 614-1642.*

After a hijacked airliner bore into a western wall of the Pentagon on 9/11, construction crews made it a point of honour to rebuild the outer wall by the one-year anniversary. Like clockwork, they did so, and visitors to the Pentagon today would scarcely notice what happened on that terrible day. The five-sided structure, headquarters of the US Department of Defense, is the largest office building in the world, and captures the grandeur and bureaucracy of the Cold War era in which it was constructed. Its size lies in its extraordinary girth rather than height, and it used to draw visitors interested in exploring the inner workings of US military and strategic might. Guided tours of the Pentagon have resumed, but they must be groups of five or more and requested in advance. US residents should contact their Congress person, and international visitors should inquire through their embassy to make arrangements at least four weeks in advance.

ROOSEVELT ISLAND

The wildlife preserve of Roosevelt Island lies along the Virginia shores of the Potomac. Named after Theodore Roosevelt, the 25th US president famous for his love of the wilderness and establishment of the National Park system, Roosevelt Island is a quiet place to escape from the city, seek out water life such as large birds and beavers, or sit along the banks and admire the city opposite. No cars are permitted on the island; park in the lot along George Washington Memorial Parkway and take the footbridge across, or walk from the Rosslyn metro station.

Suggested walk

Total distance: 2 miles (less if you arrive by car instead of metro; there are several parking garages in the vicinity, and limited street parking). Arlington, which is built for cars, is not covered in this walk.

Time: 3–4 hours with stops.

**Friendship Fire
Engine Company**
*07 S. Alfred Street;
el: (703) 838-3891. Free.*

*.yceum $ 201 S
Washington St;
el: (703) 838-4994.*

Route: From King Street metro station, walk down King St towards Washington St. This 15-minute walk has no particular sites, but the brick homes, shops and restaurants lining the road are very pleasing. Turn right on to S Alfred St, and you immediately come to the **Friendship Fire Engine Company** ❶, once a functioning fire station and now a museum. Turn left down Prince St, and after two blocks you come to the **Lyceum** ❷, a small museum containing photographs

The Athenaeum
201 S Prince Street; tel: (703) 548-0035; www. nvfaa.org; open Easter–Oct, call for hours. Free.

Torpedo Factory Art Center *105 N Union Street; tel: (703) 838-4565; www.torpedofactory.org; open daily 1000–1700. Free.*

and maps covering the history of Alexandria. Continue down Princ St. A quick one-block detour right down Fairfax St takes you to th **Old Presbyterian Meeting House ③**, another late 18th-centur church, at which George Washington's memorial service was held.

Back on Prince St, at the corner of S Lee St, take note of the peach coloured **Athenaeum ④**, once a bank and now a small art gallery. Th last block of Prince St before the river is known as **Captain's Row ⑤** with the original cobblestoned street intact. Turn left on to S Union S and walk one block back to King St, where the **Torpedo Factory ⑥** occupies a prominent piece of land by the river. Wander through th artists' studios within, and then step out to the small pier behind it fo a view of the Potomac. Take your time walking back up **King St ⑦**; is at its most quaint and enjoyable as it rolls up from the river, and i packed with antique shops, bars and restaurants. After two blocks turn right on to Fairfax St and admire **Carlyle House ⑧** befor turning left up Cameron St, past **Gadsby's Tavern Museum ⑨** and o to **Christ Church ⑩**. From here, it's an easy walk back to the metr station, or back down to one of the many restaurants along King St.

Above
Alexandria

Also worth exploring

Pope-Leighey House and Woodlawn Plantation
9000 Richmond Hwy (Rte 1 near Rte 235); tel: (703) 780-4000; http://popeleighey1940. org. and http://woodlawn1805. org; open Apr–Dec Thur–Mon 1000–1700, last tour 1600.

Eminent American architect Frank Lloyd Wright designed the **Pope-Leighey House**, near Mount Vernon, in what he termed his 'Usonian' style: simple, useful and for people of moderate means. This box-like wooden home is the only such work of his accessible to the general public and exemplifies Wright's natural aesthetic sensibility. The house sits on the grounds of the **Woodlawn Plantation**, a graceful brick plantation home in the Georgian style, dating from 1802. Both are located at the intersection of Rtes 1 and 235.

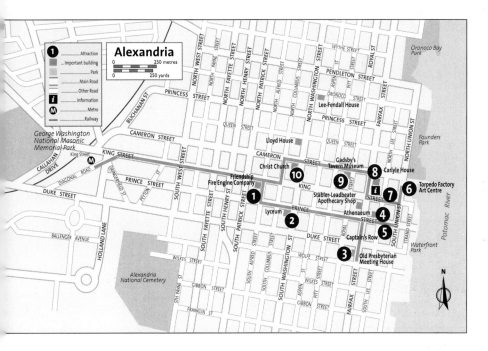

Right
Town Hall, Alexandria

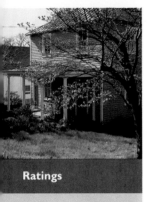

Northern Virginia

Ratings

History	●●●●●
Gastronomy	●●●●○
Shopping and crafts	●●●●○
Entertainment	●●●○○
Museums	●●●○○
Nature	●●●○○
Children	●●○○○
Beaches	●○○○○

As Washington DC grows, it increasingly swallows up northern Virginia, transforming it into a major technology centre and one of the wealthiest regions in the entire country. There are still pockets resounding with echoes of Virginia's rich history, however, such as Manassas Battlefield, site of two bloody fights during the Civil War. Beyond the suburbs, northern Virginia reveals itself as a microcosm of the entire state: head west and you are in the lovely rolling hills of northern Virginia's hunt country, spreading all the way into the foothills of the Blue Ridge Mountains. George Washington laid his hand on much of this land, living in Winchester and surveying a tiny town which now bears his name. Northern Virginia can easily be visited on a day trip from Washington DC, but with its wealth of truly fine inns, you'll probably want to stay a night.

MANASSAS BATTLEFIELD

Ⓗ Manassas Battlefield $ *Near the intersection of I-66 and Rte 234; tel: (703) 361-1339; www.nps.gov/mana; open daily 0830–1700.*

On 21 July 1861, troops of the inexperienced Union and Confederate armies clashed in the Civil War's first major battle, known to Southerners as the First Battle of Manassas and to the North as the Battle of Bull Run. Union troops had expected to burst through the hold and cut a direct path to Richmond, the capital of the South, but met their match in General Thomas Jackson – earning his nickname 'Stonewall', through the Confederates' stubborn stand. What the North had expected to be a decisive victory was in fact ferocious and deadly, and set the tone for the next four years of war. The scene repeated itself on 28–30 August 1862, when 'Stonewall' Jackson again led the South to victory at Manassas, establishing a temporary upper hand in the war. Today the battlefield is set aside as a national park: walking and driving tours lead past important sites and memorials, and an excellent museum interprets the battles through displays of musketry and uniforms and a slide show.

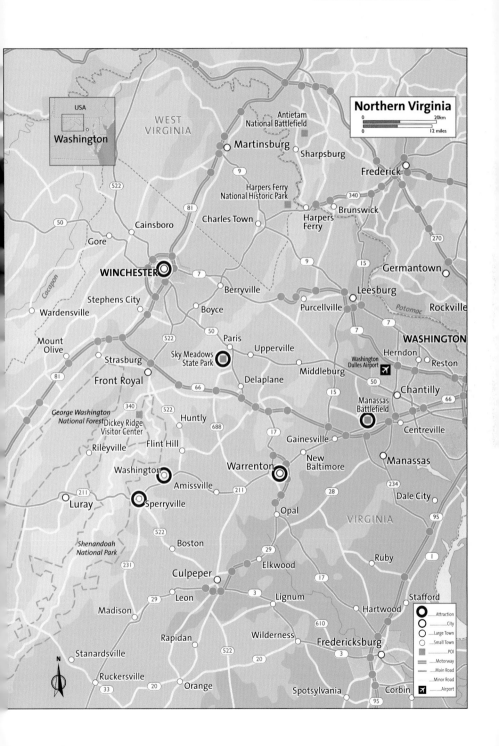

SKY MEADOWS STATE PARK

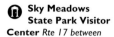
**Sky Meadows
State Park Visitor
Center** *Rte 17 between
Delaplane and Paris; park
entrance is on State Route
710; tel: (540) 592-3556;
open daily dawn to dusk.*

If you can't make it to Shenandoah National Park, the easily accessible Sky Meadows State Park offers a gorgeous alternative, without the crowds. Draped along the gentle slopes of a quiet valley, the park takes its name from open meadows reaching upward to the forests. A leisurely walk across the fields reveals sweeping farmland below, and the visitor centre, located in a 19th-century farmhouse, holds displays on the local ecology. If you want more legwork, follow the path up into the woods, which meets the 2,200-mile-long Appalachian Trail.

Accommodation and food near Sky Meadows State Park

Three excellent inns lie to the north and east of Sky Meadows State Park.

Blackthorne Inn $$ *10087 John Mosby Hwy; tel: (540) 592-3848; www.blackthorne-inn.com.* This tranquil place, a few miles away off Rte 50 in Upperville, has a British-influenced menu; many rooms come with jacuzzi® and fireplace.

The Red Fox Inn $$ *2 E Washington St, Middleburg; tel: (540) 687-6301 or (800) 223-1728; www.redfox.com.* All rooms have proud four-poster beds; breakfasts are big and Virginia dinners are hearty.

The Ashby Inn and Restaurant $$–$$$ *692 Federal St, Paris; tel: (540) 592-3900 or toll free (866) 336-0099; www.ashbyinn.com.* Just up the road in Paris, this is one of the finest of its kind in Virginia.

WARRENTON

**Warrenton Visitor
Center** *In the John
Singleton Mosby House on
Calhoun St; tel: (800) 820-
1021; www.warrentonva.gov*

Old Jail Museum $
*Corner of Main and
Ashby Sts; tel: (540) 347-
5525; www.fauquierhistory.
com; open Tue–Sun 1000–
1600. Free.*

Just beyond the grasp of Washington DC's suburbs, the town of Warrenton merits a stopover for its stately old Virginia feel. Washingtonians in fact find Warrenton an easy getaway for antique shopping and a taste of small-town Virginia. Courthouse Square is a good place to start, dominated by the heavy-set white columns of the Old Courthouse. Opposite stands the **Old Jail Museum**, a fun little place to explore, with jail buildings dating from 1808 and 1823 containing a mixed bag of Civil War weaponry, agricultural tools and a blacksmith's display. Tumble down the incline of Court St behind the Old Courthouse to view the elegant Warren Green Hotel, whose many guests over the ages have included Presidents James Monroe, Andrew Jackson and Theodore Roosevelt. Or stroll down Main Street towards the tidy red-brick Warrenton Presbyterian Church, which served as a Civil War hospital. Along the way you pass numerous antique and home décor shops, such as Sarah Belle's, at No 110.

Accommodation and food in Warrenton

Antique shop-hopping

One reason northern Virginia is such a popular escape for Washingtonians is its wealth of antique shops. It's hard not to find an antique seller, as just about every town has shops touting their wares. Given the simple fact of Virginia's age and wealth, there are plenty of goodies to go around, such as butter churns, pickling jars, picture frames and old baseball cards. Antique emporiums – warehouse-size facilities filled with a veritable combination of treasures and junk – are especially popular, and those in Strasburg and Sperryville are particularly well known.

There is no shortage of chain hotels and restaurants along Rte 29, but better options are available.

Fountain Hall $–$$ *609 S East St, Culpeper; tel: (540) 825-8200 or (800) 298-4748; www.fountainhall. com.* B&B in a pretty home 20 miles south in Culpeper.

Claire's at the Depot $$ *65 S 3rd St; tel: (540) 347-1212; www.claires restaurant.com.* On the site of Warrenton's former railroad station, it offers good American fare along with Mediterranean specialities.

Legends Restaurant and Bar $$ *67 W Lee St; tel: (540) 347-9401.* Relaxed ambience downtown. Friday and Saturday entertainment.

Black Horse Inn $$–$$$ *8393 Meetze Rd; tel: (540) 349-4020; www.blackhorseinn.com.* Refined home (though pricey) east of town, with a nice garden in which to enjoy afternoon tea.

WASHINGTON AND SPERRYVILLE

Sperryville Antique Market
Rte 211; tel: (540) 987-8050.

Nestling snugly in the foothills of the Blue Ridge Mountains is the utterly charming village of Washington, sometimes called Little Washington to distinguish itself from the nation's capital. Incorporated in 1749, it was laid out by (guess who?) George Washington, who was 17 at the time, and has since become a preferred destination for several renowned artists and politicians, many of whom live in the grand estates you see on the hillsides outside of town. Washington is tiny and there are no actual sites, but be sure to stroll the quiet streets, and, if you can afford it, indulge at the luxurious Inn at Little Washington.

Pint-size Sperryville, just 6 miles west along Rte 211, is quite a contrast to Washington's gentility. The residents are a mix of hard-working locals and transplanted hippies, and the place feels beguilingly rougher around the edges. Sperryville can be seen in an hour or less; inspect the shops on tiny Main St or step into the huge Sperryville Antique Market on the eastern edge of town.

Above
Warrenton's Old Jail Museum

Accommodation and food in Washington and Sperryville

Mountainside Market *11711 Lee Highway (Rte 211), Sperryville; tel (540) 987-9100.*

The Conyers House Country Inn & Stable $$ *3131 Slate Mills Rd, Sperryville; tel: (540) 987-8025; www.conyershouse.com.* Breakfast and six course dinners; dogs welcome with reservation.

Foster Harris House $$–$$$ *189 Main St, Washington; tel: (540) 675-3757 or (800) 666-0153; www.fosterharris.com.* Cosy rooms and pleasant gardens overlook the foothills.

The Inn at Little Washington $$$ *Middle and Main Sts; tel: (540) 675-3800; www.theinnatlittlewashington.com. Closed Tue.* A masterpiece of fine dining, to go with equally sumptuous lodging. The *prix-fixe* dinners are four-course marvels, with a grand array of seasonal selections and full range of cordials and liqueurs. The Inn has been hailed by countless commentators nationwide.

WINCHESTER

ⓘ Winchester-Frederick County Convention and Visitors Bureau *1360 South Pleasant Valley Rd; tel: (877) 871-1326; www.visitwinchesterva.com*

ⓖ George Washington's Office Museum $ *Corner of Braddock and Cork Sts; tel: (540) 662-4412; www.winchesterhistory.org; open Apr–Oct Mon–Sat 1000–1600, Sun 1200–1600.*

Stonewall Jackson's Headquarters Museum $ *415 N Braddock St; tel: (540) 667-3242; open Apr–Oct Mon–Sat 1000–1600, Sun 1200–1600.*

Old Court House Civil War Museum $ *20 S Loudoun St; tel: (540) 542-1145; www.civilwarmuseum.org; open Wed–Sat 1000–1700, Sun 1300–1700.*

Tucked right up into the northernmost tip of Virginia, Winchester is an intriguing little town for various reasons. George Washington spent several years in Winchester surveying the land and holding his first elected office here. His log-cabin headquarters is now a museum, **George Washington's Office Museum**, containing predictable personal items. More than a century later, 'Stonewall' Jackson took up residence in Winchester while leading the Confederacy through numerous Civil War operations, and his home, today **Stonewall Jackson's Headquarters Museum**, commemorates his feats. The **Old Court House Civil War Museum** right downtown has a good collection of civil war artefacts. Of a different kind of historical significance, Winchester was also the childhood home of country music legend Patsy Cline, whose many hits in the late 1950s and early 1960s included 'Crazy' and 'I Fall to Pieces', shocking the establishment with her challenging honesty. Though scorned at the time, she has since become a favourite of the tourist authorities, who

know an opportunity to make a buck when they see one. She is buried in Shenandoah Memorial Park on Rte 522 just southeast of town.

Winchester is also one of the apple capitals of America – the fruit is celebrated at the Shenandoah Apple Blossom Festival in early May, and at numerous apple harvest festivals in surrounding orchards in September and October. Beyond these attractions, the town centre is simply a pleasing place to stroll. Loudoun St downtown is a pedestrian zone that doesn't appear to have changed much since Patsy Cline's day, and there are plenty of galleries, boutiques and coffee shops into which to poke your head.

Accommodation and food near Winchester

The nicest places to stay are located outside of town.

Brewbakers $–$$ *168 N Loudoun St; tel: (540) 535-0111*. Country-saloon atmosphere and similar food.

Brownstone Cottage $–$$ *161 McCarty Lane, just off Rte 50 at Rte 723 east of Winchester; tel: (540) 662-1962; www.brownstonecottage.com*. Closest non-chain accommodation to central Winchester, in a homey setting.

Hotel Strasburg $–$$ *213 S Holliday St, Strasburg; tel: (540) 465-9191 or (800) 348-8327; fax: (540) 465-4788; www.hotelstrasburg.com*. Sitting pretty 15 miles south down either I-81 or Rte 11 in Strasburg, this feels like a grand old dame of the frontier, and has one of the best restaurants ($$) in the area.

Fuller House Inn & Carriage House $$ *220 W Boscawen St; tel: (540) 722-3976; www.fullerhouseinn.com*. Historic home, convenient downtown location; pet-friendly.

Violino Ristorante Italiano $$$ *181 N Loudoun St; tel (540) 667-8006*. Regional Italian cuisine by chefs Franco Riccardo and Marcella Stocco; reservations as highly recommended as the fare.

Suggested tour

Total distance: 230 miles from the intersection of Rte 50 and I-66 to Manassas Battlefield Park.

Time: 8–10 hours with selected stops. Allow 1^{1}/$_{2}$–2 days for more stops or if including detours.

Links: Winchester and Strasburg lie at the top of the Shenandoah Valley (*see pages 76–88*), and Front Royal is the northernmost entrance to Shenandoah National Park (*see page 82*).

Route: Coming from Washington DC, I-66 runs directly west through the heart of northern Virginia. Take exit 57 (Rte 50 west) which soon

eft
ieorge Washington's Office
luseum, Winchester

becomes very picturesque, with long white picket fences encircling beautiful horse farms. At **Middleburg**, take note of the pretty clapboard homes lining the road, then pause at a local shop or winery before continuing on to **WINCHESTER ❶**.

Detour: SKY MEADOWS STATE PARK ❷ lies just a couple of miles south of Paris on Rte 17. This is a lovely road winding down to the former railroad junction of **Delaplane**.

Retrace your steps to Rte 50 and Winchester. From Winchester, Rte 11 south is preferable to I-81, and the town of **Strasburg** offers yet more opportunities to go antiquing, most obviously at the huge Strasburg Emporium. The town was settled in the 1700s by German immigrants (hence the name), and although the original character of the town is lost, it is still a nice place to pause or stop into the self-explanatory Stonewall Jackson's Headquarters Museum or Museum of American Presidents.

From Strasburg, Rte 55 leads eastward to **Front Royal**, an inland port where you can rent canoes to paddle down the easy Shenandoah River.

Detour: From Front Royal, you can travel a good third the length of Skyline Drive through the **Shenandoah National Park** before hooking up with Rte 211 at Thornton Gap, which takes you east 7 miles into **SPERRYVILLE ❸** and back to the main route. The views are wonderful along Skyline Drive; keep in mind the $10 park entrance fee.

You can also skirt the park on Rte 522 from Front Royal, a beautiful country road heading south towards Rte 211 near **WASHINGTON ❹** Rte 211, although a four-lane highway, is soft on the eye and lightly travelled, winding its way east to **WARRENTON ❺**.

Detour: If Warrenton tickles your fancy, head south 20 miles down Rte 29 to **Culpeper**, a smaller version of the same staid brick churches and small shops.

Rte 29 north from Warrenton is no great joy to drive along, but it does lead you straight to **MANASSAS BATTLEFIELD ❻**, which itself is located just off I-66, and a quick trip back to Washington DC.

Also worth exploring

It may come as a surprise, but Virginia is the nation's seventh largest wine-producing state, and the tradition can be traced back to Thomas Jefferson, who gained a fondness for the tipple when he served as ambassador to France. Wineries are well signposted throughout northern Virginia, and some of the many offering tours and tasting include **Prince Michel Vineyards**, off Rte 29 south of Culpeper **Farfelu Vineyard** near Rte 522 in Flint Hill, **Naked Mountain Vineyard and Winery** along Rte 55 in Markham and **Piedmont Vineyards and Winery** on Rte 626 outside Middleburg.

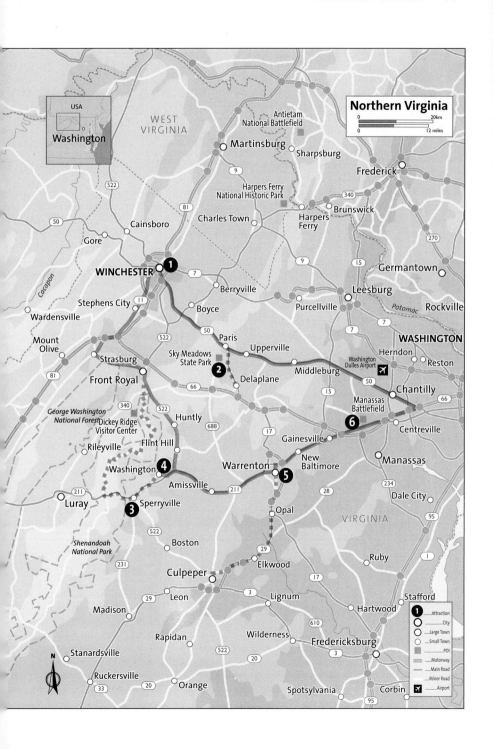

Shenandoah

Ratings

Nature and wildlife	●●●●●
History	●●●●○
Gastronomy	●●●○○
Museums	●●●○○
Shopping	●●●○○
Children	●●○○○
Entertainment	●●○○○
Beaches	●○○○○

Two distinctive geographical features lend the central portion of the Appalachian Mountains its sublime beauty and its rich historical importance. The luxuriant Shenandoah National Park (the name comes from a native American word meaning 'daughter of the stars') is one of the most visited in the nation. The mountains here are often referred to as the Blue Ridge because of their remarkable appearance: distant peaks really do look blue most days, due to the presence of a particular haze. The fertile Shenandoah Valley below was highly prized during the Civil War, and its towns today are a virtual history lesson: New Market Battlefield was the scene of a vicious battle, and towns such as Staunton and Lexington retain their proud 19th-century appearance. Numerous caves and full-season resorts provide some recreational diversion, and give this portion of the Appalachian Mountains a little something for everyone.

BATH AND HIGHLAND COUNTIES

ⓘ Bath County Chamber of Commerce Rte 22, Hot Springs; tel: (800) 628-8092; www.bathcountyva.org

Highland County Chamber of Commerce Spruce St, Monterey; tel: (540) 468-2550; www.highlandcounty.org

ⓜ Highland Maple Museum $ Rte 220, Monterey; tel: (540) 468-2550; usually open daily 0900–1700.

Much of the western edge of Virginia is made up of sections of the expansive George Washington National Forest. The hills rise again west of the Shenandoah Valley, rubbing up against the state of West Virginia, and the area west of Staunton is a visual delight. The village of Monterey in Highland County is surrounded by sheep farms – there are in fact more sheep than people here, and all local industries are derived from the land. Just south of Monterey, the **Highland Maple Museum** is an old log cabin with exhibits on how to make maple syrup. Nearby, the **Virginia Trout Company** gives tours of its hatchery.

Bath County gains its name, aptly enough, from the mineral springs that flow forth from its soil. It should come as no surprise, then, that the towns of Warm Springs and Hot Springs are built upon spa facilities, still in use today. The round white wooden bath houses you see near the intersection of Rtes 39 and 220 in Warm Springs are the **Jefferson Pools**, one for men and one for women, where you can

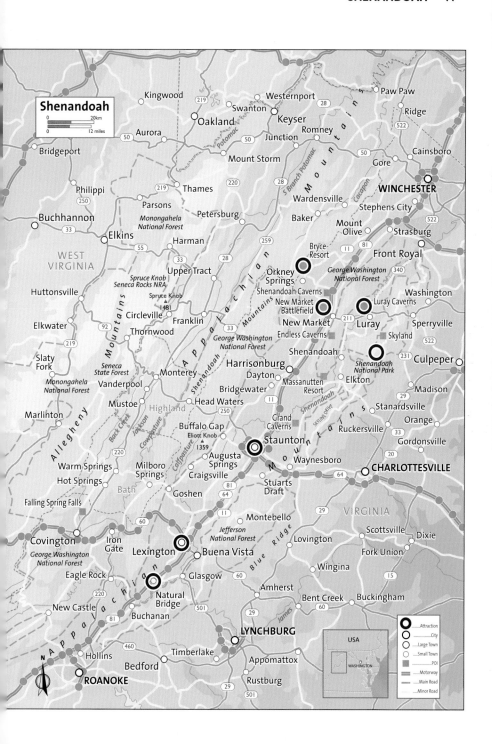

Virginia Trout Company $ *Rte 220, Monterey; tel: (540) 468-2280; call for daily tour information.*

Jefferson Pools $ *Rte 220, Warm Springs; tel: (540) 839-5346; open daily Jun–Oct 1000–1800; call for opening hours Nov–May.*

immerse yourself in the body-temperature water. The pools date from 1761 and 1836 respectively, and are not in tip-top shape – though for some, this is part of the charm. For the more traditional, over-the-top spa experience, **The Homestead**, 5 miles further south at Hot Springs, is a lavish resort with baths that are indeed a bit hotter – but be prepared to pay for the privilege.

Accommodation and food in Bath and Highland Counties

Highland Inn $ *Main St (Rte 220), Monterey; tel: (888) 466-4682, www.highland-inn.com.* Large white clapboard home with long porches on both storeys; an ageing yet highly regarded hotel and restaurant.

The Inn at Gristmill Square $$ *Rte 220, Warm Springs; tel: (540) 839-2231.* Rustic rooms and an excellent restaurant (**$$**) in a converted flour mill.

Below
The slopes of the Bryce Resort

The Homestead $$$ *Rte 220, Hot Springs; tel: (800) 838-1766, www.thehomestead.com.* Fantastic mountain resort with all the facilities and activities you could possibly think of, from the spa to golf and fine dining.

BRYCE RESORT

Bryce Resort $–$$ *Basye; tel: (800) 821-1444; www.bryceresort.com.* Slope-side lodges and self-catering apartments, and a good, if standard, bar and grill, all handled by the resort itself.

Set amid lovely rolling hills and low mountains, Bryce Resort offers low-key recreational activities just 2½ hours from Washington DC. Snow machines ensure white slopes from November to March, though the skiing is not challenging. Other amenities include 18 holes of golf, tennis, horse riding and a lake for swimming and canoeing. Just down the road, **Orkney Springs** is a lovely former spa town with a grand hotel, no longer in use but impressive all the same.

LEXINGTON

ⓘ Lexington Visitor Center
*106 E Washington St,
tel: (540) 463-3777;
www.lexingtonvirginia.com*

ⓜ Virginia Military Institute Museum $
*Campus of the Virginia
Military Institute; tel: (540)
464-7334; www4.vmi.edu/
museum; open daily
0900–1700.*

George C Marshall Museum $ *Campus of the
Virginia Military Institute; tel:
(540) 463-7103; open
Oct–Mar Mon–Sat 0900–
1700, Sun 1300–1700;
Apr–Sept daily 0900–1700.*

Stonewall Jackson House $$ *8 E Washington
St; tel: (540) 463-2552;
open Mon–Sat 0900–1700,
Sun 1300–1700.*

Lee Chapel and Museum $ *Campus of
Washington and Lee
University; tel: (540) 463-
8768; open Apr–Oct
Mon–Sat 0900–1700,
Sun 1300–1700; Nov–Mar
Mon–Sat 0900–1600,
Sun 1300–1600.*

Home to two universities and several historic brick buildings, Lexington is an agreeable place to break the journey and soak up small-town Virginia. The presence of the Virginia Military Institute (VMI) has much to do with the town's identity: it supplied the Confederacy with soldiers throughout the Civil War, and remains one of the country's most prestigious military academies.

The **Virginia Military Institute Museum** documents its history through good, if predictable, glass cases full of uniforms and weaponry. Two of VMI's most famous sons have museums here in their honour. George C Marshall, author of the Marshall Plan to rebuild countries destroyed in World War II, graduated with the Institute's class of 1901, and the **George C Marshall Museum** tells his life story. In downtown Lexington, the **Stonewall Jackson House** is a plain brick house in which the celebrated commander of the Confederate Army lived for several years while he taught at VMI.

Lexington is also a lovely place to unwind. The sprawling green campus of Washington and Lee University contains the sedate **Lee Chapel**, dedicated to Robert E Lee, another Confederate general and VMI professor, who is buried underneath the building. Streets surrounding the campus are lined with beautiful old Victorian homes, and the downtown area, particularly Main St and Nelson St, is a compact series of smart red-brick and stone shopfronts with quaint boutiques and antique shops.

Accommodation and food in Lexington

Redwood Family Restaurant $ *898 N Lee Hwy; tel: (540) 463-2168.* Daily specials include seafood and steak in this cosy family restaurant. Wi-Fi on site.

Llewellyn Lodge $–$$ *603 S Main St; tel: (540) 463-3235 or (800) 882-1145; www.llodge.com.* A pretty white home right in town with B&B and information on outdoor excursions.

Lavender Hill Farm $$ *1374 Big Spring Dr; tel: (540) 464-5877 or (800) 446-4240; www.lavhill.com.* Near Rte 60 and I-64 some 5 miles west of town, this is a working farm where you can go trout fishing or enjoy home-baked bread on the porch.

Southern Inn Restaurant $$–$$$ *37 S Main St; tel: (540) 463-3612; www.southerninn.com.* Excellent traditional Southern cooking, and a selection of good beers and Virginia wines.

*Above
Statue of General 'Stonewall'
Jackson*

LURAY CAVERNS

Luray Caverns $$$
*Rte 211 outside Luray;
tel: (540) 743-6551; open
mid-Mar–Oct 0900–1800,
Nov–mid-Mar 0900–1600.*

Shenandoah Caverns $
*Tel: (540) 477-3115. www.
shenandoahcaverns.com*

Endless Caverns $
*Tel: (540) 896-2283.
www.endlesscaverns.com*

Grand Caverns $
*Tel: (540) 249-5729.
www.uvrpa.org*

Stunning caves pock the hills surrounding the Shenandoah Valley, the largest and most heavily advertised being Luray Caverns, outside the town of Luray. The size and the quantity of stalactites and stalagmites is spectacular but be prepared for heavy commercialisation. Guided tours lead visitors along concrete footpaths, past evocative natural sculptures such as a 'gremlin' and a pair of 'fried eggs', as well as a hand-built 'pipe organ'; coloured lights heighten the beauty/kitsch. Despite the hefty admission fee, the place is always crowded, and is well and truly complemented with gift shops and a 'family-style' restaurant. If this all sounds like too much, other (albeit less dramatic) caves in the area with fewer visitors include **Shenandoah Caverns**, off I-81 near Mount Jackson, **Endless Caverns**, off Rte 11 south of New Market, and **Grand Caverns**, off Rte 340 north of Waynesboro.

NATURAL BRIDGE

The 90ft-span of this natural stone bridge is part of Rte 11, but you may scarcely notice it until you view it from the bank of Cedar Creek 215ft below. The setting is beautifully rural, but the lure of tourist dollars means an extravagant hotel, a silly wax museum and a hefty admission fee to see the archway. Despite these annoyances, the bridge is quite spectacular, and a path beneath it leads along the creek to some deep-pocket caverns. George Washington's initials are carved into the arch, and the land was once owned by Thomas Jefferson.

Accommodation and food near Natural Bridge

Natural Bridge Inn and Conference Center $–$$ *Rt 11 and Rte 130; tel: (540) 291-2121 or (800) 533-1410; www. naturalbridgeva.com*. Grandiose hotel with a decent restaurant capitalising on the location.

NEW MARKET BATTLEFIELD

New Market Battlefield State Historical Park $$ *Tel: (540) 740-8065 or (886) 15-1864; open daily 0900–1700.*

Hall of Valor $$ *Tel: (540) 740-3101; open daily 0900–1700.*

A trip through the Shenandoah Valley is a retracing of both Confederate and Union troop movements during the Civil War. Its rich soil and the long, flat north–south passage it offered through the mountains of western Virginia rendered it highly coveted land. Several battles were waged here through the course of the war, the worst and most deadly at New Market in 1864. Among those killed were Confederate cadets – some as young as 14 – from the Virginia Military Institute (VMI) in Lexington.

The site is marked today with two excellent museums. The **New Market Battlefield Military Museum** contains a chronological display of thousands of artefacts from the War such as General Custer's spurs and 'Stonewall' Jackson's bible. The nearby **Hall of Valor** commemorates those killed at New Market and provides a detailed history of the battle through films and display cases. After the museums, a tour guide takes you out onto the battlefield, including a farmhouse and slave quarters that sat right in the crossfire.

Accommodation in New Market

Cross Roads Inn $ *9222 John Sevier Rd (Rte 211); tel: (540) 740-4157 or (888) 740-4157; fax: (540) 740-4255; www.crossroadsinnva.com.* Comfortable B&B on the eastern edge of town with a large yard, views of the hills and home-made strudel.

Left
Natural Bridge

Above
The Grand Caverns

SHENANDOAH NATIONAL PARK

🅗 **Shenandoah**
National Park $
Shenandoah National Park
is open year-round, though
Skyline Drive may be
closed at times because of
bad weather conditions.
Admission to the park is
$10 per vehicle or $5 per
person on foot; no bicycles
permitted. All park
entrances are staffed with
helpful rangers, who give
out maps and information.
There are regular Visitor
Centres at Dickey Ridge
(Milepost 4) and Big
Meadows (Milepost 51),
both *open daily 0900–1700*.
For general park
information, call *(540) 999-*
3500; www.nps.gov/shen

🌙 **Aramark**
Shenandoah
National Park Lodges
$–$$ Box 727, Luray;
tel: (888) 896-3833;
www.visitshenandoah.com

Opposite
Frozen waterfall, Shenandoah
National Park

Straddling the eastern ridge of the Blue Ridge Mountains, Shenandoah
National Park extends for about 80 miles northeast to southwest, from
Front Royal to Waynesboro. Skyline Drive rides the ridges all the way
along it, linking up with the Blue Ridge Highway which continues all
the way down to Great Smoky Mountains National Park in North
Carolina. Stunning viewpoints grace both sides of the road, so you can
take the drive without getting out, but this defeats the purpose of
being in the mountains. There are some 500 miles of trails here, and
the brochure given out at the park entrance gives tips on hikes –
anything from quick jaunts to see a view or waterfall to longer circuits
taking several hours or even days. The Appalachian Trail, which
extends over 2,200 miles from Georgia to Maine, winds through the
park, marked with a white blaze.

Skyland and Big Meadows, separate administrative centres near the
midpoint of Skyline Drive, both have facilities for visitors. A pair of
short walks are suggested in this area. Just north of Skyland, the
1½-mile hike up to Stony Man Mountain reveals wonderful vistas of
40-mile-long Massanutten Mountain and the Shenandoah Valley
– especially beautiful at sunset. Just south of Big Meadows, an easy
¾-mile path runs down to Dark Hollow Falls, a grand series of falls
dropping over 70ft into a shady pool below.

Accommodation and food in Shenandoah National Park

All accommodation in the park is handled by **Aramark Shenandoah**
National Park Lodges and includes campsites, standard hotel
accommodation and pleasantly rustic cabins at Skyland Lodge
(Milepost 41), Big Meadows (Milepost 51) and Lewis Mountain
(Milepost 57). Lodges are usually open early April–November, cabins
May–late October; it is imperative to book well in advance. There are
dining facilities, all acceptable but none exceptional, every 20 miles or
so along Skyline Drive, and you can pick up groceries at Skyland, Big
Meadows and Loft Mountain (all April–October only).

Shenandoah wildlife

Shenandoah National Park is home to a wide range of wildlife, including an estimated 500 black bears.
There are two species of poisonous snake: the copperhead and timber rattlesnake. Less fearsome
creatures include Virginia white-tail deer, red and grey foxes, skunks, bobcats, raccoons, groundhogs and
chipmunks. The birds most commonly seen, especially from Skyline Drive, are the turkey vulture and black
vulture. The turkey vulture, or buzzard, has a wingspan up to 6ft and a red head; the smaller black vulture
has a pale patch on the underside of each wing. Wild turkeys, the largest of the park's bird species, are
frequently seen too, especially in the northern section. More than 1,000 species of plant life are found in
the park, including 18 types of orchid but picking flowers is forbidden. Most of the park's trees are
deciduous, predominantly oak and hickory, and a lush carpet of fern often lies underneath.

STAUNTON

Staunton-Augusta Travel Information Center *1250 Richmond Rd (at the Museum of American Frontier Culture); tel: (800) 342-7982 or (540) 332-3972; www.visitstaunton.com*

Woodrow Wilson Presidential Library *$$ 18–24 N Coalter St; tel: (540) 885-0897; www.woodrowwilson. org; open Mar–Oct Mon–Sat 0900–1700, Sun 1200–1700; Nov–Feb Mon–Sat 1000–1600, Sun 1200–1600.*

Museum of American Frontier Culture *Near intersection of I-66 and I-81; tel: (540) 332-7850; www.frontiermuseum.org; open daily mid-Mar–Oct 0900–1700; Nov–mid-Mar 0900–1600.*

Although sometimes overlooked by tourists, the unassuming city of Staunton (pronounced 'Stanton') comes as a wonderful little surprise. The town is hilly, exceedingly clean and an authentically enchanting place to visit, having preserved its character without pandering to tourists.

Staunton has been fairly wealthy since its role as an important railroad junction around the time of the Civil War. Although today it serves only one daily Amtrak train (the Washington–Chicago 'Cardinal' route), the small train station is a destination in itself for its simple elegance, and with the handsome brick warehouse buildings opposite, forms part of the so-called Wharf District, once a bustling commercial area now converted to boutiques and restaurants.

Beverley Street is Staunton's main drag, a marvellous throwback of three-storey buildings in various 19th-century architectural styles. Just beyond this central business district, the hills rise steeply and Staunton's fine array of Victorian and antebellum family homes line the streets. One of these homes was the birthplace of President Woodrow Wilson, in 1856. Today the **Woodrow Wilson Presidential Library** chronicles the life of one of the United States' greatest presidents, including a tour of his home and displays on his many achievements, along with his favoured Pierce-Arrow limousine.

On the eastern edge of town, the open-air **Museum of American Frontier Culture** displays farmhouses relocated here from Germany, England and Ireland, in order to present the life of the earliest settlers in this region. Costumed guides demonstrate how immigrants from these countries lived in the 1700s, and how they had forged a new American

Staunton Volunteer Fire Department *500 N Augusta St; tel: (540) 332-3886; open daily 0800–2100.* Free.

Trinity Episcopal Church *214 W Beverley St; tel: (540) 886-9132; www.trinitystaunton.org; tours Jun–Aug Mon–Thur 1300–1600.* Visitors welcome to attend services. Free.

identity by the 1800s. With farm animals, a blacksmith's shop and knowledgeable interpreters, this is especially good for children.

Be sure not to miss the **Staunton Volunteer Fire Department**, Virginia's oldest fire station, where there is a small museum dedicated to its fully restored 1911 Robinson Chemical Fire Engine, affectionately called 'Jumbo'. Also of note is the **Trinity Episcopal Church**, Staunton's oldest, proudly wearing Tiffany windows.

Accommodation and food in Staunton

The Pampered Palate Café $ *26 E Beverley St; tel: (540) 886-9463; www.thepamperedpalatecafe.com.* Good coffee and pastries in this central café, along with simple, filling breakfasts and lunches.

Stonewall Jackson Hotel $ *24 S Market St; tel: (540) 885-4848; www.stonewalljacksonhotel.com.* Once one of the grandest hotels in the South, it has recently been thoroughly renovated. The faded lobby and ballroom exude a past era.

Belle Grae Inn $$ *515 W Frederick St; tel: (540) 886-5151 or (888) 541-5151; fax: (540) 886-6641; www.bellegrae.com.* A neighbourhood of its own, occupying several Victorian homes with gracious rooms and suites, and a good restaurant.

The Miller House Bed and Breakfast $$ *210 N New St; tel: (540) 886-3186 or (877) 886-3186; www.millerhousebandb.com.* A truly elegant Victorian experience in a grand historic home; full gourmet breakfast served.

The Pullman $$ *36 Middlebrooke Ave; tel: (540) 885-6612.* Located in the classy old railroad station, and offering prime rib, local rainbow trout and Virginia wines, plus an old-fashioned ice-cream bar.

Suggested tour

Total distance: 205 miles from Front Royal to Strasburg via Waynesboro and Staunton. Add 152 miles for the detour to Bath and Highland Counties.

Time: 6 hours actual driving time, 9 hours including the detour. Allow 2 full days for the route, up to 3 full days including the detour.

Links: The Skyline Drive can be approached from Washington DC, via Front Royal (off I-66) or Thornton Gap (Rte 211). The latter is more interesting as it takes in some of the sights of northern Virginia (*see pages 68–75*). Charlottesville (*see pages 91–3*) also makes a good launching pad to Skyline Drive via I-64. Rte 11 and I-81 both run through the Shenandoah Valley to Roanoke (*see pages 95–6*).

Left
taunton Museum of American
rontier Culture

**ⓗ Virginia Quilt
Museum $** *301 S
Main St, Harrisonburg; tel:
(540) 433-3818;
www.vaquiltmuseum.org;
open Tue–Sat 1000–1600.*

**Shenandoah Valley
Folk Art and Heritage
Center $$** *High St,
Dayton; tel: (540) 879
2681;
www.heritagecenter.com;
open Mon–Sat 1000–1600.*

Route: This is an elongated circular route, and has two real highlights:
the roads themselves. Most sites mentioned in this chapter can be
reached by **Skyline Drive** in the Shenandoah National Park and by
Rte 11, which traverses the Shenandoah Valley.

Enter the **SHENANDOAH NATIONAL PARK ❶** at either Front Royal or
Thornton Gap. Skyline Drive takes about 3 hours, as speed limits are set
at 35 mph. Be sure to stop for at least a short hike; see the Shenandoah
National Park section (*page 82*) for details. Exit Skyline Drive near
Waynesboro, and take I 64, a short hop over to **STAUNTON ❷**

Detour: The beautiful mountain scenery and cute towns of the **George
Washington National Forest ❸** west of Staunton are worth a trip in
themselves, and all the roads through here are designated 'Virginia
scenic byways' (*see the Bath and Highland Counties section on pp76 and 78
for details*). From Staunton, follow Rte 250 west to **Monterey ❹**, then
Rte 220 south to **Warm Springs** and **Hot Springs ❺**. From Warm
Springs, Rte 39 east takes you to Goshen, linking up with Rte 42 north;
at Buffalo Gap head east on Rte 254 back to Staunton.

The quick way up the Shenandoah Valley is I-81, but the prettier way
is along Rte 11 which runs parallel. The **Shenandoah Valley Folk Art
and Heritage Center**, off Rte 42 just south in the town of **Dayton ❻**
holds a solid collection of ceramic pots, needlework, basketry and
painted chests from the region. The next large town north is
Harrisonburg ❼, a mildly interesting place with a couple of museums
on folk art traditions. The **Virginia Quilt Museum** on Main St has a
select collection of quilts, pronouncing the 'role of quilting in the
cultural life of society'.

Rte 11 continues through **NEW MARKET ❽** and on past a string of
pretty one-street towns such as Mount Jackson, Woodstock and Tom's
Brook. Just before Mount Jackson, signs point you to **Meem's Bottom
Bridge** on Rte 720, one of the last remaining covered bridges in the
state. The valley peters out at **Strasburg** and **Winchester**, which are
covered in the Northern Virginia route (*see pages 72–4*).

Also worth exploring: West Virginia

The border between Virginia and West Virginia is formed by
mountains that become increasingly rugged the further west you go.
The **Monongahela National Forest** in West Virginia is splendid and
sparsely populated, and offers fabulous opportunities for hiking, skiing
and whitewater rafting. Rte 55 from Strasburg and Rte 33 from
Harrisonburg link up at the stunning cliffs of **Seneca Rocks NRA**, a
1¹/₂-hour drive. Nearby **Spruce Knob** is the highest peak in the state
and you can drive to the top. Rte 39 from Lexington and Rte 250 from
Staunton both link up with Rte 28 in West Virginia, from which Rte 66
leads you to the historic mining town of **Cass** and the excellent ski
resort at **Snowshoe**, both roughly 1¹/₂–2 hours away.

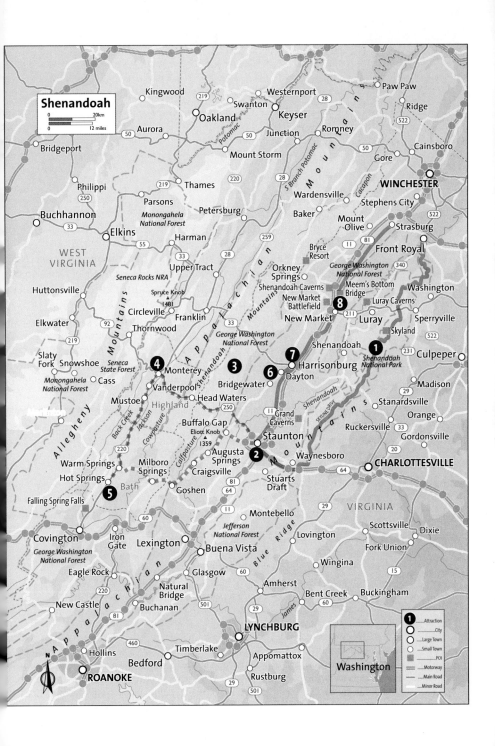

Shenandoah

0 ──── 20km
0 ──── 12 miles

The Piedmont

Ratings

Art and museums	●●●●○
Gastronomy	●●●●○
History	●●●●○
Nature	●●●●○
Shopping	●●●○○
Children	●●○○○
Entertainment	●●○○○
Beaches	●○○○○

The charming small cities of Virginia's Piedmont region offer a richly mixed bag of historical and architectural delights, with the beautiful low Blue Ridge Mountains as a backdrop. Well-heeled Charlottesville is a major draw, not least for Thomas Jefferson's extraordinary home at Monticello nearby, as well as the beautiful campus of the University of Virginia. Cities such as Lynchburg and Roanoke, once dynamic industrial centres, have gentrified historical cores and are surprisingly lively. Driving through the rolling countryside is pure joy: grand estates of old Virginia mingle with a plethora of good wineries throughout the region, and most towns retain traces of the 19th century in Main Street shopfronts, churches and courthouses. One of the real highlights, though, is the tiny settlement at Appomattox, site of the meeting between Generals Grant and Lee that brought an end to the Civil War.

APPOMATTOX

 **Appomattox Court House National Historical Park $** *Rte 24, north of Appomattox; www.nps.gov/apco; tel: (434) 352-8987; open daily 0830–1700.*

This quiet little community, set amid the brooding landscape of central Virginia, was the scene of one of the most significant events in the history of the United States – the end of the Civil War. Here, on 9 April 1865, General Robert E Lee surrendered the Army of Northern Virginia to General Ulysses S Grant, commander of the Union forces.

Appomattox Court House National Historical Park, three miles from the modern town of Appomattox (pronounced 'AP-po-MAT-tux'), encompasses the original village, which has been restored to its 1865 appearance after falling into disrepair at the end of the 20th century. This was only a tiny place at the time, with a court house, jail, tavern, store, law office and a few homes; many still stand or have been rebuilt, and can be visited on a self-guided tour. The courthouse contains the visitor centre and museum, but the momentous document signing actually took place in a private home, the McLean

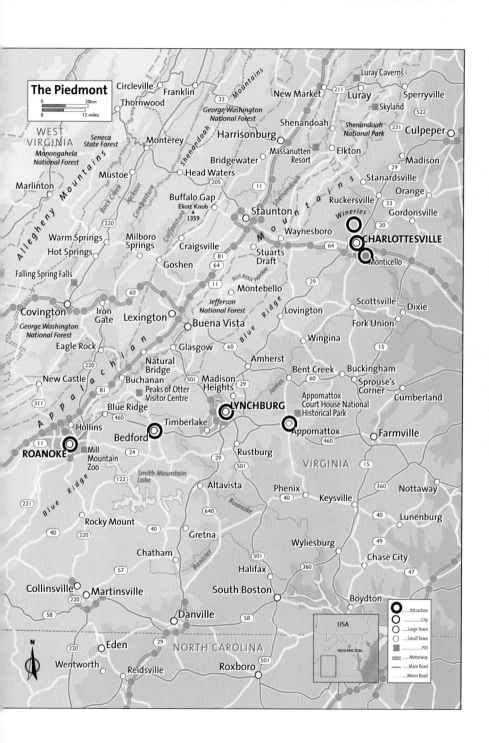

The Piedmont

0   20km
0   12 miles

WEST VIRGINIA

Monongahela National Forest

Seneca State Forest

Allegheny Mountains

Marlinton

Mustoe

Circleville

Thornwood

Franklin

Monterey

Head Waters

Buffalo Gap
Eliott Knob
1359

Bridgewater

Harrisonburg

George Washington National Forest

Shenandoah Mountains

Massanutten Resort

New Market

Shenandoah

Luray Caverns

Luray

Skyland

Shenandoah National Park

Elkton

Sperryville

Culpeper

Madison

Stanardsville

Orange

Staunton

Ruckersville

Gordonsville

Wineries

CHARLOTTESVILLE

Monticello

Warm Springs

Hot Springs

Milboro Springs

Craigsville

Goshen

Waynesboro

Stuarts Draft

Falling Spring Falls

Covington

George Washington National Forest

Iron Gate

Lexington

Buena Vista

Montebello

Jefferson National Forest

Lovington

Scottsville

Dixie

Fork Union

Wingina

Eagle Rock

Glasgow

Amherst

Bent Creek

Buckingham

Sprouse's Corner

Cumberland

New Castle

Natural Bridge

Buchanan

Peaks of Otter Visitor Centre

Madison Heights

James

Appomattox Court House National Historical Park

Blue Ridge

Hollins

Timberlake

LYNCHBURG

Appomattox

Farmville

ROANOKE

Bedford

Mill Mountain Zoo

Rustburg

VIRGINIA

Smith Mountain Lake

Altavista

Phenix

Keysville

Nottaway

Rocky Mount

Roanoke

Lunenburg

Gretna

Chatham

Wyliesburg

Chase City

Banister

Halifax

Collinsville

Martinsville

South Boston

Boydton

Danville

USA

WASHINGTON

N

Eden

NORTH CAROLINA

Wentworth

Reidsville

Roxboro

Blue Ridge

Blue Ridge Parkway

Appalachian

Shenandoah

Back Creek

Callpasture

Cowpasture

Jackson

Mountains

Blue Ridge

Attraction
City
Large Town
Small Town
POI
Motorway
Main Road
Minor Road

House, which has been reconstructed. Appomattox is really very small, but there is something haunting to the village and the gently rolling countryside around that makes it a must-see in the region.

Accommodation and food in Appomattox

Babcock House Bed and Breakfast Inn $–$$ *250 Oakleigh Ave (Rte 6); tel: (434) 352-7532 or (800) 689-6208; fax: (434) 352-9743; www.babcockhouse.com.* Nice accommodation, and the comfortable restaurant serves the usual Virginia favourites.

BEDFORD

D-Day Memorial
$$ *Rtes 460 and 122; tel: (540) 587-3619; www.dday.org; open daily 1000–1700.*

Bedford is the pretty, unassuming site of the new **National D-Day Memorial**, so chosen because this tiny town supposedly lost the highest percentage of inhabitants of any US city during the so-called D-Day invasion of the Normandy beaches in 1944. Flags of the alliance nations ring the dominant Overlord Arch, named after the war operation on Nazi-controlled France. Over 10,000 allied soldiers were killed in the raid, in which US and British air and ship battalions

Right
Charlottesville Fife and Drum
Honor Guard

stormed the beaches at Normandy, exposing themselves horribly upon landing before eventually overpowering the Germans by their sheer numbers. The memorial is well presented, with rather graphic scenes of battle that include fallen soldiers in a sloping pool of water meant to resemble a beach, and sound effects and exhibits detailing the sacrifices made. The town of Bedford is itself a relaxing place to break the trip, with a Greek-Revival church and stately city hall, and numerous antique shops and cafes along the main street.

Appomattox: the end of the war

The terrible war between North and South raged for four years, at a price of over 600,000 lives, and yet it all ended with a mere whimper. Lee's Army of Northern Virginia, the last major force in the now-decimated Confederacy, lost battles at Richmond (capital of the South) and Petersburg on 1–2 April 1865, and fled westward to reach a supply train near Lynchburg. The troops were exhausted and practically starving, however, and Grant's healthy forces cut them off on 9 April. Lee realised he had no chance, and surrendered his men at Appomattox, the nearest town with a court house. Though minor skirmishes flared up in a few more Southern states for another two months, the agreement between Lee and Grant effectively began the long period of reconciliation.

CHARLOTTESVILLE

Charlottesville/ Albemarle Convention and Visitors Bureau Rte 20 south of centre; tel: (434) 293-6789 or (877) 386-1103; fax: (434) 295-2176; www.pursuecharlottesville.com

Monticello Visitor Center Rte 20 south of centre (in the same building as the Charlottesville/ Albemarle Convention and Visitors Bureau); tel: (434) 984-9822.

Rotunda $ University of Virginia campus; tel: (434) 924-3239; open daily 1000–1600.

Monticello $$$ Rte 53 off Rte 20); tel: (434) 984-9822; www.monticello.org; open daily Mar–Oct 0800–1700; Nov–Feb 0900–1630.

The small city of Charlottesville has a spirit thoroughly dominated by the University of Virginia and its founder, Thomas Jefferson. The campus is one of the most beautiful of its kind, a stately collection of dignified red brick buildings, smooth green lawns and carefully placed trees all designed by Jefferson himself. The robust **Rotunda** stands at its centre, with a gleaming white dome and columns modelled on the Pantheon in Rome. A small museum in the basement recalls Jefferson's special pride in this institution, still today considered one of America's finest. From here you can also join a campus tour, but you need only stand on the back steps of the Rotunda to admire the truly beautiful quadrangle, a long stretch of lawn colonnaded by low brick buildings still used today as dormitories for professors and students.

Several blocks down Main St to the east, Charlottesville's centre-most area is a pedestrianised street of shops and restaurants known as the Downtown Mall. With several notable old buildings, it's a pleasant place to stroll, or stop for ice cream or coffee. Two blocks north, at 5th and Jefferson Sts, the **Albemarle County Court House** includes an 1820s chapel that was shared by Baptists, Episcopalians, Methodists and Presbyterians, when worshippers included Presidents Jefferson, Monroe and Madison.

Most visitors to Charlottesville come specifically to see **Monticello**, the stately, though eccentric, home designed by Thomas Jefferson, third president of the United States. Maintained and preserved as a national monument to Jefferson, Monticello is located on a hilltop just southeast of Charlottesville, and commands a fine view of the central Virginia countryside. If you can't make it here, you can always see the house on the back of any 5-cent coin, but a visit gives good insight into the mind of a squire who has become a revered American icon. Virginians still refer to him as 'Mr Jefferson', an indication of the esteem in which he is held in these parts, even though he has been in the news in recent years due to evidently substantiated rumours that he bore offspring with one of his slaves.

Not content to be merely a seminal figure in American politics, Jefferson was also a fine architect, astronomer, horticulturalist and inventor. Among the quirks inside are a two-storey grandfather clock, a telescope and a gadget holding two pens which allowed Jefferson to make automatic copies of the more than 20,000 letters he wrote. The grounds are equally fascinating, and include an orchard, a vineyard, a 1,000ft-long kitchen garden, the foundations of servants' quarters and Jefferson's grave.

Accommodation and food in Charlottesville

Ciboulette $ *416 W Main St; tel: (434) 295-0570.* This lovely French market offers lunches in-house or boxed, and dinners Thur–Sat. The best feature is its selection of over 60 cheeses, and the expert staff to help you choose.

English Inn $ *2000 Morton Dr; tel: (434) 971-9900; www. englishinncharlottesville.com.* This pleasant enough hotel is north of the centre, with a pool, sauna and fitness room.

Al Dente $$ *225 W Main St; tel: (434) 295-9922.* Located in the historic Downtown Mall, Al Dente prides itself in fresh-baked bread and pasta as well as a lengthy and impressive wine list.

Right
Statue of General Lee in Charlottesville

Right
Monticello, designed by
Thomas Jefferson

Michie Tavern **$$** *Rte 53, near Monticello; tel: (434) 977-1234.*
Lunchtime-only tavern appearing just as it did in Jefferson's day,
located at the base of the road up to Monticello.

Tastings **$$** *5th and Market Sts; tel: (434) 293-3663.* Combination wine
bar/wine store/restaurant, with entrées such as crab cakes and lightly
grilled meats.

The Inn at Court Square **$$–$$$** *410 E Jefferson St; (434) 295-2800 or
(866) 466-2877; www.innatcourtsquare.com.* Pretty new B&B in an old
brick townhome, well-situated near the Albemarle County Court
House and full of antiques. Each room has a private bathroom and
most have fireplaces.

200 South Street **$$–$$$** *200 South St; tel: (434) 979-0200 or (800) 964-
7008; www.southstreetinn.com.* This gracious Southern B&B is
conveniently located right downtown, although the immediate
neighbourhood is a bit drab.

The Clifton Inn **$$$** *Clifton Inn Dr, near intersection of Rtes 250 and
729, east of Charlottesville; tel: (888) 971-1800; www.cliftoninn.net.* This
award-winning country inn outside Charlottesville has an elegant
dining room, swimming pool and tennis courts.

LYNCHBURG

**Lynchburg Visitors
Center** *216 12th St;
tel: (434) 847-1811 or
(800) 732-5821; www.
discoverlynchburg.org; open
daily 0900–1700.*

Settled in 1727, Lynchburg sprawls across seven steep hills above the
James River. The city began as a ferry crossing and developed as a
tobacco town; for more than a century tobacco was processed,
auctioned and made into cigarettes and plugs for chewing. During the
Civil War, the city was a major Confederate storage depot and a burial

**Old Court House/
Lynchburg Museum**
$ 901 Court St; tel: (434)
847-1459; open Mon–Sat
1000–1600, Sun
1200–1600.

**Anne Spencer House
and Garden** $ 1313
Pierce St; tel: (434) 846-
0517; open daily by
appointment.

place for the war dead. Several streets are designated historic districts
and the city today has echoes of its former importance with several
museums and a prettified centre.

The **Old Court House** downtown dates from 1855 and contains a
decent museum on the city's history. The Community Market to the
east was a favourite of Thomas Jefferson, and is still the place to come
for fresh produce and home-made crafts. A few streets up, the **Anne
Spencer House and Garden** was once the home of this noted poet
who was part of the Harlem Renaissance, and is the only black woman
and Virginian included in the *Norton Anthology of Modern American and
British Poetry*.

In recognition of its position at a strategic crossroads, the **City
Cemetery** at 4th and Taylor Sts contains the graves of men who
fought in the Revolutionary War, but the most poignant part is the
Confederate section with the graves of 2,700 soldiers from 14 states
who died in the Civil War.

Accommodation and food in Lynchburg

Main Street Eatery $–$$ 907 Main St; tel: (434) 847-2526;
www.Mainsteatery.com. Simple but good lunches and dinners right in
the historic district.

Carriage House Inn Bed and Breakfast $$ 404 Cabell St; tel: (434)
846-1388 or (800) 937-3582; www.thecarriagehouseinnbandb.com. This
1878 mansion is the best of old-fashioned elegance with modern
treats, like the on-staff massage therapist, a three-course breakfast and
Wi-Fi connection.

Jazz St Grill $$ 3225 Old Forest Rd; tel: (804) 385-0100. Located south
of the centre, this is a local favourite for its New Orleans-inspired
cuisine.

Norvell-Otey House $$ 1020 Federal St; tel: (434) 528-1020;
www.norvelloteyhouse.com. One of several nice B&Bs on this street, with
antiques and four-poster beds throughout.

Right
Lynchburg City Cemetery

ROANOKE

i **Roanoke Valley Convention and Visitor's Bureau** *101 Shenandoah Ave NE; tel: (540) 342-6025 or (800) 635-5535; www.visitroanokeva.com*

R **Art Museum of Western Virginia** *$ Center in the Square, 1 Market St; tel: (540) 342-5760; open Tue–Sat 1000–1700, Sun 1300–1600.*

A 19th-century industrial centre which flourished with the growth of railroads and trade through the Shenandoah Valley, Roanoke today is a surprisingly urbane city with enough attractions to keep you busy for a few hours at least. It was settled by German, Welsh and Scottish immigrants in the mid-18th century, but didn't come into its own until over a hundred years later. A slight European tinge pervades, from the site of an ochre-coloured neo-classical church, to the very German-looking Hotel Roanoke in the centre, to the presence of a daily farmers' market in town. The central area has the feel of the important industrial centre it once was, and the nearby railroad tracks seem to assert its continued sense of purpose, while a magnificent new home for the **Art Museum of Western Virginia** designed by Randall Stout, a former associate of Frank Gehry, was completed in 2008.

Roanoke is also blessed with some very good museums, three of which are gathered under one roof at the Center in the Square, a restored and converted 1914 warehouse. The **Science Museum of Western Virginia** has interactive displays and a planetarium, making

Below
Hotel Roanoke

it a big hit with children, while the Art Museum of Western Virginia displays nationally important American art of the 19th and 20th centuries, as well as folk art of the southern Shenandoah. On the top floor, the very good **History Museum of Western Virginia** gives insight on the development of the area from pre-Colonial days. Roanoke was built on the railroad, and one last museum you shouldn't miss is the **Virginia Museum of Transportation** a few blocks away, a celebration of the golden age of the iron horse – with several historic steam and diesel engines on hand – along with early cars, fire trucks and bomber planes.

Outside Center in the Square, at the intersection of Market and Campbell Sts, is a daily open-air farmers' market, in operation since 1882. Campbell St is a trendy stretch of arty shops and international restaurants, and is good for a stroll and a meal.

⑪ Science Museum of Western Virginia
$$ *Center in the Square, 1 Market St; tel: (540) 342-5726; www.smwv.org; open Tue–Sat 1000–1700, Sun 1300–1700.*

History Museum of Western Virginia $
Center in the Square, 1 Market St; tel: (540) 342-5770; open Tue–Fri 1000–1600, Sat 1000–1700, Sun 1300–1700.

Virginia Museum of Transportation $ *303 Norfolk Ave; tel: (540) 342-5670; www.vmt.org; open Mon–Fri 1000–1600, Sat 1000–1700, Sun 1300–1700.*

Accommodation and food in Roanoke

Jefferson Lodge $ *616 S Jefferson St; tel: (540) 342-2951.* A reasonabl priced motel within walking distance of the centre.

Alexander's $$ *105 S Jefferson St; tel: (540) 982-6983.* One of the city' best, serving a variety of American and international cuisines.

Corned Beef & Company $$ *107 S Jefferson Street; tel: (540) 342-335₄ www.cornedbeefandco.com.* Fun American-themed place with steak₅ sandwiches, pizzas and rooftop seating. Occasional live music.

Hotel Roanoke $$ *110 Shenandoah Ave; tel: (540) 985-5900; fax: (54₀ 853-8264; www.hotelroanoke.com.* The city's granddaddy, this larg₅ historic hotel commands a presence on a downtown hillside, and ha₅ a very good restaurant as well.

Virginia Dare Cruises and Marina $$ *3619 Airport Rd, Moneta; te (540) 297-7100; www.vadarecruises.com.* Affordable dinner cruises o Smith Mountain Lake.

WINERIES

In the past few decades, the Charlottesville area has become a mir east coast Napa Valley. Dozens of wineries have tours and win tastings, amid splendid settings. These are some of the best:

Barboursville Vineyards *Rte 777, Barboursville, 17 miles northeast ₒ Charlottesville off Rte 20; tel: (540) 832-3824; www.barboursvillewine.con open Mon–Sat 1000–1700, Sun 1100–1700.* As a little bonus to th pretty setting, the grounds contain the ruins of a manor house whic₁ burned down in 1884 – and it's not hard to see that Thomas Jeffersoɪ designed it.

Horton Cellars *6399 Spotswood Trail, Gordonsville, 20 miles northea₅ of Charlottesville off Hwy 33 West; tel: (540) 832-7440; www.hvwine.con open daily 1000–1700.* Daily tastings in this stone winery, one of th largest in the state.

Jefferson Vineyards *Near Monticello on Rte 53; tel: (434) 977-304₂ www.jeffersonvineyards.com; open daily 1000–1800.* Here you can stan on the site where Jefferson planted the colony's first vines, in one ₒ the area's most accessible vineyards.

Valhalla Vineyards *6500 Mt Chestnut Rd, Roanoke; tel: (540) 72₅ 9463; www.valhallawines.com; open Fri 1600–1900, Sat 1200–1700, Su 1300–1700.* French style wines, aged in a cave 60ft underground.

White Hall Vineyards *Sugar Ridge Rd, Whitehall, 10 mile northwest of Charlottesville off Rte 810; tel: (434) 823-861₅ www.whitehallvineyards.com; open Wed–Sun 1100–1700.* Generall₁ considered the best in the area.

Suggested tour

Mill Mountain Zoo
$ JP Fishburne Pkwy
and Prospect Rd; tel: (540)
343-3241; open daily
0000–1630.

Total distance: 270 miles.

Time: 8 hours without stops. Allow 2 full days to enjoy the Blue Ridge Parkway, Roanoke and/or Lynchburg and Appomattox, as well as time to drive slowly and take in the scenery.

Links: The suggested tour for Shenandoah could be combined with this to give a lengthier tour of Western Virginia, or it might be a good follow-on from tours of the Arlington or Richmond regions.

Route: The quickest drive from **Charlottesville ①** to Roanoke is I-64 west to I-81 south, which runs through Staunton and Lexington on the way (*see pages 79–5*). But by far the prettier route is on the **Blue Ridge Parkway**, an extension of the Shenandoah National Park's Skyline Drive, and just as scenic, with grand mountain views and some good opportunities for hikes. Just off the Parkway, atop Roanoke's Mill Mountain, the accredited **Mill Mountain Zoo** exhibits 50-plus species of mammals, birds and reptiles, including rare snow leopards, red pandas and Japanese macaques. There are picnic facilities, a wildflower garden and views over the Roanoke Valley. Take I-64 or the quieter Rte 250 west from Charlottesville to the Parkway, which winds all the way down to **ROANOKE ②**, 120 miles southwest.

From Roanoke, Rte 460 provides a lovely drive through the low hills of the Piedmont to the small, attractive town of **BEDFORD ③**, with its D-day memorial. Rte 460 continues on to the fun little city of **LYNCHBURG ④**, but be sure to save time to visit the engrossing **APPOMATTOX COURT HOUSE NATIONAL HISTORICAL PARK ⑤**, near the junction of Rtes 460 and 24. There are a couple of little walks you can do here, as well as a self-guided driving tour that traces Lee's retreat.

Below
Gardens at the University of
Virginia, Charlottesville

Ⓡ Ash Lawn-Highland $$ *Rte 795 near Rte 53; tel: (434) 293-8000; www. ashlawnhighland.org; open daily Apr–Oct 0900–1800; Nov–Mar 1100–1700.*

Montpelier $$ *Rte 20, Orange; tel: (540) 672-2728; www.montpelier.org, open daily Apr–Oct 0930–1730; Nov–Mar 0930–1630.*

Below
Mill at Michie Tavern, Charlottesville

From Appomattox back to Charlottesville it's an enjoyable drive along a few back roads: take Rte 24 east 20 miles to Rte 60 east. Turn right and at Sprouse's Corner, turn left on to Rte 15 north. After one mile turn left again on to Rte 20 north, which takes you through the charming streets and grand old homes of **Scottsville** before rolling past beautiful country estates and on into Charlottesville.

Also worth exploring

If you're on the trail of the American presidents, **Ash Lawn-Highland** is an easy trip from Charlottesville and complements a visit to **Monticello**. It's because of Thomas Jefferson, in fact, that James Monroe, fifth US president, moved to this plantation home nearby in 1793. The house contains Monroe's furnishings and the grounds make a great spot for a picnic. To complete the troika, the man who served between Jefferson and Monroe also had a home in these parts. Twenty-five miles northeast of Charlottesville, James Madison's enormous estate of **Montpelier** lords over Orange County.

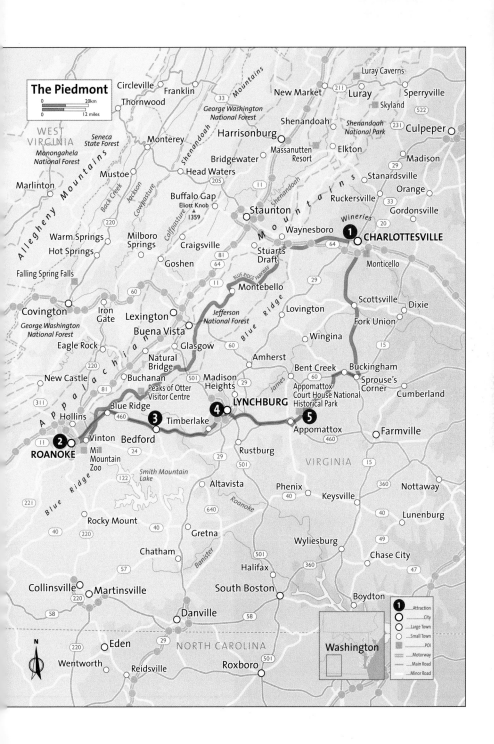

Richmond

Ratings

Art and museums	●●●●●
History	●●●●●
Entertainment	●●●●
Gastronomy	●●●○○
Children	●●○○○
Shopping	●●○○○
Beaches	●○○○○
Nature	●○○○○

The state capital is relatively small; the city's population hovers around the 200,000 mark. Both Virginia Beach and Norfolk have more citizens. But that middling size seems out of proportion to Richmond's rich and turbulent history, its distinctive old neighbourhoods, outstanding cultural institutions, notable personalities, eye-catching architecture, imposing memorials, buzzing nightlife and recreational and entertainment amenities.

Named because of a similarity between the James River bend and a curve on the Thames at Richmond, England, the city's most fateful four years began in 1861, when the Ordinance of Secession was passed, leading to Richmond's prominence as capital of the Confederate States of America – and subsequently as the rebel forces' chief armaments supplier, hospital city, military target and ultimate scene of devastating conflagration. Today, early in a new century, modern progress and an enduring air of Southern civility co-exist as prevalent attributes.

Below
Richmond State Capitol

Arriving and departing

Richmond is located at the junction of the I-95 and I-64 motorways, making it a central hub for quick, moderate-distance automobile access to and from points beyond – Washington DC (105 miles), for instance – as well as coastal locales and the Shenandoah National Park vicinity.

You can also get here via **Amtrak** rail service. The **Richmond National Airport** lies ten miles east of the city centre, off I-64. **Groome Transportation** provides service between the airport and downtown locales (*tel: (804) 222-7222; www.groometransportation. com/richmond.htm*).

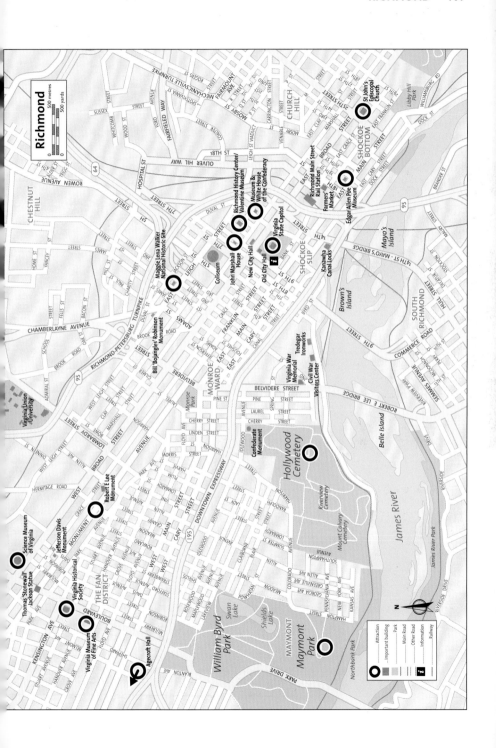

Richmond

500 metres
500 yards

St John's Episcopal Church
CHURCH HILL
SHOCKOE BOTTOM
Richmond Main Street Rail Station
Farmers' Market
Edgar Allen Poe Museum
Museum & White House of the Confederacy
Richmond History Center/ Valentine Museum
Virginia State Capitol
John Marshall House
New City Hall
Old City Hall
SHOCKOE SLIP
Kanawha Canal Locks
Coliseum
Maggie Lena Walker National Historic Site
Brown's Island
Mayo's Island
SOUTH RICHMOND
Bill 'Bojangles' Robinson Monument
MONROE WARD
Tredegar Ironworks
Virginia War Memorial
Civil War Visitars Center
BELVIDERE STREET
Monroe Park
Belle Island
Hollywood Cemetery
Confederate Monument
Robert E Lee Monument
Virginia Union University
Science Museum of Virginia
Jefferson Davis Monument
Thomas 'Stonewall' Jackson Statue
Virginia Historical Society
THE FAN DISTRICT
Virginia Museum of Fine Arts
Agecroft Hall
William Byrd Park
Swan Lake
Shields Lake
Riverview Cemetery
Mount Calvary Cemetery
MAYMONT PARK
Maymont Park
James River
Northbank Park
James River Park

Attraction
Important building
Park
Main Road
Other Road
Information
Railway

Getting around

Metropolitan Richmond Convention and Visitors Bureau 405 N 3rd St; tel: (888) 742-4666; www.richmondva.org

A Visitor Center can be found at the airport: tel: (804) 783-7450.

Civil War Visitor Center 470 Tredegar St; tel: (804) 771-2145; www.virginia.org

The Downtown Expressway (Rte 195) slices east–west through the city. Streets are laid out in a simple grid pattern. Parking is plentiful, and buses operated by the **Greater Richmond Transit Company** (*tel: (804) 358-4782; www.ridegrtc.com*) cover city-wide routes. For inexpensive self-guided sightseeing, board any of the GRTC trams at downtown stops; their routes bring you close to shopping disticts, restaurants, museums, theatres and nightclubs. Guided walking tours are available, too. For high-altitude orientation, take in panoramic views from the free-admittance observation deck atop **New City Hall** on Broad St.

Right
Richmond skyline

Sights

Agecroft Hall $
*4305 Sulgrave Rd;
tel: (804) 353-4241;
www.agecrofthall.com; open
Tue–Sat 1000–1600, Sun
1230–1700.*

**Edgar Allen Poe
Museum $** *1914–1916
E Main St; tel: (888) 213-
2763 or (804) 648-5523;
www.poemuseum.org; open
Tue–Sat 1000–1700, Sun
1100–1700.*

Hollywood Cemetery $
*412 S Cherry St; tel: (804)
648-8501; www.
hollywoodcemetery.org; open
daily 0800–1700, tours
Apr–Oct Mon–Sat 1000.*

John Marshall House $
*818 E Marshall St; tel: (804)
648-7998; www.apva.org;
open Mar–Oct Wed–Fri
1100–1500, Sat 1000–
1700, Sun 1200–1700.*

**Maggie Lena Walker
National Historic Site**
*110 E Leigh St; tel: (804)
771-2017;
www.nps.gov/malw; open
Mon–Sat 0900–1700. Free.*

Maymont $ *2201 Shields
Lake Dr; tel: (804) 358-
7166; www.maymont.org;
grounds open daily
1000–1700; house open
Tue–Sun 1200–1700.*

Agecroft Hall

This 15th-century timbered English Tudor manor house stood in Lancashire prior to being dismantled in the late 1920s. Shipped overseas, its best parts were reassembled west of downtown, at Windsor Farms alongside the James River. Featuring the original hand-carved oak panelling and leaded- and stained-glass windows, the mansion also contains furnishings from the Tudor and early Stuart periods, plus tapestries, massive fireplaces, ornate plaster ceilings, British military artefacts and a two-storey Great Hall, with woodlands and formal gardens on the 23-acre estate. An all-British museum shop is on the premises.

Edgar Allan Poe Museum

Five buildings, most notably the 1737 Old Stone House (Richmond's oldest dwelling), chronicle the melancholy writer's life and literary output. The Memorial Building displays memorabilia, manuscripts and first editions; the carriage house's gallery features James Carling's illustrations inspired by one of Poe's eeriest poems, *The Raven*.

Hollywood Cemetery

Burial place of US Presidents James Monroe and John Tyler, Confederacy President Jefferson Davis, twenty-two Confederate generals and six Virginia governors. A granite pyramid memorialises the 18,000 Confederate soldiers also interred here. The cemetery covers bluffs overlooking the James River.

John Marshall House

Built in the late 18th century for Thomas Jefferson's cousin and Revolutionary War veteran who was chief justice of the US Supreme Court from 1801 to 1835. The house retains its wide-plank pine floors, woodwork and panelling, augmented by period antiques and Marshall's personal belongings.

Maggie Lena Walker National Historic Site

Being physically impaired, black and a woman were social hindrances in 1903. Even so, Mrs Walker became the USA's first female bank president upon establishing the St Luke Penny Savings Bank (since renamed the Consolidated Bank & Trust). A leading force in Richmond's African-American community, she also published a newspaper and founded a department store. The house in which she lived from 1904 until her death in 1934 is maintained by the National Park Service.

Maymont

A 33-room Romanesque-Revival mansion dominates Major and Mrs John Henry Dooley's 100-acre James River country estate. The grounds include Japanese and Italian gardens, a herb garden, arboretum,

🅸 **Monument Avenue**
Begins in town at Lombardy St; ends at Horsepen Rd/Glenside Dr on Richmond's western outskirts.

Museum and White House of the Confederacy $ *1201 E Clay St; tel: (804) 649-1861; www.moc.org; open Mon–Sat 1000–1700, Sun 1200–1700.*

Richmond History Center/Valentine Museum $ *105 Clay St; tel: (804) 649-0711; www. richmondhistorycenter.com; open Tue–Sat 1000–1700, Sun 1200–1700; tours daily on the hour 1100–1600.*

Science Museum of Virginia $$ *2500 W Broad St; tel: (804) 864-1400; www.smv.org; exhibits open Tue–Sat 0930–1700, Sun 1130–1700; IMAX show times vary.*

St John's Episcopal Church $ *2401 E Broad St; www. historicstjohnschurch.org; guided tours Mon–Sat 1000–1530, Sun 1300–1530; re-enactments late May–early Sept Sun 1400.*

children's farm and a nature centre with a 26,000-gallon terraced river aquarium, plus wildlife habitats for native Virginian black bears, bison, elk, bobcats and birds of prey. Gilded Age goodies inside the turreted manse include stained-glass windows, Oriental carpets, Tiffany vases, porcelain, tapestries, sculptures and an art nouveau swan-shaped master bed.

Monument Avenue

Laid out in Parisian style in 1890 with its centre strip shaded by oaks and maples, this brick-paved boulevard is regarded as one of the US's most beautiful urban thoroughfares. Its easternmost mile features a block-by-block 'parade' of six statues, including a 60ft-high bronze Robert E Lee astride his horse 'Traveller'. Additional statues honour other Civil War military leaders and officers.

Museum and White House of the Confederacy

Founded in 1890, this is the nation's largest museum devoted to Confederate artefacts, documents, weapons, paintings, photographs, soldiers' diaries and battlefield sketches. Uniforms and equipment belonging to military leaders 'Jeb' Stuart and 'Stonewall' Jackson are displayed, along with a replica of Lee's field headquarters and more than 500 military and governmental flags. Also on view is *The Last Meeting of Lee and Jackson*, a 15ft-high canvas painted in 1869 by E B D Julio as a memorial to the South's lost cause.

Jefferson Davis and his family lived in the 1818 Victorian mansion next door to the museum throughout his four years as the Confederacy chief executive. Among the 11 furnished period rooms open to the public are the dining room (used for cabinet meetings), library, Davis's office and upstairs bedrooms.

Richmond History Center/Valentine Museum

A repository of Richmond's urban and social history, decorative and industrial arts, architecture and racial inter-relationships. Vintage photographs of the city are displayed, and a gallery is devoted to the South's largest costume and textile collection. 'The Valentine' incorporates the 1812 Federal-style Wickham House, featuring a freestanding circular staircase, carved ornamentation and rare neo-classical wall paintings, along with humble quarters for domestic servants and slaves.

Science Museum of Virginia

Richmond's science museum offers stationary and revolving exhibits for young and old alike, covering a wide array of topics for the curious at heart. The IMAX theatre is sure to impress even the greatest sceptic. The museum itself is set in one of the city's historical buildings.

St John's Episcopal Church

Built in 1741, Richmond's oldest church was the meeting place of the Second Virginia Convention in March 1775, attended by such influential Virginians as George Washington and Thomas Jefferson.

Rising to support a bill authorising the training of a militia to fight against Great Britain, delegate Patrick Henry delivered his famously stirring speech, concluding with: 'Is life so dear, or peace so sweet, as to be purchased at the price of chains or slavery? Forbid it, almighty God! I know now what course others may take; but as for me, give me liberty, or give me death!'

The surrounding burial ground contains the graves of a signatory of the Declaration of Independence, two Virginia governors and actress Elizabeth Arnold, Edgar Allan Poe's mother.

ght
useum of the Confederacy

🅵 **Virginia Historical Society** $ *428 N Blvd;*
tel: (804) 358-4901;
www.vahistorical.org; open Tue–Sat 1000–1700, Sun 1300–1700.

Virginia Museum of Fine Arts $ *2800 Grove Ave; tel: (804) 340-1400;*
www.vmfa.museum; open Wed–Sun 1100–1500.

Virginia State Capitol $
Capitol Sq, 9th and Grace Sts; tel: (804) 698-1788;
www.virginiacapitol.gov; open Mon–Sat 0830–1700, Sun 1300–1600.

Virginia Historical Society

A vast permanent exhibit, *The Story of Virginia, an American Experienc* covers Old Dominion history from earliest settlement and Virginia' colonial era through the Civil War, World Wars I and II and presen times. Items related to native son George Washington are extensive among them the diary he kept during his first year as US President The museum's neo-classical building opened in 1913 as Battle Abbey a shrine to Virginians who died during the Civil War.

Virginia Museum of Fine Arts

Renowned for its Fabergé collection of more than 300 *objets d'ar* including five jewel-encrusted Easter eggs crafted for Russian Tsar Alexander III and Nicholas II. In addition, the museum excels in it exhibits of Greek, Egyptian, Tibetan and South American antiquitie and contemporary American art, as well as the Mellon collection c French Impressionist and post-Impressionist paintings. Also notable ar a life-size marble statue of the Roman emperor Caligula and six Gobeli tapestries embroidered with episodes from Cervantes' *Don Quixote*.

Virginia State Capitol

Designed by Thomas Jefferson, this neo-classical building i reminiscent of the Maison Carrée – a Roman temple in Nîmes, Franc which Jefferson greatly admired. It has been in continuous use as th state capitol building since its completion in 1788. Twin-colonnade wings were added in 1906. Beneath the rotunda skylight stands Jea Antoine Houdon's life-size statue of George Washington, surrounde overhead by busts of seven other Virginia-born US presidents.

🅰 **Richmond CenterStage** *111 Virginia St; tel: (804) 327-5755.*

Theater Virginia *2800 Grove Ave; tel: (804) 340-1400.*

Theater IV *114 W Broad St; tel: (804) 344-8040; www.theatreivrichmond.org*

Landmark Theater *Laurel and Main Sts; tel: (804) 646-4213.*

Coliseum *601 E Leigh St; events tel: (804) 780-4956, box office (804) 780-4970, ext. 131; www.richmondcoliseum.net*

Opposite
Monument Avenue

Entertainment and recreation

The Thursday 'Weekend' section of the *Richmond Times-Dispatch* ha what's-on listings for shows, concerts and nightclub offerings. Listing and reviews also appear in the hip, free *Style Weekly* tabloid.

Downtown, the 2,060-seat **Richmond CenterStage**, originally 1920s' Moorish-style Loew's cinema, now hosts Broadway road show and is home to the Richmond Symphony, Richmond Ballet an Virginia Opera.

Theater Virginia, in the **Virginia Museum of Fine Arts**, is professional theatre staging five shows (musicals, comedies, dram and classical productions) each autumn to spring season. The 191 Empire Theater has become **Theater IV**, housing the US's secon largest children's theatre and a resident professional compan presenting off-Broadway plays. National touring companies appear the 3,300-seat **Landmark**, locally nicknamed 'The Mosque' becau of its exotic resemblance to an Islamic temple. Big-name showb stars and bands (also sports events) pack them in at Richmond **Coliseum**.

Richmond's historic neighbourhoods

Exploring them with a watchful eye will deepen your appreciation of the city's diversity and conservationist zeal.

Church Hill, east of downtown, covers 2 sq miles on high ground above the river. Along the brick sidewalks of this oldest Richmond neighbourhood stand some 200 18th- and 19th-century houses; many feature cast-iron ornamentation. **St John's Episcopal Church** of Patrick Henry renown is in Church Hill, as is the **Richmond National Battlefield Park Visitor Center** (see *Richmond Battlefields, pages 112–19*).

The **Fan District**, so called because its streets 'fan' out from Virginia Commonwealth University, lays claim to being the US's largest intact Victorian neighbourhood, comprising styles ranging from traditional brownstones to elegant townhouses in softly muted yellows, pinks and blues.

Shockoe Slip and **Shockoe Bottom** are side-by-side riverside districts. The 'Slip' was formerly Richmond's commercial trading centre, hence its recycled warehouses and cobblestone streets, plus Italianate brick and iron front buildings now housing shops and galleries in a half-square-mile area. Shockoe Bottom's resurgence, long hindered by James River flooding, accelerated upon completion of a floodwall. Once the city's main business and tobacco-factory district, Shockoe Bottom includes 17th St's **Farmers' Market**, in existence since 1775.

Jackson Ward became a thriving African-American cultural and entrepreneurial centre following the Civil War. Northwest of downtown, this neighbourhood features the nation's second greatest usage of architectural cast iron after New Orleans. Watch for the **Bojangles Monument**, where E Leigh St and Chamberlayne Ave intersect; it commemorates local legend Bill 'Bojangles' Robinson, Shirley Temple's tap-dancing co-star in the 1935 movie *The Little Colonel*.

Monroe Ward, on Richmond's west side, encompasses some of the city's finest 19th-century residences, with opulent domestic architecture ranging from French Renaissance to Greek Revival.

Court End, named after its proximity to federal courts of the late 1700s and early 1800s, radiates from Capitol Square. Nine National Historic Landmarks can be found amidst these elegant old residences, including the **State Capitol** and the 1813 **Governor's Mansion**, the **Valentine Museum/Wickham House** and the **Museum and White House of the Confederacy**.

Dogwood Dell
Boulevard and Idlewood Ave; tel: (804) 646-1437.

Paramount's Kings Dominion $$$ *Exit 98 off I-95, Doswell; tel: (804) 876-5000; www.kingsdominion.com*

Colonial Downs $
Exit 214 off I-64, New Kent County; tel: (804) 966-7223.

The Diamond $ *3001 N Blvd; tel: (804) 359-4444.*

Richmond Canal Cruises $ *490 Tredegar St; tel: (804) 649-2800.*

Richmond Raft Co. $$$
Tel: (804) 222-7238; www.richmondraft.com

Adventure Challenge $$$ *Tel: (804) 276-7600; www.adventurechallenge.com*

Jefferson Hotel $$–$$$ *Franklin and Adams Sts; tel: (800) 424-8014 or (804) 788-8000; www.jeffersonhotel.com*

Linden Row Inn $$ *100 E Franklin St; tel: (800) 348-7424 or (804) 783-7000; www.lindenrowinn.com*

Berkeley Hotel $$ *1200 E Cary St; tel: (888) 780-4422 or (804) 780-1300; www.berkeleyhotel.com*

Richmond Marriott $$–$$$ *500 E Broad St; tel: (800) 228-9290 or (804) 643-3400.*

Emmanuel Hutzler House $$ *2036 Monument Ave; tel: (804) 353-6900.*

If you're visiting during summertime, join the audience at William Byrd Park's **Dogwood Dell** amphitheatre for the free-admittance Festival of Arts ballets, plays and musical performances.

Paramount's Kings Dominion is a multi-attraction 400-acre theme park, 20 miles north of Richmond, including a suspended hair-raiser of a roller coaster, Volcano, the Blast Coaster and the 16-acre WaterWorks, with a wave pool and water slides. Music from Paramount movies enhances an ice-skating show, and laser beams and fireworks light up evening skies.

Fans of pari-mutuel thoroughbred racing head 25 miles east of downtown to **Colonial Downs**.

Shockoe Bottom and Shockoe Slip are Richmond's 'in' nightlife destinations for discos, comedy clubs and sundry drinking places.

Venues for spectator sports include **The Diamond**, where the Richmond Braves play AAA-level minor-league baseball. If you desire a more leisurely pace join **Richmond Canal Cruises** for a 35-minute historically narrated tour of the James River & Kanawha Canal along Richmond's historic canal walk.

For active-participation right downtown, whitewater rafting on the James River is provided by **Richmond Raft Co. Adventure Challenge** runs James River kayaking trips.

Accommodation and food

The Metropolitan CVB and the Visitor Centers are reliable sources of lodging listings in various price ranges, but making reservations is your affair. Most of the familiar US chains operate at least one hotel or motel in the metro area. Holiday Inn, for instance, has ten properties and six Days Inns.

Right
Washington statue, Richmond

Mr Patrick Henry's Inn $–$$ 2300-2302 E Broad St; tel: (804) 644-1322.

Richmond's thickest concentrations of recommendable restaurants are in Shockoe Slip, Shockoe Bottom and the Fan district.

oe's Inn $ 205 N Shields Ave; tel: (804) 355-2282; www.joesinn.com. This Fan storefront restaurant serves heaping-big breakfasts and Italian-accentuated lunches and dinners.

The Dining Room at the Berkeley Hotel $$–$$$ 1200 E Cary St; tel: (804) 225-5105; www.berkeleyhotel.com. serves French country cuisine.

ulep's New Southern Cuisine $$–$$$ 1719-1721 Franklin St; tel: (804) 777-3968; www.juleps.net. Elegant setting in historic Shockoe Bottom and the River District. Southern cuisine at its best.

Capital Ale House $–$$$ 623 E Main St; tel: (804) 780-2537; www.capitalalehouse.com. This trendy establishment offers 50 different kinds of beers from all over the world. The bar has an 'ice rail' to keep your beverage cold.

Millie's Diner $$–$$$ 2603 Main St; tel: (804) 643-5512; www.milliesdiner.com. A retro 1950s diner turned into a fine little Shockoe Bottom restaurant with an eclectic menu.

For a convenient location and gracious opulence which includes the Palm Court with a Thomas Jefferson statue beneath a stained-glass skylight, opt for what's been a landmark since 1895: the **Jefferson Hotel**. A row of Greek-Revival townhouses dating from 1847 comprises the 71-room **Linden Row Inn**. Opened in 1988, the **Berkeley Hotel** is in Shockoe Slip and offers complimentary valet parking. Five blocks from historic Court End attractions, the **Richmond Marriott** is also close to the Jackson Ward and Monroe Ward neighbourhoods.

Several in-town bed and breakfasts emanate Southern charm and hospitality. One is the Italian Renaissance-style **Emmanuel Hutzler House**. Another, a Greek-Revival beauty in historic Church Hill, is **Mr Patrick Henry's Inn**.

Suggested walks

Monument Avenue

Total distance: Viewing the monuments entails a 1½-mile walk. Backtracking by way of Main St or Grove or Stuart Ave in the Fan district adds another 1¾ miles. Opting for a return via Grove Ave enables you to visit the **VIRGINIA MUSEUM OF FINE ARTS**. Walking west along Stuart Ave brings you to the **VIRGINIA HISTORICAL SOCIETY**.

Time: Depending upon your preferred pace, allow approximately 2–3 hours, at most a full morning or afternoon.

Route: Monument Ave's eastern end begins at the Lombardy St intersection, where you'll see the first Confederate hero statue, honouring General J E B Stuart. The equestrian Robert E Lee monument stands tall at the next crossroads. Jefferson Davis, president of the Confederacy, merits an especially elaborate memorial. His sculpted likeness stands amidst 13 Doric columns representing the 11 states that seceded and two others sending delegates to the Confederate Congress. Next, at the Monument Ave/Boulevard intersection, you'll see the statue of Thomas 'Stonewall' Jackson atop his horse Little Sorrel. Tennis champion Arthur Ashe Jr, is honoured with a statue, erected in 1995 at the corner of Monument Ave and Roseneath Rd.

River walk

Total distance: Walking a bit more than 3 miles provides an overview of Richmond's portion of the US's first extensive canal system.

Time: Allow half a day for easygoing sightseeing.

Route: At **Shockoe Slip ❶**, head down 12th St to Byrd St to the **Kanawha Canal Locks**, constructed in 1854. From there, a combined canal/river walk extends 1½ miles, connecting on to pedestrian

Hyperlink Café
$–$$ *814 W Grace St;
tel: (804) 254-1942;
http://hyperlinkva.com.*
Virginia's only oxygen bar,
where inhaling claims to
boost energy and relieve
hangovers and headaches.
Also offers great food to
nosh while you go online.

**Sam Miller's
Warehouse $$–$$$**
*1210 E Cary St; tel: (804)
644-5465;
www.sammillers.com.*
Excellent Chesapeake Bay
seafood in this Slip stalwart.

Strawberry Street Café
$–$$ *421 N Strawberry St;
tel: (804) 353-6860; www.
strawberrystreetcafe.com.*
Top choice in The Fan, a
laid-back eatery and wine
bar with its salad bar
stashed inside an old-
fashioned clawfoot
bathtub.

The Tobacco Company
$$ *12th and Cary Sts; tel:
(804) 782-9555; www.
thetobaccocompany.com.*
Another 'Slip' favourite, in
a former 1860s tobacco
warehouse, specialising in
contemporary American
cuisine.

**James River
Plantations $** *Tel:
(804) 829-2480; www.
jamesriverplantations.org;
open daily 0900–1700.*
Money-saving combination
tickets can be purchased.

bridges reaching **Brown's Island ❷** and **Belle Island ❸**. A 1-mile
path on that island (site of a Civil War prison camp) passes waterfalls
and 19th-century earthworks.

Back on shore, you can view remnants of the **Tredegar Ironworks ❹**
(*see page 116*), supplier of artillery, cannonballs and armour plate for the
Confederate army and navy. Historical markers are positioned along the
walkway. You can also walk 1 mile atop the **Richmond Floodwall's**
concrete levee, with Canada geese and blue heron likely to be seen.

Also worth exploring

Four close-together, fully furnished exemplars of Old South aristocracy
can be reached by way of a scenic 30–35-mile Rte 5 drive southeast
from Richmond. **Shirley Plantation**, Virginia's oldest, was first settled
in 1613; the mansion dates from 1723. The property includes brick
outbuildings forming a unique Queen Anne forecourt. **Berkeley**, an
early three-storey Georgian mansion (1726) filled with 18th-century
antiques and heirlooms, is the birthplace of William Henry Harrison,
ninth US president. **Evelynton** has been home to the Ruffin family
since 1847; patriarch Edmund Ruffin fired the first shot of the Civil
War at Fort Sumter. The 2,500-acre property features former slave
quarters and historical markers indicating 1862 wartime skirmishes.
Sherwood Forest, surrounding a circa 1730, 300ft-wide mansion (the
country's longest frame dwelling), was owned by two US presidents,
William Harrison and John Tyler.

Right
State Capitol

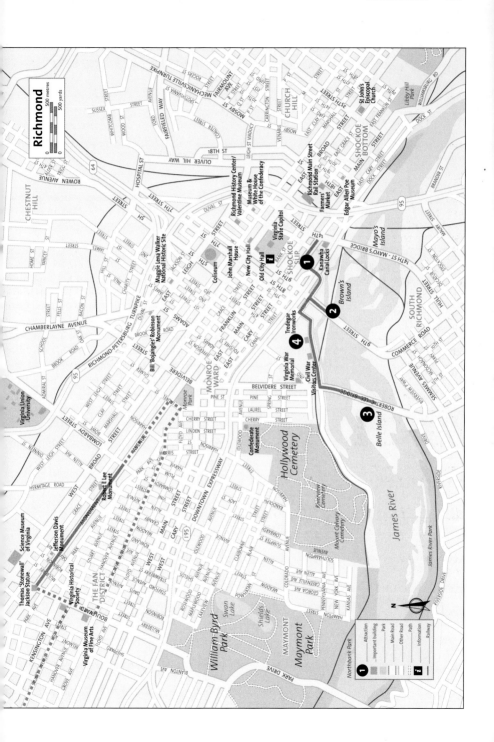

Richmond

0   500 metres
0   500 yards

CHESTNUT HILL

Virginia Union University

CHAMBERLAYNE AVENUE

RICHMOND PETERSBURG TURNPIKE

Bill 'Bojangles' Robinson Monument

Maggie Lena Walker National Historic Site

Coliseum

John Marshall House

New City Hall

Old City Hall

Richmond History Center/ Valentine Museum

Museum & White House of the Confederacy

Virginia State Capitol

Richmond Main Street Rail Station

Farmers' Market

Edgar Allen Poe Museum

St John's Episcopal Church

CHURCH HILL

SHOCKOE BOTTOM

SHOCKOE SLIP

Kanawha Canal Locks

Brown's Island

Mayo's Island

SOUTH RICHMOND

Tredegar Ironworks

Virginia War Memorial

Civil War Visitors Center

Belle Isle

James River

Hollywood Cemetery

Riverview Cemetery

Mount Calvary Cemetery

Confederate Monument

MONROE WARD

Monroe Park

THE FAN DISTRICT

Robert E Lee Monument

Thomas 'Stonewall' Jackson Statue

Jefferson Davis Monument

Science Museum of Virginia

Virginia Historical Society

Virginia Museum of Fine Arts

William Byrd Park

Swan Lake

Shields Lake

MAYMONT PARK

Maymont Park

Northbank Park

James River Park

Attraction
Important building
Park
Main Road
Other Road
Path
Information
Railway

Richmond battlefields

Ratings

History	●●●●●
Art and museums	●●○○○
Children	●●○○○
Beaches	●○○○○
Entertainment	●○○○○
Gastronomy	●○○○○
Nature	●○○○○
Shopping	●○○○○

The Confederacy's capital became the Federal forces' primary objective from the Civil War's very outset in 1861. Richmond was the South's strategic command post, medical centre, main manufacturing base and biggest supply depot for the thousands of rebel troops assigned to Robert E Lee's Army of Northern Virginia.

Overall, seven major assaults were launched against Richmond. Two, in 1862 and again in 1864, brought Union infantry and artillery within shooting range of downtown objectives. Upon evacuating their city a year later, Confederate officials authorised the burning of warehouses and supplies; fires quickly spread to the riverside commercial districts.

A visit to the Richmond National Battlefield Park puts all of that inflammatory past history into perspective. A few miles south, the smaller communities of Hopewell and Petersburg – and certainly Petersburg's nearby battlefield – also became prominent locales during the conflict that split the nation apart.

HOPEWELL

ℹ Hopewell Visitor Center *4100 Oaklawn Blvd; tel: (800) 863-8687 or (804) 541-2461; www.ci.hopewell.va.us; open daily 0900–1700.*

Ⓗ Appomattox Manor $ *Cedar Ln, City Point; tel: (804) 458-9504; open daily for visitor information and guided tours 0900–1700.*

On high ground bulging into the confluence of the James and Appomattox rivers, City Point, a compact National Historic District looms large in Civil War annals. General Ulysses S Grant made the hamlet his command post for the Union forces' relentless siege of nearby Petersburg in 1864–65 (*see page 115*). The waterways and lengthened rail lines became supply routes for 100,000 troops manning the siege lines, with Grant's headquarters functioning as his army's logistical and communications nerve centre. President Lincoln travelled twice from Washington to join in the strategy sessions. Wayside markers are informative.

On this National Park Service property, the 25 rooms of **Appomattox Manor** accommodated Grant's staff. Nearby, the general's rebuilt log headquarters cabin stands on its original site; peer inside to see his blue uniform coat, adorned with three-star epaulets, slung over a chair.

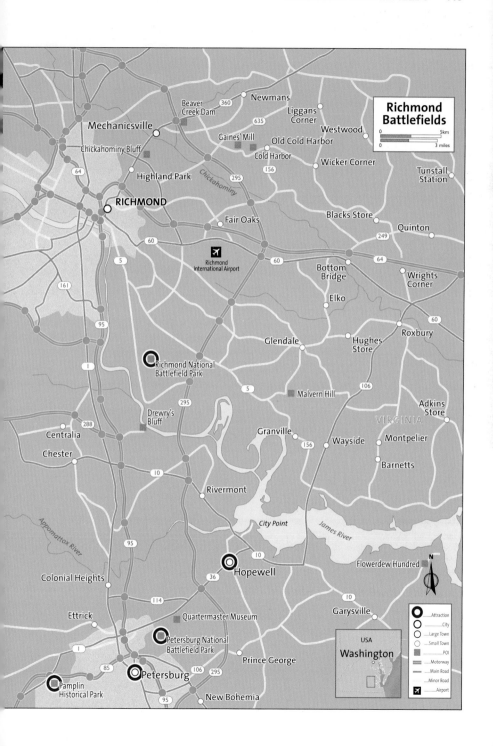

Richmond Battlefields

Newmans
Beaver Creek Dam
360
Liggans Corner
635
Westwood
Mechanicsville
Gaines' Mill
Old Cold Harbor
Chickahominy Bluff
Cold Harbor
Wicker Corner
156
Tunstall Station
64
Highland Park
Chickahominy
295
RICHMOND
Fair Oaks
Blacks Store
Quinton
60
249
60
Bottom Bridge
64
Wrights Corner
Richmond International Airport
5
161
Elko
60
Roxbury
95
Hughes Store
1
Glendale
Richmond National Battlefield Park
295
Malvern Hill
106
Adkins Store
Drewry's Bluff
VIRGINIA
288
Granville
Centralia
156
Wayside
Montpelier
Chester
Barnetts
10
Rivermont
City Point
James River
95
Appomattox River
Colonial Heights
10
Flowerdew Hundred
Hopewell
36
114
10
Garysville
Ettrick
Quartermaster Museum
1
Petersburg National Battlefield Park
85
Prince George
Pamplin Historical Park
Petersburg
106
295
New Bohemia
95

Richmond Battlefields

0 ____ 5km
0 ____ 3 miles

USA
Washington

◉ ......Attraction
◎ ......City
○ ......Large Town
○ ......Small Town
■ ......POI
━━ ......Motorway
━━ ......Main Road
━━ ......Minor Road
✈ ......Airport

Right
Confederate cavalry hero 'Jeb'
Stuart commemorated on
Richmond's Monument Avenue

Accommodation and food in Hopewell

Broadway Cafeteria $ *120 E City Point Rd; tel: (804) 458-1700.* Affordability and copious amounts of good self-service food makes a good choice for any of three daily meals.

Ginny's Café $ *222 E Broadway; tel: (804) 458-1401.* Open weekdays, antiques hanging on its walls, this café is a downtown bargain for 'home-cooked' breakfasts, lunches and dinners.

Innkeeper $ *3952 Courthouse Rd; tel: (800) 822-9899 or (804) 458-2600.* This hotel comprising 104 guest rooms is only about a 10-min drive from Hopewell town centre.

El Nopal Mexican Restaurant $–$$ *4118 Oaklawn Blvd; tel: (804) 452-0901.* Authentic recipes and homemade Mexican food. Extensive menu includes combination plates, vegetarian dishes, fajitas appetizers and desserts.

PAMPLIN HISTORICAL PARK

🏛 Pamplin Historical Park $ *6125 Boydton Plank Rd; tel: (804) 861-2408; www.pamplinpark.org; open daily 0900–1700. Café and gift shop on the premises.*

A somewhat touristy attraction but worthwhile, since it was here, on 2 April 1865, that Union infantry and cavalry regiments ended Petersburg's siege by breaking through the Confederates' formidable defence lines. A 1-mile system of trails winds through the battlefield amidst some of Virginia's best-preserved Civil War earthworks, artillery emplacements and picket posts. An interpretive centre displays uniforms, firearms and campaign flags; a fibre-optics battle map and interactive video programs turn the conflict into a high-tech learning experience.

Also in the park is Tudor Hall, an 1812 plantation house used a brigade headquarters by rebel General Samuel McGowan. The National Museum of the Civil War Soldier honours the 3 million men who served during the war under northern and southern commands.

PETERSBURG

Petersburg Visitors Center *425 Cockade Alley; tel: (800) 368-3595 or (804) 733-2400; www.petersburg-va.org*

Siege Museum $ *15 W Bank St; tel: (804) 733-2400; open daily 1000–1700.*

Old Blandford Church $ *111 Rochelle Ln; tel: (804) 733-2396; open: Mon–Sat 0900–1700, Sun 1230–1600; tours every 45 minutes until 1600.*

Quartermaster Museum *E Washington St, off Rte 36; tel: (804) 734-4203; open Tue–Fri 1000–1700, Sat & Sun 1100–1700. Free.*

Flagship Inn $ *815 S Crater Rd; tel: (804) 861-3470.*

Ragland Mansion Bed and Breakfast $–$$ *205 S Sycamore St; tel: (800) 861-8898 or (804) 861-1932; www.ragland-mansion.com*

High Street Inn $–$$ *405 High St; tel: (804) 722-0800 or (888) 474-1898.*

Mayfield Inn $–$$ *3348 W Washington St; tel: (800) 538-2381 or (804) 733-0866.*

Dixie Restaurant $ *250 N Sycamore St; tel: (804) 732-5761.*

Alexander's $–$$ *101 Bank St; tel: (804) 861-6755.*

The Brickhouse Run $ *407–409 Cockade Alley; tel: (804) 862-1815.*

The history of this little city (population 38,400) on the Appomattox River's south bank is closely linked with the final phases of the Civil War. As a manufacturing centre and railroad junction crucial to Confederate supply and transport, Petersburg became an inevitable target, with incessant Union barrages inflicting severe destruction.

Those bombardments culminated in the longest siege in US history, spanning nearly ten months and beginning in 1864. The **Siege Museum** downtown presents a tableau of citizens' endurance throughout that trying period. Petersburg-born actor Joseph Cotten narrates *The Echoes Still Remain*, a cinematic retrospective of their ordeal. A panoramic *Battle of the Crater* painting is noteworthy. The museum occupies a colonnaded Greek-Revival landmark opened in 1839 as the city's commodities exchange.

South of downtown, the 18th-century **Old Blandford Church** was used as a makeshift field hospital. Restored as a Confederate war memorial in 1901, each of its 15 stained-glass windows, including a Cross of Jewels masterpiece, was commissioned from Louis Comfort Tiffany's New York City studios. Paying respects to those who died on both the 'northern blue' and 'southern gray' sides of the conflict, America's first Memorial Day remembrance was observed here in June 1866. Some 30,000 Confederate soldiers are buried in the cemetery, where the oldest tombstone dates from 1702. Another, by contrast, marks movie-star Cotten's grave.

In the US Army's **Quartermaster Museum**, 3 miles east of Petersburg at Fort Lee, uniforms and random kinds of military gear from all the nation's wars are exhibited, and also such miscellanea as Union General Ulysses S Grant's saddle, World War II General George S Patton's custom-fitted jeep, supply wagons, field kitchens, governmental flags and one of the marcher's drums used in President John F Kennedy's funeral cortège.

Accommodation and food in Petersburg

Within walking distance of the battlefield, the 135-room **Flagship Inn** is an ordinary but satisfactory motel with an outdoor swimming pool. In the city's historic district are two gracious bed and breakfast inns, the Italianate (1850) **Ragland Mansion**, and the turreted **High Street Inn** (1893); both are tastefully appointed. South of downtown, **Mayfield Inn** epitomises 18th-century Georgian-style plantation architecture. Ask the owners about their bed and breakfast's history, which includes its use during the Civil War's final months. Essentially a chatty diner, downtown's **Dixie Restaurant** has been going strong for more than half a century. Greek and Italian dishes are **Alexander's** house specialities; sandwich takeouts can be ordered. **The Brickhouse Run** has sidewalk tables for light pleasant-weather meals.

PETERSBURG NATIONAL BATTLEFIELD PARK

Petersburg National Battlefield Park $ E
Washington St (Rte 36); tel: (804) 732-3531; Visitor Center open daily 0900–1700; battlefield open daily dawn–dusk. An audio guide for a 37-mile tour of battle sites can be rented.

Grim trench warfare was waged during the Union's Overland Campaign in June 1864 on this 1,500-acre site, which includes two forts, gun pits and miles of original earthworks. Twice-daily re-enactments and cannon firings take place during summertime (mid-June–August). From Battery Five a trail leads to the Federal artillery's 17,000-pound seacoast mortar, nicknamed the 'Dictator', which lobbed shells on downtown Petersburg. Prominent on a 4-mile tour route is the Crater, a depression measuring 170ft by 60ft and 30ft deep, created when members of the 48th Pennsylvania Infantry dug a 511-ft tunnel to a Confederate salient and ignited 4 tons of gunpowder. Poplar Grove National Cemetery is the burial place of 6,178 Union soldiers.

RICHMOND NATIONAL BATTLEFIELD PARK

Richmond National Battlefield Park 3215 E Broad St; tel: (804) 226-1981; www.nps.gov/rich/; park open daily dawn–dusk. Free.

Within the park is the **Tredegar Visitor Center** $ 470 Tredegar St; tel: (804) 771-2145; open daily 0900–1700. Audio guides can be rented for self-guided motor touring.

The park's widespread layout, in suburban and rural countryside east and southeast of central Richmond, consists of ten major battle locales and requires a 97-mile drive if covered thoroughly. Walking trails flank well-marked remains of defensive fortifications and other visible indicators of the Union forces' Peninsula (1862) and Overland (1864) Campaigns, aimed at vanquishing the Confederate capital.

On the James riverfront downtown, a visitor centre occupies a former building of the Tredegar Ironworks, the South's largest wartime arsenal.

Sites relevant to the Seven Days' Battles of 1862 include Chickahominy Bluff, where two Confederate divisions succeeded in a flanking manoeuvre that ousted the Federals from their entrenchments. At Beaver Dam Creek, North Carolinians and Georgians encountered withering gunfire during a hopeless attack. Gaines' Mill is remembered for daring Confederate onslaughts against fortified front lines along Boatswain's Creek. Despite heavy casualties, Texas and Georgia troops broke through for a rebel victory.

Massed Federal infantry and artillery defending Malvern Hill opened close-range fire (totalling 1,392 rounds) on two enemy brigades advancing across unprotected meadows and hay fields to attempt death-defying charges up the steep ridge, at a cost of 5,000 Southern casualties. A forest trail reaches the promontory's overlook.

Seven miles south of Richmond, Drewry's Bluff affords panoramas of a bend in the James River, 200ft below, protected in 1862 by clifftop batteries manned by Captain Augustus Drewry's Southside Artillery. When Union gunboats, including the famous ironclad *Monitor*, steamed upriver heading for a planned bombardment of the capital, projectiles hurled from Drewry's 8 in Columbiana and 6½ in Brooke cannons repulsed the flotilla.

Microtel Inn and Suites $ *6000 Audubon Dr, Sandston; tel: (800) 771-7171 or (804) 737-3322.*

Wingate Inn $ *491 International Center Dr, Sandston; tel: (800) 228-1000 or (804) 222-1499.*

Padow's Hams & Deli $ *8161 Atlee Rd, Mechanicsville; tel: (804) 569-1610.*

Calabash Restaurant $$ *7514 Lee David Rd, Mechanicsville; tel: (804) 746-8630. Specialising in hushpuppies, spiced shrimp, calabash pear pie, and house seafood recipes.*

Outback Steakhouse $–$$ *7420 Bell Circle Rd, Mechanicsville; tel: (804) 746-5277.*

Bill's Barbecue $ *927 Myers St, Richmond; tel: (804) 358-7763. This Richmond tradition, established in 1930, serves traditional Virginia style barbecue. Good value for money.*

General Robert E Lee's last significant field victory came in June 1864 at Cold Harbor, where his officers assembled 50,000 rebel soldiers behind 6 miles of entrenchments along ravines and tree lines. Federal attackers suffered extremely heavy casualties – more than 7,000 killed and wounded, mostly during the first hour of fighting. The maze of earthwork trenches can be viewed by way of a 1¼-mile tour road and 1-mile walking trail.

Accommodation and food in or near Richmond

Few people visiting the Civil War sites plan an overnight stay in the area; lodgings in Richmond aren't that far away. If you decide otherwise, however, two attractive and inexpensive non-chain properties in the vicinity of Richmond Airport, at about midpoint along the complete battlefield drive, are the **Microtel Inn and Suites** and the **Wingate Inn**.

Mechanicsville, close to the northernmost Richmond-area battlefields, is well situated for a lunchtime stopover. Made to order sandwiches, wraps and salads are the speciality of **Padow's Hams & Deli**. Eat in or take away with you. If you're touring the battlefields in a south-to-north direction, consider early evening dinner at Mechanicsville's **Calabash Restaurant**, which provides an opportunity to try Rappahannock oysters, Chesapeake clams, Gulf shrimp or backfin crabmeat. An Australian steakhouse is the concept for the **Outback Steakhouse**. Although beef and steak items make up a good portion of the menu, the chain offers a variety of chicken, ribs, seafood and pasta dishes too.

You'll also spot fried-chicken chains, burger franchises, pizza parlours and roadside food stores – as well as pancake and waffle houses, ubiquitous throughout Virginia.

Suggested tour

Total distance: 80–120 miles, depending upon how many sites you choose to visit.

Time: Allow a full day, which includes stopover time for an unhurried lunch.

Links: Battlefield-to-battlefield driving crosses I-64 east–west, so you could merge with the Historic Triangle route (*see pages 143–4*). You'll also cross I-295 at Mechanicsville north of Richmond. Going from that juncture to I-95 northbound provides a feasible link with the Fredericksburg area route (*see page 126*).

Route: From the Tredegar Visitor Center on Richmond's riverfront, turn left onto 9th St, then right on Broad St. Go east through the Church Hill neighbourhood to reach signposted parkland on

**ⓕ Flowerdew
Hundred $$**
*Flowerdew Hundred Rd;
tel: (804) 541-8897;
www.flowerdew.org;
open Apr–Nov Mon–Fri
1000–1600.*

Chimborazo Hill, where more than 77,800 Confederate wounded were treated in the South's largest military hospital complex. Continue by turning right on 18th St, then right on Fairfield Ave; follow signs for Rte 360 (Mechanicsville Turnpike).

On Rte 360, watch for signs indicating **Chickahominy Bluff ❶**. After returning to Rte 360, exit on to Rte 156 (Cold Harbor Rd) to reach **Beaver Creek Dam ❷** and, after 2 miles, **Gaines' Mill ❸**, then 1 mile onward to **Cold Harbor ❹**.

From that Civil War site, go left on Old Hanover Rd, then next right on to Grapevine Rd. Where it ends, steer left on to Meadow Rd, where the **Battle of Savage Station** was waged in 1862. Meadow Rd becomes Rte 156 again after you've crossed Rte 60. Following a 12-mile drive from Savage Station, you'll see roadside signs for **Malvern Hill ❺**.

Continue south via Rte 156 across the Benjamin Harrison Bridge for Hopewell. Turn right on Rte 10 (Randolph Rd); back to the left is **Flowerdew Hundred**, a 17th-century working farm where in 1864 the Union Army of the Potomac crossed a 2,000ft pontoon bridge assembled by its Corps of Engineers under combat conditions. A schoolhouse museum displays colonial Virginian artefacts. Continue to Appomattox St, then Cedar Ln to reach National Park Service site at **City Point ❻**.

Return to Rte 10 and turn right for **HOPEWELL ❼**. Drive 8 miles via Rte 36 to **PETERSBURG NATIONAL BATTLEFIELD PARK ❽** and 2½ miles to **PETERSBURG ❾**. Heading north on I-95 across the Appomattox River, take Exit 64 on to Willis Rd for a 2½-mile drive to **Drewry's Bluff ❿**. Back on I-95, drive to Richmond, thereby closing the battlefield loop. The distance from Petersburg to Richmond totals 23 miles.

Also worth exploring

Clustered in Hopewell's Crescent Hills neighbourhood, 44 prefabricated **mail-order houses** from Sears, Roebuck & Co. were erected from kits between 1926 and 1937. Most are on Oakwood and Prince George Aves. From City Point, Drive West on Broadway. An illustrated brochure is available from the visitor center.

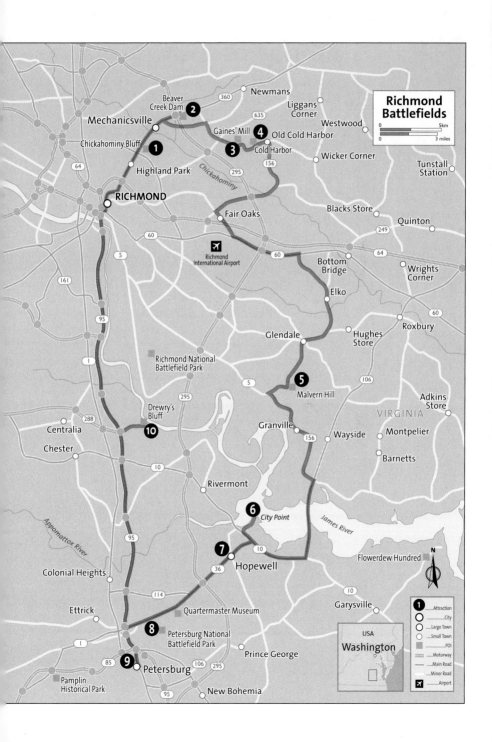

Fredericksburg area

Ratings

Gastronomy	●●●●●
History	●●●●●
Art and museums	●●●●○
Shopping	●●●●○
Children	●●○○○
Entertainment	●●○○○
Beaches	●○○○○
Nature	●○○○○

Settled in 1728, Fredericksburg's location in a fertile valley at the head of Rappahannock River navigation made it a prosperous tobacco-trading port. George Washington spent most of his boyhood years here, later purchasing a house on Charles Street for his mother, Mary Ball Washington. James Monroe, destined to become the fifth US president, set up his law office in Fredericksburg in 1786. A 40-block National Historic District encompasses more than 350 buildings from the 18th and early 19th centuries.

The city (current population about 19,000–20,000) became a Civil War armed camp and hospital for wounded troops of both the Confederate and Union armed forces. Some of that conflict's bloodiest battles were fought in town and nearby – especially in such western-vicinity locales as Chancellorsville Spotsylvania and Wilderness. All of the area's major battlefields are situated within a 17-mile radius of riverfront Fredericksburg.

FREDERICKSBURG

ⓘ Fredericksburg Visitor Center 706 Caroline St; tel: (540) 373-1776 or (800) 678-4748; http://visitfred.com. Ask about money-saving combination tickets for admittance to most-visited attractions.

Fredericksburg Area Tourism 4704 Southpoint Pkwy; tel: (540) 891-6670 or (800) 654-4118.

Get oriented at Market Square's **Fredericksburg Area Museum and Cultural Center** in the former town hall and market house, built in 1815. Six galleries on two floors – plus the upstairs Council Chamber - trace the region's natural and social history by way of artefacts, tools toys, furniture, paintings and photographs, Civil War weaponry, craf demonstrations, audiovisual presentations and special exhibits.

The **Hugh Mercer Apothecary Shop** displays 18th-century medicinal remedies (leeches and snakeroot, for example) which patients had to endure during those pre-anaesthesia days. Dr Merce closed shop upon joining the Continental Army as a brigadier genera in 1776. The **Rising Sun Tavern** was built in 1760 for Charle Washington, George's youngest brother, and was later turned into stagecoach stop and centre of Fredericksburg's social life. Costume 'wenches' welcome visitors with a touristy representation of colonia tavern jollity and serve a complimentary spiced drink.

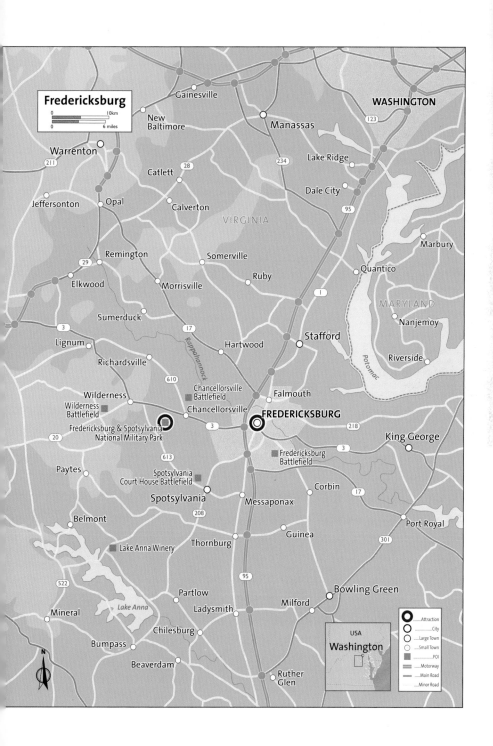

Fredericksburg

| 0 | | 10km |
| 0 | | 6 miles |

Gainesville

WASHINGTON

123

New Baltimore

Manassas

Warrenton

211

Catlett

28

Lake Ridge

234

Dale City

Jeffersonton

Opal

Calverton

95

VIRGINIA

Marbury

Remington

Somerville

29

Ruby

Quantico

Elkwood

Morrisville

MARYLAND

1

Sumerduck

17

Nanjemoy

3

Hartwood

Stafford

Lignum

Rappahannock

Riverside

Richardsville

Potomac

610

Wilderness

Chancellorsville Battlefield

Falmouth

Wilderness Battlefield

Chancellorsville

FREDERICKSBURG

Fredericksburg & Spotsylvania National Military Park

3

20

613

218

King George

3

Fredericksburg Battlefield

Paytes

Spotsylvania Court House Battlefield

Corbin

17

Spotsylvania

Messaponax

208

Belmont

Guinea

Port Royal

Lake Anna Winery

Thornburg

301

522

Partlow

Milford

Bowling Green

Mineral

Lake Anna

Ladysmith

95

Chilesburg

Bumpass

Beaverdam

Ruther Glen

N

USA

Washington

⦾	Attraction
◎	City
◯	Large Town
○	Small Town
■	POI
▬	Motorway
▬	Main Road
─	Minor Road

Fredericksburg, at a midpoint 50 miles north of Richmond and 50 miles south of Washington DC, is conveniently accessible from those metro areas via the north–south I-95 motorway. From east to west, Rte 3 connects the small city with Virginia's Tidewater and Shenandoah Valley regions. An Amtrak train station is merely three blocks south of the centrally located Visitor Center.

A trolley tour of Fredericksburg's sightseeing circuit covers nearly three dozen historic attractions in 60 minutes (tel: (540) 898-0737). Ask at the Visitor Center for five fully detailed and illustrated *Walking through History* brochures, useful for self-guided touring throughout the city centre. Two of these publications enable visitors to follow the course of the Civil War's hard-fought Fredericksburg Campaign of December 1862.

Fredericksburg Area Museum and Cultural Center $ *907 Princess Anne St; tel: (540) 371-3037; www.famcc.org; open Mar–Nov Mon–Sat 1000–1700, Sun 1300–1700; Dec–Feb Mon–Sat 1000–1600, Sun 1300–1600.*

Hugh Mercer Apothecary Shop $ *1020 Caroline St; tel: (540) 373-3362; open Mar–Nov daily 0900–1700; Dec–Feb 1000–1600.*

Right
Kenmore Plantation

For six years, from 1788, James Monroe began his illustrious career at what is now the **James Monroe Museum and Memorial Library**, which displays Louis XVI furniture purchased in Paris while he was US minister to France – along with books, portraits, correspondence and documents highlighted by a section of President Monroe's 1823 address to Congress, which became the influentially internationalist Monroe Doctrine.

After wealthy planter Fielding Lewis married George Washington's sister Betty, they lived in the mid-Georgian brick mansion at **Kenmore Plantation and Gardens**, especially noted for the gorgeously sculpted plasterwork on ceilings and above the fireplaces. The English and American furnishings are authentic 18th-century period pieces. Washington bought the modest clapboard **Mary Washington House** for his mother upon her move from nearby Ferry Farm in 1772. She lived here until her death 17 years later. Some of her belongings are on display, and boxwoods she planted still thrive in the English-style garden. Hostesses in colonial attire conduct half-hour tours.

St George's Episcopal Church, a tall-steepled structure (1849), features a memorial window dedicated to Mary Washington, plus three stained-glass windows designed at Louis Comfort Tiffany's New York City studio. In 1863, General Robert E Lee's Confederate soldiers gathered here for religious revival meetings. A year later, the church became a hospital for wounded Union troops.

Accommodation and food in Fredericksburg

Virtually every US hotel or motel chain has one or more properties in the area. One alternative, a short drive from the Mary Washington college campus and Fredericksburg Battlefield, is the **Heritage Inn**. Another, centrally located in the Old Town district, is the **Kenmore Inn**, an elegant late 1700s mansion (with full breakfasts and dinners).

Rising Sun Tavern
$ 1304 Caroline St; tel:
(540) 371-1494; open daily
Mar–Nov 0900–1700;
Dec–Feb 1000–1600.

**James Monroe Museum
and Memorial Library** $
908 Charles St; tel: (540)
654-1043; www.umw.
edu/jamesmonroemuseum;
open Mon–Sat 1000–1700,
Sun 1300–1700 (until 1600
Dec–Feb).

**Kenmore Plantation
and Gardens** $ 1201
Washington Ave; tel: (504)
373-3381; www.kenmore.
org; open daily 1000–1700
(until 1600 Nov and Dec).

**Mary Washington
House** $ 1200 Charles St;
tel: (540) 373-1569; open
Mar–Oct Mon–Sat 1100–
1700, Sun 1200–1600; Nov
& Dec daily 1200–1600.

**St George's Episcopal
Church** 905 Princess Anne
St; open Mon–Sat
0900–1700; guided tours
Mon–Fri 1000–1500.

Numerous antique
shops line downtown's
Caroline St; more are on
Sophia and William Sts.

Heritage Inn $
5308 Jefferson Davis
Hwy; tel: (540) 898-1000;
www.heritage-inn.org

Kenmore Inn $ 1200
Princess Anne St; tel: (540)
371-7622;
www.kenmoreinn.com

Richard Johnston Inn $
711 Caroline St; tel: (540)
899-7606; www.
therichardjohnstoninn.com

Right
Tiffany stained glass in
St George's Episcopal Church

A pair of 18th-century Old Town row houses comprise the eight-room **Richard Johnston Inn**. Civil War-era antiques and artefacts fill the **Inn at the Olde Silk Mill**. **La Vista Plantation**, in classical revival style, is located in the verdant Spotsylvania County countryside on Fredericksburg's southern outskirts. The grounds feature old shade trees, gardens and a fish pond on a 10-acre spread.

For lodgings in a contemporary setting with an indoor pool, fitness facility and full buffet breakfasts, consider **Wytestone Suites**. This all-suites hotel (each room includes a kitchenette) is adjacent to the Massaponax crossing shopping and cinema mall.

Among area campsites is **Fredericksburg KOA**.

For information and reservations pertaining to lodgings in the area's outlying Spotsylvania and Stafford counties, contact **Spotsylvania County Visitor Center** (*4704 Southpoint Pkwy; tel: (877) 515-6197*).

Inn at the Olde Silk Mill $$ *1707 Princess Anne St; tel: (540) 371-5666; www.fci1.com*

La Vista Plantation $-$$ *4420 Guinea Station Rd; tel: (800) 529-2823 or (540) 898-8444; www. lavistaplantation.com*

Wytestone Suites $-$$ *4615 Southpoint Pkwy; tel: (800) 794-5005 or (540) 891-1112; www. wytestone.com*

Fredericksburg KOA $ *www.fredericksburgkoa.com*

Despite its small size, Fredericksburg has an amazing number of good restaurants. **La Petite Auberge ($-$$** *311 William St; tel: (540) 371-2727)* offers traditional French dining in a cheerful garden setting. **Merriman's** *(715 Caroline St; tel: (540) 371-7723)* has attained a widespread reputation for cuisine featuring fresh Virginia produce; the menu changes seasonally.

Sammy T's ($ *801 Caroline St; tel: (540) 371-2008)* serves inexpensive soups and salads, pasta, burgers, vegetarian dishes and typically southern Brunswick stew; outdoor seating in pleasant weather.

You can find a 'ye olde' atmosphere at **Smythe's Cottage ($$** *303 Fauquier St; tel: (540) 373-1645)*, in what used to be a blacksmith's shop (1840) with a brick patio at the back. Order Virginia favourites such as peanut soup and chicken pot pie. **Brock's Riverside Grill ($$** *503 Sophia St; tel: (540) 370-1820; www.brocksgrill.com)* has chicken, seafood and beef specialities at dinnertime, overlooking the tidal Rappahannock River.

Fredericksburg's ritziest restaurant, with a top-notch wine list, is **Claiborne's ($$$** *200 Lafayette Blvd; tel: (540) 371-7080; www.clabornesrestaurant.com)* – in the city's restored railroad depot. For a quick, inexpensive bite, try **Botta Bing Bagel & Deli ($** *310 Garrisonville Road; tel: (540) 720-8777)* and for genuine Jambalaya and other bayou specialties, go to **Café New Orleans ($** *216 William St; tel: (540) 374-0404)*. **Laziza ($$** *4256 Plank Rd; tel: (540) 548-4555)* serves authentic Lebanese cuisine in an upscale setting, with belly dancing on Fridays and Saturdays.

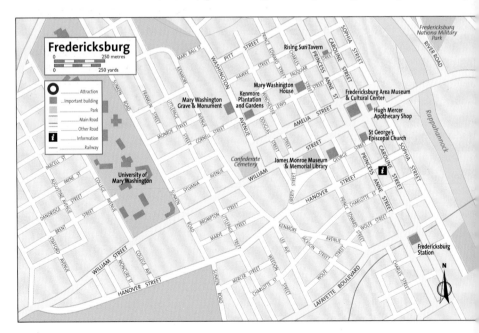

FREDERICKSBURG AND SPOTSYLVANIA NATIONAL MILITARY PARK

Each of the **four battlefield parks** as wayside exhibits, Civil War defensive earthworks, historic buildings, memorials, interpretive driving routes and walking trails in addition to picnic facilities. One admittance rice provides access to all our parks.

Fredericksburg Battlefield Visitor Center $ 1013 Lafayette Blvd (Rte 1); tel: (540) 373-6122; open mid-Jun–mid-Aug daily 0830–1830; mid-Aug–mid-Jun 0900–1700.

Chancellorsville Battlefield Visitor Center $ Rte 3 West (1001 Plank Rd); tel: (540) 786-2880; open Mon–Fri 0900–1700, Sat & Sun 0900–1800; extended summer hours. Audio tapes for self-guided tours can be rented at each centre.

Wilderness Battlefield e 20; guided tours available Apr–Sept 1100 & 1400 weather permitting. Recorded tours available at Chancellorsville Battlefield Visitor Center. Exhibit shelter with walking tour brochures.

Spotsylvania Court House Battlefield Tel: (540) 786-2880 for guide & historian information; open t, Sun & Memorial Day 1100–1800.

From the Civil War's very beginning in 1861, Northerners had an 'On to Richmond' rallying cry, anticipating a swift victory after routing defenders of that crucial 'rebel' city. However, strategically situated Fredericksburg and its field-and-stream environs – midway between the Federal and Confederate capitals – blocked any semblance of a decisive advance. Instead, opposing forces slugged it out in four epic battles over the course of the next three years. Their intense, relentless warfare resulted in estimated death tolls of 70,000 Northern soldiers and 35,000 Southerners. Overall, the park covers 16 sites on 8,400 acres.

Time-travelling begins at **Fredericksburg Battlefield** (11–15 December 1862). Despite harassment by Confederate sharpshooters, Union divisions under General Ambrose E Burnside's command managed to enter Fredericksburg by making a pontoon-bridge crossing of the Rappahannock River from Stafford Heights – meanwhile ravaging the city with short-distance artillery barrages. Robert E Lee's 'most one-sided victory' came during the following three days. The general's 78,000-man force – infantry entrenched behind Sunken Road's stone walls (an original portion of which still exists), cannon and mortar gunners on a ridge called Marye's Heights – repulsed 14 successive Union assaults. Burnside withdrew his demoralised army, retreating back across the river after nightfall on 15 December. A walking trail extends alongside Sunken Road; 15,000 Union soldiers are buried in the Fredericksburg National Cemetery atop Marye's Heights.

Next in sequence comes **Chancellorsville Battlefield** (27 April– 6 May 1863). Union General Joseph Hooker (Burnside's replacement) led another river-crossing, this time north of Fredericksburg. Following a ten-mile westward advance towards Chancellorsville, his 134,000 troops encountered Lee's 60,000-man Army of Northern Virginia at a strategic crossroads. In a surprise manoeuvre, 'Stonewall' Jackson's cavalry corps attacked the 6-mile Federal line's right flank, resulting in a major Southern victory despite heavy casualties on both sides.

A year later, General Ulysses S Grant's armies achieved a third Union crossing of the Rappahannock, then advanced 5 miles past Chancellorsville to the junction at Wilderness Tavern, locale of **Wilderness Battlefield** (5–6 May 1864). Lee advanced to meet the Northerners, marking history's first Lee vs Grant encounter. Two days of fierce fighting ensued in a forest's dense, tangled undergrowth – 60,000 Southerners holding double that number to a stalemate.

Lee and Grant faced off again a year later, near a village court house standing at the shortest roadway route to Richmond. The **Spotsylvania Court House Battlefield** (8–21 May 1864) recalls two weeks of combat – including 20 hours on 12 May at a salient known as 'Bloody Angle'. Within this square-mile area, 13,000 soldiers died during the war's longest-sustained hand-to-hand fighting. The Spotsylvania Confederate Cemetery contains 600 military graves.

Suggested tour

Total distance: 50–55 miles if you cover the four battlefields in an well beyond central Fredericksburg; 75 miles if you cover all related sites

Time: 5–6 hours' leisurely driving – but best to plan a full day morning to sunset.

Links: After your battlefields drive, connect with the Northern Virginia route (*see page 73*). From Fredericksburg and its immediate easter environs, connect with the Tidewater region route (*see pages 133–4*).

Route: From downtown's National Historic District, drive 2 mile southwest on Lafayette Blvd to reach the **FREDERICKSBUR« BATTLEFIELD VISITOR CENTER** and adjacent **Fredericksbur National Cemetery ❶**. Then head west via Rte 3 for 10½ miles; th dual carriageway passes a seemingly endless conglomeration c shopping malls, car dealerships and fast-food establishments, bt eventually opens on to rolling farmland. At **CHANCELLORSVILL BATTLEFIELD ❷**, a 10-mile roadway curves past extensive remains c Confederate trenches and earthworks. After another 6¼ miles via Rte (Plank Rd), you'll arrive at **WILDERNESS BATTLEFIELD ❸**, widespread expanse of forested acreage where you might see whiteta deer scampering through the underbrush. Reach the exhibit shelter b turning on to Rte 20. While touring this battlefield, watch for th evocative memorial to the Union Army's 5th New Jersey Infantr Regiment. Return to Rte 3 then follow Rte 613 (Brock Rd) off Rte southward for 10½ miles to reach the exhibit shelter at th **SPOTSYLVANIA COURT HOUSE BATTLEFIELD ❹**, where 'Blooc Angle' is clearly signposted. The relatively small **Spotsylvani Confederate Cemetery** is south of the battlefield, near the intersectic of Rtes 613/628. For an 11-mile return drive to Fredericksburg, take R 608 east to its junction at Rte 1.

Also worth exploring: Lake Anna State Park

Fresh-air recreation around Lake Anna can be combined with a driv to the battlefields. This public spread surrounds one of Virginia's mo popular lakes and features a sandy beach, in-season food concession pontoon boat rides and plenty of space for picnicking and hiking, pl nearby campsites. Eight marked trails with distances ranging from to 2 miles wind through the wooded terrain. From Spotsylvani follow Rte 208 (Courthouse Rd) southward via Post Oak village; tui on to Rte 601 to reach the park's entrance. For fastest, 26-mile acce direct from Fredericksburg, drive south on I-95; take Exit 118 for scenic drive through Thornburg, Snell and Post Oak via Rte 20 Country grocery stores for takeouts are reasonably numerou **Lakewood** is a combined motel and restaurant 2 miles from the pa at **Lake Anna Winery**, where tastings are offered.

🏞 Lake Anna State Park $ *6800 Lawyers Rd, Spotsylvania; tel: (540) 854-5503; open daily.*

🍴 Lakewood $ *Tel: (540) 895-5844.*

🍷 Lake Anna Winery *5621 Courthouse Rd, Spotsylvania, on Rte 208; tel: (540) 895-5085; www.lawinery.com; open Wed–Sat 1100–1700, Sun 1300–1900.*

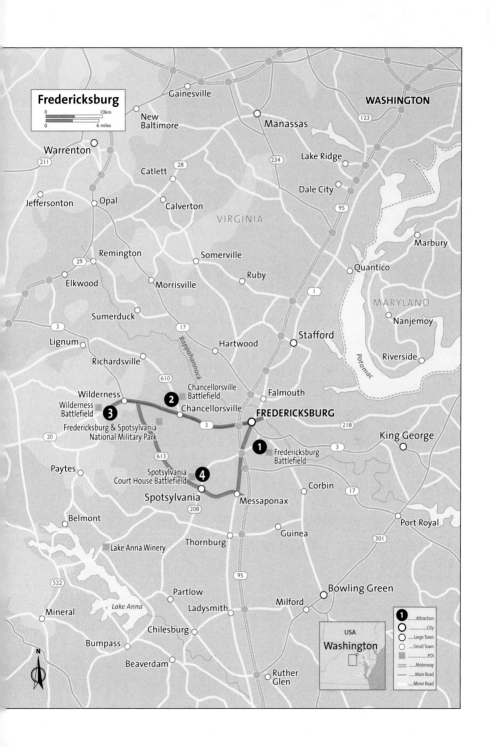

Fredericksburg

| 0 | 10km |
| 0 | 6 miles |

Gainesville

WASHINGTON

New Baltimore

Manassas

123

Warrenton

211

Catlett

28

234

Lake Ridge

Dale City

Jeffersonton

Opal

Calverton

VIRGINIA

95

Marbury

Remington

Somerville

Quantico

Elkwood

Morrisville

Ruby

1

MARYLAND

Sumerduck

17

Nanjemoy

Lignum

Hartwood

Stafford

Riverside

Richardsville

Rappahannock

610

Chancellorsville Battlefield

Falmouth

Potomac

Wilderness

2

Chancellorsville

FREDERICKSBURG

Wilderness Battlefield

3

3

218

King George

Fredericksburg & Spotsylvania National Military Park

20

1

Fredericksburg Battlefield

3

Paytes

613

4

Corbin

17

Spotsylvania Court House Battlefield

Spotsylvania

208

Messaponax

Port Royal

Belmont

Guinea

301

Lake Anna Winery

Thornburg

Lake Anna

522

95

Mineral

Partlow

Milford

Bowling Green

Ladysmith

Chilesburg

USA

Washington

Bumpass

Beaverdam

Ruther Glen

N

1 ....Attraction
○ ....City
○ ....Large Town
○ ....Small Town
.........POI
.........Motorway
.........Main Road
.........Minor Road

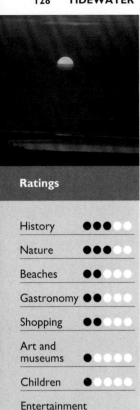

Tidewater

Ratings

History	●●●○○
Nature	●●●○○
Beaches	●●○○○
Gastronomy	●●○○○
Shopping	●●○○○
Art and museums	●○○○○
Children	●○○○○
Entertainment	●○○○○

The Potomac, Rappahannock, James and York rivers slice Virginia's low-lying coastal plain into jagged fingers of land (locals call them 'necks') poking into huge Chesapeake Bay. Each neck – indented with tidal creeks, mini-bays, inlets, coves and estuaries – comprises an ecosystem featuring nature sanctuaries. The region, in fact, is a stopover on the 'Atlantic flyway' travelled by millions of migratory birds. Because of those topographical indentations, the state's portion of bayfront shoreline (shared with Maryland) exceeds 3,300 miles. Short distance roads connect random fishing villages and country towns.

County names – King William, Richmond, Lancaster, King and Queen, Middlesex, Gloucester, York, Northumberland, Isle of Wight – stem from English colonial settlement. The Northern Neck has American history-book significance, mainly because George Washington and Robert E Lee's birthplaces are close together on the upper part of that peninsula, where the Potomac River flows into Chesapeake Bay.

BAYSHORE NORTHERN NECK

ⓘ Lancaster Chamber 506 N Main St, Kilmarnock; tel: (800) 579-9102 or (804) 435-6092; www.lancasterva.com

Ⓜ Reedville Fishermen's Museum $ 504 Main St (Rte 360); tel: (804) 453-6529; www.rfmuseum.org; open May–Oct daily 1030–1630; spring and autumn call ahead.

Northumberland and Lancaster counties comprise the eastern portion of 'The Neck', with close geographic affinity to Chesapeake Bay ecology and weather patterns. The mostly flat landscape's deepest cleft is formed by the Great Wicomico River.

In 1874, a New England ship captain named Elijah W Reed founded his namesake town of Reedville, a picturesque community with Victorian houses near the banks of Cockrell's Creek. Thanks to his foresight, citizens amassed modest fortunes by hauling in menhaden, Chesapeake Bay fish still caught and processed for crop fertiliser and protein-rich livestock feed. That endeavour's heyday is recalled in the **Reedville Fishermen's Museum**, with its permanent collection and rotating exhibits in the 1875 William Walker House and latter-day Covington Building. Boats and equipment used by the area's fishermen to harvest fish, oysters and blue crabs are displayed outdoors.

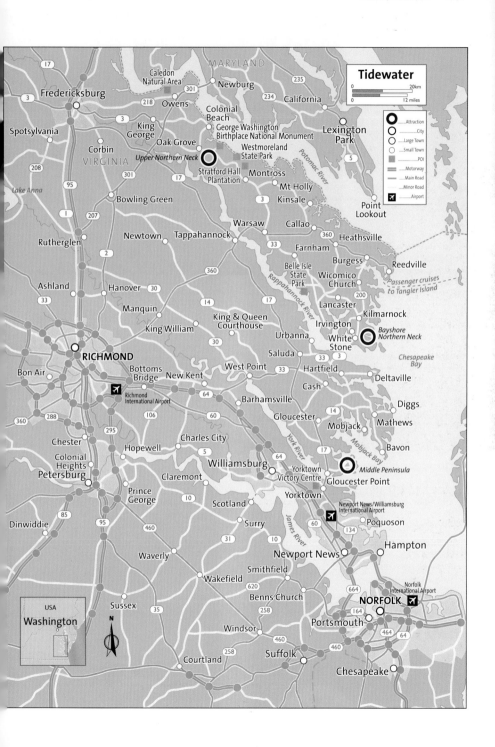

Tidewater

0		20km
0		12 miles

- ⬤ ......Attraction
- ⭕ ......City
- ◯ ......Large Town
- ○ ......Small Town
- ■ ......POI
- ━━ ......Motorway
- ━━ ......Main Road
- ─── ......Minor Road
- ✈ ......Airport

MARYLAND

Fredericksburg

Caledon Natural Area
Newburg
California

Owens
Colonial Beach
George Washington Birthplace National Monument
Lexington Park

Spotsylvania
King George
Oak Grove
Westmoreland State Park

Corbin
VIRGINIA
Upper Northern Neck
Stratford Hall Plantation
Montross

Lake Anna
Bowling Green
Mt Holly
Kinsale

Point Lookout

Warsaw
Callao
Heathsville

Rutherglen
Newtown
Tappahannock
Farnham
Burgess
Reedville

Ashland
Hanover
Belle Isle State Park
Wicomico Church
Passenger cruises to Tangier Island

Manquin
King & Queen Courthouse
Lancaster
Kilmarnock

King William
Urbanna
Irvington
White Stone
Bayshore Northern Neck

RICHMOND
Saluda
Chesapeake Bay

Bon Air
Bottoms Bridge
New Kent
West Point
Hartfield
Deltaville

Richmond International Airport
Barhamsville
Cash
Diggs

Chester
Hopewell
Charles City
Gloucester
Mobjack
Mathews

Colonial Heights
Petersburg
Williamsburg
Yorktown Victory Centre
Middle Peninsula
Bavon

Claremont
Gloucester Point
Mobjack Bay

Prince George
Scotland
Yorktown

Dinwiddie
Surry
Newport News/Williamsburg International Airport
Poquoson

Waverly
Hampton

Smithfield
Newport News

USA
Washington
Wakefield
Benns Church
Norfolk International Airport

Sussex
NORFOLK
N
Windsor
Portsmouth

Courtland
Suffolk
Chesapeake

Historic Christ Church $ *Rte 200; tel: (804) 438-6855; www.christchurch1735.org; open daily 0900–1700, weekends vary seasonally.*

The Tides Inn $$$ *480 King Carter Dr, Irvington; tel: (800) 843-3746 or (804) 438-5000.*

Hope and Glory Inn $$ *65 Tavern Rd; tel: (800) 497-8228 or (804) 438-6053.*

The Bell House Bed & Breakfast $$–$$$ *821 Irving Ave, Colonial Beach; tel: (804) 224-7000; www.thebellhouse.com*

The Morris House $–$$ *826 Main St, Reedville; tel: (804) 453-7016.*

Cedar Grove $–$$ *2743 Fleeton Rd; tel: (800) 497-8215 or (804) 453-3915.*

Inn at Levelfields $ *10155 Mary Ball Rd, Lancaster; tel: (800) 238-5578 or (804) 435-6887.*

Elijah's $$ *729 Main St, Reedville; tel: (804) 453-3621.*

Crazy Crab $–$$ *902 Main St, Reedville; tel: (804) 453-6789.*

The Trick Dog Café $–$$ *4357 Irvington Rd, Irvington; tel: (804) 438-1055; www.trickdogcafe.com*

Sandpiper Restaurant $–$$ *850 Rappahannock Dr, White Stone; tel: (804) 435-6176.*

Above
Local crabs a speciality

A mile from the Rappahannock River docks in Irvington, th cruciform **Historic Christ Church** has stood virtually unchange since its completion in 1735. Visitors can admire the marble baptisma font, Queen Anne holy table, the original Communion silver, th 'triple-decker' pulpit and 26 high-backed pews. On the north coast Yeocomico River, Kinsale was settled in 1708, making this tiny sailing boat haven and long-ago steamboat landing the oldest port town o Virginia's side of the Potomac.

Accommodation and food in Bayshore Northern Neck

Northern Neck's poshest and best-known waterfront resort i **The Tides Inn**, with a superlative marina-view dining room Irvington's bed and breakfast alternative is an 1890s elementar school impressively remade into the **Hope and Glory Inn**. A Virgini Historic Landmark and National Historic Property, the **Bell House** wa the summer home of American inventor Alexander Graham Bell.

Built in 1895, **The Morris House** is a turreted Queen Anne-styl Victorian bed and breakfast on Reedville's 'millionaire's row'. Anothe in-town bed and breakfast with water views is **Cedar Grove**. Souther graciousness also defines the 1857 **Inn at Levelfields**.

One of the area's choicest restaurants for seafood and prime cuts o beef is a former cannery in Reedville, now **Elijah's**. The laid-bac **Crazy Crab** features a wraparound deck overlooking the harbour. In pink cottage, known as "the best place to eat on the Northern Neck **The Trick Dog Café** is an upscale café with an innovative menu.

An amiable establishment in White Stone is the **Sandpipe Restaurant**. Nearby Burgess has folksy **Rosie Lee's** (*$ Rte 360; tel: (80 453-6211*). The aptly named **Good Eats Café** (*$ jct Rtes 202/203; te (804) 472-4385*) adds to the enjoyment of a stopover in Kinsale.

MIDDLE PENINSULA

ⓘ Gloucester Visitor Center *6467 Main St; tel: (804)693-0014; www.gloucesterva.info*

Tappahannock-Essex Chamber of Commerce *205 S Cross St, Tappahannock; tel: (804) 443-5241; www.essex-virginia.org*

Ⓜ Virginia Institute of Marine Science *1208 Greate Rd, Gloucester Point; tel: (804) 684-7000; www.vims.edu; open Mon–Fri 0900–1630.*

Ⓛ Linden House Plantation $ *11770 Tidewater Trail, Champlain; tel: (804) 443-1170 or (804) 445-4526.*

Inn at Urbanna Creek $–$$ *210 Watling St, Urbanna; tel: (804) 758-4661.*

Ⓛ Lowery's $$ *528 Church Lane, Tappahannock; tel: (804) 443-2800.*

Rivahside Café $ *221 Prince St, Tappahannock; tel: (304) 443-2333.*

River's Inn $$ *8109 Yacht Haven Rd, Gloucester Point; tel: (804) 642-9942.*

Jessica's Sweet Shop Café & Bakery $ *6558 Main St, Gloucester; tel: (304) 693-5235.*

Its mouth opened wide by deep-water Mobjack Bay, this chunky peninsula looks like the head of a snapping turtle. The Rappahannock and York rivers form the top-to-bottom contours. Three towns in particular – Gloucester, Tappahannock and Urbanna – have well-preserved historic districts. Urbanna's Oyster Festival, held annually during the first weekend of November, attracts upwards of 100,000 people. On the York River, Gloucester Point's **Virginia Institute of Marine Science** maintains eight aquariums containing saltwater fish indigenous to Virginia, plus endangered sea crabs; a touch tank enables visitors to handle hermit crabs, starfish and sea urchins. Farmers raise soya beans, wheat, barley, oats and rye on wide expanses of inland terrain; you'll also see occasional horse ranches. And you'll come upon country stores purveying takeout food, a chance to try Virginian oyster and crab cake sandwiches.

Accommodation and food in the Middle Peninsula

Dating from the 1750s, **Linden House Plantation** in Champlain is a bed and breakfast amidst English gardens. Located within walking distance of marinas, restaurants and shops is the **Inn at Urbanna Creek**, a circa 1870 colonial-style inn and cottage.

Eat in or order a takeout at **Lowery's**, thriving as a family restaurant in Tappahannock since 1938. A more intimate downtown eatery is the **Rivahside Café**.

At Gloucester Point's marina, **River's Inn** cooks freshly caught Chesapeake Bay seafood.

To get a jolt of caffeine, stop by **Jessica's Sweet Shop Café & Bakery** famous for their gourmet coffees, sweets and speciality sandwiches.

In Urbanna, **The River's Edge** (*217 Virginia St; tel: (804) 758-1447*) is a snack bar and ice-cream parlour. For heartier fare such as clam chowder and oyster stew, stroll to the **Virginia Street Café** (*Virginia and Pearl Sts; tel: (804) 758-3798*).

Above
Sunset over Middle Peninsula

UPPER NORTHERN NECK

Northern Neck Tourism Council
479 Main St, Warsaw; tel: (800) 393-6180 or (804) 333-1919; www.northernneck.org

Westmoreland County Visitor Center
Courthouse Sq, Montross; tel: (888) 783-9282 or (804) 493-0130.

George Washington Birthplace National Monument $ Rte 204; tel: (804) 224-1732; open daily 0900–1700.

Stratford Hall Plantation $$ Rte 214; tel: (804) 493-8038; www.stratfordhall.org; open daily for guided tours 0900–1630. Actor Jason Robards narrates an introductory 14-minute film, The Lees of Stratford.

Caledon Natural Area $ Rte 218, King George County; open daily 0800–dusk.

Westmoreland State Park $ State Park Rd, off Rte 3; tel: (804) 493-8821; open daily 0800–dusk.

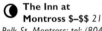 **The Inn at Montross** $–$$ 21 Polk St, Montross; tel: (804) 493-0573.

Mount Holly Steamboat Inn $$ Rte 202, Mount Holly; tel: (804) 472-9070.

Driving eastward from Fredericksburg's outskirts brings you to this rural, fertile chunk of Virginia Tidewater country. The most notable attractions are either on or near the Potomac River frontage, with southerly stretches of Maryland's coast visible across the water.

The 'Founding Father' of the US entered this world on 22 February 1732, at his ancestral 538-acre plantation on Pope's Creek in what is now the **George Washington Birthplace National Monument**. In the Memorial House, built to replace the burned-down original, costumed guides point out furnishings and utensils typifying the period. The acreage includes a Colonial Living Farm with livestock, crops and a herb garden. A *Childhood Place* is an informative 14-minute film.

Close by, **Stratford Hall Plantation** was home to four generations of Lees, one of the South's most illustrious families – but it's best known as the birthplace in 1807 of Robert E Lee, fated to be commissioned the Confederate army's commander-in-chief. Sloping down to the river, Stratford Hall's 1,600-acre spread includes woodlands, meadows, gardens and a working farm, plus more than 2 miles of nature trails bordering the Potomac and the plantation's mill pond. The patrician, H-shaped manor house is a classic example of Colonial architecture on a grand scale. Among the furnishings are some of the Lee family's original pieces, notably infant Robert's crib.

Two nature-reserve parks, both atop Potomac cliffs, attract outdoor enthusiasts. The **Caledon Natural Area** is summer habitat for one of the East Coast's largest concentrations of American bald eagles. In this woods-and-wetland environment, the big birds can be spotted as they forage around Boyd's Hole and Caledon Marsh. The park includes picnic facilities and 5 miles of trails winding through marshlands and an old-growth forest. Hikers exploring 1,311-acre **Westmoreland State Park** are rewarded with river panoramas from the Horsehead Cliffs, with beachfront picnic grounds on-site.

Accommodation and food in Upper Northern Neck

Several of the region's bed and breakfasts are historic and recommendable, for instance, **The Inn at Montross**, a 1790s structure with the original John Minor's Pub of 1685 downstairs; the innkeepers serve lunches and gourmet dinners. Alongside the Nomini Bridge, **Mount Holly Steamboat Inn** features breakfasts and dinners on a screened patio.

At the tip of a wooded Potomac peninsula, **Cole's Point Plantation** offers a marina, 110 campsites, swimming pool and restaurant.

On Stratford Hall's sprawling acreage, **The Plantation Dining Room** excels in home-style Virginia cooking for afternoon and evening meals. Outrageously rich chocolate peanut-butter cake is

Cole's Point Plantation $ Rte 612 Cole's Point; tel: (804) 472-3955.

The Plantation Dining Room $ tel: (804) 493-8038.

Driftwood Restaurant $–$$ Rte 612, Cole's Point; tel: (804) 472-3892.

Wilkerson's $$ 3900 McKinney Blvd, Colonial Beach; tel: (804) 224-7117.

Monroe Bay Landing $$ 11 Monroe Bay Ave, Colonial Beach; tel: (804) 224-7360.

Eckhard's $$ Rte 3, Topping; tel: (804) 758-4060.

Right
Yorktown battlefield

Tangier and Chesapeake Cruises $$ 468 Buzzard Point Rd, Reedville; tel: (804) 453-2628; www.tangiercruise.com. Operates between Reedville and Tangier Island (May–mid-Oct).

dessert speciality. In Cole's Point, the **Driftwood Restaurant** is a seafood-and-steak hangout. On the Colonial Beach shorefront **Wilkerson's** seafood, steak and chicken entrées dominate the lunch, dinner and weekend buffet menus. Also pleasantly situated is **Monroe Bay Landing**. Near Montross, **Eckhard's** is a *gemütlich* German restaurant with a Bavarian accent.

Suggested tour

Total distance: 175 to 190 miles, including detours, to reach all notable points of interest.

Time: With side-road shorefront locales to entice you, allow at least one full day, but preferably two.

Links: Begin a south-to-north Tideway region tour after leaving Yorktown on the Virginia's Historic Triangle route (*see pages 143–5*). Starting instead at uppermost Northern Neck connects you with the Fredericksburg area route (*see page 126*).

Route: From Yorktown, cross the Rte 17 toll bridge spanning the York River to reach the **MIDDLE PENINSULA** at **Gloucester Point ❶**; drive 13 miles to **Gloucester ❷** and its photogenic, early 19th-century Courthouse Square Historic District. Continuing 19 miles on Rte 17

**Belle Isle State
Park** *Rte 354; tel:
(804) 462-5030.* Camping
and visitor's centre, as well
as luxury accommodations
available at the Bel Air
Mansion.

brings you to Saluda. From there, head 4 miles north via Rtes 33/227 to reach charming little **Urbanna** ❸, a tobacco-trading port founded in 1680. Backtracking to Rte 33, drive east to Rte 3 for a 14½-mile drive via the 2-mile-long Rappahannock River bridge to White Stone at the southern tip of **BAYSHORE NORTHERN NECK** ❹, 14½ miles overall.

Turn left on to Rte 200 for a 2-mile drive to **Irvington** ❺. North from there, watch for signs leading to historic **Christ Church** on a side road. Then tour onward to **Kilmarnock** ❻, Lancaster County's commercial hub, and another 12 miles through Wicomico Church to Burgess, just beyond the Great Wicomico River bridge. Steer right on to Rte 360; after 6 miles, you'll be in **Reedville** ❼, port of embarcation for passenger (not car-ferry) cruises to **Tangier Island** ❽ midway between the Northern Neck and Virginia's Eastern Shore. Backtrack from Reedville to Burgess; take Rte 360 through Heathsville, Lottsburg and Callao. Reach placid Kinsale by meandering several miles north on Rte 621.

Detour: At Kilmarnock's crossroads, head 7½ miles west on Rte 3 to **Lancaster** ❾. As in Gloucester, you'll come upon a Historic Courthouse District. Mary Ball, George Washington's mother, was born at a nearby Epping Forest farmstead. For an exercise break, hike the town's 2½-mile **Hickory Hollow Nature Trail**. Find it by turning off Rte 3 on to Rte 604. A bit further from town, via Rte 354, **Belle Isle State Park** ❿ has picnicking and boating facilities. A 5-mile trail through fields and marshes (hunting grounds for herons and egrets) reaches the Rappahannock River. Return to Rte 3 via Rte 201, passing backwoods creeks, swamps and mill ponds.

Taking Rte 202 at Callao, travel 20½ miles north by way of Mount Holly to **Montross** ⓫ in the **UPPER NORTHERN NECK**. Montross is 5 miles south of **Stratford Hall Plantation** – and from there it's a 9½-mile jaunt on Rte 3 to **George Washington Birthplace National Monument** and **Westmoreland State Park** ⓬. Further north in Oak Grove, **Ingleside Plantation Vineyards** ⓭ has been producing premium wines and sparkling wines for more than a century. From Oak Grove, go 6 miles north on Rte 205 to the Potomac resort town of **Colonial Beach** ⓮, then to the **Caledon Natural Area** ⓯ off Rte 218. On that highway, continue 29 miles west to reach the bridge leading directly into Fredericksburg.

Also worth exploring

Across the Rappahannock River from the Northern Neck, **Tappahannock** was originally called New Plymouth upon settlement in 1680. Colonial and Victorian houses and public buildings, along with antique shops and Essex County's history museum, embellish the historic district. Reach this mini-city by driving 17 miles west via Rte 360 from Callao.

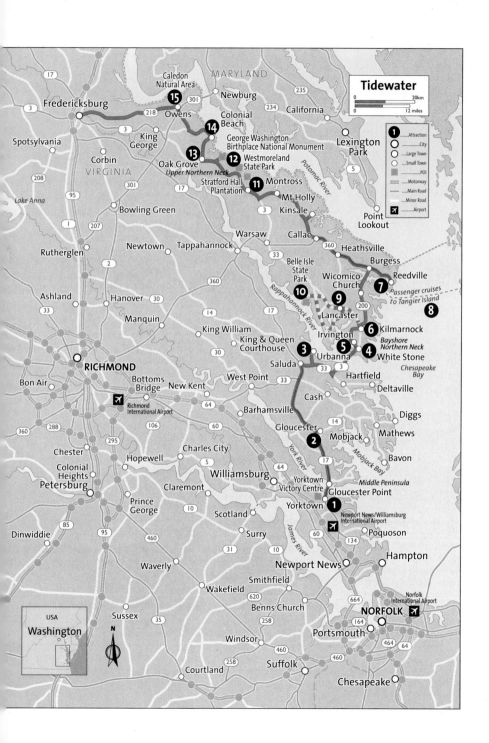

Virginia's historic triangle

Ratings

Children	●●●●●
History	●●●●●
Shopping	●●●●○
Art and museums	●●●○○
Gastronomy	●●●○○
Entertainment	●●○○○
Nature	●●○○○
Beaches	●○○○○

In 1607, colonists from the Virginia Company of London established the New World's first permanent English settlement, naming it Jamestown to honour King James I. The introduction of tobacco cultivation in 1612 brought a small measure of prosperity and, seven years later, America's earliest representative government – the House of Burgesses – convened here. But daily existence remained harsh and perilous; two years after the founding, only 60 of the 214 settlers had survived disease and starvation. This capital of colonial Virginia eventually moved into a planned city called Williamsburg, named after England's William III.

Yorktown, a Tidewater tobacco port founded in 1691, completes the time-line triangle. Joined by French allies, George Washington's troops defeated General Charles Cornwallis' entrapped British redcoats in 1781 for the decisive victory in America's War of Independence. Less than a century later, Yorktown was embroiled in the Civil War's land-and-sea Peninsula Campaign.

BUSCH GARDENS

Busch Gardens $$$
1 Busch Gardens Blvd off Rte 60; tel: (757) 253-3350; www.buschgardens.com; opening times vary seasonally, so call ahead.

Visitors to this multi-activity theme park can dine, shop and be entertained in fantasy versions of 17th-century English, Scottish, Irish, French, German and Italian villages. And they can whoop and yell on 40 thrill rides – among them Apollo's Chariot, a 'hypercoaster' that plunges 825ft at speeds exceeding 70mph.

JAMESTOWN SETTLEMENT AND YORKTOWN VICTORY CENTER

Jamestown-Yorktown Foundation *Williamsburg; tel: (757) 253-4838; www.jamestown-yorktown.state.va.us*

These sites draw equal attention to two of the US's epochal events marking the beginning and end of Colonial America. Both have exhibition galleries with excellent orientation films, *Jamestown: The Beginning* and Yorktown's *A Time of Revolution*.

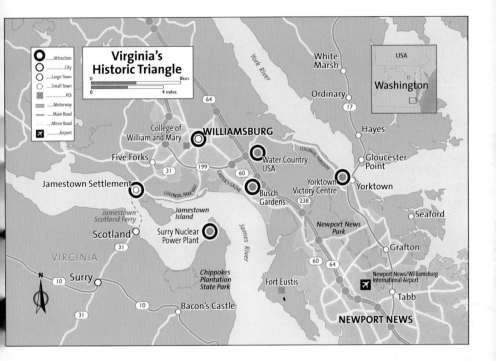

Jameston Settlement $$$ and Historic Jamestown $

Rte 31; tel: (888) 593-4682 or (757) 253-4838; www.jamestown-yorktown.state.va.us; open daily mid-Aug–mid-Jun 0900–1700; mid-Jun–mid-Aug 0900–1800.

Yorktown Victory Center $$

Rte 238; tel: (888) 593-4682 or (757) 253-4838; www.jamestown-yorktown.state.va.us; open daily mid-Aug–mid-Jun 0900–1700; mid-Jun–mid-Aug 0900–1800.

Yorktown Battlefield $

Colonial Pky; tel: (757) 898-2410; Visitor Center open daily 0900–1700. Save money by purchasing a combination ticket for admittance to all four locales.

Jamestown's acreage includes a Powhatan Indian Village with reed-covered dwellings and crafts demonstrations, plus a re-creation of the settlers' palisaded James Fort. In 1607, 104 of them made it to the New World aboard three ships: the *Susan Constant,* the *Godspeed* and the *Discovery.* Full-scale replicas can be boarded.

On adjacent Jamestown Island, Colonial National Historical Park rangers point out the excavated remnants of the settlers' **Original Settlement**, with a 5-mile loop drive for self-guided touring.

Continental Army soldiers re-enact daily regimental routines – parade-ground drills, weaponry cleaning, preparation of rations, medical care – in **Yorktown Victory Center's** encampment. Barnyard fowl and livestock inhabit a 1780s 'living history' farm where tobacco and corn are cultivated.

A film, *Siege of Yorktown,* is shown in the Visitor Center at **Yorktown Battlefield** on the opposite (eastern) side of town from the Victory Center. A signposted 7-mile tour passes American and French siege lines, earthwork fortifications, artillery emplacements and British surrender sites. Along a separate 9-mile drive, descriptive markers indicate American and French encampment areas.

A marble Victory Monument, dedicated in 1884, stands 98ft tall in the centre of Yorktown.

Accommodation and food in Jamestown and Yorktown

Duke of York $ *508 Water St, Yorktown; tel: (757) 898-3232.* Motel with a river view.

York River Inn $$ *209 Ambler St, Yorktown; tel: (800) 884-7003 or (757) 887-8800; www.yorkriverinn.com.* A local bed and breakfast alternative.

Edgewood Bed & Breakfast $$–$$$ *4800 John Tyler Memorial Hwy, Charles City; tel: (800) 296-3343 or (804) 829-2962; www.edgewoodplantation.com.* Relive Virginia's Golden Age by staying at a National Register Landmark plantation.

Below
Yorktown Victory Center

Opposite
Jamestown Settlement's
replica of the *Discovery*

Indian Fields Tavern $$$ *9220 John Tyler Memorial Hwy Rte 5, Charles City; tel: (804) 829-5004; www.indianfields.com.* Off the beaten path but worth the drive for exceptional food and service.

WATER COUNTRY USA

Water Country USA $$$ *Rte 199; tel: (757) 253-3350 or (800) 343-7946; www. watercountryusa.com; open May–mid-Sept. Hours vary seasonally, so call ahead.*

Designed for swimmers and splashers of all ages. Malibu Pipeline is a two-person tube ride; families in giant inner tubes raft down Big Daddy Falls; white-water excursions surge through the Atomic Breakers; Nitro Racer, a speed slide, features a 320ft-long drop. Cow-A-Bunga is a children's play area, and aquacade shows happen daily.

WILLIAMSBURG

Williamsburg Area Convention and Visitors Bureau *421 N Boundary St; tel: (800) 368-6511 or (757) 253-0192; www.visitwilliamsburg.com*

Two **Colonial Williamsburg Visitor Centers** provide information on admission charges, attractions and events. Take Exit 238 off I-64 to reach the main one by car (*tel: (757) 220-7615; www.history.org; open daily 0900–1700*). A smaller facility is in town at Merchants Square (*Duke of Gloucester St; tel: (757) 229-1000; open Sun–Thur 0830–1800, Fri & Sat 0830–1900*).

Thanks to preservation and restoration projects primarily funded by zillionaire John D Rockefeller Jr, a sizeable city-centre tract was resurrected as immensely popular colonial Williamsburg in the 1920s. Staffed by costumed 'townsfolk' and interpreters, this Historic Area emulates the appearance and lifestyles of what was Virginia's capital from 1699 to 1780. Nearly 600 buildings – government edifices, stores, artisans' workshops, taverns, an apothecary, a parish church, a courthouse, a guardhouse and gaol, a grocery, a printing office, a public hospital and residences – are 18th-century originals or faithful look-alikes. Some 90 acres of gardens adhere to period landscaping concepts. In resplendent regalia, a fife and drum corps makes periodic marching appearances down Duke of Gloucester St, the mile-long main thoroughfare. Programmes of events (entertainment and otherwise) are published in a weekly *Visitor's Companion* tabloid.

Three **museums** are on-site, too. The **Abby Aldrich Rockefeller Folk Art Center** displays an outstanding assemblage of early-American folk art. Colonial-era **Bassett Hall** became the Rockefellers' 1930 abode, sumptuously furnished with Chippendale, Federal and Empire pieces. Artisans' works in the **DeWitt Wallace Decorative Arts Gallery** include the largest collection of English pottery outside the UK and the world's foremost collection of antique Virginia furniture.

Facing broad Palace Green, the Georgian-style **Governor's Palace** replicates the 1722 original, occupied by seven royal governors, then by Patrick Henry and Thomas Jefferson – the Virginia Commonwealth's first two governors. Visitors guided through the Capitol, where America's first representative assembly convened, learn about the heated debates and defiant speeches that preceded warfare for independence from British rule.

Granted a royal charter in 1693 (therefore America's second-oldest university after Harvard), Williamsburg's **College of William and Mary** features a harmonious campus layout complete with a lake amidst Crim Dell's wildflower refuge. The **Wren Building**, its architecture influenced by England's Sir Christopher Wren and completed in 1695, is the nation's oldest academic structure in continuous use. Three Virginia-born W&M alumni went on to become US presidents: Thomas Jefferson, James Monroe and James Tyler.

Right
Governor's Palace, Williamsburg

Accommodation and food in Williamsburg

The **Colonial Williamsburg Foundation** arranges reservations fo lodgings and restaurants situated within the Historic Area (*tel: (800* *447-8679 or (757) 229-1000*).

Four hotels are official Colonial Williamsburg properties; al share the above telephone numbers, and all offer free parking. Th quartet's poshest and priciest is **Williamsburg Inn** (**$$$** *136 Francis St*), a golf-and-tennis resort with a ritzy Regency dinin room, indoor/outdoor swimming pools and fitness facilities. Mor rustic **Williamsburg Lodge** (**$$–$$$** *305 S England St*) has comparabl amenities. On 44 wooded acres, **Williamsburg Woodlands** (**$** *102 Visitor Center Dr*) is casual and family-oriented. So is th more modest, 200-room **Governor's Inn** (**$** *506 N Henry St*).

Visitors can choose from a range of accommodation close to th Historic Area – hotels, motels and bed and breakfasts. Th **Williamsburg Hotel and Motel Association** provides a fre reservation service (*tel: (757) 220-3330 or (800) 899-9462*).

Williamsburg Hospitality House (**$$** *415 Richmond Rd; tel: (800* *932-9192 or (757) 229-4020*), comprising 297 guest rooms, is tw blocks from the Historic Area and across the street from the College o William and Mary campus. The **Homewood Suites Hotel** is a mil away (**$$** *601 Bypass Rd; tel: (757) 259-1199*). Camellias and magnolia embellish 10 acres of grounds at the **Governor Spottswood Motel** (**$** *1508 Richmond Rd; tel: (800) 368-1244 or (757) 229-6444*).

Location and ambience make **A Primrose Cottage** an especiall recommendable bed and breakfast (**$–$$** *706 Richmond Rd; tel: (800* *522-1901 or (757) 229-6421*), and also **Governor's Trace** (**$$** *30. Capitol Landing Rd; tel: (800) 303-7552 or (757) 229-7552*).

Outlying campsites include **Fair Oaks Campground** (**$** *901 Lightfoo Rd; tel: (800) 892-0320 or (757) 565-2101*), 5 miles west of town.

Four non-smoking restaurants with 'ye olde' tavern atmosphere ar inside the Colonial Williamsburg Historic Area. They share reservation number (*tel: (757) 229-1000*). **Chowning's Tavern $$–$$** replicates an 18th-century English ale house. Steaks and chop highlight the **King's Arms $$–$$$** menu. **Christiana Campbell' $$–$$$** focuses on seafood. **Shields $$–$$$** is a good choice fo traditional Virginian fare such as crayfish soup, rôtisserie-roaste chicken and Surry County pork chops.

Eateries galore line Williamsburg's busiest thoroughfares. Fo Chesapeake Bay and Atlantic Ocean seafood, dine at **Berret's** (**$$–$$** *199 S Boundary St; tel: (757) 253-1847*). Down-home Virgini specialities (including peanut soup and Smithfield ham) are favoure selections at the **Jefferson Restaurant** (**$$** *1453 Richmond Rd; tel: (757* *229-2296*). Experience plantation cooking in an 18th-century dinin room at **Old Chickahominy House** (**$$** *1211 Jamestown Rd; tel: (757* *229-4689*). Close to the college, sandwiches are served at the **Gree Leafe Café** (**$** *765 Scotland St; tel: (757) 220-3405*).

Free ferryboat crossing

Right alongside Jamestown Settlement, the Colonial Parkway and Rte 31 converge at the river's edge, where the **Jamestown Scotland Ferry** takes on passengers and automobiles for its 15-minute crossing to the landing at Scotland in Surry County, long-existent farmland for cotton, peanuts and tobacco. There's no charge for what's been a state-run operation since 1945 – providing holidaymakers with a chance to imagine what the earliest English settlers saw and felt when they ventured upstream. Four ferryboats – the *Williamsburg, Surry, Virginia* and *Pocahontas* – make the year-round James River crossing (*for schedules, tel: (757) 294-3354; www.virginiadot.org*).

From the landing, Rte 31 leads south to Surry, a crossroads village close to **Smith's Fort** (*Smith's Fort Ln, off Rte 31*), where in 1609 Capt John Smith constructed defensive barricades in what was then part of the New World's uncharted wilderness frontier. Now the site features an 18th-century plantation house with a boxwood and herb garden.

After driving 3 miles east from Surry, you'll reach **Chippokes Plantation State Park** (*695 Chippokes Park Rd, off Rte 10*), its farm started by Capt William Powell – one of the Jamestown settlers – and cultivated continuously since 1619. On-site there is a plantation house containing displays of household antiques, plus a working sawmill, cropland and a Farm and Forestry Museum. The park's rambling terrain includes hiking trails and picnic grounds.

From there, continue another 3 miles to reach a side road leading to triple-chimneyed **Bacon's Castle** (*465 Bacon's Castle Trail, off Rtes 10/617*), claimed to be among North America's oldest documented brick houses. Built in 1665 by English immigrant Arthur Allen, its name stems from a rebellion against royal colonial governor Sir William Berkeley that erupted 11 years later, when the property was seized and occupied by troops loyal to firebrand organiser Nathaniel Bacon. The castle garden was laid out in 1680.

In sharp contrast, there is the free-admittance **Surry Nuclear Information Center** (*Hog Island Rd, off Rtes 10/650; tel: (757) 357-5410; open Mon–Fri 0900–1600*). Outside is a game refuge, and inside the nuclear power station are interactive displays.

Surrey House $$ (*11865 Rolfe Hwy, Surry; tel: (757) 294-3389*) is a recommendable stop for Virginian lunch or dinner.

Suggested tour

Total distance: 23 miles

Time: At most half a day, even allowing time for stopovers at noteworthy turnouts along Colonial Parkway.

Links: Richmond (*see pages 100–11*) is 50 miles northwest of Williamsburg via the I-64 motorway – slightly more if you prefer following Rte 5 (the John Tyler Hwy) through Charles City by way of the James River Plantations, slightly less if you link the Richmond Battlefields route (*see pages 117–18*) with the Historic Triangle.

After crossing the Coleman Bridge from Yorktown to Gloucester Point you can begin the Tidewater region route (*see pages 133–4*) by continuing north on Rte 17.

Heading south from Williamsburg on I-64 gets you to Newport News and Hampton on the Hampton Roads route (*see pages 153–4*).

Route: The very scenic 23-mile **Colonial Parkway** curves across narrow peninsula, between **JAMESTOWN SETTLEMENT** ❶ on the Jamestown River and **Yorktown** on the York River. At mid-point is **WILLIAMSBURG** ❷, where the three-lane parkway tunnels beneath the Colonial Williamsburg Historic Area. Williamsburg is 8 miles from **Jamestown** sites; Williamsburg to Yorktown entails 13 miles of parkway driving.

Detour: If you start at the parkway's western (Jamestown) end, a short-distance deviation via Rte 199 and then Rte 60 southbound gets you to **BUSCH GARDENS** ❸. Beyond there the scenic **Carter's Grove Road** ❹ meanders 6 miles north to Williamsburg.

Unspoiled landscape

Note that petrol stations and other public service facilities (and also unsightly billboards) are non-existent along the Colonial Parkway's entire length. The route features numerous turnings signposted with explanatory markers, and you'll travel through an unspoiled realm of forests, fern groves, marshes, creeks and ravines, plus riverside meadows at the western and eastern ends. One turning overlooks Jones Mill Pond and its flock of resident geese.

Right
Gloucester St, Williamsburg

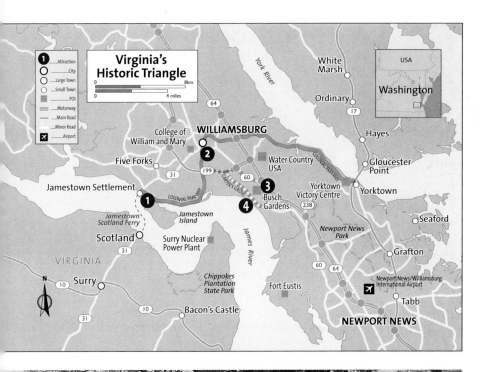

Hampton Roads

Ratings

Beaches ●●●●●

History ●●●●○

Art and museums ●●●○○

Children ●●●○○

Nature ●●●○○

Gastronomy ●●○○○

Entertainment ●○○○○

Shopping ●○○○○

Named after England's third Earl of Southampton, the general Hampton Roads area covers a sizeable expanse of waterways and heavily urbanised terrain in Virginia's southeastern corner. This is also the southernmost section of Virginian Tidewater country, where Chesapeake Bay and the Atlantic Ocean converge. Navigable sea lanes brought English settlers at the early 17th-century beginning of North American colonisation. Two and a half centuries later, a historic Hampton Roads naval engagement involved Union and Confederate 'ironclad' warships.

Present-day US Navy vessels amount to a highly visible presence, offshore and in one of the world's best-situated deepwater harbours. (In marine terminology, a 'road' is a place of safe anchorage.)

Virginia Beach is aptly named: the state's most populous city features 28 miles of fine surf-washed beachfront, plus 3 miles of oceanside boardwalk and an in-town state park — hence its popularity as a summer holiday destination.

HAMPTON

The region is served by **Norfolk International Airport**, 1½ miles north of I-64, and by **Newport News/Williamsburg International Airport** on Newport News' northern outskirts, also accessed via the I-64 motorway. In addition, that James River city is on the **Amtrak** rail route.

Diverse elements make this an interesting little city. Among them are a fishing-boat fleet, Langley Air Force Base and Fort Monroe's still active army installation, crucial Civil War connections, Hampton University's pioneering importance in educating African-Americans, 1959 space training for the first US astronauts, whale-watching excursions, recreation at Buckroe Beach and a 1920 carousel spinning in a pleasant riverfront park.

Downtown's **Virginia Air and Space Center** features vintage and experimental aircraft and aeronautic and space exhibits (many are interactive), including the *Apollo 12* command module and a chunk of 3-billion-year-old moon rock. Films are shown in a giant IMAX theatre.

Completed in 1834, Fort Monroe's moat-surrounded bastion remains the largest rock fortification ever built in America. In its **Casemate Museum, Fort Monroe** ($ tel: (757) 788-3391; open daily

ⓘ Hampton Roads Convention and Visitor Bureaus *Suite 290, 1919 Commerce Drive; tel: (757) 722-1222 or (757) 487 8778; fax: (757) 896-4600; www.hamptoncvb.com or www.visithamptonroads.com*

ⓡ Virginia Air and Space Center $ *600 Settlers Landing Rd; tel: (757) 727-0900; www.vasc.org; open 21 May–7 Sept Mon–Wed 1000–1700, Thur–Sun 1000–1900; 8 Sept–20 May daily 1000–1700.*

Right
Hampton waterfront

1030–1630), visitors view Civil War memorabilia and the cell where Confederate President Jefferson Davis endured two years imprisonment after the conflict.

Accommodation and food in Hampton

The Jewish Mother $ *3108 Pacific Ave; tel: (757) 422-5430.* Nosh or deli sandwiches, smoked fish and milkshakes.

Grey Goose $$ *101A W Queens Way; tel: (757) 723-7978.* Virginian home-style cooking.

Little England Inn $$ *4400 Victoria Blvd; tel: (800) 606-0985 or (757) 722-0985.* Turn-of-the century restored Victorian inn, centrally located, walk to shops, restaurants and attractions. Breakfast included in room rate.

Havana $$–$$$ *1423 Great Neck Rd; tel: (757) 496-3333.* Hip innovative Cuban cuisine.

NEWPORT NEWS

ⓘ Newport News Visitor Center *13560 Jefferson Ave; tel: (888) 493-7386 or (757) 886-7777; www.newport-news.org*

ⓡ Mariners' Museum $$ *100 Museum Dr; tel: (757) 596-2222 or (800) 581-7245; open Mon–Sat 1000–1700, Sun 1200–1700.*

Virginia War Museum $ *9285 Warwick Blvd; tel: (757) 247-8523; www.warmuseum.org; open Mon–Sat 0900–1700, Sun 1300–1700.*

The Shipbuilding and Drydock Company has dominated this city's economy and James River vistas since 1886. Contrast that industriousness with the élite North End/Huntington Heights neighbourhood, art galleries and riverside Victory Arch of 1919. The beautifully situated comprehensive **Mariners' Museum** is the best of its kind in America, and don't miss the equally first-class **Virginia War Museum**.

Outdoors, roam through the 8,065-acre **Newport News Park** (America's second-largest municipal park; bicycle rentals available) and observe diverse wildlife via woodland trails at the **Virginia Living Museum**.

Accommodation and food in Newport News

Boxwood Inn $ *10 Elmhurst St; tel: (757) 888-8854; www.boxwood-inn.com.* An 1896 B&B with meals served in its charming Blue Willow Tea Room.

Mulberry Inn $ *16890 Warwick Blvd; tel: (800) 223-0404 or (757) 887. 3000.* Some of the 101 rooms have self-catering facilities.

Newport News Park $ *13564 Jefferson Ave; tel: (757) 886-7912; open daily dawn–dusk.*

Virginia Living Museum $$ *524 J Clyde Morris Blvd; tel: (757) 595-1900; www.thevlm.org; open daily 0900–1700.*

Al Fresco **$$** *11710 Jefferson Ave; tel: (757) 873-0644.* Go Italian.

The Crab Shack **$$** *7601 River Rd; tel: (757) 245-2722.* Seafood.

The Train Station **$$** *2295 Harbor Rd; tel: (757) 247-7512.* Seafood.

Das Waldcafé **$$** *12529 Warwick Blvd; tel: (757) 930-1781.* Germanic fare.

NORFOLK

Norfolk Convention and Visitors Bureau *9401 E View St; tel: (800) 368-3097 or (757) 664-6620; www.norfolkcvb.com*

Norfolk Naval Station $ *Tour Office, 9079 Hampton Blvd; tel: 757) 444-7955.* Phone ahead for guided tour schedules, and 'open house' visits aboard designated warships.

Chrysler Museum of Art $ *245 W Olney Blvd; tel: (757) 664-6200; www.chrysler.org; open Tue–Sat 1000–1700, Sun 1300–1700.*

Douglas MacArthur Memorial $ *MacArthur Sq (City Hall Ave and Bank St); tel: (757) 441-2965; open Mon–Sat 1000–1700, Sun 1100–1700.*

Hampton Roads Naval Museum *1 Waterside Dr; tel: (757) 322-2987; open summer daily 1000–1700; rest of year varies greatly. Free.*

Virginia Zoological Park $ *3500 Granby St; tel: (757) 441-2374; www.virginiazoo.org; open 1000–1700.*

Home port of the US Atlantic Fleet and the world's largest **naval station**, Norfolk burgeoned as a sailor's haven during the two World Wars. That's still a fact of local life, but the city has simultaneously evolved into the region's business, mercantile and cultural capital.

Following several depressed decades, downtown's resurgence began when the Waterside marketplace pavilion opened in 1983, overlooking riverfront promenades, amidst a backdrop of high-rise buildings. Then, in 1999, came the MacArthur Center, a huge, strikingly designed shopping/dining complex.

Two distinctive neighbourhoods are worth visiting: old Freemason and gentrified Ghent (named after the 1814 Treaty of Ghent, which ended the British-American War of 1812).

For high-class prestige, nothing matches Norfolk's **Chrysler Museum of Art**, especially renowned for its world-class glass collection, including gorgeous creations by Tiffany, Gallé and Lalique. Also well represented are 19th- and 20th-century French and American paintings and sculptures, and art-nouveau furniture. The old City Hall, an 1850 Classical-Revival landmark, houses the **Douglas MacArthur Memorial**, a museum devoted to the epochal life and times of five-star general Douglas MacArthur. He and his wife are entombed in the rotunda.

Massive battleship-grey metallic architecture makes Nauticus impossible to miss on its riverfront site. Subtitled the National Maritime Center, with an upstairs **Hampton Roads Naval Museum**, exhibits delve into naval and aquatic lore. Open to the public, the battleship USS *Wisconsin* and a 1933 tugboat are permanently anchored at adjoining piers.

Weather permitting, head for the Norfolk Botanical Garden – noted for its 250 varieties of azaleas and interlaced with 12 miles of pathways – or the **Virginia Zoological Park**, the state's biggest and best.

Accommodation and food in Norfolk

Eaton Gogh $–$$ *806 Harringtor Ave; tel: (757) 640-0233.* Light fare

Castaldi's $$ *Tel: (757) 627-8700* For Italian cooking in the MacArthur Center.

Freemason Abbey $$ *209 W Freemason St; tel: (757) 622-3966* Originally a Presbyterian church lobster is the speciality.

Kincaid's $$ *Tel: (757) 622-8000* A fish, chop and steakhouse, also in the MacArthur Center.

Monastery $$ *443 Granby St; tel (757) 625-8193.* Czech-Hungariar food.

Page House Inn $$ *333 Fairfa: Ave; tel: (800) 599-7659 or (757 625-5033.* A resplendent B&B ir an 1889 mansion.

Wild Monkey $$ *1603 Colle; Ave; tel: (757) 627-6462.* Hip favourite.

Freemason Inn $$–$$$ *411 W York St; tel: (866) 388-1897 or (757 963-7000; www.freemasoninn.com* Located in the quiet Histori Freemason District.

On stage and screen

Norfolk's Chrysler Hall is home to the Virginia Symphony, with additional concert dates in Virginia Beach's modernistic Amphitheater, and also Hampton and Newport News. Also in Norfolk is the Harrison Opera House, a premier facility for Virginia Opera productions. The Virginia Stage Company, in residence at the historic Wells Theater, receives critical acclaim for its performances, both contemporary and Shakespearean. There's a Peninsula Community Theater in Newport News, and Hampton has its American Theater for stage shows, jazz concerts and classic films. Portsmouth's cinematic venue is unique. Light meals are served while films are shown on the big screen in the 1945 Commodore Theater. And watch for schedules of performing arts festivals throughout this maritime region.

PORTSMOUTH

ⓘ Portsmouth Convention and Visitors Bureau
801 Crawford Pky, Suite 2; tel: (800) 767-8782 or (757) 393-5111; www.portsva.com

ⓜ Naval Shipyard Museum $ *2 High St; tel: (757) 393-8591; open Tue–Sat 1000–1700, Sun 1300–1700.*

Children's Museum of Virginia $ *221 High St; tel: (757) 393-5258; open Tue–Sat 1000–1700, Sun 1300–1700.*

Separated by deep sea lanes from Norfolk, with that city's skyline in view, Portsmouth was established in 1752. The Gosport Shipyard became the nation's largest in the 18th and 19th centuries – subsequently launching America's first battleship (USS *Texas*) in 1892 and first aircraft carrier (USS *Langley*) 30 years later.

But a Civil War 'first' is better known. Confederate shipbuilders converted the wooden frigate *Merrimac* into the CSS *Virginia* – naval warfare's earliest armour-plated vessel – destined to battle the ironclad USS *Monitor* off Newport News on 9 March 1862.

High Street is lined with restaurants, pubs and antique shops. Stroll the brick sidewalks of Olde Towne, a square-mile showpiece of Colonial, neo-Georgian, Greek Revival and Victorian domestic architecture.

Discover titbits about historic, 'seaworthy' Portsmouth in its **Naval Shipyard Museum**. Even grown-ups enjoy the **Children's Museum of Virginia**, mainly due to the amazingly sizeable Lancaster Antique Toy and Train Collection.

Accommodation and food in Portsmouth

Bier Garden $–$$ *434 High St; tel: (757) 393-6022.* For German food and imported beer.

Glen Coe Inn $–$$ *222 North St; tel: (757) 397-8128; www.glencoeinn.com.* Sits on the Elizabeth River in Historic Downtown.

Lobscouser Restaurant $–$$ *337 High St; tel: (757) 397-2728.* Daily seafood specials.

Café Europa $$ *319 High St; tel: (757) 399-6652* is recommendable for Portuguese-Mediterranean dishes.

Above
Portsmouth naval base

Opposite
Chrysler Museum of Art

VIRGINIA BEACH

ⓘ Virginia Beach Convention & Visitors Bureau *2100 Parks Ave; tel: (800) 822-3224 or (757) 437-4919; www.vbfun.com*

ⓘ First Landing/ Seashore State Park $ *2500 Shore Dr; tel: (757) 412-2300; open daily 0800–dusk; visitor centre open Apr–Nov 0900–1800.*

Cheasapeake Bay Center *2500 Shore Dr; tel: (757) 412-2316; open daily 0900–1700. Free.*

Back Bay National Wildlife Refuge/False Cape State Park $ *4005 Sandpiper Rd; tel: (757) 721-2412; open daily dawn–dusk.*

Virginia Aquarium & Marine Science Museum $$ *717 General Booth Blvd; tel: (757) 425-3474; www.vmsm.com; open daily 0900–1800.*

Old Coast Guard Station Museum $ *24th St and Atlantic Ave; tel: (757) 422-1587; open Mon–Sat 1000–1700, Sun 1200–1700; closed rest of year Mon.*

Ocean Breeze Water Park $$–$$$ *General Booth Blvd; tel: (757) 422-4444; www. oceanbreezewaterpark.com. Call ahead for admittance prices and hours of various attractions.*

Nearly 3 million visitors flock here annually, drawn to the lengthy beachfront and boardwalk – now concrete-surfaced, with a parallel bicycle path – begun in 1888. To accommodate the throng, 'the Beach' has 11,000-plus guest rooms; 53 hotels and motels line both sides of Atlantic Avenue.

Vacation popularity inevitably breeds T-shirt shops, salt-water taffy (a sweet consisting of molasses, brown sugar and butter) stands, tacky souvenirs, miniature golf and other such stuff. But you can also go ecotour kayaking and deep-sea fishing, feast on fresh seafood and choose from 'something-for-everyone' entertainment.

Vast **First Landing/Seashore State Park**, Virginia's most-visited natural area, features salt-marsh habitats, a maritime forest, freshwater ponds where Spanish moss 'drips' from cypress trees, nearly 20 miles of scenic hiking trails and the **Chesapeake Bay Center**, an interactive visitor's centre. Further south, nature trails wind through oceanic barrier-island terrain in **Back Bay Natural Wildlife Refuge** and **False Cape State Park**.

The **Virginia Aquarium & Marine Science Museum**, the state's largest aquarium, includes sharks, sea turtles, bottlenose dolphins, harbour seals, stingrays, horseshoe crabs and river otters, along with feathered creatures. Galleries recalling shipwrecks in rough seas fill Virginia Beach's **Old Coast Guard Station Museum**, a life-saving station dating from 1903. For crazy contrast, **Ocean Breeze Water Park** offers pursuits such as a shipwreck-themed mini-golf course, Wild Water Rapids wave pool and bungee-jumping.

Accommodation and food in Virginia Beach

The big-name chains are omnipresent along and near the boardwalk. Independently operated hotels and motels are even more plentiful.

First Landing/Seashore State Park $ *Tel: (800) 933-7275.* Has 233 campsites.

Mary's $ *616 Virginia Beach Pky (17th St); tel: (757) 428-1355.* Home cooking six blocks inland from the surf.

Rockafeller's $ *308 Mediterranean Ave; tel: (757) 422-5654.*

Barclay Cottage $–$$ *400 16th St; tel: (757) 422-1956.* A bed and breakfast alternative in an 1895 boarding school.

Thunderbird Motor Lodge $–$$ *35th St and Oceanfront; tel: (800) 633-6669 or (757) 428-3024.*

Cavalier $$ *42nd St and Oceanfront; tel: (888) 446-8199 or (757) 425-8555.* Virginia Beach's classic hotel with a 1970s oceanside adjunct.

Colonial Inn $$ *2809 Atlantic Ave; tel: (800) 344-3342 or (757) 428-5370.*

Laverne's Seafood $$ *701 Atlantic Ave; tel: (757) 428-6836.*

Rudee's on the Inlet $$ *227 Mediterranean Ave; tel: (757) 425-1777.* Waterfront restaurant with an outdoor terrace.

Waterman's Beachwood Grill $$ *415 Atlantic Ave; tel: (757) 428-3644.* Newly remodelled boardwalk-bordering restaurant.

Suggested tour

Total distance: 105 to 110 miles; add a total of 45–50 miles for drives to Great Dismal Swamp and Smithfield.

Time: Not counting those side trips, non-stop motoring between Norfolk, Portsmouth, Hampton and Newport News would take less than a full day. But, of course, allow adequate 'out-of-the-car' time for stopovers.

Links: Newport News and Hampton are on the same Tidewater peninsula as the Historic Triangle's Williamsburg–Jamestown–Yorktown route (*see pages 143–4*). From Williamsburg, exit off Colonial Parkway on to I-64 for a 23-mile southbound drive to Newport News. From Rte 13 on Virginia's Eastern Shore (*see page 188*), you can reach the Hampton Roads conurbation via an engineering wonder: the 17½-mile Chesapeake Bay Bridge-Tunnel; toll payment required.

Route: With **NORFOLK** ❶ as your starting point, drive west along Waterside Drive. Follow Rte 264 West signs to **PORTSMOUTH** ❷ via the Downtown Tunnel; after 3 miles, you'll reach Crawford St, then Water St (alongside the Elizabeth River) in the downtown district, where High St is the main thoroughfare. Then backtrack to Norfolk.

Drive 20–22 miles east from Norfolk to **VIRGINIA BEACH** ❸ by way of Rte 264. Watch on your right for 68ft Mount Trashmore, a solid-waste landfill site transformed into a recreational park with lakes and playgrounds. The otherwise featureless expressway becomes residential 22nd St, leading straight to oceanfront Atlantic Ave.

Depart Virginia Beach by driving north on Atlantic Ave to its 89th St terminus; turn on to Rte 60, curving past **First Landing/Seashore State Park**. Three miles beyond, you'll cross a bridge spanning northside Virginia Beach's Lynnhaven Inlet – you will be in Norfolk's Ocean View district after another 8 miles.

Rte 60 meets Rte 64 for access through the Hampton Roads Bridge-Tunnel to **HAMPTON** ❹. Loop via Rte 258 through Hampton's Phoebus neighbourhood to reach Fort Monroe and its **Casemate Museum**. Hampton's other stellar attraction, the **Virginia Air and Space Center**, is right downtown.

From Hampton, drive 8–9 miles west on Rte 258 (Mercury Blvd, lined with shopping malls, fast-food places and petrol stations) to

ⓘ Smithfield & Isle of Wight Convention & Visitors Bureau *335 Main St, Smithfield; tel: (866) 889-0688 or (757) 301-4007; www.smithfield-virginia.com.* Available: Old Town walking-tour brochures.

Above
Virginia Beach

NEWPORT NEWS ❺ , where James River shipbuilding works com
into view. Turn right on to Jefferson Blvd to reach the **Mariners**
Museum and – further north – **Newport News Park**. Return te
Hampton via Rte 64 and from there back into Norfolk via tha
highway's bridge-tunnel.

Detour: From Newport News, cross the James River Bridge to arrive ir
Isle of Wight County. Reaching Rte 10, drive 5½ miles to **Smithfield**
one of Virginia's most photogenic communities with its Colonia
Federal and Victorian architecture, and home of Smithfield hams
famous state-wide. Fifteen houses and four public buildings are o
18th-century vintage; fourteen predate the Revolutionary War.

Also worth exploring

Great Dismal
Swamp National
Wildlife Refuge $
Headquarters at 3100
Desert Rd, Suffolk; tel: (757)
968-3705; open daily
sunrise–sunset.

Despite its less than alluring name, the **Great Dismal Swamp** is
national wildlife refuge of considerable scope (223,000 acres, partiall
extending into North Carolina) and unspoiled beauty, reached b
driving a short distance south beyond metro Norfolk–Portsmouth
Wildlife inhabitants include black bears, wildcats, foxes, whitetaile
deer and otters, plus more than 200 species of birds. Woodland
consist of bald cypress, juniper, black gum, red maple and yellov
poplar trees. Nature trails and an interpretive boardwalk extend te
centrally situated Lake Drummond, surrounded by an eerie forest o
gnarled, moss-draped cypresses.

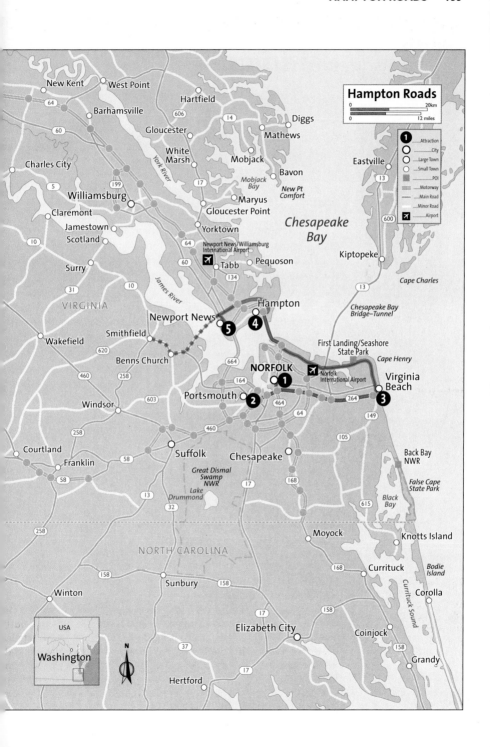

Baltimore

Ratings

Art and museums	●●●●●
Children	●●●●○
Entertainment	●●●●○
Gastronomy	●●●●○
History	●●●●○
Shopping	●●○○○
Beaches	●○○○○
Nature	●○○○○

The Port of Baltimore's Colonial-era prominence and development as a rail-to-shipping centre made the city a major industrial centre, and in turn America's second largest port of entry for immigrants. These factors have given Baltimore the lively, vibrant and somewhat gritty blue-collar and ethnic character that visitors find so appealing today.

On a steady rise from its port's decline, Baltimore has reinvented its waterfront around the centrepiece of the newly restored USS *Constellation*, a 19th-century sailing ship. Once dilapidated docks have been transformed into the brand new and beautiful Inner Harbor, its sturdy brick warehouses and sparkling new buildings filled with museums, trendy shops, entertainment stages and dozens of places to eat and drink. In the neighbourhoods around it, old ethnic enclaves remain, now studded with dining places. Today's Baltimore is fun, upbeat, historic and filled with activity.

Arriving and departing

❶ Baltimore Area Convention and Visitors Association *On the Inner Harbor opposite Constellation Pier; tel: (410) 837-INFO(4636) or (877) 225-8466; www.baltimore.org*

❷ Baltimore-Washington International Airport *Tel: (410) 859-7111 or (800) 435-9294; www.bwiairport.com*

Amtrak *Tel: (800) 872-7245; www.amtrak.com*

Baltimore is linked to Washington by I-295, the Baltimore-Washington Parkway, and to Wilmington (Delaware) and Washington by I-95, which passes through the city. Rte 2 joins it with Annapolis to the south. The Baltimore Beltway, I-695, surrounds the city.

Baltimore-Washington International Airport (BWI) is 10 miles south of the city centre, served by most major carriers, including budget-stretching Southwest Airlines.

Amtrak and Maryland Area Rail Commuter (MARC) connect the airport with Baltimore's Penn Station, a 20-minute ride. Mass Transit Administration (MTA) bus No 17 connects downtown Baltimore and the airport. More expensive, but convenient for those with luggage, BWI Airport Shuttle and Baltimore Airport Shuttle link Inner Harbor hotels to the airport. Frequent Amtrak trains connect Baltimore and BWI Airport to both New York and Washington DC, while MARC runs between Baltimore and Washington, a 1-hour trip.

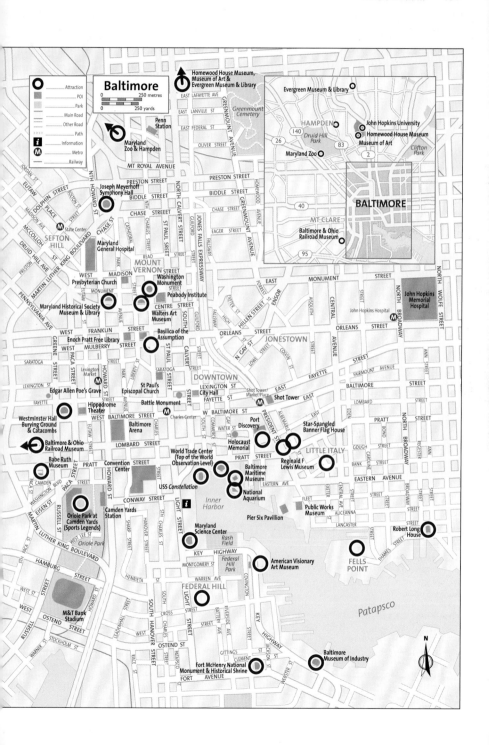

Baltimore

0 ___ 250 metres
0 ___ 250 yards

Attraction
POI
Park
Main Road
Other Road
Path
Information
Metro
Railway

Homewood House Museum, Museum of Art & Evergreen Museum & Library

EAST LAFAYETTE AVE
EAST LANVILLE ST
EAST FEDERAL ST
OLIVER STREET

Greenmount Cemetery

Evergreen Museum & Library

HAMPDEN

John Hopkins University

Homewood House Museum

Museum of Art

Clifton Park

Maryland Zoo

BALTIMORE

MT CLARE

Baltimore & Ohio Railroad Museum

Penn Station

Maryland Zoo & Hampden

MT ROYAL AVENUE
PRESTON STREET
PRESTON STREET
Joseph Meyerhoff Symphony Hall
BIDDLE STREET
BIDDLE STREET
CHASE STREET
CHASE STREET
State Center

SEFTON HILL

Maryland General Hospital

MOUNT VERNON
WEST MADISON STREET
Presbyterian Church
Washington Monument
MONUMENT
Peabody Institute
Maryland Historical Society Museum & Library
CENTRE STREET
Walters Art Museum
WEST FRANKLIN STREET
Enoch Pratt Free Library
WEST MULBERRY STREET
Basilica of the Assumption

SARATOGA STREET
LEXINGTON STREET
Lexington Market
Edgar Allen Poe's Grave
St Paul's Episcopal Church
FAYETTE STREET
Hippodrome Theater
Battle Monument
Westminster Hall Burying Ground & Catacombs
WEST BALTIMORE STREET
Baltimore & Ohio Railroad Museum
Baltimore Arena
LOMBARD STREET
Babe Ruth Museum
Convention Center
PRATT STREET
World Trade Center (Top of the World Observation Level)
USS Constellation
CONWAY STREET
Camden Yards Station
Oriole Park at Camden Yards (Sports Legends)
Oriole Park
MARTIN LUTHER KING BOULEVARD
HAMBURG STREET
M&T Bank Stadium
OSTEND STREET
WEST OSTEND ST

DOWNTOWN
LEXINGTON ST
City Hall
FAYETTE ST
Shot Tower/Market Place
Shot Tower
W BALTIMORE STREET
Charles Center
Port Discovery
Holocaust Memorial
Star-Spangled Banner Flag House
Baltimore Maritime Museum
Reginald F Lewis Museum
National Aquarium
EASTERN AVE
Inner Harbor
Public Works Museum
Pier Six Pavillion
LITTLE ITALY
Maryland Science Center
Rash Field
Federal Hill Park
American Visionary Art Museum
KEY HIGHWAY
FEDERAL HILL
Robert Long House
FELLS POINT
Patapsco

JONESTOWN
ORLEANS STREET
John Hopkins Hospital
John Hopkins Memorial Hospital
MONUMENT STREET
BALTIMORE STREET
FAIRMOUNT AVENUE
PRATT STREET
EASTERN AVENUE

Fort McHenry National Monument & Historical Shrine
Baltimore Museum of Industry

N

**Maryland Area Rail
Commuter (MARC)**
*Tel: (410) 539-5000 or
(800) 325-RAIL;
www.mtamaryland.com*

**Ⓜ Maryland Transit
    Administration
(MTA)**
*Tel: (410) 539-5000;
www.mtamaryland.com*

BWI Airport Shuttle
*Tel: (800) 776-0323 or
(410) 381-2772;
www.theairportshuttle.com*

Right
Washington Monument

Getting around

**Ⓜ Many of downtown
    Baltimore's streets**
are designated by a
compass point. The
north–south division is
Baltimore St, while
Charles St separates east
from west.

Nearly everyone begins a Baltimore visit at the Inner Harbor, where
many of the museums are located. To its north is the elegant old
neighbourhood of Mount Vernon, dominated by the tall monument
to George Washington. East of the harbour is Little Italy, south of
which is lively Fells Point. Rising from the opposite side of Inner
Harbor is historic Federal Hill, with more museums at its base. Most
places visitors want to see are in or close to these areas.

   While in Baltimore, you will certainly want to explore at least one
of its old neighbourhoods, residential sections that retain their distinct
flavours and their commercial cores, with shops, restaurants, churches
and community spirit.

P The many well-marked car parks may be crowded during weekdays. Commuter Rail stations at Beltway exits have Park-and-Ride lots, but if you are staying in the city, your hotel will have moderately priced or free parking.

Ed Kane's Water Taxi Tel: (410) 563-3901 or (800) 658-8947; www.thewatertaxi.com. An inexpensive way to get around the city and have a harbour tour at the same time. A single ticket ($) allows unlimited access to the boats all day. In summer boats run every 15–20 minutes.

Baltimore Ghost Tours Tel: (410) 522-7400; www. baltimoreghosttours.com. Haunted walking tours of Fell's Point and Mount Vernon, and Haunted Pub Walks.

Public transport

MTA bus and rail travel often involves several transfers, but MARC's bus and Metro map lists major attractions and hotels, with their best connections. You need the exact change, but for more than two rides in a day, buy the $3 day pass. To signal a stop, push the yellow stripe on the wall.

Water taxis and shuttles offer a cheap, fast, year-round service with 17 stops near major sights. Day passes include multiple reboarding, trolley connections to Fort McHenry, and discounts to attractions.

Tours

Mount Vernon Walking Tour Tel: (410) 605-0462; www.mvcd.org. An exploration of the sites and history of the neighbourhood's two most famous romances: Jerome Bonaparte and Betsy Patterson, and the Duke and Duchess of Windsor.

Inner Harbor Cruises $$ Tel: (410) 800-4998; www.clippercity.com; Mon–Sat 1200 & 1500, Sun 1500 & 1800. This schooner offers 2-hour and longer sailing tours from Inner Harbor, next to the Science Center.

Ride the Ducks $$$ Inner Harbor Promenade (south of the Light St Pavilion); tel: (410) 727-3825; www.baltimoreducks.com; Jun–Labor Day, 1000–1900, shorter hours Apr, May, Oct & Nov. An 80-minute street and harbour tour in a 1945 Army amphibious vessel that navigates on land or water.

Right
Inner Harbor

Sights

American Visionary Art Museum $$ 800 Key Hwy, under Federal Hill; tel: (410) 244-1900; www.avam.org; open Tue–Sun 1000–1800.

Baltimore and Ohio Railroad Museum $$ 901 W Pratt St, at Poppleton St; tel: (410) 752-2490; www.borail.org; open Mon–Sat 1000–1600, Sun 1100–1600.

Babe Ruth Museum $$ 216 Emory St; tel: (410) 727-1539; www. baberuthmuseum.com; open daily 1000–1700 (until 1900 on game days).

Baltimore Maritime Museum $$ Pier 3, E Pratt St, on the Inner Harbor; tel: (410) 396-3453; ships usually open daily 1000–1800, longer summer hours, weekends only in winter. Maritime attractions have joined as **National Historic Seaport of Baltimore** (tel: (410) 783-1490) and sell combined admission passes with water transportation.

Baltimore Museum of Art Art Museum Dr, Charles St at 31st St; tel: (443) 573-1700; www.artbma.org; open Wed–Fri 1100–1700, Sat & Sun 1100–1800. Free.

Baltimore Museum of Industry $ 1415 Key Hwy; tel: (410) 727-4808; www.thebmi.org; open Tue–Sat 1000–1600, Sun 1100–1600.

American Visionary Art Museum
The artworks, by untrained or self-taught artists, range from brilliant to bizarre, and the materials used can be surprising.

Baltimore and Ohio Railroad Museum
The roundhouse of America's first passenger railway station contains beautifully restored steam and diesel locomotives, passenger cars and freight wagons. Excursion trains run on weekends.

Babe Ruth Museum
The baseball great was born here in 1895. The house celebrates The Babe's Life.

Baltimore Maritime Museum
The floating collection includes the US Coastguard cutter *Taney*, the only ship surviving from the Japanese attack on Pearl Harbor in 1941. The US submarine *Torsk* (11,884 dives) was the last warship to sink an enemy vessel in World War II. Lightship *Chesapeake* served as a floating lighthouse in the Chesapeake Bay.

Baltimore Museum of Art
The museum's displays rotate through its premier 85,000-piece permanent collection. The Matisse, Picasso and Cézanne paintings are outstanding, as are collections of ancient mosaics, African folk art and eight galleries of Old Masters.

Baltimore Museum of Industry
The museum is located in an 1870 oyster cannery complete with belt-driven machine shop and giant pressure cooker. Baltimore's garment, printing and other major industries are represented with displays and demonstrations of actual working machinery. Children can enjoy hands-on experiences and the 1906 steam tugboat moored outside.

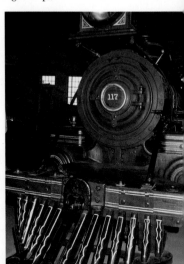

Basilica of the Assumption
The first Roman Catholic cathedral in the US was designed by Benjamin Latrobe, and is considered one of the world's top examples of neo-classical building.

Basilica of the Assumption 409 Cathedral St; tel: (410) 727-564; www.baltimorebasilica.org; open Mon–Fri 0700–1700, Sat & Sun 0700–1830; museum open daily 0900–1500. Free. Tours are given after the 1045 Sunday mass (about 1200).

Evergreen Museum & Library $$ 4545 N Charles; tel: (410) 516-0341; www.museums.jhu.edu; open Tue–Fri 1100–1600, Sat & Sun 1200–1600. Tours hourly until 1500.

Federal Hill Off Light St, across Inner Harbor from the World Trade Center.

Fells Point is reached by Water Taxi from Inner Harbor or by following Caroline St south from Little Italy.

Star-Spangled Banner Flag House 844 E Pratt St, at Albermarle; tel: (410) 837-1793; www.flaghouse.org; open Tue–Sat 1000–1600. Parking free on Albermarle St.

The Maryland Zoo in Baltimore $$ Druid Hill Park; tel: (410) 396-7102; www.marylandzoo.org; open daily 1000–1600.

Reginald F Lewis Museum $ 830 E Pratt St; tel: (443) 263-1800; www.africanamericanculture.org; open Tue–Sat 1000–1700, Sun 1200–1700.

Opposite
B & O Railroad Museum

Evergreen Museum & Library

This 48-room Italianate mansion contains collections of Japanese netsuke, Tiffany glass, Chinese porcelain and post-Impressionist paintings. You can also tour the gardens and spacious grounds.

Federal Hill

These gentrified old row houses, with antique shops, restaurants and the boisterous Cross Street Market, are a National Historic District. The best view of the Inner Harbor and city skyline is from the park at its northern end.

Fells Point

Dating from the 1700s, Fells Point is an early maritime community, with homes of merchants, carpenters and shipwrights built close to the busy harbour. This lively neighbourhood of shops, antique stores, pubs and restaurants is a weekend favourite of young people and students, and shoppers at the markets on Broadway.

Star-Spangled Banner Flag House

Built in 1793 and furnished to that period, this was the home of Mary Pickersgill, maker of the 30-by-42ft flag that survived the British bombardment of Fort McHenry during the War of 1812. A driving map of sites connected with the War of 1812 is available from tourist information offices.

The Maryland Zoo in Baltimore

The zoo includes an African watering hole, home to rhinoceros, zebras and gazelles. Siberian tigers are among the rare species. Hands-on activities earned it ratings as America's best zoo experience for children.

Reginald F Lewis Museum

African-American history and culture in Maryland is explored through displays, a theatre and interactive learning opportunities.

The Star-Spangled Banner

Francis Scott Key was on board a British ship negotiating the release of an American doctor, when the British fleet attempted to take Baltimore. Throughout the night of steady rocket fire he waited, until 'by the dawn's early light' he saw the huge American flag that Mary Pickersgill had sewn still 'gallantly streaming' over Fort McHenry. So moved was he by the sight of its 'broad stripes and bright stars' that he wrote a verse describing it which later became the national anthem, 'The Star-Spangled Banner'. The original hand-written poem is on display at the Maryland Historical Society Museum and Library (see page 162).

🏛 **Fort McHenry National Monument & Historic Shrine** $ *2400 E Fort Ave; tel: (410) 962-4290; www.nps.gov/fomc/; open daily 0800–1645.* Grounds, earthworks and the Visitor Center are free. Water-taxi tickets include free shuttle to the fort.

📍 **Hampden** W 36th St, just west of Johns Hopkins University campus, is Hampden's central street.

🏛 **Homewood House Museum** $$ *3400 N Charles St, Johns Hopkins University; tel: (410) 516-5589; www.museums.jhu.edu; open Tue–Fri 1100–1600, Sat & Sun 1200–1600, last tour 1530.*

📍 **Little Italy** Follow Pratt St east from Inner Harbor for two blocks, and Little Italy is just south, between Pratt St and Eastern Ave.

🏛 **Maryland Historical Society Museum and Library** $ *201 W Monument St; tel: (410) 685-3750; www.mdhs.org; open Wed–Sun 1000–1700.*

Maryland Science Center $$ *601 Light St; tel: (410) 685-2370; www.mdsci.org; open summer Sun–Thur 1000–1800, Fri & Sat 1000–2000; shorter hours and closed Mon in winter.*

Previous page
Baltimore Museum of Industry

Above
Fells Point

Fort McHenry National Monument and Historic Shrine
During the War of 1812, this 1790 brick fort withstood the British bombardment of Baltimore. The Visitor Center has a film and exhibits, and inside the fort are officers' quarters, guardrooms, the powder magazine, earthworks and cannons. On summer weekends costumed actors re-enact life in the garrison.

Hampden
Many visitors miss this neighbourhood away from the city centre that is like the Baltimore of several decades ago. Women there will call you 'Hon' (short for honey), and the laid-back pace is epitomised at the **Café Hon** (*see page 165*), the neighbouring Hometown Girl shop and in the not-too-old merchandise of Hampden's antique shops.

Homewood House Museum
Built in 1801, this is an outstanding example of Federal architecture and is notable for the exceptional craftsmanship of its interior ornamentation and period furnishing.

Little Italy
Baltimore's lively Italian community is filled with restaurants, two parish churches, colourful festivals and a Bocce court on Stiles St. St Anthony's Festival in mid-June and Columbus Day in early October are especially active times.

Maryland Historical Society Museum and Library
This packed museum includes the Radcliffe Maritime Museum, a Children's Gallery and Civil War and War of 1812 rooms. The original manuscript of 'The Star-Spangled Banner' is here, and its star attractions are the collections of American decorative arts and 19th-century American silver.

Maryland Science Center
Learn about the Chesapeake Bay environments, the Hubble Space Telescope and space research, the world of dinosaurs, electricity and

Mount Vernon
Charles and Monument ts, north of Inner Harbor.

National Aquarium in Baltimore $$$ *Pier 3, 01 E Pratt St; tel: (410) 76-3800; www.aqua.org; pening hours vary, usually ummer 0900–1700, later ri & Sat; Sept–Jun 1000– 700. Purchase a timed cket early in the day.*

Port Discovery $$ *5 Market Pl; tel: (410) 727-120; www.portdiscovery.org; pen summer Mon–Sat 000–1700, Sun 1200– 700; off-season hours vary.*

Robert Long House $ *12 S Ann St, Fells Point; el: (410) 675-6750; www. reservationsociety.com; ours Thur 1000, 1300 & 500.*

Sports Legends at Camden Yards $$ *301 V Camden St; tel: (410) 27-1539; www.sports egendsatcamdenyards.com; pen Apr–Oct daily 1000– 800 (1930 on baseball ame days); Nov–Mar ue–Sun 1000–1700 (2000 n football game days).*

other sciences through hands-on exhibits and hourly live demonstrations (*weekdays 1030–1330, weekends 1030–1730*). The IMAX Theater and the Davis Planetarium also have regular shows.

Mount Vernon

Once the centre of Baltimore's high society, Mount Vernon is a well-kept mecca for arts and culture. Museums, fine shops, galleries and 'Restaurant Row' cluster around the genteel parks at the foot of the Washington Monument, and it is the best place to get a feel for the Baltimore of a century ago.

National Aquarium in Baltimore

The aquarium is a centre for education about the marine environment and conservation, and exhibits thousands of creatures – over 600 species of fish, birds, reptiles, amphibians and marine mammals. Stars include a giant octopus, electric eels, an Atlantic coral reef, a 16ft anaconda and a rainforest alive with sloths, parrots, monkeys, frogs and fish. Dolphins perform in the Marine Mammal Pavilion, in 25-minute shows.

Port Discovery

Port Discovery is an exciting interactive activity and learning museum for children aged 5 to 13, who will love crawling into a giant kitchen sink to learn about environmental issues or starring in a show in the TV studio.

Robert Long House

The city's oldest urban residence dates from 1765. Headquarters of Baltimore's Preservation Society, the restored brick house is furnished with period antiques as befits an 18th-century merchant's home.

Sports Legends at Camden Yards

An historic railway station has been restored and transformed into a sports museum, taking some of the visitor pressure off Babe Ruth's

ight
laryland Historical ociety Museum

USS *Constellation*
$$ *Pier 1, Constellation Dock at 301 E Pratt St; tel: (410) 539-1797; www.constellation.org; open for tours Apr–Oct daily 1000–1730; off-season 1000–1630. May be open evenings Jul & Aug.*

Walters Art Museum
600 N Charles St; tel: (410) 547-9000; www. thewalters.org; open Wed–Sun 1100–1700, Fridays until 2000. Free.

Washington Monument
$ *N Charles St at Mt Vernon Pl; tel: (410) 837-4636; open daily 0900–1700.*

Westminster Hall Burying Ground and Catacombs *W Fayette and Greene Sts; tel: (410) 706-2072; www. westminsterhall.org. There are free tours on the first and third Fri and Sat of each month (by reservation Apr–Nov).*

Top of the World Observation Level $
401 E Pratt St, 27th Floor; tel: (410) 837-8439; open Apr–Oct Mon–Sat 1000–1700, Sun 1200–1700.

birthplace. Explored in upbeat and active exhibits are a variety c sports themes in addition to The Babe and baseball: lacrosse, wome in sports, Baltimore teams and players, the Preakness horse race an college sports.

USS *Constellation*
On the waterfront this is the star attraction. Its 1999 restoratio yielded new information on the sailing ship's age and history, whic included capturing slave-trade ships off Africa and carrying famine relief supplies to Ireland.

Walters Art Museum
The gallery's 30,000 objects cover five millennia of Fine and Applie Arts, ranging from ancient Egyptian sculpture and decorative arts t Fabergé eggs and Asian arts.

Washington Monument
This was the first architectural monument in the United State honouring George Washington. Climb its 228 steps for a view of th skyline and rooftops of Mount Vernon or see the small museum at i base.

Westminster Hall Burying Ground and Catacombs
The burial place of the writer Edgar Allen Poe, whose monument is i the corner plot, is among Baltimore's oldest cemeteries, with rar underground crypts, at an 1852 Presbyterian church.

Top of the World Observation Level
From the top of the 423ft tower of the world's tallest pentagona building, you can get a long view of the city and a short view c Baltimore's history.

Festivals and events

Artscape *Tel: (410) 752-8632; www.artscape.org.* In late July Baltimor celebrates all the arts with a lively programme of dance, theatre, oper film, music, street performances and foods.

Independence Day Several days of activities celebrate 4 July, with fireworks display at Inner Harbor.

Star-Spangled Banner Weekend *Tel: (877) 225-8466.* In early–mi Sept Fort McHenry has re-enactments, ending with Saturday firework

Fells Point Fun Festival *Tel: (410) 675-6756; http://fellspoint.us.* In ear October, this is a big street fair with crafts, music and lots of food.

Thanksgiving Parade *Tel: (410) 837-4636.* In late November, th parade has equestrian units, marching bands, clowns and floats.

Accommodation and food

Restaurants gather in neighbourhoods, with most near the waterfront, Little Italy, Fells Point and along Charles Street in Mount Vernon.

Amicci's $ *231 S High St, Little Italy; tel: (410) 528-1096; www.amiccis.com.* Its checked tablecloths and the warm, kindly atmosphere epitomise traditional family Italian restaurants.

Café Hon $ *1002 W 36th St, Hampden; tel: (410) 243-1230; www.cafehon.com.* This is a relaxed restaurant with home-style favourites, including lasagne, meatloaf and good crab cakes. Specials might be fried chicken (*Tue*) or fish and chips (*Fri*).

Vaccaro's $ *222 Abermarle St, Little Italy; tel: (410) 685-4905; www. vaccarospastry.com.* The restaurants in Little Italy get their desserts from this café; expect a wait on weekend evenings.

James Joyce Irish Pub & Restaurant $–$$ *616 President St, Inner Harbor; tel: (410) 727-5107; www.thejamesjoycepub.com.* Frequent live music and imported ales on tap.

Abercrombie Badger Bed and Breakfast $$ *58 W Biddle St; tel: (410) 244-7227 or (888) 9BADGER; fax: (410) 244-8415; www.badger-inn.com.* Directly opposite Joseph Meyerhoff Symphony Hall, elegantly decorated lodgings range from cosy singles to large rooms.

The Admiral Fell Inn $$ *888 S Broadway, Fells Point; tel: (410) 522-7377 or (800) 292-4667.* This quietly elegant inn overlooks the harbour. Outstanding breakfast buffet, and accommodating staff.

Babalu Grill $$ *32 Market Pl, Downtown; tel: (410) 234-9898; www.babalugrill.com.* Flavours of the Caribbean spice up long-roasted pork or steak in tomatoes and rum.

Bertha's $$ *734 S Broadway, Fells Point; tel: (410) 327-5795; www.berthas.com.* The mussels are famous, although it serves other dishes. Sunday brunch (*1130–1400*; **$**) offers country sausages or creamed oysters. Mrs McKinnon's Scottish afternoon tea (*Mon–Sat 1500–1700*; **$**) is by reservation.

DaMimmo Italian Restaurant $$ *217 S High St, Little Italy; tel: (410) 727-6876; www.damimmo.com.* Open daily for lunch and dinner, DaMimmo is a friendly, family-owned Baltimore institution, anchoring the city's lively Italian neighbourhood.

The Inn at Henderson's Wharf $$ *1000 Fell St, Fells Point; tel: (410) 522-7777 or (800) 522-2088; www.hendersonswharf.com.* On the waterfront, this inn has 38 well-furnished rooms overlooking the water or garden courtyard.

True $$ *888 S Broadway, Fells Point; tel: (410) 522-2195.* Working with local farmers to use the freshest produce for the fullest flavour and, when possible, organically raised ingredients, True changes its menu as often as necessary to present everything in season. Expect dishes such as Amish farm-raised duck breast, with raw milk cheddar and corn grits.

Gertrude's $$–$$$ *Baltimore Museum of Art, 10 Art Museum Dr, off Charles St; tel: (410) 889-3399; www.johnshields.com.* Bookings are almost essential at this smart restaurant owned by a local legend chef specialising in the products of the Chesapeake Bay and the farms that surround it.

Joy America Café $$–$$$ *American Visionary Art Museum, 800 Key Hwy, Inner Harbor; tel: (410) 244-6500; www.avam.org.* Local ingredients (especially seafood) cooked with a Caribbean/south of the border accent, served overlooking the city from across the harbour.

Charleston $$$ *1000 Lancaster St; tel: (410) 332-7373, www.charlestonrestaurant.com.* Chef Cindy Wolfe creates 'Low Country' cuisine the way we wish Southern food always tasted.

Entertainment

Baltimore Symphony Orchestra *Joseph Meyerhoff Symphony Hall, 1212 Cathedral St; tel: (410) 783-8000; www.baltimoresymphony.org*

Peabody Institute *1 E Mt Vernon Pl; tel: (410) 659-8100; www.peabody.jhu.edu*

Pier Six Pavilion *Pier 6, Pratt St; tel: (410) 837-4636; summer; www.pier6pavilion.com*

The Hippodrome Theatre $$ *10 N Eutaw St; tel: (410)837-7400; www.france-merrickpac.com*

Baltimore is known for the broad range of its cultural life. The **Baltimore Symphony Orchestra** has a steady schedule of top popular and classical performers such as Yo-Yo Ma, Pinchas Zukerman and Itzhak Perlman. The **Peabody Institute**, part of The Johns Hopkins University, has a full schedule of concerts featuring classical, jazz and other music styles. The Inner Harbor has several venues for performances, in all price ranges, many free, including **Pier Six Pavilion**, a tent-theatre for rock, blues, country and jazz.

The **Hippodrome Theatre** presents Broadway shows in its fully restored glory as an early 20th-century vaudeville stage. The venue is located on the campus of the University of Maryland Baltimore, at the France-Merrick Performing Arts Center.

Shopping

Fells Point is filled with artists' studios, craft shops and antique shops. **Bay and Country Crafts** (*1635 Lancaster St*) specialises in Chesapeake Bay crafts, including carved wooden duck decoys. **The Silver Store** (*1640 Thames St*) sells sterling silver jewellery. Baltimore's many museums all have outstanding gift shops.

North Charles St in Mount Vernon has art and craft galleries and **Woman's Industrial Exchange** (*333 N Charles St; www womansindustrialexchange.org*) where they sell homely handwork, such as knitted mittens and baby gifts. **Antiques Row** (*N Howard and W Reed Sts*) has several shops with silver, Victoriana and pricey furniture.

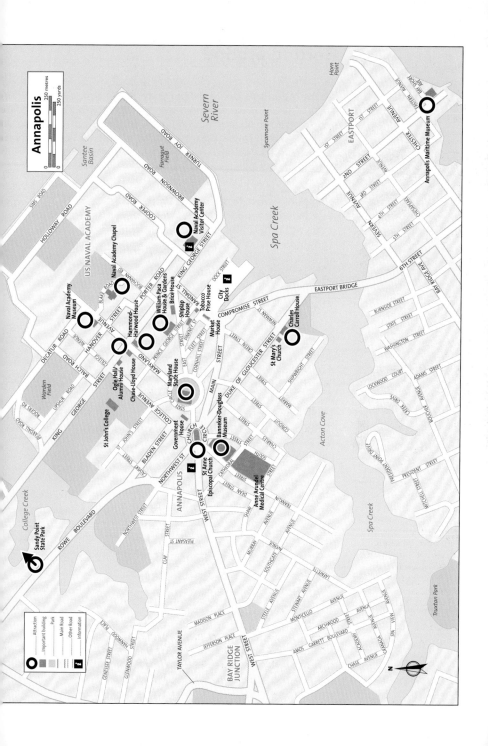

Annapolis

0 ____ 250 metres
0 ____ 250 yards

Severn River

Santee Basin

Horn Point

Spa Creek

EASTPORT

Annapolis Maritime Museum

EASTPORT BRIDGE

Acton Cove

Spa Creek

Truxtan Park

College Creek

Sandy Point State Park

US NAVAL ACADEMY

Naval Academy Museum

Naval Academy Chapel

Naval Academy Visitor Center

Hammond-Harwood House

William Paca House & Gardens

Brice House

Shiplap House

Tobacco Prise House

City Docks

Charles Carroll House

St Mary's Church

Ogle Hall/Alumni House

Chase-Lloyd House

St John's College

Maryland State House

Government House

St Anne Epicopal Church

Banneker-Douglass Museum

Anne Arundel Medical Centre

BAY RIDGE JUNCTION

Warden Field

Farragut Field

Sycamore Point

Attraction
Important building
Park
Main Road
Other Road
Information

N

Getting around

Ⓦ **Watermark Water Taxi** *City Dock; tel: (410) 263-0033.* Provides transport from boats and between land points.

Festivals and events

Independence Day *Tel: (410) 263-1183.* A 4 July parade, Naval Academy band concert and waterfront fireworks.

Maryland Seafood Festival *Sandy Point State Park; tel: (410) 268-1437; www. mdseafoodfestival.com.* A September celebration of the official state food – steamed hardshell crabs, crab cakes and more.

Maryland Renaissance Festival *$$$ Rte 178, Crownsville; tel: (410) 266-7304 or (800) 296-7304; www.renfest.com; open late Aug–Oct, weekends.* A permanent recreation of a medieval and Renaissance English market fair, featuring jousting, a replica Globe Theatre, craft booths, minstrels, magicians, food, ales and mead. Rollicking good fun.

Christmas in Annapolis *Tel: (410) 268-8828; open Nov & Dec.* Homes and historic houses are decorated, and there are a lighted boat parade, house tours, and concerts.

Life in Annapolis centres around City Dock, from which Main S climbs the hill to the Maryland State House. Its narrow winding Colonial streets make Annapolis a charming place to walk. Driving i difficult, with snarled traffic and limited parking. Most attractions are close to downtown, best reached on foot. Other parts of Annapolis such as restaurants along Spa and Back Creeks, are connected by wate taxi, but are not a long walk from the central dock area.

Tours

Annapolis Carriage $$ (*Market Sq at Main St; tel: (410) 267-6656 www.annapoliscarriage.com*) provides a leisurely ride around the ol centre with a historical narrative.

Annapolis Tours $$ (*48 Maryland Ave; tel: (410) 263-5401; ope Apr–Oct daily, Nov–Mar Sat*) conduct 2-hour walking tours of th Historic District, leaving from the Visitors Bureau.

Annapolis Walkabout $$ (*223 S Cherry Grove Ave; tel: (410) 263-8253 open Apr–Oct Sat and Sun*) is led by an architectural historian.

Capital City Colonials $$–$$$ (*101 Severn Ave; tel: (410) 295-9715 www.capitalcitycolonials.com; 90-minute tours Tue & Wed 1000, Thur–Sa 1000 and 1430, Sun 14.30; short orientation tours Tue–Sat 1700)* Costumed guides give a good background to the historic sites, wit special attention to everyday life in Colonial times.

Discover Annapolis Tours $$ (*tel: (410) 626-6000; www discoverannapolis.com; open Apr–Nov daily, Dec–Mar most weekends*) ha daily 1-hour trolley tours leaving from the Visitor Center on West St.

Historic Annapolis Foundation $ (*77 Main St; tel: (410) 268-5576 open Mon–Sat 1000–1700, Sun 1200–1700*) rents recorded self-guide tours, one highlighting African-American history.

Kayak Annapolis $$ (*tel: (443) 949-0773*) leads guided kayak tour around the scenic harbour and Naval Academy.

Schooner *Woodwind* Cruises $$$ (*tel: (410) 263-7837; www schoonerwoodwind. com; open May–Sept*) has 2-hour sailing cruises fro the Marriott Hotel, next to City Dock. The cruises on the 74ft *Woodwir* take in waterfront views of the Naval Academy and pass under Ba Bridge, and the Wed evening sail includes watching sailing-boat races.

Sights

Annapolis Maritime Museum

Maritime collections and material give an interesting insight into th cultural history of the neighbourhood, once home to boat-builde and watermen, and on local marine history.

Banneker-Douglass Museum

In the former Mount Moriah African Methodist Episcopal Churcl

**Annapolis
Maritime Museum**
723 2nd St, Eastport;
tel: (410) 295-0104; open
Sat & Sun. Free.

**Banneker-Douglass
Museum** 84 Franklin St;
tel: (410) 216-6180; www.
bdmuseum.com; open
Tue–Fri 1000–1500, Sat
1200–1600. Free.

Charles Carroll House
$ 107 Duke of Gloucester
St; tel: (410) 269-1737;
www.charlescarrollhouse.com

Chase-Lloyd House $
22 Maryland Ave; tel: (410)
263-2723; open Mar–Dec
Mon–Sat 1400–1600.

The signers

In Maryland much is
made of those who
signed the Declaration
of Independence,
pledging 'our lives, our
fortunes and our sacred
honor'. The four
Annapolis men who
signed for Maryland
joined counterparts
from other colonies to
lead a cause which
would cost many their
lives and even more
their fortunes. Charles
Carroll of Carrollton,
important in both
Annapolis and
Baltimore, was the only
Catholic and one of the
few lucky ones. He
outlived all the others
and continued to be one
of the wealthiest and
most influential men of
his time.

there are changing exhibits of photographs and collections relating to Maryland's Black heritage and the art of Africa and African-Americans.

Charles Carroll House
The birthplace and home of Declaration of Independence signer Charles Carroll of Carrollton, a wealthy and influential man who helped found America's first railroad. The house, in restoration, sits above 18th-century terraced gardens and has frequent interactive programmes with costumed interpreters.

Chase-Lloyd House
Begun in 1769 and completed by William Buckland on an unlimited budget, within its outstanding interior is possibly the finest cantilevered stairway built in the colony; ornate carvings and silver fixtures decorate the dining room.

Hammond-Harwood House
The last work of architect William Buckland, the house was built in 1774 at the height of Annapolis's Golden Age. In almost entirely original condition, it is among the most beautiful examples of late colonial architecture in America. The highlight is the dining room, with a rococo carved overmantel, finely detailed mouldings and carved window shutters. The quoined window above the stairway is inspired by the church of St Martin-in-the-Fields in London. The house has several Peale portraits and outstanding furniture by Charles Shaw, one of Colonial America's finest cabinetmakers.

Maryland State House
America's oldest State House in continuous use, and the only one to have served as the US Capitol. In this building the congress met in 1783 and 1784, George Washington resigned his command of the Continental Army and the Treaty of Paris was ratified, officially ending the American Revolution. The 1788 dome is the largest wooden dome in the United States.

The Naval Academy Chapel
The imposing dome forms a backdrop for Annapolis's Historic District, and contains impressive stained-glass windows, several by Tiffany. The baptismal font in St Andrew's Chapel is made of wood from the USS *Constitution*. Underneath the Rotunda lies the Crypt of John Paul Jones, the Revolutionary War hero.

The Naval Academy Museum
Though small, the museum is filled with artefacts of naval history and academy traditions, such as the desk from the battleship *Missouri* on which Fleet Admiral Chester Nimitz signed the Japanese surrender in Tokyo Bay in 1945. One room contains ship models made contemporaneously with the original ships, dating back as far as 1650.

Hammond-Harwood House $$
*19 Maryland Ave; tel: (410)
263-4683; www.
hammondharwoodhouse.org;
hourly tours usually Apr–Oct
daily, but changes frequently.*

Maryland State House
*State Circle; tel: (410) 974-
3400; open Mon–Fri 0830–
1700, Sat & Sun 1000–
1600; free 30-minute tours
daily 1100 and 1500. Free.*

**The Naval Academy
Chapel** *Near Gate 3,
Maryland Ave; open
Mon–Sat 0900–1600, Sun
1300–1600. Free. Visitors
over age 16 must show
photo identification to
enter the Naval Academy
grounds.*

**The Naval Academy
Museum $** *Near Gate 3,
Maryland Ave; open Mon–
Sat 0900–1700, Sun 1100–
1700; www.navyonline.com*

**The Naval Academy
Visitor Center** *Gate 1,
King George St; tel: (410)
293-8687; www.navyonline.
com; open daily Mar–Dec
0900–1700; Jan & Feb
0900–1600.*

**William Paca House
and Gardens $$** *186
Prince George St; tel: (410)
990-4543 or (800) 603-
4020; house open Apr–Dec
Mon–Sat 1000–1700, Sun
1200–1700; Jan–Mar call
for hours. Last tour begins
1530. Garden open Apr–Oct
until 1700.*

**St Anne Episcopal
Church** *Church Circle; open
daily 0800–1730.*

**Sandy Point State Park
$** *E College Pwy, signposted
from US-301/50 west of Bay
Bridge; tel: (410) 974-2149.*

A most unusual collection of intricate ship models was carved from bone by French sailors interned in British prison ships between 1756 and 1815.

The Naval Academy Visitor Center
The academy trains over 4,000 cadets as Navy or Marine Corps officers and is filled with history and tradition. Guided tours (**$$**) begin here where there are also exhibits and a film on the academy. Self-guided tours of the grounds are free.

St Anne Episcopal Church
In Colonial days this was the royal governor's parish; King William presented the silver communion service in 1695, which is still in use. Three parishioners signed the Declaration of Independence. See the Tiffany stained-glass window, the needlepoint kneelers and the colony's last royal governor's grave in the churchyard.

Sandy Point State Park
A day-use beach park, with changing facilities, food vendors, trails, boats for hire, picnic areas and excellent windsurfing off the long beach. The waterfront is prime birding territory during spring and autumn migrations.

William Paca House and Gardens
The restored home of a signer of the Declaration of Independence and Governor of Maryland is combined here with the city's premier historic garden. Thirteen period furnished rooms include an outstanding collection of antique American silver and decorative arts.

The beautiful gardens drop gently in terraces, and feature boxwood parterre with topiary centrepieces and potted standards, five tall cone-shaped holly trees, a medicinal herb garden and a domed summer house. A visitors' centre has displays on historical garden themes. The re-creation of the original garden has been based on the site's archaeology and on a contemporary painting.

Accommodation and food

Country Inn and Suites $$ *2600 Housley Rd; tel: (410) 571-6700 or (800) 456-4000; www.countryinns.com.* Has spacious suites in a location convenient to Rte 2, US-301/50 and I-97, just east of the city, with bus shuttles to and from downtown Annapolis.

Flag House Inn $$ *24 Randall St; tel: (410) 280-2721 or (800) 437-4825; www.flaghouseinn.com.* Historic District house, between City Dock and the Naval Academy, which has off-street parking and serves English breakfasts. Its brochure includes an excellent illustrated map of attractions, shops and restaurants.

Gibson's Lodgings $$ *110 Prince George St; tel: (410) 268-5555 or (877) 330-0057; www.gibsonslodgings.com.* Close to City Dock, in historic district houses, with parking. The beautifully decorated rooms have period antiques.

Historic Inns of Annapolis $$ *58 State Circle; tel: (410) 263-2641 or (800) 847-8882; www.historicinnsofannapolis.com.* Includes four 18th- and 19th-century buildings close to the Capitol, with combined check-in at the Governor Calvert House. Rooms vary from slightly dowdy to newly renovated and period furnished, as in Robert Johnson House.

Loews Annapolis Hotel $$ *126 West St; tel: (410) 263-7777 or (800) 526-2593; www.loewsannapolishotel.com.* A modern hotel within walking distance of the Naval Academy and City Dock, with a pool, tennis courts, health club and business centre.

The Charles Inn $$–$$$ *74 Charles St; tel: (410) 268-1451; www.charlesinn.com.* Close to Church Circle, a nicely restored Civil War-era home with off-street parking. The three rooms have feather beds and private baths with antique deep tubs or whirlpools. A full breakfast is elegantly served.

State House Inn $$–$$$ *25 State Circle; tel: (410) 990-0024; www.statehouseinn.com.* Charming inn located in the Historic District, with views of the Chesapeake and the Capitol.

Most Annapolis restaurants are in the dock area, along Main St or in nearby Eastport, which is a short walk along the waterfront from the docks. Several more line West St, at the top of the hill past the Capitol. All the restaurants listed below are open daily unless otherwise noted.

Aromi d'Italia Café $ *8 Dock St, behind the information kiosk; tel: (410) 263-1300; www.aromiditalia.com.* Specialises in Italian ice cream, sandwiches, salads and pizza, with a few daily full meal specials.

Buddy's Crabs and Ribs $$ *100 Main St; tel: (410) 626-1100.* Known for these two Maryland specialities, but serves a full seafood menu.

bove
nnapolis Post Office

pposite
he Naval Academy

Right
Annapolis Historic District

All-you-can-eat lunch buffets on weekdays. Sunday breakfast buffet includes hearty seafood dishes.

Carrol's Creek Café $$ *410 Severn Ave, Eastport; tel: (410) 263-8102* Commands a fine harbour view. Fresh seafood is prepared in elegant and innovative styles, with a new way each day for rockfish (bass), and a four-course Bay Dinner (**$$$**) including several of their specialities such as Maryland crab soup.

Phillips $$ *City Dock; tel: (410) 990-9888.* One of several in this small local chain, dependable for seafood. Crab cake platters and dishes of crab cakes with grilled fish are a good way to sample local fare.

Ram's Head Tavern and Fordham Brewing Co $$ *33 West St; tel: (410) 268-4545; www.ramsheadtavern.com.* The microbrewery includes the original cosy pub, a tiny tearoom or patio tables in fair weather. A cosmopolitan menu includes shepherd's pie, crab cakes, Jambalaya and shellfish pie. Live performances are a weekly feature.

Treaty of Paris Restaurant $$ *16 Church Circle; tel: (410) 263-2641.* Offers Old Country favourites, such as Beef Wellington, as well as updated American dishes, served in an 18th-century setting. Three meals are served daily.

Sam's on the Waterfront $$–$$$ *2020 Chesapeake Harbor Dr E; tel: (410) 263-3600; www.samsonthewaterfront.com.* Follow Bay Ridge Ave from Eastport to find this local secret at the Chesapeake Harbor Marina. The owners are dedicated to using fresh produce from local farms, emphasising organic and sustainable ingredients. The result is superlative, from the cream of crab bisque to silky diver scallops speared on a lemon grass stalk. Sam's serves lunch, light fare and dinners, including tasting dinners with wine pairings.

Annapolis Farmers' Market
Riva Rd at Truman Pkwy, accessible from Exit 22 off US-301/50; open Sat 0700–1200.

Pennsylvania Dutch Farmers' Market
Annapolis Harbor Center, Solomons Island Rd; tel: (410) 573-0770; open Thur 1000–1800, Fri 0900–1800, Sat 0830–1500. Country foods, baked goods, vegetables, cheese and cured meats.

Shopping

Main St and nearby streets are lined with boutiques and shops. Short Maryland Ave, between State Circle and the Academy Gate 3, has more, especially antique shops. Most are open Mon–Sat 1000–1500, Sun 1200–1700, often with longer summer evening hours.

Historic Annapolis Foundation Museum Store (*77 Main St*) offers quality crafts and historic reproductions, many with a maritime theme. At **Annapolis Pottery** (*40 State Circle*), across from the State House

Maryland Hall
for the Creative
Arts 801 Chase St;
tel: (410) 263-5544;
www.marylandhall.org

Annapolis Opera
Company 801 Chase St;
tel: (410) 267-8135; www.
annapolisopera.org

Annapolis Symphony
Orchestra 801 Chase St;
tel: (410) 269-1132;
www.annapolissymphony.org.
Performances Oct–May.

Ballet Theater of
Maryland 801 Chase St;
tel: (410) 263-8289; www.
marylandballet.org

The Annapolis Chorale
801 Chase St;
tel: (410) 263-1906;
www.annapolischorale.org;
Sept–Apr.

Annapolis Summer
Garden Theater 143
Compromise St; tel: (410)
268-9212; www.
summergarden.com.
Performances late May–Aug
Thur–Sun.

Colonial Players 108
East St; tel: (410) 268-7373;
www.cplayers.com; open year
round.

Bay Theatre Company
275 West St; tel: (410) 268-
7333; www.baytheatre.org

Annapolis Sailing
School 601 6th St;
tel: (800) 638-9192 or (410)
267-7205; www.
annapolissailing.com. Adults
and children are taught how
to handle a sailing boat. To
try without committing
yourself to formal lessons,
go any morning at 1000
or 'Try-Sail'.

demonstrations show stoneware pottery being made. **The American Craftworks Collection** and **League of Maryland Craftsmen** (*189B Main St*) sells pottery, glass, wood, fibre arts and baskets. Shortly beyond Academy Gate 3, at the end of Maryland Ave, is the **Naval Institute Bookstore** (*open Mon–Sat 0900–1700, Sun 1100–1700*) on the ground floor of the museum, with books on every aspect of the sea and the US Navy, nautical gifts and Naval Academy insignia items.

Ron Snyder Antiques (*2011 West St*) is where 40 antique dealers show their best furniture, china, quilts, decoys and other collectables.

Entertainment

Annapolis offers a rich and varied programme of performing arts events. Major performances are held at **Maryland Hall for the Creative Arts**, including grand operas, operetta and Broadway musicals presented by **Annapolis Opera Company**, classical concerts by the **Annapolis Symphony Orchestra** and classical and modern dance by the professional **Ballet Theater of Maryland**. Popular and classical works can also be heard here, performed by **The Annapolis Chorale**.

The **Annapolis Summer Garden Theater** presents Broadway musicals in an outdoor setting and the **Colonial Players** have five theatre-in-the-round productions a year. **Bay Theatre Company** offers Equity theatre in Annapolis with year-round performances. For complete listings of clubs, bars and restaurants with live music, pick up the free *Chesapeake Music Guide*.

Suggested walk

Distance: 2–3 miles, 3–4 with both detours.

Time: A leisurely stroll looking at the sights will take about 2 hours; but to explore the attractions thoroughly allow for a whole day.

Route: Begin at **City Docks** ❶, the historic heart of Annapolis, where you may see the *Stanley Norman*, a skipjack belonging to Save the Bay Federation, or possibly the sailing ship *Pride of Baltimore*, with its raked masts. Several harbour and river excursions begin at City Docks.

After touring the docks, head to the right-hand corner of Market Square, behind the market building, next to Maria's Restaurant. At the corner of Pinkney St is the **Tobacco Prise House** ❷, a warehouse from the early 1800s, and next door the **Shiplap House** ❸, built about 1715, and one of the oldest in the city. Follow Pinkney St to East St, where a right and a quick left turn will bring you to the **WILLIAM PACA HOUSE AND GARDENS** ❹, on Prince George St.

London Town and Gardens $$
London Town Rd, off Rte 253, Edgewater; tel: (410) 222-1919; www. historiclondontown.com; open Tue–Sat 1000–1600, Sun 1200–1600. To reach Edgewater, follow Rte 2 south from the city.

Maps

The free *Destinations* guide to Annapolis includes a good map, keyed to descriptions of 40 numbered sites, each coded to show its historic period. The list shows significant private buildings as well as those open for tours. The smaller but also excellent map inside the **Flag House Inn** brochure includes restaurants and other points of interest.

Art walk

Each August the Annapolis Gallery Association hosts an open tour of over 20 galleries downtown, with artist demonstrations and discussions. **Annapolis Gallery Association** *215 Main St, tel: (410) 267-7077; www.artinannapolis.com*

Detour: Take a few moments to wander through the narrow old streets that ascend the hill, including Cornhill and Fleet Sts.

Continue on Prince George St to Maryland Ave, turning right to pass the 1774 **HAMMOND-HARWOOD HOUSE ❺**, around the corner, an excellent example of late Colonial architecture.

Across the street is the 1769 **CHASE-LLOYD HOUSE ❻**, known for its fine interior. Maryland Ave leads on to Gate 3 of the US Naval Academy. (Visitors over age 16 need photo ID.) Through the gate on your right is the grand dome of the **NAVAL ACADEMY CHAPEL ❼**, and the entrance to the **Crypt of John Paul Jones ❽**. On the left is the **NAVAL ACADEMY MUSEUM ❾**. Return to the gate and turn right, walking one block to College Ave, following it past the campus of **St John's College ❿**, where buildings date from as early as 1722.

A left turn on North St brings you to State Circle and **MARYLAND STATE HOUSE ⓫**. In its grounds are a treasury building from 1737 and a cannon that arrived with the first settlers aboard the *Dove*, in 1634. Continue around State Circle to School St, on the corner of which is **Government House ⓬**, official residence of Maryland's Governor.

School St leads directly into Church Circle, with **ST ANNE EPISCOPAL CHURCH ⓭** in its centre. Directly opposite School St is West St, in which there are several restaurants as well as the **Annapolis Visitors Bureau ⓮**.

Head downhill from Church Circle on Duke of Gloucester St to St Mary's Church ⓯, a Victorian Gothic building with ribbed vaulting and a carved altar screen, usually open during daylight. The cornerstone was laid in 1858 by Saint John Neuman. Next to the church, **CHARLES CARROLL HOUSE ⓰** at No 107 has terraced gardens. From the end of Duke of Gloucester St, a left turn on to Compromise St leads back along the waterfront to your starting point at City Dock.

Detour: Those with energy to spare can turn right on Compromise St, crossing the bridge over Spa Creek to explore the old fishermen's and boat-building neighbourhood of Eastport.

Also worth exploring

Historic London Town and Gardens overlooks South River at the major ferry to Annapolis, where George Washington always crossed. Ships loaded tobacco from area plantations in a town of 300 people. But by 1800 London Town had almost disappeared. Today you can watch archaeologists uncover artefacts beneath **Rumney's Tavern**.

Only the large brick **William Brown House** remains, restored to 18th century condition. The authentic household linens include embroidered bed hangings. Gardens surround the visitors' centre, above a dell filled with azaleas. The rare 1720 tobacco house was relocated here.

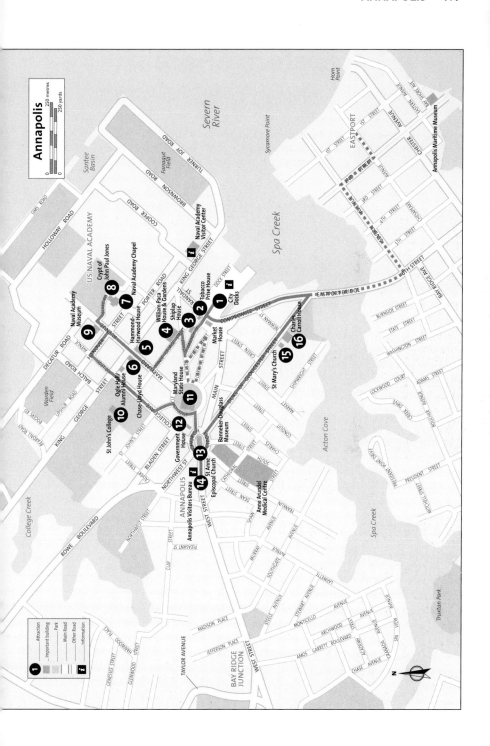

Ratings

Nature and wildlife	●●●●●
Beaches	●●●●
Children	●●●
Gastronomy	●●●
Shopping and crafts	●●●
Art and museums	●●
Entertainment	●●
Historical sights	●●

Eastern Shore

Maryland's Eastern Shore joins with the state of Delaware and a tiny piece of Virginia to form the Delmarva Peninsula, based on the names of the three states. The landscape is flat or, at the most, gently rolling. Wide tidal rivers and estuaries cut it deeply, and the shore is further broken by islands and long fingers of water-surrounded land.

Facing the Atlantic Ocean to the east, a long strip of barrier island extends along all three states. Its smooth beaches, dunes and marshes provide a habitat for shore birds and for the famous wild horses, often called Chincoteague ponies. Historic small towns dot the peninsula, many of them fishing villages whence fishermen once sailed in search of the Chesapeake's rich store of shellfish.

CAMBRIDGE

 Dorchester County Visitors Center *Sailwinds Park; tel: (410) 228-1000 or (800) 522-8687; www.tourdorchester.org*

Muddy Marsh Outfitters *Tel: (410) 228-2770.* Rents canoes and kayaks and leads paddling tours into the tidal marshes and estuaries.

The High Street's elegant Federal, Queen Anne, Second Empire and High Victorian homes give Cambridge an air of grace and make strolling a pleasure. The **Richardson Museum** (*401 High St; tel: (410) 221-1871; open Apr–Oct Wed, Sat & Sun 1300–1600*) records a rich maritime heritage and celebrates the art of wooden boat building with a replicated boat shop and watermen's tools. Learn about skipjacks and bugeyes, and how they evolved, then visit the Richardson Boatworks on Hayward St.

LaGrange Plantation (*LaGrange Ave; tel: (410) 228-7953; tour Thur–Sat 1000–1600*) complex includes the 1760 Meredith House furnished in fine antiques, with doll and toy collections. The adjoining Neild Museum preserves rural and agricultural tools

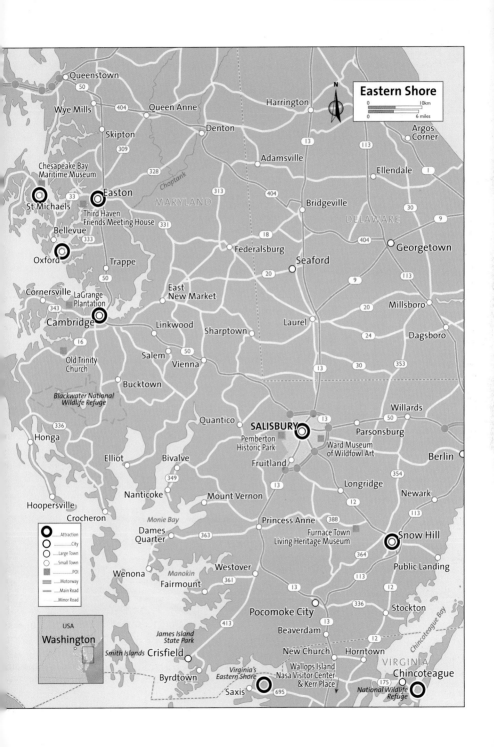

Blackwater National Wildlife Refuge $ *Rte 335, Church Creek; tel: (410) 228-2677; Visitors' Center open Mon–Fri 0800–1600, Sat & Sun 0900–1700.*

Dorchester Arts Center *321 High St; tel: (410) 228-7782; open Mon–Sat 1000–1400.* On sale are the works of local artists and craftsmen.

Brooks Barrel Company *5228 Bucktown Rd; tel: (410) 228-0790.* Watch them work or buy barrels and buckets in the factory store.

Antique Aircraft Fly-in *Dorchester Heritage Museum, off Rte 343; tel: (301) 228-1000.* In late May antique and classic planes are put through their paces.

The free *Historic Walking Tour of Cambridge* is an illustrated booklet explaining not only the history, but the architecture of the old waterfront neighbourhoods.

Nathan of Dorchester **$$$** *Long Wharf, at the foot of High St; tel: (410) 228-7141; www.skipjack-nathan.org.* Built in 1994 to preserve traditional wooden boat-building skills of the Chesapeake Bay, the *Nathan* tours local ports on educational cruises.

maritime trades and Native American artefacts. The Goldsborough Stable contains early vehicles and blacksmith, wheelwright and harnessmakers' tools.

Blackwater National Wildlife Refuge is a vast tideland where you can drive, walk or canoe amid profuse bird life. Bald eagles are common and between October and March tundra swans, snow geese and 20 duck species winter here. Trails lead to a marsh boardwalk and overlook platform.

Accommodation and food in Cambridge

Several chains have lodgings in Cambridge, including Days Inns, Hyatt and Holiday Inn Express. For a complete list and contact information, *visit www.tourdorchester.org*

Cambridge House Bed & Breakfast $–$$ *112 High St; tel: (410) 221-7700.* Located in the historic district.

The Inn on Locust Street $–$$ *707 Locust Street; tel: (410) 961-3321.*

Portside Seafood Restaurant $–$$ *201 Trenton St; tel: (410) 228-9007 open Tue–Sun lunch and dinner.* Overlooks the water and serves local seafood.

Snappers Waterfront Café $–$$ *112 Commerce St; tel: (410) 228-0112 www.snapperswaterfrontcafe.com.* Serves local seafood as well as more exotic dishes.

Canvasback Restaurant $$ *420 Race St; tel: (410) 221-5177.* Popular with locals for its well-prepared seafood and meat dishes.

Right
Boats moored in Cambridge

EASTON AND OXFORD

Talbot County Office of Tourism
11 S Harrison St, Easton; tel: (410) 770-8000; www.tourtalbot.org

Self-guided walking tour maps are available from the **Historical Society.**

Oxford–Bellevue Ferry *5 Morris St, Oxford; tel: (410) 745-9023; www.oxfordbellevueferry.com; open Jun–Aug.*

Historical Society of Talbot County *25 S Washington St, Easton; tel: (410) 822-0773; www.hstc.org; open Mon–Sat 1000–1600. Free.*

Third Haven Friends Meeting House *405 S Washington St, Easton; tel: (410) 822-0293.*

Antique shops are on N Harrison St opposite the Tidewater Inn, on S Harrison, Washington and along US-50.

Wheel Doctor *1013 S Talbot St, St Michaels; tel: (410) 745-1676; www.wheeldrbicycle.com.* Delivers rental bikes to the trailhead or your accommodation and picks them up.

Avalon Theater *40 E Dover St; tel: (410) 822-7299.*

The old Quaker settlement of Easton made its mark as a 19th-century steamboat port, a period recalled by the **Historical Society of Talbot County** at three homes surrounding Federal-style gardens. The fine brick Federal James Neall House, the 1795 Joseph's Cottage and Ending of Controversie, a reconstruction of a 17th-century house, are all furnished. **Third Haven Friends Meeting House** is probably the oldest active religious building in the US.

Nearby Oxford was a thriving trading port long before the Revolution, and its quiet streets are lined with old homes. A ferry established in 1683 crosses the Tred Avon River to Bellevue.

Accommodation and food in Easton and Oxford

Oxford Market and Deli $–$$ *203 S Morris St, Oxford; tel: (410) 226-0015.* Has sandwiches, freshly baked breads, cheeses and meats for picnics, and also hand-dipped ice cream.

The Robert Morris Inn $$ *314 N Morris St, Oxford; tel: (410) 226-5111, fax: (410) 226-5744; www.robertmorrisinn.com; dinner daily, lunch Apr–Nov.* A local landmark, with rooms in the historic inn and newer waterside building. The restaurant features local seafood in gracious surroundings.

Tidewater Inn $$ *101 E Dover St, Easton; tel: (410) 822-1300 or (800) 237-8775; www.tidewaterinn.com. Buffet brunch Sat & Sun.* Eastern Shore gentry to the core, catering for wildfowl hunters with details such as an 0430 autumn breakfast. The dining room (**$$**) deserves its excellent reputation, and is the place to sample crab cakes.

Mathilda's $$$ *103 Mill St, Oxford; tel: (410) 226-0056; open from 1700 Mon–Sat.* An elegant venue for Mediterranean cuisine.

SALISBURY

ⓘ Wicomico County Visitors Center
8480 Ocean Hwy (US-13); tel: (410) 548-4914 or (800) 332-8687; www.wicomicotourism.org; open daily summer 0800–1800; winter 0830–1700.

🐾 Salisbury Zoo S
Park Dr; tel: (410) 548-3188; www. salisburyzoo.org; open daily summer 0800–1930; winter 0800–1630. Free.

Ward Museum of Wildfowl Art $$ *909 S Schumaker Dr; tel: (410) 742-4988; www. wardmuseum.org; open Mon–Sat 1000–1700, Sun 1200–1700.*

Pemberton Historic Park *Rte 349 West; tel: (410) 860-2447; www. pembertonpark.org*

⬣ Salisbury Pewter
2611 N Salisbury Blvd (US-13); tel: (410) 546-1188; open Mon–Fri 0900–1700, Sat 1000–1700. Pewter is spun using Colonial techniques, which you can watch in the workshop. Prices may be half retail.

⚆ All tennis courts, many lit at night, are free, often without reservations.

◭ Salisbury Festival, in the first week of May, sees the town filled with a colourful display of blooming dogwood and azaleas.

Above
Salisbury Historic District

Walking and cycling path follow the river through Salisbury Zoo, an outstanding community nature centre that introduces 90 species of native and exotic wildlife. Raised boardwalks and natural habitat enclosures make it easy to watch buffalo, spider monkeys, prairie dogs, sloths, otters, black jaguars and spectacled bears. The **Ward Museum of Wildfowl Art** features historic decoy displays and collections of award-winning art.

Newtown Historic District is a living catalogue of Victorian, Queen Anne, Second Empire, Eastlake, Colonial Revival and cottage architecture.

Pemberton Historic Park combines history with nature at an early plantation set in several ecosystems that provide the habitat for nearly 160 bird species. Programmes examine Colonial and Native American life.

Accommodation and food in and near Salisbury

Adam's The Place For Ribs $–$$ *219 Fruitland Blvd, Fruitland; tel: (410) 749-6961.* Excellent ribs and other local barbecue specialities.

Watermen's Cove $–$$ *925 Snow Hill Rd, Salisbury; tel: (410) 546-1400; open daily for lunch and dinner.* Stands out for its treatment of seafood, prepared in a variety of tasty ways.

Whitehaven Hotel $–$$ *River St & Whitehaven Rd, Whitehaven; tel: (410) 873-2000 or (877) 809-8296; http://whitehaven.tripod.com.* The inn is a recently restored 19th-century hotel, right on the water near the ferry landing, and has two kayaks available to guests.

Waterloo Country Inn $$ *28822 Mt Vernon Rd, Princess Anne; tel: (410) 651-0883; fax: (410) 651-0883.* Combines elegance with sublime comfort on the bank of a tidal creek where guests are welcome to use the inn's canoes.

SNOW HILL

Worcester County Tourism *104 W Market St; tel: (410) 632-3110 or (800) 852-0335; www.visitworcester.com*

Furnace Town Living Heritage Museum *$ Old Furnace Rd; tel: (410) 632-2032; open Apr–Oct daily 1100–1700.*

Pocomoke River State Park *US-113 (Worcester Hwy); tel: (410) 632-2566, reservations (888) 432-2267; www.dnr.state.md.us. Free.*

Captain Bruce Wooten *6661 Snow Hill Rd; tel: (410) 632-1431; www.captbrucewooten. com. Takes anglers on 3-hour fishing trips with as much instruction as needed.*

Pocomoke River Canoe Company *$–$$$ 312 N Washington St; tel: (410) 632-3971 or (800) 258-0905; www.atbeach.com; open daily Apr–Nov. The company rents kayaks and canoes, provides shuttles and runs guided trips.*

Snow Hill sits astride the meandering Pocomoke River, which flows through a beautiful wilderness of cypress swamps. Bird life is abundant, and cypresses form a watery scene of tall trunks and knobbly half-submerged knees. Explore by canoe or on boardwalks in the Nassawango Creek Cypress Swamp Preserve, reached through **Furnace Town Living Heritage Museum**. Worth seeing for its giant brick iron furnace, this museum village thrived around the furnace in the early 1800s.

Pocomoke River State Park has several sections along the river, with cypress swamps and forests and, at Shad Landing, swimming, fishing, camping, hiking and boat rentals.

Accommodation and food in Snow Hill

The Mansion House $$ *4436 Bayside Rd; tel: (410) 632-3189; http://mansionhousebnb.com.* Swim, fish or paddle from their waterfront or cycle the country roads (bikes, canoes and kayaks provided) from this 1835 planters mansion overlooking the bay.

River House Inn $$ *201 E Market St; tel: (410) 632-2722; fax: (410) 632-2866; www.riverhouseinn.com.* Overlooks the river, with its own canoe landing and nicely decorated rooms furnished in antiques. Bicycles are free for guests' use.

Right
Pocomoke River State Park

Next page
St Michaels

St Michaels

ⓘ St Mary's Square Museum *St Mary's Sq; tel: (410) 745-9561; open May–Oct Sat & Sun 1000–1600.*

ⓘ Chesapeake Bay Maritime Museum *$$ 213 N Talbot St; tel: (410) 745-2916; www.cbmm.org; open daily summer 1000–1800; spring & autumn 1000–1700; winter 1000–1600.*

◉ Artiste Locale *112 N Talbot St; tel: (410) 745-6580. Local crafts.*

Chesapeake Bay Maritime Museum Store *Mill St; tel: (410) 745-2098.*

ⓘ Chesapeake Lighthouse Tours *$$–$$$ 5907 Tilghman Island Rd, Tilghman Island; tel: (410) 886-2215 or (800) 690-5080; www.chesapeakelights.com. Half and full-day boat tours featuring local lighthouses.*

◉ Tilghman Island Marina *6140 Mariners Ct, Tilghman Island; tel: (410) 886-2500; www.tilghmanmarina.com. Rents canoes, kayaks, pontoon boats and bicycles. Kayak tours with naturalists.*

St Michaels Marina *305 Mulberry St; tel: (410) 745-2400 or (800) 678-8980; www.stmichaelsmarina.com. Hire a bicycle by the hour ($) or day ($$$).*

◉ Chesapeake Folk Festival *Tel: (410) 745-2916; www.cbmm.org; last Sat in Jul. Local and regional food, music and boat rides.*

Tilghman Island Day *www.tilghmanisland.com. Exhibits, skipjack races, music and food in mid-Oct.*

Chesapeake Bay Maritime Museum shows the breadth of the bay's influence on Eastern Shore life, history and culture through historic boats, exhibits on decoys, fishing, Native Americans, ship-building, steamboating and watermen's skills. At its heart is the 1879 Hooper Straight Lighthouse with its restored keeper's cottage.

Tilghman Island has the last working fleet of skipjacks engaged in oyster dredging. Look for these sailing craft at Dogwood Harbor, after you cross the drawbridge.

St Michaels boasts of being 'the town that fooled the British' for tricking British ships during the War of 1812. Lanterns atop ship masts and in treetops above an otherwise darkened town caused the British to aim too high and most of the cannon fire flew over the rooftops.

Accommodation and food in St Michaels

Victoriana Inn $ *205 Cherry St; tel: (410) 745-3368.* Has three rooms with shared baths, one private, close to the Maritime Museum.

Black Walnut Point Inn $$ *Tilghman Island; tel: (410) 886-2452, fax. (410) 886-2053; www.tilghmanisland.com/blackwalnut.* Fills its own private point, surrounded by the bay. A waterside cottage has a kitchen.

Harrison's $$ *Rte 33, Tilghman Island; tel: (410) 886-2123.* A combination of fishing centre and restaurant, serving seafood fresh from its own fleet's catch in a casual atmosphere.

VIRGINIA'S EASTERN SHORE

ℹ️ **New Church Welcome Center**
US-13, New Church; tel: (757) 824-5000.

Chincoteague Chamber of Commerce 6733 Maddox Blvd; tel: (757) 336-5161; www.chincoteaguechamber.com

🅘 Every place in this narrow peninsula is close to US-13.

🅗 **Chincoteague National Wildlife Refuge** $ Tel: (757) 336-512. Visitors Center open winter 0900–1600, longer in summer.

NASA Visitor Center Wallops Island, Rte 175; tel: (301) 286-3978; www.wfl.nasa.gov/vc; open Thur–Mon 1000–1600. Free.

Kerr Place $ Onancock; tel: 757) 787-8012; open Mar–Dec Tue–Sat 1000–1600.

🅐 **Hopkins & Bro. Store** 2 Market St, Onancock; tel: (757) 787-8100. In business since 842.

🅟 **Capt'n Bob's Marina** $$$ Chincoteague; tel: (757) 336-6654; www.captbobsmarina.com. Rent a boat here.

Hopkins & Bro. Store see above. Bicycle hire.

🅐 **Assateague Pony Penning** Jul last Wed and Thur. The wild horses swim the channel to Chincoteague.

Rural character pervades Virginia's Delmarva, where tourism is largely confined to Chincoteague and to motorists short-cutting south via the Chesapeake Bay Bridge-Tunnel.

Assateague Island extends from Maryland, and **Chincoteague National Wildlife Refuge**, which occupies much of it, is named after the smaller neighbouring Chincoteague Island just west, with resort facilities. The refuge on the fragile barrier island is a prime bird-watching area also famous for wild horses, although these are easier to spot on Maryland's end of the island. A 1¼-mile trail leads to the 1867 Assateague Lighthouse.

NASA Visitor Center follows the history of flight and rockets. See a piece of the moon, satellite photos of a hurricane and launch rockets. **Kerr Place** is a mansion dating back to 1799, with finely detailed plasterwork and woodwork, furnished and decorated to its period.

Accommodation and food in Virginia's Eastern Shore

Don's Seafood Restaurant $ 4113 Main St, Chincoteague; tel: (757) 336-5715; www.donsseafood.com. Serves three casual meals daily, with chicken, shrimp and other Chesapeake specialities.

1848 Island Manor House B&B $–$$ 4160 Main St, Chincoteague; tel: (757) 336-5436 or (800) 852-1505; fax: (757) 336-1333; www.islandmanor.com. Offers six antique-furnished rooms with shared and private baths.

Garden & Sea Inn $–$$ 4188 Nelson Rd, New Church; tel: (757) 824-0672 or (800) 824-0672; fax: (757) 824-5605; www.gardenandseainn.com. Built in 1802 and furnished with fine antiques and oriental rugs, some rooms with whirlpools. The dining room ($$) is among the Delmarva's best, serving Chincoteague oysters in peppercorn sauce and filling trout with Crab Imperial.

Miss Molly's Inn $–$$ 4141 Main St, Chincoteague; tel: (757) 336-6686 or (800) 221-5620; fax: (757) 336-0600; www. missmollys-inn.com. Built in 1886, serves fresh scones and trifle for tea.

Right NASA Visitor Center

Suggested tour

St Michael's: Dockside Express Tours & Shuttles $ *Tel: (410) 886-2643; open mid-Apr–mid-Nov.* Leads general and themed historic walking tours.

Express Princess $$$ *Tel: (410) 886-2643.* Reservations are suggested for these morning 90-minute nature cruises, sunset and moonlight cruises.

Patriot $$ *Maritime Museum Dock; tel: (410) 745-3100; www.patriotcruises.com; cruises Apr–Oct daily 1100, 1230, 1430 & 1600.* A large tour boat explores the Miles River.

Rebecca T Ruark $$$ *Dogwood Harbor, Tilghman Island; tel: (410) 886-2176; www.skipjack.org.* Built in 1886, this ship makes 2-hour sailing tours.

Crisfield Visitors Center and J Millard Tawes Historical Museum $ *Somers Cove Marina; tel: (410) 968-2501; open May–Oct Mon–Fri 0900–1630, Sat & Sun 1000–1500.*

Smith Island Cruises *Somers Cove Marina; tel: (410) 425-2771; www.smithislandcruises.com; Jun–Oct daily 1230.*

Tangier Island Cruises *City Dock; tel: (410) 968-2338; www.tangierislandcruises.com; open mid-May–mid-Oct daily 1230.*

Right
Bison in Salisbury Zoo

Total distance: 202 miles.

Time: 5 hours driving time. Allow 2–3 days, longer with canoe or boat trips. Those with limited time should concentrate on Furnace Town Living Heritage Museum and the Maritime Museum at St Michaels, if possible adding a skipjack sailing tour.

Links: From Norfolk the Chesapeake Bay Bridge-Tunnel leads north to the Eastern Shore. Snow Hill and Salisbury are close to Ocean City and the Delaware Coast, and US-50 leads directly from Easton to Annapolis or to US-301 and the Northern Chesapeake itinerary.

Route: From the Chesapeake Bay Bridge-Tunnel, follow US-13 past **Kiptopeke State Park**, **Cape Charles** and **Onancock** to Rte 175 turning right to **CHINCOTEAGUE ❶**.

Backtrack to US-13, turning right on to US-113 near **Pocomoke City** and continuing to **SNOW HILL ❷**. Follow Rte 12 to **SALISBURY ❸**.

Head west on US-50 to **CAMBRIDGE ❹**, continuing over the Choptank River to **EASTON ❺**. Follow Rte 333 to **OXFORD ❻** crossing the **Oxford–Bellevue Ferry** and turning left on Rte 33 to **ST MICHAELS ❼**. Return to US-50, heading north to the Bay Bridge.

Also worth exploring

Already a sailing port in the late 17th century, **Crisfield** prospered on fishing and by 1910 had the nation's largest sailing fleet. **Janes Island State Park** (*tel: (410) 968-1565*), accessible by shuttle or rented boats, has canoe and walking trails through marshes and pine forests. The campsite and marina are on the mainland. Ferries leave Crisfield for **Smith** and **Tangier Islands**.

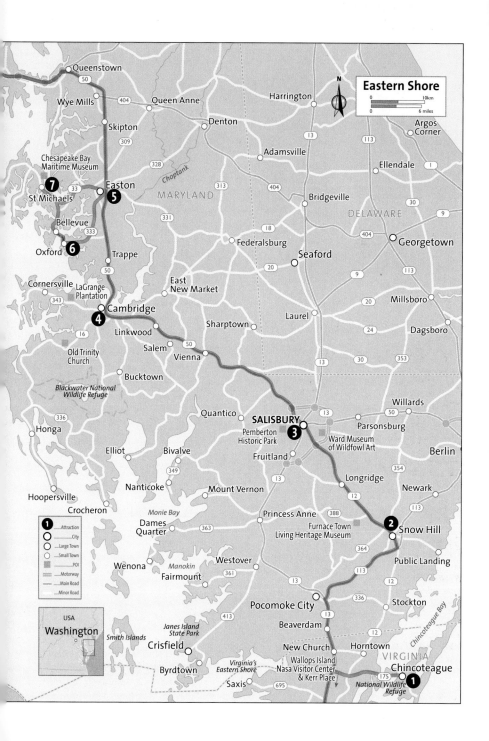

Rockville to Frederick

Ratings

Historical sights	●●●●
Shopping and crafts	●●●●
Gastronomy	●●●
Art and museums	●●
Children	●●
Entertainment	●●
Nature and wildlife	●●
Beaches	●

History is the hallmark of this area north of Washington DC The C&O Canal begins here (and began building here i 1828), bypassing one of the region's premier natural feature: the torrential Great Falls of the Potomac. Today the canal is th focus of a linear National Park that protects its 184-mile length.

The region was a corridor through which both armies course in the Civil War, as General Lee sought to demoralise the Unio and surround its capital. Frederick was an important crossroac and storage centre for Union supplies, and a crucial battle a Monocacy saved Washington from invasion. More peacefu today, Frederick's history is evident in its streets of beautiful ol homes.

CATOCTIN MOUNTAIN

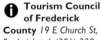 **Tourism Council of Frederick County** *19 E Church St, Frederick; tel: (301) 228-2888 or (800) 999-3613; www.fredericktourism.org; open daily 0900–1700.*

Catoctin Mountain Park Visitor Center *Rte 77, Thurmont; tel: (301) 663-9388; www.nps.gov/cato*

Catoctin Mountain Park is set in wild mountainous landscape, wher 'moonshine' whiskey was made secretly during the prohibition er. The restored remains of Blue Blazes Whiskey Still, destroyed b 'revenuers' in the 1930s, is reached by a short trail. Hog Rock Natu Trail is under 1 mile-long, with interpretive nature signs.

Cunningham Falls State Park lies directly south, named after th 70ft Cunningham Falls, which cascade over a series of rock ledges. Th 1½-mile trail to the falls has several uphill sections. A large lake offe swimming and canoes for hire and the park runs outdoor and natu programmes as well as having picnic areas and playgrounds.

Catoctin Wildlife Preserve and Zoo is designed for family outing with a blend of pettable and exotic creatures, including golden tiger

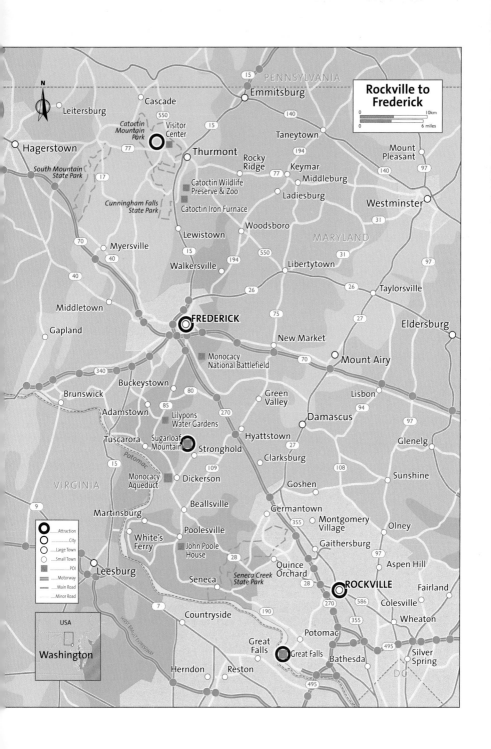

Cunningham Falls State Park $ *Rtes 77 and 15, Thurmont; tel: (301) 271-7574.*

Catoctin Wildlife Preserve and Zoo $$ *13019 Catoctin Furnace Rd (Rte 806), Thurmont; tel: (301) 271-3180; www.cwpzoo.com; open May–Sept daily 0900–1700; off-season hours vary.*

Catoctin Iron Furnace *Catoctin Furnace Rd (Rte 806), Thurmont; tel: (301) 271-7574; www.dnr.state.md.us*

Catoctin Mountain Orchard *15036 N Franklinville Rd, Thurmont; open Jun–Oct daily 0900–1700.* You can buy berries, cherries, apricots, peaches, apples and grapes in season.

Catoctin Colorfest In the second weekend in Oct at Thurmont Community Park the work of over 350 craftspeople is on show and for sale.

black jaguars, monkeys, bears, alligators and a giant tortoise. Th emphasis is on learning about the animals and interacting whe possible.

Catoctin Iron Furnace, almost across the road, was built in 1776 make cannonballs for the Revolution, providing 100 tonnes of shel used at Yorktown alone. The ruins of the ironmaster's house hav been stabilised and can be toured. Three of Maryland's five covere bridges cluster nearby – the closest to US-15 is Roddy Road Cover Bridge.

Accommodation and food in Catoctin Mountain

Mountain Gate Convenience Store $ *130 Frederick Rd (just off US-1 Thurmont.* Has takeaway lunches and dinners at extremely low prices

Mountain Gate Family Restaurant $ *133 Frederick Rd (just off US-1 Thurmont; tel: (301) 271-4373.* Serves unbelievably cheap turkey, ha roast beef and roast pork dinners, sandwiches and breakfasts.

Cozy Country Inn $–$$ *103 Frederick Rd (Rte 806), Thurmont; tel: (30 271-4301; restaurant (301) 271-7373; www.cozyvillage.com.* Used journalists and government officials accompanying US presidents nearby Camp David. Rooms are themed on past presidents ar Winston Churchill, a guest in the 1940s, and the inn has an exhib about Camp David. The popular restaurant, hardly cosy, serv traditional dishes and an all-you-can-eat buffet ($) on Sun.

Above
Catoctin Zoo

FREDERICK

ⓘ Tourism Council of Frederick County (TIC) 19 E Church St; tel: (301) 228-2888 or (800) 999-3613; www.fredericktourism.org; open daily 0900–1700.

Ⓖ Guided Walking Tours $ Tel: (301) 663-1188; tours May–Nov at and Sun 1330. These start from the TIC, which also publishes an excellent walking tour map.

Frederick Carriage Company $$$ TIC or tel: (301) 845-7001. Horse-drawn carriages tour the old city.

Ⓝ National Museum of Civil War Medicine $ 48 E Patrick St; tel: (301) 695-1864; www.civilwarmed.org; open Mon–Sat 1000–1700, Sun 1100–1700.

Rose Hill Manor $$ 1611 N Market St; tel: (301) 600-1650; www.rosehillmuseum.com; open Apr–Oct Mon–Sat 1000–1600, Sun 1300–1600; Nov weekends.

Schifferstadt Architectural Museum 1110 Rosemont Ave; tel: (301) 663-6088; open mid-Apr–mid-Dec Tue–Sun 1000–1600.

Monocacy National Battlefield Rte 355, southeast of Frederick; tel: (301) 662-3515; www.nps.gov/mono; open Apr–Oct daily 0800–1630; Nov–Mar Wed–Sun 0800–1600.

Frederick's streets are lined with well-kept commercial blocks and residences from the Civil War era and earlier. The city's role in that war is portrayed uniquely at the **National Museum of Civil War Medicine**, whose innovative displays show period medical practices.

Barbara Fritchie House recalls its 90-year-old owner, who challenged Confederate troops to tear down her Union flag. They didn't. Collections of The Historical Society of Frederick County are shown in an 1820s home, and include fine furniture, paintings and decorative arts. The Community Bridge, a *trompe-l'oeil* mural incorporating hundreds of images from the community, spans a canalised river, with a promenade and entertainment space.

Rose Hill Manor is a classic 18th-century plantation with a Farm Museum exhibiting early agriculture, and a Children's Museum with hands-on programmes teaching about life in the manor house and plantation. The 1756 **Schifferstadt Architectural Museum**, an example of a German colonial home, has thick stone walls, a built-in iron stove, wishbone chimneys and other unusual features.

Monocacy National Battlefield is the site of the 1864 Civil War battle that, although it was 'lost', stopped the Confederate march on Washington DC, and saved the capital. The Visitor Center has an orientation programme and self-guided tour maps.

Accommodation and food in Frederick

Brewers Alley Restaurant & Brewery $–$$ *124 N Market St; tel: (301) 631-0089.* Includes pub fare and more upmarket dishes, such as Louisiana *boudin* with jumbo shrimp. The atmosphere is bright, busy, noisy and youngish.

Hollerstown Hill B&B $$ *4 Clark Pl; tel: (301) 228-3630; www.hollerstownhill.com.* The High-Victorian interior is decorated with period furniture – rosewood chairs and a cameo sofa in the parlour – and the owner's doll collection.

Firestone's $$–$$$ *105 N Market St; tel: (301) 663-0330; www.firestonesrestaurant.com.* Steaks and chops dominate the menu and live entertainment is featured Fri and Sat evenings (when bookings are essential).

Tyler Spite Inn $$–$$$ *112 W Church St; tel: (301) 831-4455.* Dates from 1810, a fine antique-furnished mansion in a beautiful historic downtown neighbourhood. More rooms in the adjacent mansion are just as comfortable, with fireplaces and feather beds.

ROCKVILLE AND GREAT FALLS

ℹ Conference and Visitors Bureau of Montgomery County
111 Rockville Pike; tel: (240) 777-2060 or (877) 789-6404; www.visitmontgomery.com

➋ Rockville is an amorphous commercial and residential area just north of the Beltway, bisected by I-270, which leads north to Frederick. To reach Great Falls from Rockville, take Exit 5 to Rte 189, Great Falls Rd.

🏛 Weiner Judaic Museum *6125 Montrose Rd, just west of Rockville Pike (Rte 355); tel: (301) 881-0100; open Sun–Thur 0900–2200, Fri 0900–1700, except Jewish holidays. Free.*

Charles F Mercer $
Tel: (301) 767-3714; www.nps.gov/choh; mid-Apr–Oct. A replica canal boat adapted for passengers is drawn by mules along the C&O Canal from Great Falls Tavern, rising through the canal lock.

C&O National Historic Path *11710 MacArthur Blvd, off Great Falls Rd (Rte 189); tel: (301) 739-4000; www.nps.gov/choh; open daily 0900–1700. Free.*

Swain's Lock *Swain's Lock Rd, off River Rd (Rte 190), Potomac; tel: (301) 299-9006; canoe lessons ($) Thur 1900.*

Above
Great Falls lock hands

The jazz-era literary stars F Scott and Zelda Fitzgerald are buried at St Mary's Church Cemetery (*Viers Mill Road (Rte 586) and Rte 355*). Collections of the **Weiner Judaic Museum** focus on Judaic history from archaeological artefacts to contemporary culture and art.

The **C&O Canal National Historic Park** follows the Potomac River northwest from Washington. George Washington envisioned this canal to bypass the river's unnavigable parts and open the western frontier. One of the major obstacles was the thundering Great Falls of the Potomac, as impressive today as in Washington's time, plunging over jagged rocks into a gorge where bald eagles circle. **Great Falls Tavern Visitor Center** explains the canal and its locks. For the best view of the falls, follow the path to Olmstead Bridges.

Swain's Lock (Lock 21), about 2 miles from Great Falls Tavern, is an original lockmaster's house, now a small recreational area with picnic tables, bicycle and canoe rentals. The canal has water in it for several miles here, perfect for quiet paddling, and the tow path is a favourite of walkers and cyclists.

Accommodation and food in Rockville and Great Falls

Cabin John Regional Park $ *7400 Tuckerman Ln, Rockville; tel: (301) 299-0024; www.mc-mncppc.org/parks.* Camp pitches and a full range of recreational facilities for campers.

Woodfin Suites Hotel $$ *1380 Piccard Dr, at I-270 Exit 8; tel: (301) 590-9880 or (888) 433-9407.* Has tasteful suites and studios, some with kitchens, in a motel-style building.

Old Angler's Inn $$$ *10801 MacArthur Blvd, near Great Falls, Potomac; tel: (301) 365-2425; www.oldanglersinn.com.* Serves well-prepared upmarket cuisine in a historic setting long favoured by sporting fishermen, including President Theodore Roosevelt.

SUGARLOAF MOUNTAIN

To explore this region's C&O Canal locks, gate houses and aqueducts from the well-kept and wide towpath trail, rent a bicycle from **Swain's Lock** (*Swain's Lock Rd, off River Rd (Rte 190), Potomac; tel: (301) 299-3613*).

Lilypons Water Gardens *6800 Lilypons Rd, off Rte 85, Buckeystown; www.lilypons.com; open Nov–Feb Mon–Sat 0930–1630; Mar–Oct Mon–Sun 0930–1730. Free.*

Sugarloaf Mountain has scenic picnic areas with tables near the parking area on top and in wooded groves surrounding its rocky outcrops.

President Franklin Roosevelt tried to buy Sugarloaf Mountain as a presidential retreat, but its owner wouldn't sell. Trail maps for the surprisingly steep ascent are in a box at the entrance or you can drive to the top to explore its rocky summit and admire the views from its lookouts. The building stone for nearby Monocacy Aqueduct was quarried here, and although this bridge which carried the canal over the river is now in poor condition, the quartzite blocks are as good as the day they were cut. The seven-arched aqueduct, built 1828–33 and an icon of American transportation history, is under restoration.

Lilypons Water Gardens are among America's leading growers of water lilies and aquatic plants. Small show gardens demonstrate the use of water plants in the landscape and large pools form the nurseries for a collection of flowers in shades of yellow, pink and red. It is a favourite haunt of blue herons.

Food in Sugarloaf Mountain

Meadowlark Inn $$ *19611 Fisher Ave, Poolesville; tel: (301) 428-8900; closed Mon.* A country restaurant serving home-made breads and traditional foods.

Right
Lilypons Water Gardens

Suggested tour

The ferry *Jubal A Early* crosses the Potomac River at White's Ferry daily 0500–2300.

Carroll County Tourism *210 E Main St, Westminster; tel: (301) 848-1388 or (800) 272-1933; www. carrollcountytourism.org; open Mon–Sat 0900–1700, Sun 1000–1400.*

Frederick has over 20 **antique shops** along *E Patrick St, Carroll St and corner of 2nd E St.*

New Market *I-70 east of Frederick.* Over two dozen antique shops.

Carroll County Farmers Market *700 Agriculture Center Dr, Westminster; tel: (410) 848-7748; Jun–Sept Sat 0800–1300.*

Westminster Inn *$–$$ 5 S Center St, Westminster; tel: (410) 876-2893.* Antique-furnished rooms each have a whirlpool.

National Shrine of St Elizabeth Ann Seton *333 S Seton Ave, Emmitsburg; tel: (301) 447-6606.*

Union Mills Homestead *$ 3311 Littlestown Pike (Rte 97), Westminster; tel: (410) 848-2288; open Jun–Aug Tue–Fri 1000–1600, Sat & Sun 1200–1600.*

White's Ferry Store *24801 White's Ferry Rd, Dickerson; tel: (301) 349-5200.* Hire canoes or rowing boats here.

Total distance: 80 miles, 104 with detours.

Time: Allow 2 days with or without detours, 3 if you explore Frederick in depth or add Westminster to the itinerary. Those with limited time should stop to see Great Falls and the C&O Canal, then concentrate on Frederick.

Links: From Washington DC, Rte 355 leads to Rockville, or from the Beltway, take I-270. US-340 connects Frederick to Harpers Ferry and I-70 connects it to Hagerstown.

Route: Leave **ROCKVILLE ❶** on Rte 189, Great Falls Rd, which crosses I-270 at Exit 5, and follow it to MacArthur Blvd, following signs to **GREAT FALLS ❷**. Take Rte 189 back to Rte 190, River Rd, turning left, with a diversion left on Swain's Lock Rd. Continue past **Seneca Creek State Park** to the attractive old town of **Poolesville**.

Detour: From Poolesville, follow an un-numbered road signposted **White's Ferry**, to the last ferry across the Potomac. Confederate troops controlled this crossing point during the Civil War.

Follow Rte 109 to **Beallsville**, then Rte 28 to **Dickerson**, following Sugarloaf Rd, right immediately after the railway underpass, to **SUGARLOAF MOUNTAIN ❸**. Return to Dickerson and turn right on Rte 28, making a short diversion left to **Monocacy Aqueduct**. North of Dickerson, go right on Rte 85, and right again on Lilypons Rd to the **GARDENS**, returning to Rte 85, which leads north to **FREDERICK ❹**.

From Frederick, follow US-15 north past **Cunningham Falls State Park** and **CATOCTIN MOUNTAIN ❺**, to **Thurmont**. For variety, return to Frederick by following Rte 77 east to **Keymar** and heading south on Rte 194.

Detour: From Thurmont, continue north on US-15 to **Emmitsburg**, visiting the **National Shrine of St Elizabeth Ann Seton**, honouring the first American Roman Catholic saint.

Also worth exploring

Westminster, east of Frederick via Rtes 26 and 31, is a charming town filled with historic buildings, which you can explore on a guided or self-guided walking tour from the tourist information centre. **Uniontown**, west of Westminster, is lined by buildings that span the entire 19th century. To the north, in Union Mills, **Union Mills Homestead** assembles over 200 years of history in a 1797 home, gristmill and saw mill.

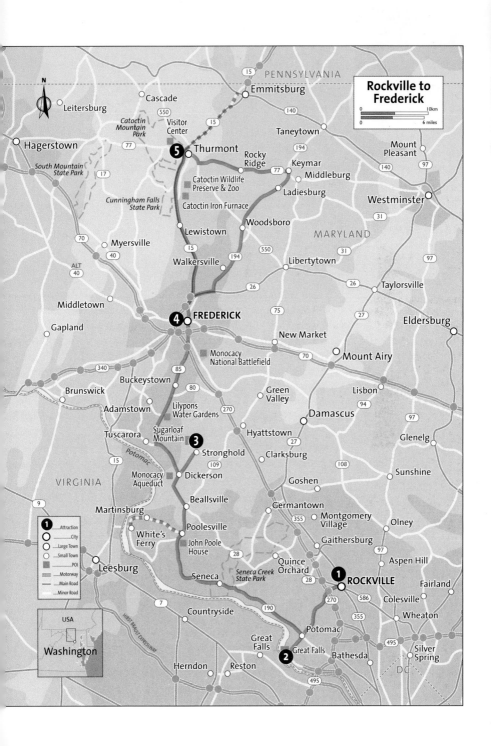

Western Maryland and borderlands

Ratings

Art and museums	●●●●○
Historical sights	●●●●○
Nature and wildlife	●●●●○
Children	●●●○○
Entertainment	●●●○○
Gastronomy	●●●○○
Shopping and crafts	●●●○○
Beaches	●●○○○

To Americans, the names of Antietam and Harpers Ferry are synonymous with the Civil War, and that era's history still pervades the region. Western sites reflect earlier history: the French and Indian Wars stronghold of Fort Frederick and George Washington's first command at Cumberland. While here Washington envisioned the C&O Canal, which borders the Potomac River, its entire length marked by a National Park and multi-use towpath trail.

Rolling mountain roads further west are less explored, except by fishermen, hikers and whitewater enthusiasts, to whom the area's vast public parklands are well known. Beautiful in any season, this landscape is most glorious in autumn, when maple paint the hillsides red and orange.

CUMBERLAND

Allegany County Visitor and Convention Bureau
13 Canal St; tel: (301) 777-5132 or (800) 425-2067; www.mdmountainside.com

Rocky Gap Information Center *Exit 50, I-68, Rocky Gap; open daily 0830–1800.*

Washington St is lined by fine old homes built in Cumberland's glory days, a living catalogue of American Victorian architectural styles from turreted brick and patterned slate to 'painted ladies'. A prime example is the 1867 **History House**, a tour of which is filled with stories of life in that opulent era.

Fort Cumberland, George Washington's first command, sat at Washington St's crest, and at Prospect Sq is a plan of the fort, its outer walls marked by paving stones. Emmanuel Church sits directly over the site of this French and Indian war fort and is a very early Gothic-Revival church, redesigned by Louis Comfort Tiffany with three large Tiffany windows. The sole remnant of Fort Cumberland is the tiny **George Washington's Headquarters**, from 1755, now on Greene St below.

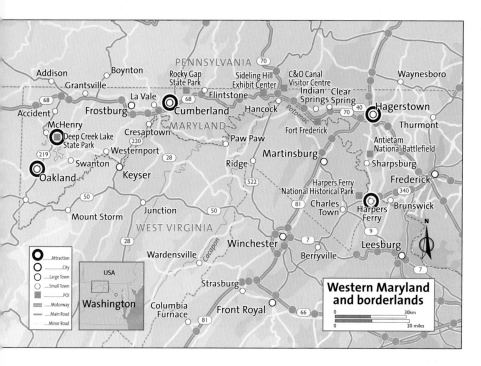

Map legend:
- Attraction
- City
- Large Town
- Small Town
- POI
- Motorway
- Main Road
- Minor Road

USA · Washington

Western Maryland and borderlands

0 — 30km
0 — 20 miles

i A *Self-Guided Walk into History*, free at History House, leads along Washington St and through the historic centre. *Fort Cumberland Walking Tour*, free from the Visitor Center, lists 28 stops with descriptions. Corresponding audio tours are available.

Western Maryland Scenic Railroad
$$ *Cumberland Station, 3 Canal St; tel: (301) 759-400 or (800) 872-4650; www.wmsr.com; May–Dec 100 or 1130, reservations recommended.* Scenic steam and diesel rail excursions travel to Frostburg.

Right
The entrance to Rocky Gap State Park

Rocky Gap State Park is highly developed, featuring a luxury hotel, Jack Nicklaus golf course and polished facilities, along with more rustic camp pitches, hiking trails, fishing, swimming, boats for hire and scheduled activities (*see page 200*).

Rocky Gap State Park *12500 Pleasant Valley Rd, Flintstone, I-68, exit 50; tel: (301) 722-1480 or (800) 724-0828; www. dnr.state.md.us.* Free.

The Gallery *8 Greene St.* Art and fine crafts are on display.

Historic Cumberland Antique Mall *55–57 Baltimore St.* Many dealers occupy this five-storey shop.

The Inn at Walnut Bottom *120 Greene St; tel: (301) 777-0003 or (800) 286-9718; www.iwbinfo.com.* You can hire bicycles for use in the area and the inn arranges bikes and shuttles for towpath trips.

Allegany Expeditions *10310 Columbus Ave; tel: (301) 722-5170 or (800) 819-5170; www.allegany expeditions.com.* You can hire kayaks, canoes and camping gear or take guided canoe trips on the Potomac.

Cumberland Theater *$$$ 101 N Johnson St; tel: (301) 759-4990; www. cumberlandtheater.com; mid-Jun–Oct.* The theatre produces professional plays and musicals.

Railfest *Tel: (301) 759-4400 or (800) 872-4650; www.wmsr.com; mid-Oct.* There are special train excursions (by reservation) to Oakland and railroading events plus dining and musical celebrations.

Accommodation and food in Cumberland

The Bourbon St Café **$** *82 Broadway; tel: (301) 722-1116; lunch and dinner Mon–Sat.* Blends Cajun flavours with Maryland ingredients, a happy marriage indeed.

Uncle Tucker's **$** *I-68, exit 46; tel: (301) 777-7232.* Serves generously embellished pizza and baby back ribs, with entertainment on the deck during summer weekends.

When Pigs Fly **$** *18 Valley St; tel: (301) 722-7447.* Serves updated home-style dishes with an emphasis on pork ribs, in a bright casual setting. The sausage chilli is delicious.

The Inn at Walnut Bottom **$–$$** *120 Greene St; tel: (301) 777-0003 or (800) 286-9718; www.iwbinfo.com.* Has the flavour of a European inn, with nicely decorated rooms and a large pleasant common area. Most rooms have private baths, all have TV and telephone. The owners will arrange bike towpath trips with shuttle.

Rocky Gap Lodge and Golf Resort **$$** *16701 Lakeview Rd, Flintstone; tel: (301) 784-8400 or (800) 724-0828; fax: (301) 784-8408; www.rockygapresort.com.* Sits above a long lake, surrounded by hills. Rooms are spacious, the dining room excellent, and a full range of activities and sports is offered. Camp pitches (**$**) are available across the lake in a wooded setting.

DEEP CREEK

Garrett County Chamber of Commerce
Rte 219, McHenry;
tel: (301) 387-4386;
www.garrettchamber.com;
open daily 0900–1700.
Publishes an excellent magazine-style guide with a detailed map.

Deep Creek Lake State Park and Discovery Center $
898 State Pk Rd; tel: (301) 387-7067; www.deepcreeklake.org

Wisp Resort 296 Marsh Hill Rd, McHenry; tel: (301) 387-4911; www.wispresort.com. Downhill skiing, snowboarding, golf, mountain biking.

High Mountain Sports US-219; tel: (301) 387-4199; www.highmountainsports.com. Equipment for hire and lessons in mountain biking, flatwater paddling, water skiing and other water sports. Specialises in teaching beginners.

Deep Creek Lake is the nucleus of a surprisingly sophisticated resort region, offering skiing and golf, world-class fly-fishing and miles of hiking trails in state parks and forests. One of these leads to the beautiful **Swallow Falls** and a rocky, scenic river canyon. **Deep Creek Lake State Park** adjoins the man-made lake with a sandy beach, marina, fishing pier, bike paths and a playground. The Discovery Center offers hands-on activities and programmes, including field trips. An aquarium there shows native fish and historical exhibits describe mining and lumbering.

Accommodation and food in Deep Creek

Arrowhead Deli $ *Rte 219 opposite tourist information centre; open 24 hours.* Has inexpensive hot and cold foods for picnics, trail lunches or a whole dinner.

Canoe on the Run Café $ *Rte 219 near the tourist information centre; tel: (301) 387-5933.* Serves soups, sandwiches and salads at lunch and dinner, plus a few breakfast favourites.

Point View Inn $ *Rte 219; tel: (301) 387-5555; www. pointviewinn.com.* Combines motel-style rooms with a good restaurant, overlooking the lake and serving three meals daily.

The Casselman Hotel and Restaurant $–$$$ *113 E Main St, Grantsville; tel: (301) 895-5055; www.thecasselman.com.* Wonderful food and lodgings in a historic building.

Carmel Cove $$ *Glendale Rd; tel: (301) 387-0067; www. carmelcoveinn.com.* Sits above a cove where the inn keeps canoes for guests. Individually decorated rooms have queen-size beds and phones, and some have whirlpool tubs, fireplaces or decks. Breakfasts are bountiful.

Streams and Dreams $$ *8214 Oakland-Sang Rd, Hoyes Landing; tel: (301) 387-6881; www. streams-and-dreams.net.* A B&B that specialises in fishing. Offers fly-fishing trips; guests can fish in the private pond.

Opposite
Washington St, Cumberland

Right
Swallow Falls

HAGERSTOWN

Hagerstown Convention and Visitors Bureau *16 Public Sq; tel: (301) 791-3246; www.marylandmemories.org*

Hagerstown is near the crossroads of I-70 and I-81. US-40 passes through its centre.

A large garage ($, free at weekends) is off N Potomac St in the town centre.

Neatly arranged in a grid, Hagerstown streets have quadrant designations to help you locate addresses.

The tourist information centre has several free *Hagerstown Downtown Walking Tour* maps, including one featuring 20 Civil War sites and another of 18 churches.

Washington County Museum of Fine Arts $ *City Park, Key St; tel: (301) 739-5727; www.wcmfa.org; open Tue–Sun 0900–1700.*

Hager House $ *City Park, Key St; tel: (301) 739-8393; www.hagerhouse.org; open Apr–Nov Tue–Sat 1000–1600, Sun 1400–1700.*

Miller House $ *135 W Washington St; tel: (301) 797-8782; open Apr–Nov Wed–Sat 1300–1600.*

Maryland Theater *21 S Potomac St; tel: (301) 790-2000; www.mdtheater.org*

Above
Doll collection, Miller House

The **Washington County Museum of Fine Arts** far exceeds the collections of many big city art museums. See works by Titian, Tintoretto and Veronese, a Lalique gallery, Tiffany and Steuben art glass, Whistler graphics, Rodin and Daumier bronzes, Peale portraits, American silver, folk art and fine furniture.

Within sight is the period-furnished stone **Hager House**, built in 1739–40 by the city's founder, a German immigrant; an adjacent small museum shows hundreds of artefacts from excavations. Also in City Park is the 1912 Engine 202 Steam Locomotive and Caboose, the last of its type, joined by eight cabooses.

A tour of **Miller House** explores not only its many rooms of collections, but its own fascinating architectural and social history beginning in 1818 as a potter's home and shop. The elegantly furnished parlour, Civil War collections, pottery, toys, 19th-century European dolls and over 150 clocks are notable.

Accommodation and food in Hagerstown

The Plum $ *6 Rochester Pl, off W Washington St; tel: (301) 791-1717 open 0730–1430.* Makes generous sandwiches to order, which you can eat in the quilt-decorated café or take away.

Wingrove Manor $–$$ *635 Oak Hill Ave; tel: (301) 733-6328 www.wingrovemanor.com.* A grand mansion surrounded by a columned porch, where continental breakfast is served in good weather.

Inn on the Potomac $$ *400 N Potomac St; tel: (301) 739-5679 or (800) 761-8313; www.innonpotomac.com.* Comfortable guest rooms in a century-old home, an easy walk from restaurants and activities.

Schmankerl Stube Bavarian Restaurant $$ *58 S Potomac St; tel: (301) 797-3354; open lunch Tue–Fri, dinner Tue–Sun.* Serves *haupt*-German cuisine, with a few nods to lighter American tastes. In the summer there's a beer garden.

Old South Mountain Inn $$–$$$ *6132 Old National Pike, Boonsboro; tel: (301) 432-6155; www.oldsouthmountaininn.com.* Seafood and beef Wellington in a historic setting.

Western Maryland Blues Fest *Tel: (301) 739-8577 ext 116; www.blues-fest.org.* The first weekend in Jun fills the city with some of the best current Blues artists.

Maryland Symphony *80 W Washington St; tel: (301) 797-4000; www.marylandsymphony.org.* Bring a picnic to their annual concert at the Antietam National Battlefield on Independence Day.

Washington County Playhouse Dinner Theatre *Tel: (301) 739-7469; www.washingtoncountyplayhouse.com; Fri and Sat 1800, Sun 1300.* Professional theatre productions with an 'all you can eat' buffet.

Discovery Station $ *101 W Washington St; tel: (301) 790-0076 or (877) 790-0076; www.discoverystation.org; open Tue–Sat 1000–1600, Sun 1400–1700.* Hands-on explorations of dinosaurs, maths and anatomy, with a special learning centre for younger children.

Augustoberfest *Tel: (301) 739-8577 ext 116; www.augustoberfest.org.* A sister-city celebration with Wesel, Germany.

Right
Miller House

HARPERS FERRY

The Shenandoah and Potomac rivers merge under tall cliffs, and the town of Harpers Ferry grew along the least steep of the junction's plunging hillsides. Also through this break in the Appalachian Mountains passes a historic route west, the train line and the C&O Canal, reached by a footbridge from the historic district.

**ⓘ West Virginia
Welcome Center**
*US-340 at Washington St;
tel: (304) 535-2627 or
(800) 848-8687.*

ⓟ Follow signs to the
National Historic
Park car park, from which
buses shuttle to the
restored area. There is no
parking in the Historic
District.

**ⓗ Harpers Ferry
National Historical
Park $** *Visitors Center,
Shenandoah St; tel: (304)
535-6223; www.nps.gov/
hafe; open daily 0800–
1700.*

**Antietam National
Battlefield $** *Rte 65,
Sharpsburg; tel: (301) 432-
7331; www.nps.gov/antil.* A
2-hour tour in your own
car, led by a ranger, is
included with park
entrance fee.

ⓠ In order to
understand the Battle
of Antietam better, and to
follow the route taken by
Confederate forces under
Gen Robert E Lee, look in
TICs for the excellent
brochure *1862 Antietam
Campaign*, which provides
a detailed map keyed to
events.

River Riders $$ *408
Alstadts Hill Rd; tel: (304)
535-2663 or (800) 326-
7238; www.riverriders.
com.* Full service outfitter
and excursion provider for
rafting, canoeing, kayaking,
cycling, fishing and more.

Above
Harpers Ferry National
Historical Park

Harpers Ferry National Historical Park includes restored building
housing static displays occasionally enlivened by costumed
interpreters. John Brown's Fort is the relocated brick armoury where
Brown's band made their stand and were captured. Beyond is a river
overlook with signs relating local Civil War history, quite literally a tug
of war as the town passed between Union and Confederate control.

Other stops include the Civil War Museum, John Brown Museum,
industry displays, a dry goods store and a building showing historic
construction techniques. Most compelling is the small Black Voices
Museum, which chronicles the lives of slaves and freed black people in
antebellum Harpers Ferry. Harper House, the oldest in town and
furnished with Civil War-era antiques, is reached by steps from High
St. The message at Harpers Ferry is a puzzling one, seeming to make a
hero of John Brown for waging civil insurrection.

North of Harpers Ferry is **Antietam National Battlefield**, scene of
the bloodiest single-day battle of the Civil War. A vivid film shown at
the Visitors Center describes it, giving meaning to Sunken Road and
Burnside Bridge, where Union troops finally forced the southern
withdrawal. The loss at Antietam stopped Lee's northward advance
and dissuaded the British from supporting the Confederacy.

Accommodation and food in Harpers Ferry

Cliffside Inn $ *Rte 340; tel: (304) 535-6302 or (800) 782-9437.* Serves
three home-style meals daily with weekend buffet.

The Anvil $–$$ *1270 Washington St; tel: (304) 535-2582.* Features
seafood, chicken, steak and veal in a rustic setting – lunch and
dinner daily.

Harpers Ferry's place in history

George Washington chose Harpers Ferry as the site for a new Federal Armory in 1796. It was this armoury, with its musket and rifle factories and two arsenals, that attracted John Brown, a violent abolitionist. Gathering followers on 16 October 1859, his troop crossed the rail bridge over the Potomac and seized the armoury, holding it for two days before he was wounded, captured, tried for treason and hanged. His raid was a prelude to the Civil War.

Harpers Ferry Flea Market *Rte 340 t Millville Rd; tel: (304) 725- 141; open Mar–Nov veekends only, dawn–dusk.* local institution, offering acres of vendor space nd a snack bar serving breakfast, lunch and supper.

Right Colonial building, near Harpers Ferry

Hilltop House $–$$ *400 E Ridge St; tel: (703) 771-6301 or (800) 338-8319.* A large traditional country inn overlooking the rivers from a high bluff. The menu is equally traditional, serving three meals daily and specialising in fried chicken.

Hostelling International Harpers Ferry $–$$ *19123 Sandy Hook Rd, Knoxville; tel: (301) 834-7652; fax: (301) 834-7652; www.harpersferryhostel.org; open mid-Mar–mid-Nov.* Reached from Rte 340 in Maryland via Keep Tryst Rd, has bunks and private rooms, kitchen, washer and dryer.

Jacob Rohrbach Inn $–$$ *138 W Main St, Sharpsburg; tel: (877) 839-4242 or (301) 432-5079.* A comfortable 1832 home with engaging innkeepers. Antiques and reproductions furnish guest rooms and a summer kitchen now houses a hot tub.

OAKLAND

Garrett County Visitors Center *S-219, McHenry; tel: (301) 87-4386; open Sun–Thur 900–1700, Fri & Sat 900–1800.*

Greater Oakland Business Association *el: (301) 334-2691; www.oaklandmd.com*

Welcoming the many prestigious guests who came to Oakland's resorts by train was the elegant 1884 B&O Railroad Depot, now under restoration. So many dignitaries visited that St Matthew's Church, across the street, was called 'The Church of Presidents'. The nearby **Garrett County Historical Museum** is like a county attic, filled with bits and pieces of local history that include Archaic period Native American artefacts, folk art, coal-mine tools and Civil War items.

A number of Amish farms are south of Oakland on US-218, some with bakery or dairy shops. You will know when you are near Amish settlements when you encounter cautionary road signs for buggies.

Right
Oakland railway station

Accommodation and food in Oakland

The free *Walking Guide* to Downtown points out interesting sights in Oakland.

Garrett County Historical Museum
107 S 2nd St; tel: (301) 334-3226; open Jun–Sept Mon–Sat 1100–1600, or by appointment. Free.

The Oakland Farmers' Market
Near the old railway station; open Wed–Sat 1000–1300. Browse around for farm produce and baked goods.

Sugar and Spice Bakery and Cheese 8672 Garrett Hwy; tel: (301) 334-1559; open Mon–Sat 0700–1730. Try the home-made cheese along with breads and delicious apple dumplings.

Oak and Apple B&B $–$$ *208 N 2nd St; tel: (301) 334-9265 www.oakandappleinn.com.* A comfortable home with four guest rooms, two of which share a bath. Continental breakfast includes home-made breads and fresh fruit.

Cornish Manor Restaurant $$ *830 Memorial Dr; tel: (301) 334-6499 fax: (301) 334-7848; www.cornishmanor.net.* Also ranks high in the fine dining class, with a continental (but never stodgy) menu. Eclectic décor and friendly hosts add to the evening.

Deer Park Inn $$ *65 Hotel Rd, Deer Park; tel: (301) 334-2308 www.deerparkinn.com.* Occupies one of the Victorian 'cottages' of the long-gone Grand Deer Park Hotel. The elegant dining room serves innovative New American cuisine (by reservation).

Suggested tour

Total distance: 294 miles.

Time: 8 hours' driving time. Allow 4 days minimum, 5 if you plan to enjoy any of the sports or activities.

Links: The tour begins in Frederick, a point on the North of Washington itinerary or easily reached from the capital by I-270. I-70 connects Frederick to Baltimore.

Route: Leave **FREDERICK** on US-340 to **HARPERS FERRY** ❶ following the un-numbered Scenic Route (designated by yellow flower

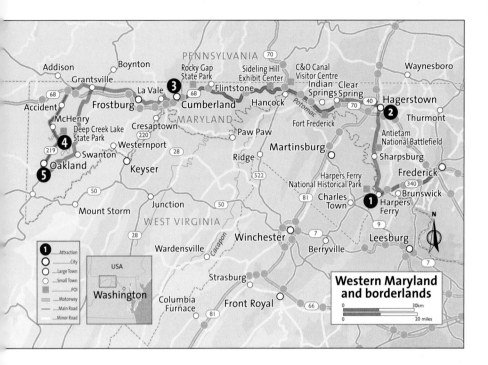

Western Maryland and borderlands

Sideling Hill Information Center I-68, Harvey; open daily 0830–1800.

Fort Frederick State Park $ Rte 56, Big Spring; tel: (301) 842-1155; www.dnr.state.md.us. Here you can find a picnic area, tent pitches and access to the C&O Canal towpath.

C&O Canal Hancock Visitors Center 326 E Main St; tel: (301) 582-813; open daily Jun–Aug; Wed–Tue spring and autumn.

Thrasher Carriage Museum 19 Depot St, Frostburg; tel: (301) 689-3380; www. thrashercarriage.com; open May–Sept Tue–Sun 1100–1500; Oct daily; Nov & Dec Sat & Sun.

signs) to Sharpsburg, where Rte 65 takes you past **Antietam Battlefield** to HAGERSTOWN ❷. Leave town on US-40 past historic stone Wilson Bridge to **Indian Springs**, following Rte 56 left to **Fort Frederick**, a rare stone Vauban-type defence built by the British during the French and Indian Wars. Backtrack to I-70/US-40 and continue west to **Hancock**, where the C&O Canal Visitor Center shows an excellent 1917 film with rare old footage.

From Hancock, US-40 and I-68 sometimes join, passing through **Sideling Cut**, an 800ft notch carved through the mountain, exposing a 20-million-year slice of geological history. Displays in **Sideling Hill Exhibit Center** explain this. Continue past **Rocky Gap State Park** to CUMBERLAND ❸. Leave via US-40, passing tiny **Toll Gate House** in La Vale and stopping in **Frostburg** to visit the outstanding **Thrasher Carriage Museum**, filled with restored horse-drawn vehicles.

Continue on US-40, crossing the **Eastern Continental Divide** at Meadow Mountain east of **Grantsville**. West of Grantsville, turn south (left) on US-219, along a scenic ridge to **Accident**, stopping to see the **Drane House**, a 1797 log farmhouse. Pass DEEP CREEK LAKE ❹ before arriving in OAKLAND ❺. From Oakland, follow Rte 135 east to Rte 495, following it north (left) to Grantsville and I-68, which returns you to Hancock and I-70, back to Frederick.

Southern Maryland

Ratings

Art and museums	●●●●○
Beaches	●●●●○
Nature and wildlife	●●●●○
Children	●●●○○
Entertainment	●●●○○
Historical sights	●●●○○
Gastronomy	●○○○○
Shopping and crafts	●○○○○

Separated from neighbouring land by the Chesapeake Bay and the broad Potomac River, Southern Maryland's wide peninsula is itself cut by several wide tidal rivers. The traveller in this relatively low and flat land is never far from water. This is the oldest part of the state, where its first settlers came in 1634 on two small ships, the *Ark* and the *Dove*, to establish a colony under Lord Baltimore.

Although the area has much of the charm and attraction of the Eastern Shore, it is one of Maryland's best-kept secrets, so you will find its beaches and parks uncrowded and the people you meet there will most likely be native to the area. Those who enjoy fishing, fossil hunting or history will like this area especially, for it offers all three in abundance.

CHESAPEAKE BEACH

Breezy Point Beach $ *Breezy Point Rd, off Rte 261; tel: (410) 535-1600; open May–Oct 0800–2100.*

Chesapeake Beach Railway Museum *4155 Mears Ave; tel: (410) 257-3892; www.cbrm.org; open May–Sept daily 1300–1600; Apr & Oct Sat–Sun 1300–1600. Free.*

Beaches are what made Chesapeake Beach a popular resort in the 19th century, and they still bring people to the area. North Beach, just north of Chesapeake Beach, has a small public beach with a half-mile boardwalk. Bay Front Park, known locally as Brownie's Beach, is just south of Chesapeake City. You may find fossils there. **Breezy Point Beach** is a half-mile stretch of sand lapped by the Chesapeake, with picnic areas, a bathhouse, playground and a fishing and crabbing pier.

Chesapeake Beach Railway Museum occupies the former station of the Chesapeake Beach Railroad, once the favoured way to arrive at this seaside resort. Old photographs and artefacts show the resort in its heyday. A 1914 Model-T Ford Depot Hack and half an 1889 railway

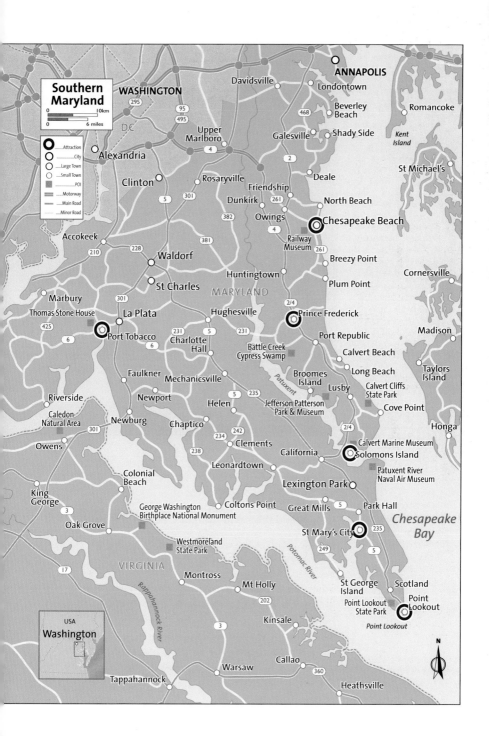

Right
Chesapeake Beach Railway
Museum

At North Beach:
Chesapeake
Antique Center *4133*
7th St. Stocks collectibles
and Victoriana.

Nice and Fleazy
Antique Center *7th St*
and Bay Ave. Sells fine
silver, nautical items,
jewellery.

Chesapeake Beach
Fishing Charters
Tel: (301) 855-4665 or
(800) 532-9246; www.
chesapeakefishingcharters.
com. Fifteen boats are
represented, including the
Mary Lou II *(tel: (301)*
855-0784). Half-day, full-day
and evening trips Jun–Sept.

Bayside History
Museum *9006*
Dayton Ave, North Beach;
tel: (410) 495-8386; open
Sun 1300–1600. Shows
how the bay shaped local
culture from prehistoric
times to today.

Chesapeake Beach
Water Park *4079 Gordon*
Stinnett Ave; tel: (410) 257-
1404; www.
chesapeakebeachwaterpark.
com; open 1100–1900
during summer. A favourite
for children on a hot day.

carriage complete the collection. Fishing charters abound, an
Chesapeake Beach is close enough to prime fishing grounds for
6-hour trip to be productive.

Accommodation and food in Chesapeake Beach

Breezy Point Campground $ *Breezy Point Rd, off Rte 261; tel: (41(*
535-0259 or (410) 535-1600 out of season for reservations – call in mi
Jan for Jul & Aug weekends; open May–Oct. Has caravan sites on th
water, with or without electric hookup, with a playground, 300
fishing and crabbing pier and a half-mile beach.

Chesapeake Beach Hotel and Spa $$ *4165 Mears Ave; tel: (410) 25.*
5596 or (866) 312-5596; www.chesapeakebeachresortspa.com. Full servic
modern hotel right on the waterfront.

Rod 'n' Reel Restaurant $$ *Rte 261 and Mears Ave; tel: (410) 257-275*
or (301) 855-8351. Serves traditional seafood, many dishes grille
instead of fried.

POINT LOOKOUT

Point Lookout State Park $ *Rte 5, Scotland; tel: (301) 872-5688.*

Scheible's Fishing Center *48342 Wynne Rd, Ridge; tel: (301) 872-5182 or (800) 895-6132; http://scheibles.homestead.com.* Scheible's is a major outfitter for fishing in the Potomac and Chesapeake, with 15 charter boats and an 80-passenger headboat.

Blue and Gray Days *Fort Lincoln, Point Lookout State Park; tel: (301) 872-5688.* Civil War battles are re-enacted in May or Jun.

elow Point Lookout Civil War camp

Point Lookout State Park is at the tip of the peninsula where the Potomac meets Chesapeake Bay. Along with good canoeing (rentals available) and swimming, there is fishing from the shore and from a pier extending 250m into Chesapeake Bay. Fort Lincoln served as a prisoner-of-war camp for Confederate soldiers during the Civil War, and monuments honour the 3,364 buried there. The earth embankments of the old fort are open to the public, and some of the buildings have been reconstructed. The park's Visitors Center has displays on the Civil War camp, as well as nature exhibits, including live reptiles and amphibians. At its very tip, Point Lookout Lighthouse is replete with ghost stories.

Accommodation and food in Point Lookout

Point Lookout State Park $ *Rte 5, Scotland; tel: (301) 872-5688.* Has a large camp-pitch, one area of it on the water. Inland sites may have annoying biting insects.

Scheible's Crab Pot Restaurant $–$$ *48342 Wynne Rd, Ridge; tel: (301) 872-5185.* Serves seafood, plus Maryland fried chicken. Look for bargains weeknights and by ordering 'basket'-style meals.

PORT TOBACCO

ⓘ Charles County Tourism Division
103 Centennial St, Suite C, La Plata; tel: (301) 645-0558 or (800) 766-3386; www.explorecharlescomd.com

ⓗ Port Tobacco Courthouse and Museum $ Chapel Point Rd, off Rte 6; tel: (301) 934-4313; open Apr–Oct, Sat & Sun 1200–1600.

Thomas Stone House $ 6655 Rose Hill Rd, between Rtes 225 and 6; tel: (301) 392-1776; www.nps.gov/thst; open Apr–Oct Mon–Sun 0900–1700; rest of the year Wed–Sun 0900–1700.

St Ignatius Church 8855 Chapel Point Rd; tel: (301) 934-8245; www.chapelpoint.org. Mass Sat 1700, Sun 0730, 0900, 1100 & 1800, weekdays 0800.

ⓦ Reel Bass Adventures 406 Butternut Ct, La Plata; tel: (301) 932-1509. Charter fishing trips are tailored to individual skills and interests, all led by expert fishermen. They provide top-notch equipment and lures.

ⓢ Blessing of the Fleet First Sat in Aug 1530. This is part of the Potomac River Festival.

Port Tobacco, founded in 1634 was a thriving seaport, but all that is left of it now is a pretty cluster of 18th-century homes and a reconstruction of the brick **Courthouse**, now a museum. A museum gift shop has local crafts and books. **Thomas Stone House** is a gracious five-part Georgian plantation built around 1770 by Thomas Stone, a signer of the Declaration of Independence and Articles of Confederation. The beautifully panelled East Room is the highlight.

Overlooking Chapel Point, **St Ignatius Church** dates from 1798, on the site of the first Catholic services, which were then illegal. It is the oldest continuously active Roman Catholic parish in the US, with a relic of the True Cross brought by its founder. Beside St Thomas Manor, a Jesuit residence built 100 years later, the small Cook's House has an open bulkhead leading to a tunnel out to the hillside. Originally used to smuggle priests, it later hid slaves on the Underground Railroad. The sunset view from the church, the stones of its churchyard silhouetted against the orange sky, is outstanding.

Accommodation and food in Port Tobacco

La Plata Best Western Inn $ 6900 Crain Hwy (Hwy 301), La Plata; tel: (301) 934-4900 or (800) 528-1234. A modern and comfortable hotel on the major route through the region.

Captain Billy's Crabhouse $–$$ Pope's Creek Rd, off Rte 301 Newburg, tel: (301) 932-4323; www.captbillys.com. Renowned for its big trays of hardshell crabs 'in the rough'. Don't be shy, they will show you how to attack these delicacies with a mallet and extract every last morsel. Crab cakes, fried oysters, scallops and fried chicken are on the menu if you don't relish this quintessential Maryland feast.

**Casey Jones Restaurant $$** 417 E Charles St, La Plata; tel: (301) 932-6226. Has fine (very fine indeed) dining and a separate pub ($) serving unique pizzas. In the restaurant expect the likes of grilled duck with foie gras.

Brictoria Cottage at Charlotte Hall $$–$$$ 7535 Poplar St, Charlotte Hall; tel: (301) 884-8699; www.brictoriacottage.com. Lovely cottage set on 8 acres with all modern amenities including washer and dryer.

Above
St Ignatius Church

PRINCE FREDERICK

Fairview Information Center 8120 S Maryland Blvd, Owings; tel: (410) 257-0381; www.co.cal.md.us/visitors

Battle Creek Cypress Swamp Gray's Rd, off Rte 506; tel: (410) 535-5327; www.calvertparks.org; open Apr–Sept Tue–Sat 1000–1700, Sun 1300– 1700; Oct–Mar until 1630. Free.

Calvert Cliffs State Park $ Rte 765, off Rte 4, Lusby; tel: (301) 743-6613; www.dnr.state.md.us; open dawn–dusk.

Jefferson Patterson Park and Museum 10515 Mackall Rd (Rte 56), St Leonard; tel: (410) 586-8501; www.jefpat.org; open year-round; Visitors center mid-Apr–mid-Oct Wed–Sun 1000–1700. Free.

Chesapeake Market Place 5015 St Leonard Rd, St Leonard; tel: (410) 586-3725; www.chesapeakemarketplace.com; open Wed–Sun 1000–1700; auctions Wed & Fri. Seventy dealers ply their wares here.

Calvert County Market Prince Frederick Shopping Center, 985 Solomons Island Rd; www.calvertcountrymarket.com; open Mon–Sat 0700–1900, Sun 0900–1600. Fresh produce, seafood, fruit, baked good and crafts.

Right
Jefferson Patterson Park, Native American dwelling

Battle Creek Cypress Swamp is a fascinating, if somewhat spooky world of tall cypress trees whose knobbly knees poke up through the water. The Nature Center shows the life cycles of the trees and the swamp, which a boardwalk takes you through with dry feet. At **Calvert Cliffs State Park**, few can resist the lure of a beach strewn with fossils from the Miocene Epoch, teeth of sharks that swam there millions of years ago. The beach is accessed by a woodland trail.

Evidence of human history dates back 12,000 years at **Jefferson Patterson Park and Museum**. Trails and exhibits show how people used the land, and the Discovery Room provides binoculars, field guides and Indian and Colonial tools and games you can use outside. Other excellent hands-on activities teach about early life and archaeologists' work. Exhibits illustrate the conservation of artefacts, underwater archaeology, the Battle of Leonard's Creek and local ecology. A replica Native American campsite with a reed house is on the Woodland Trail. At the Agricultural Center old tools are displayed and often demonstrated.

Accommodation and food in Prince Frederick

Old Field Inn $$ 485 Main St; tel: (410) 535-1054 or (301) 855-1054; www.oldfieldinn.com. The menu is evenly split between meat and seafood, with choices such as filet mignon, crab imperial, potato crusted sea bass and veal Florentine.

SOLOMONS ISLAND

Tourist Information *14175 Solomons Island Rd; tel: (410) 326-6027; open daily 0900–1700; www.ecalvert.com*

Calvert Marine Museum and Drum Point Lighthouse *$$ 1415 Solomons Island Rd; tel: (410) 326-2042; www.calvertmarinemuseum. com. Tour times vary.*

Elizabeth S *$$ 105 Charles St; tel: (301) 997-0852; www.headboatfishing. com. Full service cruise boat for 77 passengers, offering two trips daily plus special events.*

J C Lore and Sons Oyster House *$ Solomons Island Rd; open Jun–Aug daily 1000–1630; May and Sept weekends.*

Cove Point Lighthouse *$ Shuttle bus from Calvert Marine Museum; tel: (410) 326-2042; open Jun–Aug daily; weekends May & Sept 1000–1600.*

Annmarie Garden *$ Dowell Rd, off Rte 2/4; tel: (410) 326-4640; www.annmariegarden.org; open daily 1000–1600.*

Sea Dive and Bicycle *13876 Solomons Island Rd, Solomons Island; tel: (410) 326-4386.*

Bunky's Charter Boat Rentals *$$$ 14448 Solomons Island Rd, Solomons; tel: (410) 326-3241; www. bunkyscharterboats.com. The headboat Marchelle leaves at 0700 and 1300 daily, as well as charters.*

Almost completely surrounded by water, Solomons Island is popular for fishing, boating and the outstanding **Calvert Marine Museum** whose well-designed exhibits illuminate the natural and human history of the Chesapeake, covering everything from the Miocene Sea to the Triangle Trade and the War of 1812. Underwater exploration vehicles, the Navy in World War II, watermen and oyster packing are all explored and fossil collections help recognise those found on the beaches. An aquarium and river otters are highlights for children.

Drum Point Lighthouse stands outside on tall stilts, and you can climb inside to see the keepers' quarters and light. In the water and sheds below are vintage craft, including the *Wm B Tennison*. **J C Lore and Sons Oyster House** is a working 1888 cannery with all of its original equipment. A video tells the story of the island, fishermen and packers.

Annmarie Garden combines gardens with public art space, a series of outdoor rooms, each by a prominent artist or sculptor. One is a small dance stage, another a series of wooden ramps leading to treetop level in the lovely wooded grounds.

Accommodation and food in Solomons Island

CD Café $–$$ *14350 Solomons Island Rd, Solomons; tel: (410) 326-3877; www.cdcafe.info.* Offers espresso and pastries or creative dinners using fresh local ingredients. It may be crowded at dinnertime.

Solomons Victorian Inn $–$$ *125 Charles St, Solomons; tel: (410) 326-4811; www.solomonsvictorianinn.com.* Eight rooms and a suite have private baths; those in the new Carriage House have private entrances. A full breakfast is served in a glass-enclosed porch overlooking the harbour and gardens.

ST MARY'S CITY

ⓘ St Mary's County Tourism *23115 Leonard Hall Dr, Leonardtown; tel: (301) 475-200 ext 1404 or (800) 327-9023.*

ⓗ Historic St Mary's City $$ *Rte 5; tel: (240) 895-4990 or (800) 762-1634; www.stmaryscity.org; opening dates and hours vary.*

Patuxent River Naval Air Museum *Pegg Rd, Lexington Park; tel: (301) 863-7418; open Tue–Sun 1000–1700. Free.*

St Mary's County Crab Festival *Leonardtown; tel: (301) 475-200 ext 1404; www. stmaryscrabfestival.com; mid-Jun. As well as the obvious, this includes an antique car show and craft sale.*

Tidewater Archaeology Dig Days *Historic St Mary's City; tel: (800) 762-1634; www.stmaryscity.org; late Jul. Visitors can join in archaeological excavations.*

Grand Militia Muster *Historic St Mary's City; tel: (800) 762-1634; 3rd weekend Oct. The largest 17th-century military re-enactment in the country.*

If you look for the 'city' in tiny St Mary's City, you are not alone: archaeologists and historians have been digging it up for years, trying to reconstruct what was once Maryland's thriving first settlement. Costumed interpreters at **Historic St Mary's City** re-create the setting, even speaking in early 1600s language.

Buildings are being reconstructed on their original sites in four main areas connected by roads and wide walking paths. Begin at the Visitors Center for background displays and film, then visit the nearby cluster of reconstructed bark and thatch longhouses. A farmhouse shows homely arts and period farm skills.

Around the reconstruction of the imposing brick 1676 State House are the Ordinary, an early lodging, and the merchant ship *Dove*, replicating the one that brought the original settlers from England. The house skeletons along the roads mark the sites of buildings identified by archaeologists, to be reconstructed by costumed interpreters.

Patuxent River Naval Air Museum will fascinate anyone interested in the space programme or flight, with collections of aircraft and air-related hardware and exhibits. Learn how a jet engine works, what test pilots do, how gear and equipment are tested. Ask to see the films, especially the one on the Blue Angels, the US Navy's Red Arrow counterpart.

Accommodation and food in St Mary's City

See Solomons Island for all tourist services.

Opposite
Archaeologist at work in Calvert Marine Museum

Right
Historic St Mary's City

Suggested tour

Cecil's Old Mill
Indian Bridge Rd, Great Mills; tel: (301) 994-1510; www.stmarysart.com; open mid-Mar–Oct Thur–Sun 1000–1700; Nov & Dec daily 1100–1700.

St Clement's Island – Potomac River Museum $ *38370 Point Breeze Rd, Coltons Point; tel: (301) 769-2222; open Mon–Fri 0900–1700, Sat & Sun 1200–1700.*

Below
St Mary's City

Total distance: 182 miles.

Time: Driving time 5–6 hours. Allow 3 days with sightseeing. Those with limited time should see Historic St Mary's City, Calvert Cliffs and the Calvert Marine Museum.

Links: From Baltimore, follow Rte 2 south. From Fredericksburg, Virginia, US-301 crosses the Potomac and joins the route south of Port Tobacco. From Washington DC, Rte 5 (Beltway Exit 7) connects Washington to the end of the suggested route.

Route: Travel south from **Annapolis** on Rte 2, diverting east on Rte 260 to **CHESAPEAKE BEACH** ❶ and following Rte 261 south past **Breezy Point Beach** to Rte 263. Rejoin Rte 2, now 2/4, and continue south to **PRINCE FREDERICK** ❷. Continue south on the 2/4 past **Calvert Cliffs State Park** towards **SOLOMONS ISLAND** ❸ just before the bridge over the Patuxent River. Cross the bridge and turn southwest onto Rte 235.

Follow Rte 235 south past the **Patuxent River Naval Air Museum** to its junction with Rte 5, following Rte 5 left (south) to its end at **POINT LOOKOUT** ❹. Retrace your route to the intersection, then continue north on Rte 5 to **ST MARY'S CITY** ❺. Stay on Rte 5, which heads west, through Great Mills, worth a stop for historic **Cecil's Old Mill**, an artisan's shop selling and demonstrating Maryland-made crafts.

Rte 5 continues through **Leonardtown**, boasting a museum in an old jail. Shortly past Leonardtown, bear left on to Rte 234 through the town of **Clements**.

Continue west on Rte 234 until it ends at US-301, turning north. In about miles, turn left onto Rte 6 (Port Tobacco Rd), continuing to **PORT TOBACCO** ❻, checking out **St Ignatius Church** in the village. Back at Rte 6, take Rose Hill Rd north to visit the **Thomas Stone House**. Continue to Rte 225, turning right to **La Plata** then left on US-301, which will return you to Annapolis or take you to Rte 5, north to the Beltway or into Washington DC.

Farthing's Ordinary

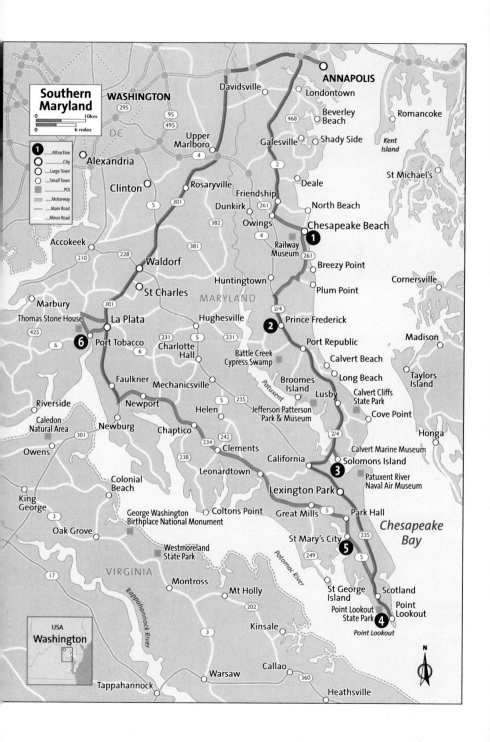

Southern Maryland

0	10km
0	6 miles

- ① Attraction
- ○ City
- ○ Large Town
- ○ Small Town
- ▨ POI
- Motorway
- Main Road
- Minor Road

WASHINGTON

295

95

495

D.C.

Alexandria

Clinton

Accokeek

210

228

Marbury

Thomas Stone House

425

6

Waldorf

St Charles

La Plata

Port Tobacco

301

231

6

Faulkner

Riverside

Caledon Natural Area

Newburg

Owens

301

King George

3

Oak Grove

Colonial Beach

Westmoreland State Park

VIRGINIA

17

Tappahannock

Rappahannock River

Montross

Mt Holly

202

Kinsale

Warsaw

Callao

360

Heathsville

Upper Marlboro

4

Rosaryville

301

5

Dunkirk

Friendship

261

Owings

382

4

Hughesville

231

5

231

Charlotte Hall

Mechanicsville

Newport

Helen

5

235

Chaptico

234

242

238

Clements

Leonardtown

California

Coltons Point

Great Mills

5

St Mary's City

249

Potomac River

St George Island

Point Lookout State Park

Point Lookout

Davidsville

MARYLAND

Huntingtown

Battle Creek Cypress Swamp

Broomes Island

Jefferson Patterson Park & Museum

Lexington Park

Park Hall

235

5

Scotland

Point Lookout

ANNAPOLIS

Londontown

Beverley Beach

468

Galesville

2

Shady Side

Deale

North Beach

261

Chesapeake Beach ①

Railway Museum

261

Breezy Point

Plum Point

2/4

Prince Frederick ②

Port Republic

Calvert Beach

Long Beach

Lusby

Calvert Cliffs State Park

Cove Point

2/4

Calvert Marine Museum

Solomons Island ③

Patuxent River Naval Air Museum

Patuxent

Romancoke

Kent Island

St Michael's

Cornersville

Madison

Taylors Island

Honga

Chesapeake Bay

⑤

⑥

Faulkner

Newburg

USA

Washington

N

North Chesapeake Bay

Ratings

Entertainment	●●●●○
Historical sights	●●●●○
Beaches	●●●○○
Children	●●●○○
Gastronomy	●●●○○
Nature and wildlife	●●●○○
Art and museums	●●○○○
Shopping and crafts	●●○○○

The land at the head of the Chesapeake lies between wide rivers that feed the bay, and the entire shore is deeply cut by tidal estuaries: the Wye, the Chester, the Sassafras, the Elk and the Northeast. Kent and Wye islands form stepping stones that narrow the bay enough for a bridge to span it. Few cities, none of any size, intrude on the rural land and seascapes of the Eastern Shore's northern reaches.

Apart from the destruction of Havre de Grace and Georgetown in the War of 1812, this corner of the bay has enjoyed a relatively quiet history. Today its towns look much as they have for the last century, with gracious old homes, the harbours on their tidal rivers now filled with pleasure boats instead of the skipjacks that once formed the core of the economy.

CHESAPEAKE CITY

P Chesapeake City is famed for police who ticket non-residents at any excuse, even while unloading luggage. Use only your lodging, restaurant or the museum car parks.

ℹ C&D Canal Museum *815 Bethel Rd, beside the canal; tel: (410) 885-5622; www. nap.usace.army.mil; open Apr–Sept Mon–Sat 0800– 1615, Sun 1000–1800.*

The Chesapeake and Delaware Canal saves ships bound for Baltimore about 300 miles and the local amusement is watching barges go by. Learn more about this interesting waterway at the well-designed **C&D Canal Museum**, where an animated model shows how locks work. The town's historic buildings centre around Bohemia Ave.

Accommodation and food in Chesapeake City

The Blue Max $–$$ *300 S Bohemia Ave; tel: (410) 885-2781 or (877) 725-8362; www.bluemaxinn.com.* Has large attractive rooms and a lovely guest parlour, as well as a long front veranda for relaxing.

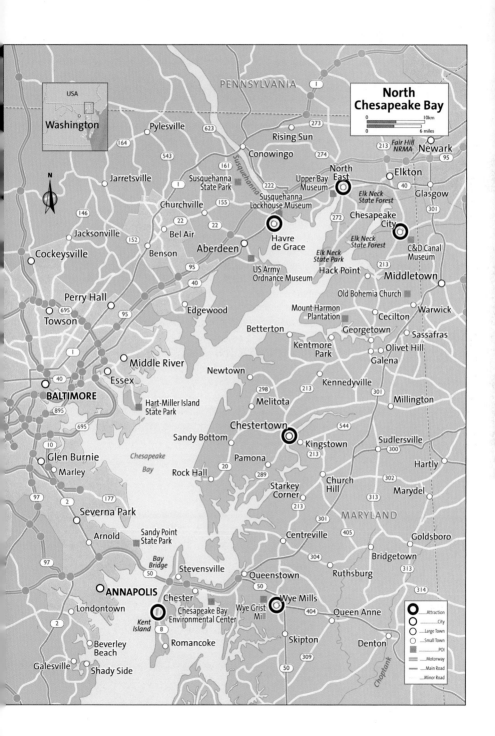

Boutiques, craft shops and antique emporia fill historic buildings along Bohemia Ave.

Chesapeake Inn Restaurant $$ *605 2nd St; tel: (410) 885-2040; www.chesapeakeinn.com.* Skilfully blends Italian culinary traditions with local seafood. In summer lighter dishes of soft-crab or crab cake sandwiches, pasta and creative pizzas are served on the deck.

Bayard House $$$ *11 Bohemia Ave; tel: (410) 885-5040; www.bayardhouse.com.* Does wonderful things with local seafood, such as stuffing chillies with crab and shrimp.

CHESTERTOWN

Kent County Tourism *400 High St, 2nd Floor; tel: (410) 778-0416; www.kentcounty.com*

Historic Walking Tours $ *High St; tel: (410) 778-2898.* Tours of Chestertown begin at the park.

Geddes-Piper House Museum $ *101 Church Alley; tel: (410) 778-3499; open May–Oct Sat & Sun 1300–1600.*

On Memorial Day weekend, Chestertown commemorates its own 'Tea Party' in 1774, similar to Boston's, when crates of tea were dumped into the Chester River, with costumed re-enactments, crafts and a parade.

Prim rows of homes from the Colonial and later eras form Chestertown's historic district, highlighted by the restored 1780s **Geddes-Piper House Museum**, furnished with fine period pieces. Widehall is an elaborate 1770 town home next to the town landing, where Chestertown's Tea Party took place. Queen and Water Sts are lined by tradesmen's and merchants' homes from the 18th and early 19th centuries.

Accommodation and food in Chestertown

Play It Again Sam $ *108 S Cross St; tel: (410) 778-2688; open Mon–Sat 0700–1530, Sun 0900–1600.* Serves bountiful croissant sandwiches, pie, cake, gourmet coffees and ice cream.

Imperial Hotel $–$$ *208 High St; tel: (401) 778-5000 or (800) 295-0014; fax: (410) 778-9662; www.imperialchestertown.com.* Restored Victorian hotel with verandahs overlooking downtown.

Right
Chestertown boardwalk

White Swan Tavern $–$$ *231 High St; tel: (410) 778-2300; fax: (410) 778-4543; www.whiteswantavern.com.* Dates from 1733, with beautifully restored rooms and suites furnished in period antiques. The original kitchen has a walk-in fireplace. Afternoon tea is included, also served to the public (*Thur–Tue 1500–1700*), reservation recommended.

Blue Heron Café $$ *226 Cannon St; tel: (410) 778-0188; www.blueheroncafe.com.* Features regional ingredients in creative New American dishes, for lunch and dinner Mon–Sat.

HAVRE DE GRACE

ⓘ Havre de Grace Visitor Center *450 Pennington Ave; tel: (410) 939-2100; www. havredegracemd.com.* The center offers maps, events listings, a visitors' guide and tours.

ⓠ Skipjack *Martha Lewis* *Congress Ave; tel: (410) 939-4078; www. skipjackmarthalewis.org; tours every 2 hours Sat and Sun 1200–1800.* A rare working oyster boat offers sailing tours focusing on the environment, oysters, birds and marine life.

ⓝ Concord Point Lighthouse *700 Concord St; www. lighthousefriends.com; tel: (410) 939-3213; open Apr– Oct Sat & Sun 1300–1700.*

Decoy Museum $ *215 Giles St; tel: (410) 939-3739; www.decoymuseum. com; open daily 1100–1600.*

Susquehanna Lockhouse Museum $ *Erie St; tel: (410) 939-5780; open Thur–Mon 1300–1700.*

US Army Ordnance Museum *Aberdeen Proving Grd, Rte 22 Aberdeen; tel: (410) 278-3602; www.ordmusfound.org; open daily 1000–1645.*

British travellers are far more welcome today than they were in 1813, When they torched the town. Only the Flemish-bond brick Episcopal Church and a few homes remained, but the result was the town rebuilt in the elegant Victorian mansions that you see today, especially on Union St.

Granite **Concord Point Lighthouse** was built in 1827 and the stone house opposite was the keeper's house. A boardwalk promenade through a bird-filled tidal marsh connects to the **Decoy Museum**, where displays show the history of decoy-making and their artists. Tydings Park, at the end of the promenade, has picnic tables and a playground.

At the opposite side of town, the **Susquehanna Lockhouse Museum** was home and office to the lock-keeper. A reconstructed pivot bridge is at the site.

In neighbouring Aberdeen, the **US Army Ordnance Museum** explores the history of firearms with collections of rare breech-loaders, Sharps and other early arms. Outside, the 'Mile of Tanks' fills fields row on row.

Accommodation and food in Havre de Grace

Currier House Bed and Breakfast $–$$ *800 S Market St; tel: (410) 939-7886 or (800) 827-2889; www.currier-bb.com.* One of the few homes to survive the War of 1812, in a quiet neighbourhood with a view of the lighthouse.

Price's Seafood $–$$ *654 Water St; tel: (410) 939-2782.* A really old-fashioned crab house, with no pretensions and lots of character.

The Crazy Swede $$ *400 N Union Ave; tel: (410) 939-5446.* Gives Chesapeake seafood dishes a new look, combining veal with shrimp and crabmeat and offering many non-seafood choices. One- and two-bedroom suites include breakfast.

MacGregor's Restaurant & Tavern $$ *331 St John St; tel: (410) 939-3003; www.macgregorsrestaurant.com. Open every day for lunch and supper, Sun for brunch too.* Every table has a view of the water.

Havre de Grace Maritime Museum
$ 100 Lafayette St; tel: (410) 939-4800, www. hdgmaritimemuseum.org. Explores the rich seafaring and shipping heritage of the Chesapeake Bay.

Tidewater Grille $$ *300 Franklin St; tel: (410) 939-3313.* Overlooks the bay, serving lunch and dinner from a varied menu that includes fried or broiled (grilled) crab cakes.

Vandiver Inn $$ *301 S Union Ave; tel: (410) 939-5200 or (800) 245 1655; www.vandiverinn.com.* Occupies a grand and elegantly decorated 1886 mansion, listed on the National Historic Register.

KENT ISLAND AND WYE MILLS

Queen Anne's County publishes an excellent free *Explore Our History and Heritage* packet covering the area from its aboriginal inhabitants. Available at (888) 400-7787 or at www.historicqac.org

The River Plantation $$$ *511 Pintail Point Ln, Queenstown; tel: (410) 827-7029 or (800) 679-1777.*

Chesapeake Bay Environmental Center $ *600 Discovery Ln, Grasonville; tel: (410) 827-6694.*

Terrapin Nature Park *Exit 37 on Rte 50/301, Stevensville; tel: (703) 324-8702.*

Chesapeake Exploration Center *Chester (Kent Narrows); tel: (410) 604-2100; open Mon–Fri 0830–1630, Sat & Sun 1000–1600.*

Wye Grist Mill $ *Wye Mills; tel: (410) 827-3850; open Apr–Oct Mon–Thur 1000–1300, Fri–Sun 1000–1600 (check hours before traveling a distance), mill operates first and third Sat.*

Prime Outlets is a giant mall filled with cut-price shops, on US-50 near its split from US-301.

The River Plantation, in a beautiful bayside setting offers a sporting clays (clay pigeons) shooting course both fresh and saltwater fly fishing, waterfowl and upland bird hunting and two golf courses, both open to the public. **Chesapeake Bay Environmental Center** preserves bird habitats for great horned owls, ospreys and a variety of others Trails lead through coastal forest to a marsh boardwalk and blinds.

Historic **Stevensville** is filled with craft and antique shops, with plenty of places to eat. Rent bicycles here to explore the 6-mile trail that spans Kent Island from **Terrapin Nature Park** to the **Chesapeake Exploration Center** at Kent Narrows.

Wye Grist Mill still grinds grain as it has since the Revolution. A small museum has displays on local agriculture. Old Wye Church was built in 1721, with box pews, a graceful centre pulpit and a rare royal coat of arms. Most were destroyed during the Revolution.

Accommodation and food in Kent Island and Wye Mills

Tuckahoe State Park $ *13070 Crouse Mill Rd, Queen Anne; tel: (410) 820-1668; open mid-Apr–mid-Oct.* Has caravan sites and tent pitches, no reservations.

Harris Crab House $–$$ *Kent Narrows, Grasonville; tel: (410) 824-9500 www.harriscrabhouse.com; open daily from 1100.* Big, noisy and busy, so expect to wait in the evening for a brown-paper-covered table and a tray of crabs – messy, but delicious and a quintessential Chesapeake experience.

Matapeake State Park $ Kent Island; tel: (410) 479-1619. Picnic tables overlook a long fishing pier, especially scenic at sunset. Free picnic sites are at Wye Grist Mill and Wye Oak.

Hemingway's $$ *US-50/301, Pier One Marina, Kent Island; tel: (410) 643-CRAB (2722); open daily from 1100.* Brings unusual flair to seafood favourites, with Caribbean and Florida Keys influences in the fruity sauces and tongue-tingling spices. The fried oysters are excellent.

Kent Manor Inn $$ *500 Kent Manor Dr, Kent Island; tel: (410) 643-5757 or (800) 820-4511.* Occupies a beautifully restored plantation home on a tidewater farm, with its own docks and walking trails, and serves peerless crab cakes, and other delicacies at lunch and dinner daily.

NORTH EAST

Cecil County Tourism 68 Heather Ln, Suite 43, Perryville; tel: (800) 232-4595; www.seececil.org

Upper Bay Museum 219 Walnut St; tel: (410) 287-2675; open Wed–Sun 1200–1600. Free.

Elk Neck State Park $ Rte 272; tel: (410) 287-5333. Has a beach on the Susquehanna which is shallow water for some distance, especially good for children.

Day Basket Factory 714 Main St; tel: (410) 287-6100. Baskets are made entirely by hand, starting with white oak planks. Watch the process and buy these individually crafted signed baskets at the shop.

A Decoy Show takes place at the Upper Bay Museum (see above) on the third weekend in Oct.

The **Upper Bay Museum** records the culture of the upper bay, along with collecting boats, watermen's tools, decoys and Native American stone weapons.

Elk Neck State Park crowns the high point that separates Elk River from the Susquehanna at the head of the Chesapeake. Turkey Point Lighthouse guards the tip, its steady solar-powered beacon still active. The main C&D Canal channel is to the left, a good place to watch ships and barges. Walk the trail around the point, but shun the dangerously undercut cliffs.

Accommodation and food in North East

Woody's Crab House $ *29 Main St; tel: (410) 287-3541; open Mar–Dec.* A casual waterside eatery with trays of hardshell crabs and fried fish.

The Mill House Bed and Breakfast $–$$ *102 Mill Lane; tel: (410) 287-3532.* In the town centre, dating from the early 1700s.

Best Western Northeast Inn $$ *39 Elwoods Rd; tel: (410) 287-5450 or (800) 780-7234; http://book.bestwestern.com.* Modern hotel, indoor pool, hot tub, exercise room and guest laundry.

Opposite
Kent Manor Inn, Kent Island

Right
Lighthouse at Turkey Point

Suggested tour

Skipjack Cove Marina Tel: (410) 275-2122; www.skipjackcove.com. On the Sassafras River in Georgetown, you can hire a kayak or take a guided trip up the tidal creeks.

Mount Harmon Plantation $ 600 Mt Harmon Rd (off Grove Neck Rd, Earleville; tel: (410) 275-8819; open for tours May–Oct Thur–Sun 1000–1500.

Waterman's Museum $ 20880 Rock Hall Ave, Rock Hall; tel: (410) 778-6697; open daily. Enquire at adjacent Marina for key.

Rock Hall Museum Town Hall, Main St, Rock Hall; tel: (410) 778-1399; open Sat & Sun 1100–1400.

Tolchester Revisted Museum $ Main St, Rock Hall; tel: (410) 639-9133; open Sat & Sun 1100–1500. Captures the spirit of the amusement park and resort that brought thousands of visitors by steamboat.

Kitty Knight House $ Rte 213, Georgetown; tel: (410) 648-5200 or (800) 404-8712; fax: (410) 275-1800. Overlooks the Sassafras River with a variety of rooms and some suites for families. The dining room ($$) is popular, serving dishes such as cashew-crusted chicken breast or tomato-basil crab crêpes.

Total distance: 160 miles, 208 with detours.

Time: 4 hours' driving time – allow 2–3 days. Those with limited time should concentrate on Chestertown and Havre de Grace.

Links: Baltimore and Annapolis are on the route. At the eastern end of Bay Bridge in Annapolis, follow US-50 south to Easton to begin the Eastern Shore itinerary, or connect to the Ocean City–Dover itinerary in Chestertown via Rte 291, which becomes Delaware Rte 6, meeting US-13 north of Dover.

Route: From **Baltimore** follow Rte 2 to US-50/301 East, crossing Bay Bridge to **KENT ISLAND ❶** and **WYE MILLS ❷**. Head north on Rte 213 to **CHESTERTOWN ❸** and continue to follow it north, crossing the Sassafras River at Georgetown.

Detour: In Cecilton, turn left on to Rte 282 to **Mount Harmon Plantation**, at the end of a long lane, its terraced boxwood parterre gardens framed by wisteria vines. The Georgian manor house dates from 1730 and is furnished with American and British antiques.

Continue on Rte 213 to **CHESAPEAKE CITY ❹** and north to **Elkton** where a left turn on to Rte 7 leads to **NORTH EAST ❺**.

Detour: Rte 213 continues north to Fair Hill, and the large **Fair Hill Natural Resource Management Area**, known for its thoroughbred racing centre and excellent fishing in Big Elk Creek. The 1860 Tawes Drive Covered Bridge is in the northern section.

From North East, Rte 272 leads south into **Elk Neck State Park**. Backtrack to Rte 7, going west to **HAVRE DE GRACE ❻**. US-40 continues south past Aberdeen and back to Baltimore.

Also worth exploring

Rock Hall, west of Chestertown on Rte 20, celebrates its roots at the **Waterman's Museum**, where exhibits show tools used by the crabbing, fishing and oyster fleets that worked from its harbour. The **Rock Hall Museum** continues the theme, with models and displays on shipping, plus Native American artefacts. Beyond, Eastern Neck Wildlife Refuge is a place to spot migrating and nesting birds and enjoy views of the bay.

Right
Chestertown

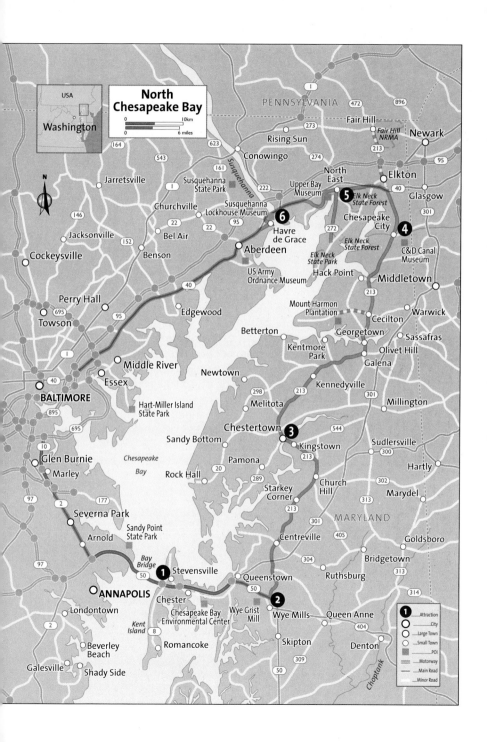

Ratings

Beaches	●●●●●
Children	●●●●●
Nature and wildlife	●●●●●
Entertainment	●●●○○
Gastronomy	●●●○○
Historical sights	●●●○○
Shopping and crafts	●●●○○
Art and museums	●○○○○

Ocean City and Delaware Shore

Beaches are what the area does best, and travellers can choose between two sharply contrasting styles. The major resorts of Ocean City and Rehoboth Beach are filled with activity, entertainment and people, while the state and national parks of Assateague, Fenwick Island and Cape Henlopen offer miles of beach with quiet stretches even in mid-summer.

A long narrow barrier island lies offshore from Cape Henlopen to Assateague, a national park known best for its wild horses. During a hurricane in 1933, the ocean cut an inlet between Ocean City and Assateague, but this is the only break. Between the barrier island and mainland are wide salt ponds that provide bird habitats and opportunities for water sports.

ASSATEAGUE ISLAND AND BERLIN

ⓘ Assateague Island National Seashore Visitor Center *Rte 611, Berlin; tel: (401) 641-1441; www.nps.gov/asis; open daily 0900–1700.*

Inside the federally managed Assateague National Seashore is Assateague Island State Park, both with tourist services, such as campgrounds and canoe/bicycle rentals. At the Visitor Center are exhibits, several excellent films and a touch tank where you can play with sea creatures. Adjacent is a picnic area. To see the wild horses which roam freely, drive slowly along the park roads. On hot summer days, look for them on the beach.

Three short nature trails explore the park ecosystems, including dunes, forest and marsh, a habitat rich in song and wading shore birds. Three miles of bike paths explore other areas. Several historic sites are marked by signs, one explaining the remains of a shipwreck.

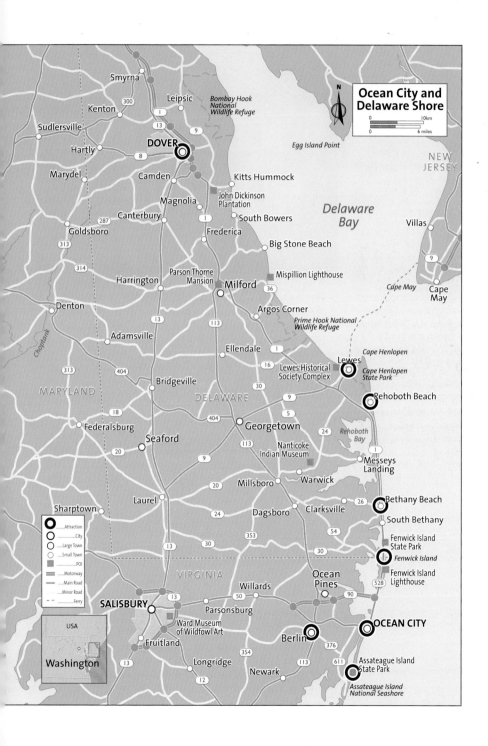

P The only car parks on Assateague Island are at the Visitor Centers, from which you can walk or cycle into the park, or at the beaches. There are few roads on the island.

M **Taylor House Museum** $ *Main and Baker Sts; tel: (410) 641-1019; www. taylorhousemuseum.org; open Jun–Oct Mon, Wed, Fri & Sat 1300–1600.*

In the Berlin–Ocean City area more than a dozen golf courses are open to the public.

Assateague Island National Seashore
Tel: (401) 641-2120; www.assateagueisland.com. Crabbing and bay explorations in canoes furnished by the park need to be reserved beforehand. Canoes may be hired at the Bayside picnic area, past the campsite.

Rainy Day Canoe *Race Track Rd, Berlin; tel: (410) 641-5029; open daily 0700–1600.* Also a local bait and tackle shop.

On Assateague Island, bicycle hires are at the end of Bayside Dr, near the picnic area.

The **Globe Theater** in Berlin has a crafts gallery on the second floor, with baskets, pottery, woodenware, quilts, decoys and more. Downstairs is a bookstore and gourmet food shop.

Often used as a film set, Berlin has attractive historic buildings in the town centre, including the art deco Globe Theater, now a venue for crafts, a café, shops and classic films. The **Taylor House Museum** is known for interior decorative features, with furnished rooms and local artefacts. A short nature trail with boardwalks enters the waterfowl nesting habitats at the Stephen Decatur Memorial Park.

Accommodation and food in Assateague Island and Berlin

The Atlantic Hotel $–$$ *2 N Main St; tel: (410) 641-3589 or (800) 814-7672; www.atlantichotel.com.* A historic hotel with restored Victorian rooms furnished with marble-topped and other Victorian pieces. The elegant dining room (**$$$**) updates a continental menu. The informal **Drummer's Café ($$)** serves lunch and dinner daily.

Holland House $–$$ *5 Bay St, Berlin; tel: (410) 641-1956; www.hollandhousebandb.com.* Friendly B&B.

Assateague Crab House $$ *Rte 611 near the park entrance; tel: (410) 641-4330.* Serves seasonal seafood dishes, including calamari, along with hard and soft-shelled crabs.

Assateague Island $$ *Tel: (410) 641-3030 or (410) 641-1441.* Camp pitches face both the bay and ocean sides of the island; open, unshaded and insect-ridden, but close to beaches, fishing, canoeing, biking and walking trails.

Merry Sherwood Plantation $$ *US-113; tel: (410) 641-2112 or (800) 660-0358; fax: (410) 641-9528; www.merrysherwood.com.* An eye-catching plantation house surrounded by trees and gardens. The interior is sumptuous, decorated with fine antiques and works of art and a full breakfast is served.

Above
The Taylor House Museum

DOVER

ℹ Delaware State Visitor Center *Duke of York and Federal Sts; tel: (302) 739-4266; www.history.delaware.gov; open Mon–Fri 0830–1630, Sat 0900–1700, Sun 1330–1630.*

Ⓒ Victorian Dover Historic District Tour *Tel: (302) 678-2040; daily by appointment.*

Ⓜ Meetinghouse Galleries $ *316 S Governors Ave; tel: (302) 739-4266.*

Delaware Agricultural Museum and Village $ *866 N DuPont Hwy (US-13); tel: (302) 734-1618; www. agriculturalmuseum.org; open Tue–Sat 1000–1600, Sun 1300–1600.*

John Dickinson Plantation *340 Kitts Hummock Rd, off US-113; tel: (302) 739-3277; open Tue–Sat 1000–1530, Sun 1330–1630. Free.*

Bombay Hook National Wildlife Refuge $ *2591 Whitehall Neck Rd, Smyrna; tel: (302) 653-6872; www.fws.gov/ northeast/bombayhook*

Ⓢ Spence's Bazaar *550 S New St; tel: (302) 734-3441; open Tue and Fri. This flea market also has auctions and an Amish food market.*

Public gardens bloom all over town, with the biggest display in the Plaza on Loockerman St. **Meeting House Galleries**, in a 1790 church, shows Delaware archaeology and small town life.

Delaware Agricultural Museum and Village demonstrates farm life throughout the state's history, with exhibits and historic buildings. **John Dickinson Plantation** is furnished with 18th-century antiques, and reconstructed outbuildings show life on a plantation of the time.

Bombay Hook National Wildlife Refuge preserves coastal habitat for birds migrating on the Atlantic Flyway. Roads and trails lead to observation towers.

Accommodation and food in Dover

Chain lodgings run the gamut from Budget Inn to Sheraton, with few other choices.

Tango's Bistro $–$$ *Sheraton Hotel, 1570 N DuPont Hwy; tel: (302) 678-8500.* Serves contemporary dishes with an emphasis on fresh produce and lighter cooking styles.

Right
Victorian house in Dover

FENWICK ISLAND AND BETHANY BEACH

ⓘ Bethany-Fenwick Area Chamber of Commerce *Rte 1, north of Fenwick Island; tel: (302) 539-2100 or (800) 962-7873; www.bethany-fenwick.org*

ⓘ Fenwick Island State Park $ *Rte 1; tel: (302) 227-2800; www.destateparks.com; open daily 0800–sunset.*

Assawoman Wildlife Area $ *Bayville; tel: (302) 739-5297.*

DiscoverSea Shipwreck Museum *708 Ocean Hwy, Fenwick Island; tel: (302) 539-9366 or (888) 743-5524; www.discoversea.com; open daily Jun–Aug 1100–2000; Sept–May Sat & Sun 1100–1600.*

◖ Bethany Beach Boardwalk There are often art and craft shows in the summer.

Seaport Antique Village *Rte 54; tel: (302) 436-8962.* The merchandise is shown off in a museum-house setting of fully furnished rooms.

Far less crowded and commercialised than the big beach resorts to its north and south, this area features quiet dune-backed beaches enjoyed primarily by residents. Fenwick Island Lighthouse, built in 1859, is open alternate Wednesdays. At the northern edge of **Fenwick Island State Park** is a round World War II coastal defence observation tower with views as far as Cape May. The park has boat rentals, fishing, bathhouses and miles of beach. **Assawoman Wildlife Area**, on the bay enclosed by the barrier island, invites birds with its variety of habitats, and people with an observation tower and nature trails for good viewing.

Coins, jewellery, pottery, weapons and gold bars recovered from local shipwrecks fill the **DiscoverSea Shipwreck Museum**, collected by a local underwater archaeologist.

Accommodation and food in Fenwick Island and Bethany Beach

Delvecchio's Bakery $ *Bayville Shopping Center, Rte 54, Fenwick Island, tel: (302) 436-9618.* Bakes bread, pastries and doughnuts, serving them with tea or coffee at café tables.

Fenwick Inn $–$$ *13801 Coastal Hwy; tel: (410) 250-1100 or (800, 492-1873; http://fenwickinn.com.* Modern high-rise resort close to the beach; check their website for special summer week rates.

DiFebo's Restaurant $$ *789 Garfield Pkwy, Bethany Beach; tel: (302, 539-4550, take-away (302) 539-4914; www.difebos.com.* Italian restaurant with a good variety of moderately priced options.

Catch 54 $$–$$$ *Route 54, Fenwick Island; tel: (302) 436-8600, www.catch54.com.* Interesting, innovative fresh seafood menu, three-course Sunday dinner special ($$); discount on Wed and Thur evenings.

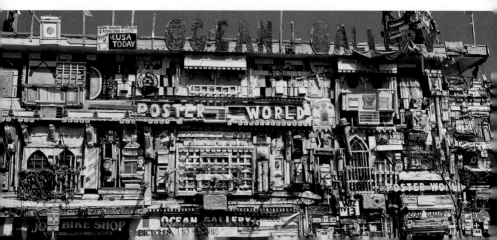

OCEAN CITY

ℹ Ocean City Convention and Visitors Bureau *4001 Coastal Hwy (Rte 528) at 40th St; tel: (410) 289-2800 or (800) 626-2326; www.ococean.com; open Mon–Fri 0830–1700, Sat 0900–1700, Sun 0930–1700; later in summer.*

ℚ *Rte 1/Coastal Hwy widens to eight lanes in the northern part of the city, with numbered short streets branching off like centipede legs. You can't possibly get lost, although trying to drive in the summer is a nightmare. A public tram ($) circles the beach and business district.*

Bike World *6 Caroline St and the boardwalk at 15th and 17th Sts; tel: (410) 289-2587; open 0600–1600. You can hire bicycles here.*

Discovery Nature Cruises $$$ *1st St Pier; tel: (410) 289-2700; Jun–Aug. There are five daily naturalist-led 90-minute trips, landing on Assateague Island.*

ℹ Ocean City Lifesaving Station Museum $ *8139 Boardwalk at the Inlet; tel: (410) 289-4991; www.ocmuseum.org; open Jun–Sept 1000–2200; call for winter hours.*

Ocean Gallery *Boardwalk and 2nd St; tel: (410) 289-5300; www.oceangallery.com*

Opposite
Ocean Gallery

Above
The boardwalk in Ocean City

Ocean City seems about to sink the narrow strip of sand it occupies, with the sheer weight of its high-rise condos and hotels, which line the 10-mile white sand beach, crowded and lively in the summer, spring and autumn. A 3-mile boardwalk stretches from the Inlet to 27th St, open to bicycles in the early morning.

The 1898 carousel at Trimper's Rides has the original hand-carved and painted animals, although it is now run by electricity. **Ocean City Lifesaving Station Museum**, an 1891 Lifesaving Station, shows the original beach resort and describes lifesaving in the region, with photographs of storm damage.

Accommodation and food in Ocean City

Commander Hotel $–$$ *1404 Baltimore Ave; tel: (410) 289-6166 or (888) 289-6166; www.commanderhotel.com.* Offers modern beachfront suites with refrigerators, microwave ovens and in-room safes, all wheelchair accessible.

Nick's Original House of Ribs $–$$ *4410 Coastal Hwy; tel: (410) 250-1984; www.nickshouseofribs.com.* Excellent crabcakes in addition to famously huge portions of ribs.

Fager's Island $$ *201 60th at Bay St; tel: (410) 524-5500.* Serves Pacific Rim cuisine. Locals gather at sunset to hear the *1812 Overture* played.

Harrison's Harbor Watch Restaurant and Raw Bar $$ *on the Inlet; tel: (410) 219-5121.* Far from intimate, but a good reliable destination for traditional and some innovative seafood dishes.

Inn on the Ocean $$ *1001 Atlantic Ave; tel: (410) 289-8894 or (877) 466-6662; www.innontheocean.com.* Also overlooks the boardwalk, each luxurious room decorated in a different colour scheme and theme.

REHOBOTH BEACH AND LEWES

ℹ Rehoboth Beach–Dewey Beach Chamber of Commerce
501 Rehoboth Ave; tel: (302) 227-2233 or (800) 441-1329; www.beach-fun.com

🚋 The Rehoboth Beach Jolly Trolley connects beaches, hotels and restaurant areas.

Queen Anne's Railroad
730 Kings Hwy, Lewes; tel: (302) 644-1720 or (888) 456-8668. You can combine a train excursion with a lunch or dinner trip in 1940s dining carriages.

Fisherman's Wharf Lewes *Tel: (302) 645-8862; www.fishlewes.com; cruises Jul and Aug.* This is the centre for whale – and dolphin – watching cruises and daily sunset cruises.

🏛 The Homestead $
12 Dodds Ln, Henlopen Acres; tel: (302) 227-8408; www.rehobothartleague.org; open Mon–Sat 1000–1600, Sun 1300–1600.

Lewes Historical Society Complex $ *110 Shipcarpenter St; tel: (302) 645-7670; www.historiclewes.org.* Several sites are included on a combined ticket.

Zwaanendael Museum $ *Kings Hwy and Savannah Rd; tel: (302) 645-1148; open Tue–Sat 1000–1630, Sun 1330–1630.*

Above
Lewes, historic house

On summer weekends, it seems as though the entire population of Washington DC has migrated to Rehoboth, which is sometimes called 'The Nation's Summer Capital'. The beach is superb, although not a place for quiet contemplation. **The Homestead**, built in 1743, is surrounded by formal boxwood gardens, a medicinal herb garden and one commemorating the coronation of Queen Elizabeth II in 1953.

Lewes is Delaware's oldest town, settled by the Dutch in 1631. It was bombarded during the War of 1812, and Cannonball House, hit in the attack, is part of the **Lewes Historical Society Complex**, along with Burton-Ingram House, Blacksmith Shop, Thompson Country Store and an early plank house. Also included is Lightship Overfalls Museum, a former seagoing beacon. **Zwaanendael Museum** tells the story of HMS *DeBraak*, a British warship sunk near Lewes in 1798.

Cape Henlopen State Park is among the east coast's finest birding sites, with forest, beach, marsh and saltwater lagoon habitats. The seaside Nature Center has an aquarium and information on current bird sitings and nature trails.

Accommodation and food in Rehoboth Beach and Lewes

Just in Thyme Square $–$$ *31 Robinson Dr, Rehoboth Beach; tel: (302) 227-3100.* Pleases all tastes with both traditional and innovative dishes featuring veal, lamb and local seafood.

The Bellmor Inn $$–$$$ *6 Christian St, Rehoboth Beach; tel: (302) 227-5800 or (800) 425-2355; www.thebellmoor.com.* A small, elegant 32-room inn on the beach, with lake access. Complimentary breakfast and afternoon tea, luggage storage and free Wi-Fi.

Eden Restaurant $$$ *23 Baltimore Ave, Rehoboth Beach; tel: (302) 227-3330; www.edenrestaurant.com.* Impeccable Asian fusion cuisine in an elegant setting.

The Inn at Canal Square $$$ *122 Market St, Lewes; tel: (302) 644-3377 or (888) 644-1911; www.theinnatcanalsquare.com.* Has waterfront rooms with balconies, breakfast included.

Cape Henlopen State Park $ US-9; tel: (302) 645-6852; www.destateparks.com; open daily 0800–sunset; Nature Center daily 0900–1600.

Millpond Paddler
Rte 26, Millville; tel: (302) 539-2339. Tours several nearby bays and ponds in sea kayaks.

Free concerts are held on weekend evenings in the summer, in the bandstand on the boardwalk at Rehoboth Ave.

Right
Dutch-style architecture at the Zwaanendael Museum

Suggested tour

Nanticoke Indian Museum $ Rtes 24 and 5; tel: (302) 945-3400; www.nanticokeindians.org; open May–Oct Tue–Sat 1000–1600; Apr Fri & Sat 1000–1600.

Cape May–Lewes Ferry Tel: (800) 643-3779; www. capemaylewesferry.com; operates year-round, with 12 daily departures in the summer.

The Mainstay Inn $$–$$$ 635 Columbia Ave, Ocean City; tel: (609) 884-8690; www.mainstayinn.com. The inn stands out for its elegantly decorated rooms in a distinguished 1872 mansion. Afternoon tea is served to guests and to the public by reservation.

Above
Fisher-Martin House, Lewes

Total distance: 88 miles, with detour 118 miles.

Time: 2–3 hours' driving time, depending on seasonal beach traffic. Allow 1–2 days with sightseeing. Those with limited time should concentrate on Assateague Island and the Historic Complex of Lewes.

Links: Berlin and Ocean City are close to Salisbury and Snow Hill, both on the Eastern Shore itinerary, and from US-13 north of Dover, Rte 6 (which becomes Rte 291 in Maryland) connects to Chestertown on the Northern Chesapeake itinerary.

Route: Leave **BERLIN ❶** via Rte 376 to **ASSATEAGUE ISLAND ❷** continuing to **OCEAN CITY ❸** on Rte 611. Rte 528 leads to **FENWICK ISLAND ❹**, where it becomes Delaware Rte 1 from **BETHANY BEACH ❺** to **REHOBOTH BEACH ❻**.

Detour: From Bethany Beach, follow Rte 26 west to Millsboro and Warwick, to visit the **Nanticoke Indian Museum**.

Rte 1 continues north, past **LEWES ❼** and Cape Henlopen, and on to **DOVER ❽**.

Also worth exploring

From Lewes, you can take the 70-min **Cape May–Lewes Ferry** across Delaware Bay to visit the Victorian seaside town in New Jersey. Leave your car in Lewes and ride on the trolley or buses that meet arriving boats. Along with its streets of well-manicured Victorian cottages, the village offers shopping, carriage rides, sailing and a lighthouse.

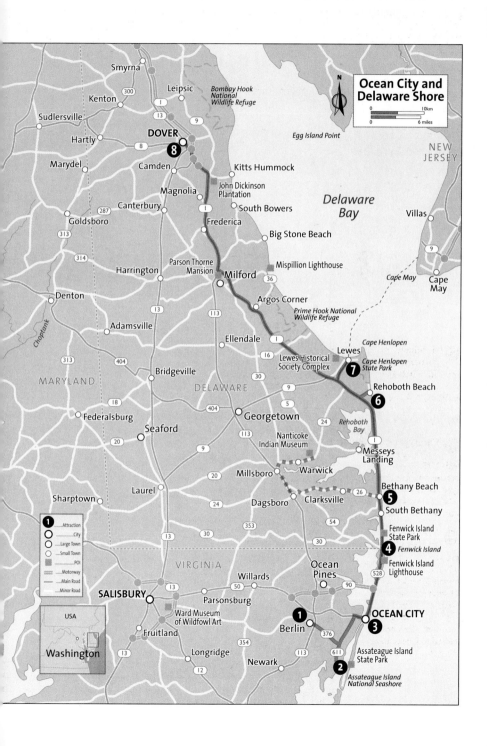

Ratings

Art and museums	●●●●○
Historical sights	●●○○○
Nature and wildlife	●●○○○
Shopping and crafts	●●○○○
Beaches	●○○○○
Children	●○○○○
Entertainment	●○○○○
Gastronomy	●○○○○

Wilmington

With Delaware's business-friendly tax policies and Wilmington's strategic location almost exactly 100 miles from Washington DC and New York, the city has evolved into a financial capital and the titular home of some of America's largest corporations, most notably E I Du Pont de Nemours. The du Pont family settled here in 1803 and flourished. Scions of the family built great mansions, constructed some of America's finest gardens and endowed the region's museums and other cultural attractions. Their estates constitute the most-visited attractions in and near Wilmington. Although Swedes founded Wilmington in 1638, the Dutch soon took over and were succeeded by the British by 1665. Quakers laid out the current city in 1731, and their legacy of social justice and business acumen remains Wilmington's guiding spirit. The main residential sections of the city have shifted towards the surrounding countryside, making Wilmington's centre very quiet at night.

ⓘ Greater Wilmington Convention and Visitors Bureau 100 W 10th St; tel: (302) 295-2210 or (800) 489-6664; www.visitwilmingtonde.com; open Mon–Fri 0900–1700.

Ⓟ Community Services Parking (jct Orange and 11th Sts) is convenient for central Wilmington sightseeing.

Getting around

DART buses (www.dartfirststate.com) service central Wilmington and surrounding attractions frequently on weekdays and Saturdays, but streets are well signposted, making it simplest for visitors to drive their own vehicles.

Sights

Brandywine Park

Stretching along 1 mile of Brandywine Creek, the park is renowned for its classic bridges and is popular with cyclists, joggers and dog-walkers

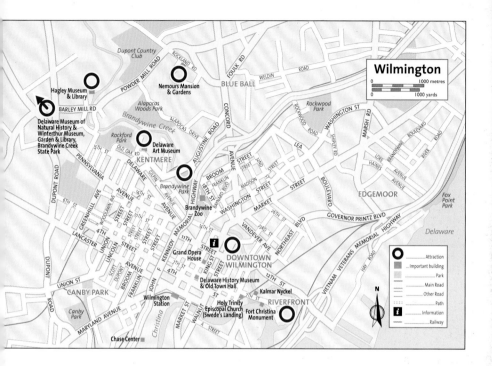

Brandywine Park $
Park Dr; open dawn to dusk.

Brandywine Zoo $ *1001 N Park Dr; tel: (302) 571-7747; www.brandywinezoo. org; open daily 1000–1600.*

It also serves as the centrepiece of the 1¾-mile Brandywine Nature Trail, which continues west to Rockford Park and east to the ornate concrete Market St bridge. Within the park are the dramatic Josephine Garden of roses and the **Brandywine Zoo**, which houses many mammals, as well as birds, reptiles and amphibians.

Delaware Art Museum
The museum was created to house works by Wilmington native Howard Pyle, who operated an influential school for illustrators. Reopened in 2005, after extensive renovations added two floors

Brandywine Christmas

The fascination with grand houses and gardens so typified by the various du Pont family properties finds its most lavish expression at Christmas, when the museums and museum houses of Wilmington and the surrounding Brandywine Valley go all out for the holidays. These annual extravaganzas include:

- Brandywine River Museum (see pages 244–5): o-gauge model railroad and Victorian dolls' houses.

- Hagley Museum (see page 239): du Pont family Christmas decorations on display.

- Longwood Gardens (see pages 247–8): lavish poinsettia displays in conservatory; holiday concerts.

- Winterthur (see page 240): period rooms show three centuries of holiday décor.

Delaware Art Museum $$ *2301 Kentmere Pkwy; tel: (302) 571-9590; www.delart.org; open Wed–Sat 1000–1600, Sun 1200–1600.*

Delaware Museum of Natural History $$ *4840 Kennett Pike; tel: (302) 658-9111; www.delmnh.org; open Mon–Sat 0930–1630, Sun 1200–1630.*

Delaware History Museum and Old Town Hall $ *504 Market St; tel: (302) 656-0637; www.hsd.org; open Wed–Fri 1100–1600, Sat 1000–1600.*

of galleries and an outdoor sculpture garden in a new landscape design, the facility has rich holdings of English Pre-Raphaelite art, early paintings by American Realist artists of the 'Ashcan School', and paintings and illustrations by Pyle, N C Wyeth and Maxfield Parrish. A new light installation brightens the façades at dawn and dusk.

Delaware Museum of Natural History

Serving scholars with its specimen collection and schoolchildren with its interpretive exhibits, the natural history museum spotlights Delaware's fauna and has a nature trail and butterfly garden in the grounds. Thematic environmental exhibits feature birds, mammals, shells and child-pleasing dinosaur displays.

Downtown Wilmington

The high-rise office buildings empty daily at 1700, and the city centre virtually closes. But by day it bustles on the pedestrianised stretch of Market St between Rodney Sq and the Delaware History Museum. Rodney Sq, marked by an equestrian statue of Delaware's signer of the Declaration of Independence, is anchored by the Hotel du Pont. The du Pont industrial family constructed the hotel in 1913 and it remains a centre for civic activities, complete with lavish public rooms and an active theatrical stage. The nearby Grand Opera House, an 1871 marvel of cast-iron design, hosts a range of performance events.

The **Delaware History Museum**, set in a renovated 1940s Woolworth's 'dime store', features interactive exhibits tracing the city's growth from its 1638 trading-post origins to its present role as a corporate capital. The adjacent Georgian-style **Old Town Hall** was the site of abolitionist meetings, although the jail beneath often held 19th-century fugitive slaves. The northernmost city in a border state between the 'free' north and the 'slave' south, Wilmington was often the final stop on the Underground Railroad, the network used by slaves to escape to freedom.

Wilmington's most active anti-slavery neighbourhood was Quaker Hill, reached by walking up 4th or 5th Sts from Market St. Settled in 1738, it is the city's oldest residential neighbourhood, and boasts fine examples of 19th-century brick town house architecture on the verge of gentrification. Central to Quaker Hill is the Friends Meeting House. The New-Wark Meeting, formed in 1682, built this structure in 1816. In the graveyard rests Quaker abolitionist Thomas Garrett, who worked with Harriet Tubman and others to guide more than 2,700 fugitive slaves to freedom.

Hagley Museum and Library

The Hagley Museum and Library chronicles the American origins of the du Pont family and their industrial legacy, the E I Du Pont de

Hagley Museum and Library $$ *Rte 141 (3¹/₂ miles north of Wilmington); tel: (302) 658-2400; www.hagley.org; open mid-Mar–Dec daily 0930–1630; Jan–mid-Mar Sat & Sun 0930–1630. Mon–Fri tour 1330.*

Nemours Mansion and Gardens $$$ *1600 Rockland Rd; tel: (302) 651-6912; www.nemours.org/mansion. Open May–Dec Tue–Sat 0900–1500, Sun 1100–1500; tour reservations recommended.*

Nemours company, which grew from a single gunpowder mill in 1804 to the largest manufacturer of black powder in the US to the modern petrochemical giant. Five generations of du Ponts lived in the Georgian-style home built by E I du Pont in 1803 to overlook his first powder mills on the Brandywine River. In addition to the house and formal gardens, the 235-acre property includes a preserved workers' community with costumed guides and a working 19th-century machine shop. A shuttle bus delivers visitors to each site, and a map details nature trails and a riverside walk through blooming azaleas, dogwoods and rhododendrons in the spring.

Nemours Mansion and Gardens

The du Pont legacy takes a decidedly French twist at this Louis XVI-style château constructed by Alfred I du Pont in 1909–10 and surrounded by some of the finest French-style formal gardens in North America. The guided tour highlights the antique furniture, paintings and decorative arts on three levels of the house, while a bus tour through the gardens concludes at the garage to see the family's collection of antique cars.

Right
Old Swede's Church, on the waterfront.

Riverfront

Swede's Landing commemorates the March 1638 landing of Swedish settlers on the north bank of the Christina River. This first successful European settlement of the Delaware Valley is poignantly reflected in Old Swede's Church (**Holy Trinity Episcopal Church**), built in 1698 and the 1690 **Hendrickson House**, built by Swedish settlers in Pennsylvania and moved here as a museum. The shipyard at the foot of 7th Street has been a fixture since the 1600s and now houses the **New Sweden Center**, which provides tourist information on local Swedish history. The shipyard's sail loft museum adjoins the 136ft replica of a vessel that brought the first settlers, the *Kalmar Nyckel*. The ship is available for occasional public sails between April and October and for winter weekend tours.

Winterthur

Winterthur legend holds that one Sunday in the 1920s Henry Francis du Pont skipped church to look for antiques. He came home with a 1737 Pennsylvania walnut chest, and turned his attention and fortune to acquiring and displaying American decorative arts. Today Winterthur holds one of the country's leading collections of American furniture and decorative arts and even offers a PhD degree in American Studies in conjunction with the University of Delaware. The two museum buildings (one with 175 period rooms) and the 965-acre estate (including 60 acres of gardens) can be overwhelming. Scholars and connoisseurs spend days at Winterthur. Admission includes a tour of selected rooms in the mansion, as well as access to the decorative arts galleries and a tram tour of the gardens. Specialised theme tours are also available.

Kalmar Nyckel
$–$$$ 1124 E 7th St;
tel: (866) 659-7447 or
(302) 429-7447;
www.kalmarnyckel.org; call
for schedule.

New Sweden Center
Kalmar Nyckel Shipyard,
1124 E 7th St;
www.colonialnewsweden.org

**Winterthur Museum,
Garden and Library** $$$
Rte 52 (6 miles NW of
Wilmington); tel: (302) 888-
4600 or (800) 448-3883;
www.winterthur.org; open
daily 1000–1700. Garden
tram operates Mar–Dec.
Reservations required for
some seasonal tours.

Above
Winterthur in spring

Right
Winterthur house

Wilmington's house
museums sponsor a vast
number of seasonal
special events that reach
a frenzied peak at
Christmas time.

Point to Point Races
Tel: (800) 448-3883.
First Sun in May, a 3-
and an 8-mile
steeplechase course in
the grounds of the
Winterthur estate.

**St Anthony's Italian
Festival** 8th St and
Bancroft Pkwy; tel: (302)
421-3100; open
May–Sept Sat 0800–
1200. Week-long ethnic
festival in June with
cafés, music, rides and a
farmers' market.

**Brandywine Arts
Festival** Tel: (302) 983-
5460; www.
brandywineartsfestival.org.
During Sept, 230
exhibitors set up along
the Brandywine River in
central Wilmington.

**Delaware Antiques
Show** Tel: (800) 448-
3883. Mid-Nov show at
Chase Center on the
Riverfront, with the
emphasis on cultivating
connoisseurship.

Shopping

No sales tax on goods makes Delaware a shoppers' mecca.

Shipyard Outlets 900 S Madison St – on riverfront; tel: (302) 425-
5000; www.riverfrontwilm.com; open May–Dec Mon–Sat 1000–2100, Sun
1100–1700; Jan–Apr Mon–Thur 1000–1800, Fri & Sat 1000–2100, Sun
1100–1700. Features brand-name outlets.

Winterthur Museum Store Rte 52 – 6 miles NW of Wilmington; tel:
(302) 888-4822; open Tue–Sun 1000–1730. Has extraordinary displays
of decorative art objects for sale, displayed in co-ordinated rooms.

Accommodation and food

The Wilmington area has the usual selection of business hotel chains,
including Sheraton, Marriott, Best Western, Days Inn, Doubletree,
Hilton, Holiday Inn and Quality Inn. Some central city hotels offer
substantial discounts on weekends.

Bed and Breakfast Delaware Tel: (302) 478-1437; www.
visitdelaware.com. Co-ordinates reservations for bed and breakfast
operations in the area.

Domain Hudson Wine Bar & Eatery $$ 1314 N Washington St; tel:
(302) 655-9463; open for dinner Mon–Sat. More than 50 wines by the
glass complement an American bistro menu.

Hotel du Pont $$$ 11th and Market Sts; tel: (800) 441-9019 or (302)
594-3100; www.hoteldupont.com. The elegant grande dame of Rodney
Sq. has 206 rooms, 11 suites and outstanding public spaces.

The Market St mall is lined with casual eateries for breakfast and lunch
on weekdays. Trolley Sq (Delaware St between Rodney and Union Sts) has
the city's best concentration of contemporary restaurants serving
evening meals.

Iron Hill Brewery $–$$$ 710 S Madison St; tel: (302) 472-2739; open
daily for lunch and dinner, Sun brunch. Seasonal beers complement a
casual American grill and barbecue menu.

Tavola Toscana $$–$$$ Rockford Shopping Center, 14th and DuPont Sts;
tel: (302) 654-8001; www.toscanakitchen.com; open for lunch weekdays,
dinner nightly. Elegant, updated northern Italian fare with crisp white
linen table settings and choice of pizza, pasta or more elaborate dishes.

Green Room $$$ Hotel du Pont, 11th and Market Sts; tel: (302) 594-
3154; open Mon–Sat for breakfast, lunch and dinner, Sun brunch. Perhaps
Wilmington's most elegant dining, the Green Room serves French
cuisine with a seasonal accent, drawing on the farms and truck
markets of the region. Sunday brunch is a popular city institution.

Above
Hagley Museum

⚙ **DuPont Theatre**
*10th and Markets Sts;
tel: (800) 338-0881 or
(302) 656-4401;
www.duponttheatre.com.*
Known as 'Wilmington's
Little Broadway', this
classically designed theatre
presents touring shows
and productions for
children.

Grand Opera House *818
N Southwest down Market St;
tel: (800) 374-7263 or (302)
652-5577;
www.grandopera.org.*
Presents a range of classical
and popular music, opera
and dance.

Suggested tour

Length: 1 mile walking; 12 miles driving.

Duration: 2–3 days.

Walking route: This tour of **DOWNTOWN WILMINGTON** ❶ begins
at Rodney Sq and takes in the city's historic roots. After an
appreciative look at the lavish lobby of the Hotel Du Pont, continue
southwest down Market St, which becomes a pedestrian way, past the
Grand Opera House for a quarter of a mile to the **Delaware History
Museum** and **Old Town Hall**.

Detour: Continue two blocks southwest down Market St then turn left
on 4th St, walking six blocks to N Church St. Turn left and then, after
400 yards, turn right along 7th St and continue another 400 yards to
Swede's Landing ❷.

From Market St, turn uphill (northwest) on 5th St and walk four
blocks to Quaker Hill. Turn right on West St to walk through the
neighbourhood to 10th St, turning right to return to Rodney Sq.

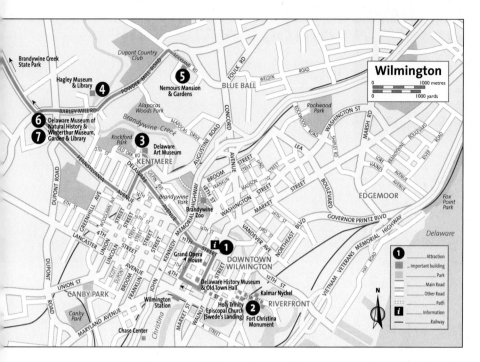

Wilmington

0 ___ 1000 metres
0 ___ 1000 yards

1 .... Attraction
.... Important building
.... Park
.... Main Road
.... Other Road
.... Path
i .... Information
.... Railway

Delaware Theatre Company 200
Water St; tel: (302) 594-1100;
www.delawaretheatre.com.
Adventurous company occupying state-of-the-art facility near the riverfront.

Driving route: This portion of the tour passes through a bucolic landscape to visit some of the great mansions and gardens of the DuPont clan. Although it's possible to stop briefly at each in a 1-day drive, the mansions deserve at least 3–4 hours each to see them properly.

From Downtown Wilmington follow Delaware Ave 1¼ miles to Union St, turn right and follow signs for three blocks to **DELAWARE ART MUSEUM ❸**. From the parking lot, follow signs for half a mile to Rte 52 (Pennsylvania Ave/Kennett Pike) and turn right. Follow Rte 52 for 3 miles north to Rte 141; turn right and drive ¼ mile to **HAGLEY MUSEUM ❹**. Continue east on Rte 141 to the junction with Rte 202 to visit **NEMOURS MANSION AND GARDENS ❺**. Backtrack to Rte 52, turn right (north) and continue 2 miles to **DELAWARE MUSEUM OF NATURAL HISTORY ❻** or 2¼ miles to **WINTERTHUR ❼**. Return to Wilmington on Rte 52.

Also worth exploring

Brandywine Creek State Park $
Off Rte 100, 5 miles north of Wilmington; tel: (302) 577-3534; open daily 800–sunset.

Brandywine Creek State Park was created from part of the Winterthur estate. Fourteen miles of walking trails snake through Tulip Tree Woods, a stand of tulip poplars nearly 200 years old. The park's fresh watermarshes teem with bog turtles and wading birds.

Brandywine Valley

Ratings

Art and museums	●●●○○
Historical sights	●●●○○
Shopping	●●●○○
Wildlife	●●●○○
Gastronomy	●●○○○
Beaches	●○○○○
Children	●○○○○
Entertainment	●○○○○

Genteel country living is the theme of the Brandywine Valley communities north of Wilmington where it seems that every third shop sells either country home décor, garden accessories or antiques. The rolling green countryside and lush farmlands of this area straddling the Pennsylvania–Delaware border have fascinated landscape painters for two centuries and the pastoral visions of American Realist Andrew Wyeth are especially prized here. Most visitors never see the modest town centres of Brandywine Valley communities, as principal attractions lie on the Baltimore Pike, Rte 1. The Delaware River towns south of Wilmington complement the Brandywine Valley with a more pervasive sense of history, augmented by the preservation of an entire early Colonial town and an important Union fortress from the Civil War. Both areas boast superb birdwatching, as they lie along the principal migratory flyway of North America's Atlantic coast.

CHADDS FORD, PENNSYLVANIA

ⓘ Chester County Visitors Center
Greenwood Rd, off Rte 1, Kennett Sq; tel: (800) 228-9933 or (610) 388-2900; www.brandywinevalley.com; open Apr–Oct daily 1000–1800; Nov–Mar daily 1000–1700.

The heart of 'Wyeth country' in the Brandywine Valley, Chadds Ford boasts three attractions that summarise the appeal of the region: history, art and agriculture. **Brandywine Battlefield Historic Site** is the location of a critical American defeat in the Revolutionary War. At the Visitors Center, displays and videos explain how General William Howe outmanoeuvred George Washington's attempt to block the British advance on Philadelphia, leaving the colonials to spend the winter of 1777–78 at nearby Valley Forge (*see page 274*). Visitors can drive through the battlefield and tour the Quaker farmhouses that served as headquarters for Washington and the Marquis de Lafayette, who saw his first military action in America here.

Setting, collections and architecture make the **Brandywine River Museum** a quintessential regional experience. The building is an artfully modern adaptation of a Civil War-era grist mill. The museum

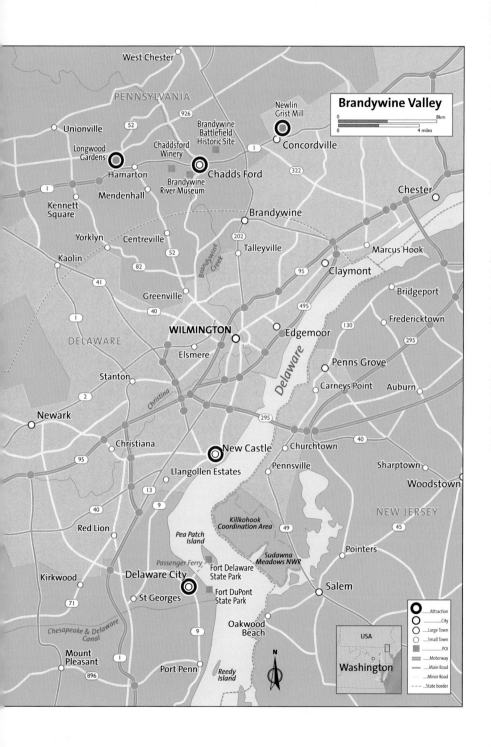

Brandywine Valley

West Chester

PENNSYLVANIA

926

Unionville

52

Longwood Gardens

Hamarton

Chaddsford Winery

Mendenhall

Kennett Square

Brandywine Battlefield Historic Site

Newlin Grist Mill

1

Concordville

322

Brandywine River Museum

Chadds Ford

Chester

Yorklyn

Centreville

52

Kaolin

82

41

1

Greenville

40

DELAWARE

Talleyville

95

Claymont

Marcus Hook

Bridgeport

Fredericktown

202

Brandywine

Brandywine Creek

495

WILMINGTON

Elsmere

Stanton

2

Christina

Newark

Christiana

95

40

13

9

Red Lion

40

Kirkwood

71

Chesapeake & Delaware Canal

Mount Pleasant

896

1

Edgemoor

130

Penns Grove

Carneys Point

Auburn

Delaware

295

New Castle

Churchtown

40

Pennsville

Sharptown

Woodstown

Llangollen Estates

NEW JERSEY

45

Killkohook Coordination Area

49

Pea Patch Island

Passenger Ferry

Delaware City

St Georges

9

Sudawna Meadows NWR

Pointers

Salem

USA

Washington

Fort Delaware State Park

Fort DuPont State Park

Oakwood Beach

N

Port Penn

Reedy Island

Attraction
City
Large Town
Small Town
POI
Motorway
Main Road
Minor Road
State border

0   8km
0   4 miles

Right
The Brandywine River Museum

Brandywine Battlefield Historic Site $$ *Rte 1; tel: (610) 459-3342; www.ushistory.org/ brandywine; open mid-Mar–Nov Tue–Sat 0900–1630, Sun 1200–1630; Dec–mid-Mar Thur–Sat 0900–1630, Sun 1200–1630.*

**Brandywine River Museum $$** *Rte 1, just south of Rte 100; tel: (610) 388-2700; www. brandywinemuseum.org; open daily 0930–1630. Additional charge ($$) for shuttle bus and tour of N C Wyeth studio.*

Chaddsford Winery *632 Baltimore Pike (Rte 1, 5 miles south of Rte 202); tel: (610) 388-6221; www.chaddsford.com; open daily 1200–1800. Free; tour tasting $$.*

Pennsbury-Chadds Ford Antique Mall *Rte 1; tel: (610) 388-1620; open Thur–Mon 1000–1700.* The displays of antique furniture, jewellery and other collectibles are unusually spacious.

Annual Fall Harvest Market *Tel: (610) 388-2700; weekends from mid-Sept–mid-Oct.* More than 20 regional artisans exhibit their work in the courtyard of Brandywine River Museum.

A Bed and Breakfast Connection *Tel: (800) 448-3619; www.bnbphiladelphia.com.* Makes reservations for B&Bs in Brandywine Valley.

holds the largest collection of work by American Realist painters and illustrators N C, Andrew and Jamie Wyeth. Also on display are works by regional 19th-century landscape painters and key American illustrators, including Howard Pyle, Maxfield Parrish and Rockwell Kent. Tours of the N C Wyeth studio are available Apr–Nov.

The **Chaddsford Winery** pioneered the production of serious table wines in Pennsylvania in the early 1980s. As the European varietal vines have matured, the wines compete well with California offerings. Tastings and winery tours are available daily.

Accommodation and food in Chadds Ford

Hank's Place $ *Rtes 1 and 100; tel: (610) 388-7061; closes at 1600 Mon, 1900 Tue–Sat, 1500 Sun.* Serves classic American grill food, starting with breakfast before dawn. Locally famous for home-made sausages.

Brandywine River Hotel $$–$$$ *Rtes 1 and 100; tel: (800) 274-9644 or (610) 388-1200; www.brandywineriverhotel.com.* An elegant interpretation of Colonial-Revival style, decorated extensively with prints and paintings in the regional Realist tradition.

The Gables at Chadds Ford $$$ *423 Baltimore Pike (Rte 1); tel: (610) 388-7700; open Mon–Fri for lunch, daily for dinner.* Serves bright contemporary New American food in stylish surroundings.

Art runs in the family

Three generations of Wyeths have made the world intimately familiar with the rural landscape of the Brandywine Valley. Illustrator and painter N C Wyeth (1882–1945) studied with the famous illustrator of fantasy romances, Howard Pyle, and developed an expressive and atmospheric style much favoured for boys' adventure novels. He settled in Chadds Ford in 1906, and his commission to illustrate *Treasure Island* in 1911 launched a very successful career. (A re-issue of this edition and many other Wyeth books are available at the Brandywine River Museum shop.) N C Wyeth was the sole teacher of his son, Andrew Wyeth (1917–2009). Andrew painted primarily in watercolours and tempera, infusing a precise naturalism with a studied visionary light. The most famous Wyeth painter, he was a member of the French Académie des Beaux-Arts and Britain's Royal Academy. Andrew's son, Jamie, born in 1946, continues the Realist painting tradition, often working in extreme close-up views, and illustrates children's books.

DELAWARE CITY, DELAWARE

Fort DuPont State Park $ *Off Rte 9, south of Delaware City; tel: (302) 834-7941; open daily 0800–sunset.*

C&D Canal Wildlife Area *Off Rte 9, south of Delaware City; tel: (302) 834-8433; open daily dawn–dusk.*

Fort Delaware State Park *Pea Patch Island; tel: (302) 834-7941; open late-Apr–Sept Sat & Sun, holidays; mid-Jun–early Sept Wed–Sun 1000–1730. Three Fort Ferry ($$) to Pea Island departs from foot of Clinton St.*

Kathy's Crab House $ *107 5th St; tel: (302) 834-2279; open Apr–Oct daily for lunch and dinner. Ultra-casual spot near the public marina with extensive picnic grounds.*

Delaware City has three chief attractions: sport fishing, bird-watching and a Civil War living history museum. The C&D Canal joins the waters of the Chesapeake Bay to the Delaware River in marshy lowlands, creating ideal conditions for striped bass, white perch and channel catfish. Many fishermen simply drop their lines at Battery Park in the centre of town. More than 200 migrant and nesting species of birds have been documented in the marshlands on the edges of **Fort DuPont State Park** and in the adjacent **C&D Canal Wildlife Area**, where grasslands attract vireos and other songbirds.

A ferry makes the 10-minute crossing to **Fort Delaware State Park** on Pea Patch Island, where interpreters recreate life during the Civil War, when the fort served as a Union prison. The ramparts provide close-up views of large sea-going vessels heading upriver. The park includes a picnic area with tables and grills, a hiking trail and a bird-watching observation tower. Nine species of herons, egrets and ibis nest on Pea Patch Island, making it the largest nesting ground for wading birds on the Atlantic coast north of Florida.

LONGWOOD GARDENS, PENNSYLVANIA

Longwood Gardens $$$ *Rte 1, Kennett Square; tel: (610) 388-1000; www.longwoodgardens.org; open daily Oct–Mar 0900–1700; Apr–Sept 0900–1800; conservatory opens 1000, some extended evening hours in Jul, Aug & Dec.*

Above
Longwood Gardens

Longwood Gardens is a vast 1,050-acre complex of 20 outdoor gardens, woodlands and meadows and an additional 20 gardens under glass. In all, more than 11,000 varieties of plants grow at Longwood, attracting garden enthusiasts from around the globe. An English Quaker family named Peirce bought the Longwood property from William Penn in 1700 and had begun planting ornamental trees by 1798. Pierre S du Pont (of the Wilmington family) purchased Longwood in 1906 to save the trees from destruction, and constructed elaborate gardens and built the vast conservatory over the next three decades. Three spectacular fountains, each with hundreds of jets lit by coloured lights on summer nights, dot the property. Exhibits at the Peirce-du Pont House trace the evolution of the property.

Accommodation and food in Longwood Gardens

Gateway Stables Riding Center $$$
949 Merrybell Ln, Kennett Square; tel: (610) 444-1255; www.gatewaystables.com.
Guided trail rides through woods and fields.

Mushroom Festival
Tel: (888) 440-9920; early Sept. Kennett Square bolsters its claim as the mushroom capital of the eastern US with a festival featuring cooking and growing demonstrations and mushroom farm tours.

Bed & Breakfast at Walnut Hill $$ *541 Chandler's Mill Rd, Kennett Square; tel: (610) 444-3703; www.bbonline.com/pa/walnuthill.* Three guest rooms in a mill house built around 1840, a short drive from Longwood Gardens.

Terrace Restaurant $$ *Longwood Gardens; tel: (610) 388-6771; open late May–Aug daily for lunch; Thur–Sat for dinner; call for off-season hours.* For garden ticket holders only. Does speciality salads and gourmet American fare.

Inn at Mendenhall $$–$$$ *Rte 52 – 1 mile south of Rte 1, Mendenhall, tel: (610) 388-2100; www.mendenhallinn.com.* A modern country hotel near Longwood Gardens.

Right
Longwood Gardens

NEW CASTLE, DELAWARE

New Castle Information *Tel: (302) 322-9802; www. newcastlecity.org; open Mon–Fri 0830–1630.*

Local lore claims that the New Castle town fathers rebuffed early 19th century preservationists, forcing them to settle for the Virginia site that became Colonial Williamsburg. Old New Castle's handsome 18th and 19th-century buildings are filled with 21st-century life. No museum village, New Castle bustles with boutiques, antique dealers, cafés and restaurants.

New Castle Court House *211 Delaware St; tel: (302) 323-4453; www.history.delaware.gov/ museums.ncch/ncch_main. shtml; open Tue–Sat 1000–1530, Sun 1330–1630.*

Dutch House $ *32 E 3rd St; tel: (302) 322-2794; www.newcastlehistory. org; open Apr–Dec Wed–Sat 1100–1600, Sun 1300–1600.*

Amstel House $ *4th and Delaware Sts; tel: (302) 322-2794; open Apr–Dec Wed–Sat 1100–1600, Sun 1300–1600.*

Read House $$ *42 The Strand; tel: (302) 322-8411; open Mar–Dec Wed–Fri & Sun 1100–1600, Sat 1000–1600.*

Separation Day *Tel: (302) 322-9802; early Jun. A celebration of Delaware's separation from England, with a parade, re-enactments and fireworks.*

Concerts in Battery Park *Tel: (302) 322-9802; late Jun–mid-Aug Wed evenings. A regular series of free concerts at Battery Park.*

Located 6 miles south of Wilmington on the Delaware River, New Castle had great strategic importance during the struggles of European nations to colonise the region. The **New Castle Court House** flies the flags of Sweden, the Netherlands, Great Britain and the US, a reminder of the world powers who have laid claim to the site since 1609. New Castle was the capital of Delaware until 1777 and the interior shows a British courtroom of the colonial era. Vintage portraits of William Penn and other early settlers hang in a ground-level hallway and changing historical exhibits are mounted upstairs.

Old New Castle begins at the waterfront with The Strand, a broad street with brick sidewalks, and progresses three blocks up from the river. This compact district contains more than 60 well-preserved historic buildings. Three homes open to the public illustrate the town's history. The **Dutch House** is a home typical of the early colonists around 1700. The Georgian **Amstel House** of about 1738, built when New Castle was the seat of colonial government, served as the governor's home. The **Read House**, a 22-room mansion built in 1801, represents the height of Federal grandeur and the wealth of New Castle's merchant class. The 2½-acre formal garden, added in 1847, is the oldest surviving garden in the region.

Accommodation and food in New Castle

New Castle has a Travelodge and a Rodeway Inn.

Jessop's Tavern $$ *114 Delaware St; tel: (302) 322-6111; open Mon–Sat for lunch, daily for dinner.* A renovated 1724 colonial tavern that serves contemporary updates on traditional fare, including wild mushroom potpie and fried oyster sandwiches.

Terry House Bed and Breakfast $$ *130 Delaware St; tel: (302) 322-2505; www.terryhouse.com.* Has five queen-bedded rooms in a Federal-Revival town house with capacious rooms.

The Arsenal at Old New Castle $$–$$$ *30 Market St; tel: (302) 323-1812; open Tue–Sat for lunch and dinner.* Set in the historic arsenal constructed in the run-up to the War of 1812, this restaurant features formal dining on Continental fare in the 1812 Room and more casual atmosphere in the Eagle and Cannon Tavern.

NEWLIN GRIST MILL, PENNSYLVANIA

Newlin Grist Mill is a low-key yet charming historic site. The water-powered grist mill built in 1704 is the oldest active mill in the US, still grinding cornmeal for sale at the Visitors Center. Other buildings on the Concordville property include the 1739 miller's house and a blacksmith shop. Three miles of walking paths follow the mill race and pass trees that predate European settlement.

Left
Newlin Grist Mill

Newlin Grist Mill and Park $–$$
219 S Cheyney Rd
(jct Rte 1, S Cheyney Rd);
tel: (610) 459-2359;
www.newlingristmill.org. Park
open daily 0800–dusk; grist
mill tours, call for hours.
Trout fishing Mar–Oct
weekends 0900–1600 ($).

Concordville has a
Best Western.

Buckley's Tavern
$$ 5812 Kennett Pike,
Centreville (Rte 52); tel:
(302) 656-9776. Open
Mon–Sat for lunch; daily for
dinner, Sun brunch. Casual
tavern fare and upmarket
American-continental
dining room.

QVC Studio Tour
$$ Off Wilson Rd; tel:
(800) 600-9900; www.
qvctours.com; tours daily
1030–1600.

Suggested tour

Length: 40 miles, 45 miles with detour.

Duration: 3 driving hours, 2 days with stops.

Route: From Wilmington, Delaware, follow Rte 52 (Kennett Pike) north for 6 miles to **Centreville**, Delaware. The community of venerable country homes dates from 1750 and 17 of its structures are on the National Historic Register. More than 30 small speciality shops, mostly devoted to home décor and antiques, line Rte 52.

Continue north to Rte 1, turning west for 2½ miles to **LONGWOOD GARDENS** ❶. Back on Rte 1, drive east for 5 miles towards **CHADDS FORD** ❷, stopping at the Chaddsford Winery and the excellent antiques mall next door. Continue 1½ miles east on Rte 1 to the **Brandywine River Museum**. Another 1 mile north is the **Brandywine Battlefield Historic Site**. Retrace your steps to Rte 1 and continue an additional 1½ miles east to the junction with Rte 202.

Detour: Continue north on Rte 1 for 2½ miles to **NEWLIN GRIST MILL** ❸ for a leisurely woodland walk along the mill stream.

Turn south on Rte 202 to I-95. Follow I-95 south to exit 6 and follow I-295 east towards Delaware Memorial Bridge, taking the Rte 9 exit. Rte 9 meanders southward 2 miles through marshlands to **NEW CASTLE** ❹. The road hugs the often-industrial marshy bank of the Delaware River for another 10 miles to **DELAWARE CITY** ❺.

Also worth exploring

West Chester, Pennsylvania, is only 7 miles north of Longwood Gardens on Rtes 100 and 52 or 7 miles north of Rte 1 on Rte 202. The drive winds through rustic countryside with calendar picture vistas. The extensive shopping district in the city centre teems with bistros and coffee bars. Yet most visitors come to see the studios of **QVC** the cable-shopping network that bills itself as the 'world's largest electronic retailer'. Call for reservations to be part of the live studio audience.

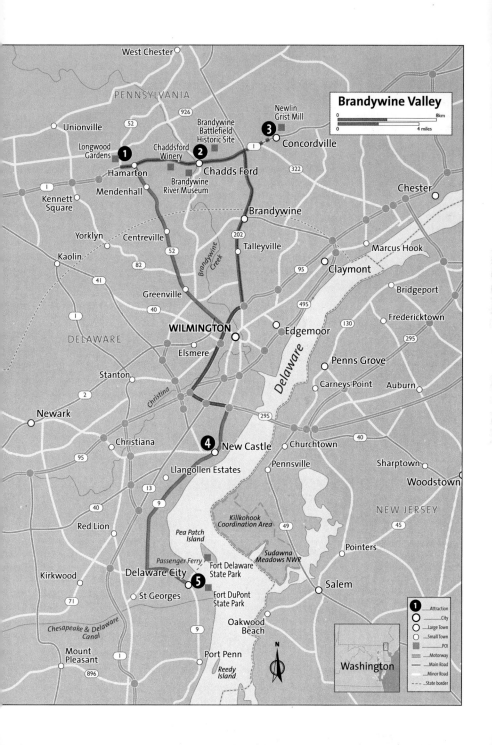

Brandywine Valley

West Chester

PENNSYLVANIA

926

Unionville

52

Longwood Gardens **1**

Chaddsford Winery

Hamarton

Mendenhall

Kennett Square

Brandywine Battlefield Historic Site

2

Chadds Ford

Brandywine River Museum

Newlin Grist Mill

3

Concordville

322

Chester

1

Yorklyn

Centreville

52

82

Kaolin

41

1

Greenville

40

DELAWARE

Brandywine

202

Talleyville

Marcus Hook

95

Claymont

Bridgeport

495

Fredericktown

295

WILMINGTON

Edgemoor

130

Elsmere

Stanton

2

Christina

Penns Grove

Carneys Point

Auburn

Delaware

Newark

Christiana

95

13

9

40

Red Lion

Llangollen Estates

4 New Castle

Churchtown

Pennsville

40

Sharptown

Woodstown

NEW JERSEY

45

Killkohook Coordination Area

49

Sudawna Meadows NWR

Pointers

Pea Patch Island

Passenger Ferry

Kirkwood

Delaware City

5

St Georges

Fort Delaware State Park

Fort DuPont State Park

Salem

71

Chesapeake & Delaware Canal

Oakwood Beach

Mount Pleasant

1

896

Port Penn

9

Reedy Island

N

Washington

1 ......Attraction
○ ......City
○ ......Large Town
○ ......Small Town
▦ ......POI
━ ......Motorway
━ ......Main Road
━ ......Minor Road
┅ ......State border

0 _____ 8km
0 _____ 4 miles

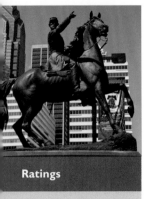

Ratings

Historical sights	●●●●●
Art	●●●●○
Entertainment	●●●●○
Gastronomy	●●●●○
Children	●●●○○
Shopping	●●●○○
Beaches	●○○○○
Nature	●○○○○

Philadelphia

Founded in 1682 by Quaker William Penn as the 'City of Brotherly Love', Philadelphia was the second largest English-speaking city in the world at the outbreak of the American Revolution and served as the insurgent colonies' first seat of 'national' government. The Declaration of Independence and the US Constitution were written here, and the city remained the capital of the new US until 1800. Often overshadowed today by New York and Washington, Philadelphia has much to offer in addition to its venerable historic sites. It boasts lively performing and visual arts scenes, bustling marketplaces and even its own eponymous fast food, the 'Philadelphia cheesesteak'. Laid out on a grid on the flat lands between the Delaware and Schuylkill rivers, Philadelphia is a walker's delight. Most attractions lie close to each other, and other interesting quadrants of the city can be reached quickly by public transport.

ⓘ Independence Visitor Center 6th and Market Sts; tel: (215) 965-7676 or (800) 537-7676; www.gophila.com. Serves as visitor centre for Independence National Historical Park and Philadelphia. City info booth open summer daily 0830–1900, call for off-season hours.

✈ Philadelphia International Airport Tel: (215) 937-6800; www.phl.org

Ⓐ Amtrak Tel: (800) USA–RAIL; www.amtrak.com

Arriving and departing

More than 20 US and international airlines service Philadelphia International Airport. The taxi fare from the airport to the central city is about $26. The convenient train service is about $5. Amtrak stops in Philadelphia as part of its Northeast Corridor and Metroline service between Boston, Massachusetts and Washington DC. Trains arrive at 30th St Station, close to central city hotels and the convention centre. Greyhound provides bus services from all parts of the US.

Drivers approaching Philadelphia from the south on I-95 or from the west on the Pennsylvania Turnpike should look for exits marked 'Central Phila./I-676' and follow signs to '15th St/Central City'.

Parking

Limited metered on-street parking is available and most larger hotels have parking lots. Private lots are well distributed throughout the city.

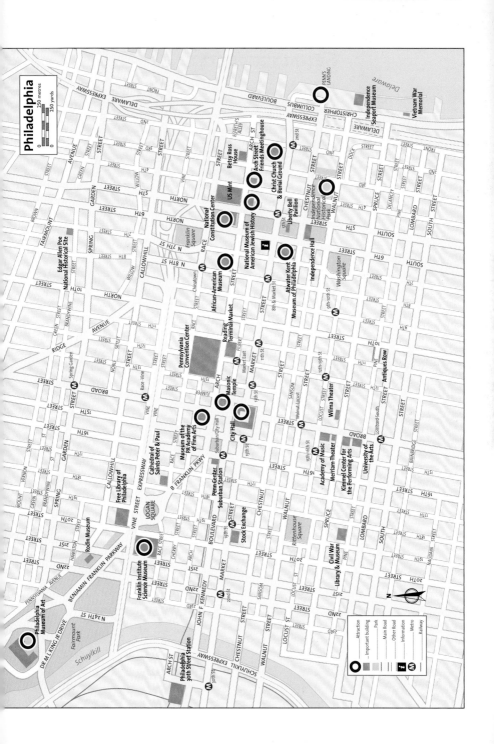

Getting around

Greyhound *1001 Filbert St; tel: (800) 231-2222 or (215) 931-4075; www.greyhound.com*

Phlash minibuses $ *Tel: (215) 4-PHLASH or (215) 238-8687; late May–Oct 1000–1800.*

SEPTA *Tel: (215) 580-7800; www.septa.org*

Philadelphia Trolley Works $$–$$$ *Tel: (215) 389-TOUR; www.phillytour.com*

Philadelphia is laid out on a strict grid formation and most attractions are found in clusters. As a result, walking is often the best way to get around. The **Phlash** minibuses also circle among most hotels and attractions. For non-attraction destinations, use the buses and streetcars operated by Southeastern Pennsylvania Transit Authority (**SEPTA**). Exact change is required. Discounted day passes can be purchased at the Visitors Center.

The **City Pass ($$$)** offers reduced-price admission to five museums, including the National Constitution Center, the Franklin Institute Science Museum, Philadelphia Zoo and a trolley tour. It is available at the Visitors Center and participating attractions.

Philadelphia Trolley Works offers a 90-minute city tour with free reboarding all day. The Fairmount Park tour, available separately, is a good way to get to Philadelphia Zoo and some of the park mansions.

Communications
Philadelphia uses 10-digit dialling, which means that local calls are dialled *with* the area code.

Below
Carriages at the Independence National Historical Park

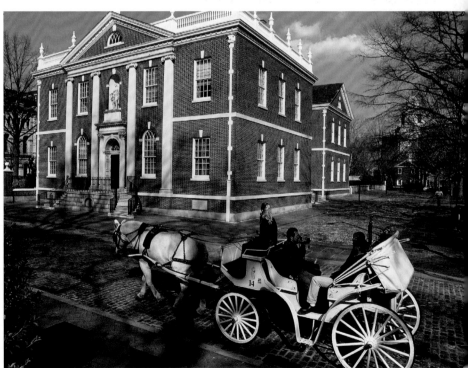

Right
Love, the motto of Philadelphia

Sights

African-American Museum
African-American Museum $$ 701
Arch St; tel: (215) 574-
9380; www.
aampmuseum.org; open
Tue–Sat 1000–1700, Sun
1200–1500.

Artefacts, artwork and multimedia presentations document the history and culture of African-Americans, with an emphasis on the 20th and 21st centuries. The museum shop has a small selection of original contemporary art.

**Arch St Friends
Meetinghouse** 320 Arch
St; tel: (215) 627-2667;
open Mon–Sat 1000–1600.
Donations welcome.

Arch St Friends Meeting House

Although Pennsylvania was open to all faiths, the Quakers were the most numerous and prominent in the early years of its settlement. The Friends have used this property since 1693 and the current annual meetinghouse dates from the early 1800s, when Quaker women demanded equal facilities. The resulting structure, with separate men's and women's halls, is the world's largest Quaker meetinghouse.

**Atwater Kent Museum
of Philadelphia $$** 15 S
7th St; tel: (215) 685-4830;
www.philadelphiahistory.org;
re-opens March 2010, call
or hours.

Atwater Kent Museum of Philadelphia

The renovation and expansion of the original 1826 Franklin Institute building allow this city history museum to display more of its 80,000-artefact collection and feature interactive exhibits that bring Philadelphia's local history and popular culture to life.

Christ Church $ 20 N
American St; tel: (215) 922-
1695; open Mon–Sat
0900–1700, Sun
1300–1700.

Christ Church and Burial Ground

Completed in 1754, Christ Church was attended by Benjamin Franklin, George Washington and other prominent early Americans. It remains an active Episcopal parish. A Palladian window covering most of the altar wall highlights the graceful, voluminous interior. Two blocks west, the burial ground contains the graves of Benjamin Franklin and four other signers of the Declaration of Independence.

Burial Ground $
Mon–Sat 1000–1600, Sun
1200–1600.

City Hall $–$$ *Penn Sq (Broad and Market Sts); tel: (215) 686-2840.* A 90-min tour of public rooms and tower *(Mon–Fri 1230)* departs from Room 121. The tour of the tower *(Mon–Fri 0930–1615)* is sometimes reserved for groups.

Franklin Institute Science Museum $$$ *Benjamin Franklin Pkwy at 20th St; tel: (215) 448-1200; www.fi.edu; open daily 0930–1700.* IMAX Theater tickets (**$$$**) are additional; advance reservation is recommended *(tel: (215) 448-1254).*

City Hall

Begun in 1871 and completed in 1901, City Hall occupies Penn Square and is the US's largest municipal building. Constructed in the effusive French Empire style widely used for grandiose American public statements in the late 19th century, the building is an undeniable engineering feat, although architects and art historians are divided about its aesthetic merits. The 538ft tower is the world's tallest masonry structure without steel reinforcement. Many visitors assume the 37ft, 27-ton bronze statue on top is Benjamin Franklin, but it is Philadelphia's founder William Penn. A gentlemen's agreement capped all other buildings at the brim of Penn's hat until a few towers from the 1980s reached a trifle higher. The City Hall tower observation deck, located just below Penn's feet, provides a spectacular 360° view of the central city. Call on the day of your visit to reserve a time slot.

Franklin Institute Science Museum

Founded in 1824 to promote invention and mechanical arts, the Franklin Institute established a museum in 1934 to augment its activities. The current complex rates as one of the US's finest general science museums, living up to polymath Benjamin Franklin's own observation 'watching, playing, asking questions – that's where all my inventions began'. Electricity exhibits and the walk-through heart are especially popular with children. The massive marble rotunda includes an oversized marble statue of Franklin and many of his effects. Franklin inventions on display include the glass armonica (an 18th-century musical instrument), bifocal glasses, cast-iron fireplace and swim fins. The Mandell Center relates sciences to contemporary technology (especially high-speed computers) with an accent on social implications. The Institute also has a major planetarium and a four-storey dome-screen IMAX Theater.

Benjamin Franklin

Born in Boston in 1706, Benjamin Franklin spent his adult life in Philadelphia, where he became the American embodiment of the Enlightenment. A prodigious inventor and thinker, he was known by his contemporaries as a leading researcher on the properties of electricity. Nominally a printer by trade, Franklin advocated the establishment of the city's first library in 1731, the American Philosophical Society in 1743 and the Academy of Pennsylvania (now the University of Pennsylvania) in 1751. In 1753, Franklin became deputy postmaster general for the British colonies in charge of the mail for the northern colonies, expanding his political thinking beyond the merely parochial. A key figure in deciding on revolution against the English king and in drafting the Constitution, Franklin served the US as postmaster general and as ambassador to France. French economist Anne-Robert-Jacques Turgot wrote of Franklin that 'he snatched the lightning from the skies and the sceptre from tyrants'.

ℹ **Independence National Historical Park** *Visitors Center at 6th and Market Sts; tel: (215) 965-2305 or TTY: (215) 597-1785; www.nps.gov/inde; Visitor Center open 0830–1800; most park buildings open daily 0900–1700 (extended hours in summer). Free. Check for schedule of tours. Due to security concerns all visitors must enter Independence Mall at Market and Walnut Sts. All bags will be screened. Free timed tickets required for Independence Mall Mar–Dec. Available day of visit at Visitors Center. Reserve in advance at (877) 444-6777; www.recreation.gov*

Independence National Historical Park

Philadelphia sites associated with the American Revolution and the formation of the country lie within a few blocks of each other in 'America's Most Historic Square Mile'. Within these modest brick structures surrounded by green lawns in the heart of a busy city, the US took shape. More than a dozen sites come under the park's purview, including some surviving colonial residences, but most visitors concentrate on a handful of buildings. The Independence Visitors Center shows an overview film and has excellent displays. The Second Bank of the United States, in the Greek Revival style chosen to associate the young country with classical democracy, houses a portrait gallery of early patriots, many painted by Philadelphia portraitist Charles Willson Peale. Carpenters Hall, still owned and operated by the Carpenters Company, was the meeting hall for the First Continental Congress, the colonial assembly which met in 1774 to address grievances against the king.

The cluster of buildings on Independence Square, however, were the crucible of the US. Graceful Independence Hall was built between 1732 and 1756 as the Pennsylvania State House. The Second Continental Congress began meeting here in 1775 to authorise and approve the Declaration of Independence, first read to the public in Independence Square on 4 July 1776. The business of American government, including the drafting of the Articles of Confederation and the US Constitution, continued here (with brief hiatuses) until 1790. In that year, Congress moved next door to Congress Hall, where it remained until the US Capitol in Washington was ready in 1800. Timed tour tickets are issued for Independence Hall. Unescorted visits are not allowed.

Over the generations, the Liberty Bell has become a patriotic icon. Cast in London in 1752 for the Pennsylvania State House, it cracked on arrival and was recast twice by a Philadelphia foundry. Rung for major national events – the surrender of Cornwallis at Yorktown, the

Opposite City Hall

signing of the Treaty of Paris that ended the Revolution and the deaths of George Washington and Lafayette – the bell cracked again in 1835. It has not been rung since Washington's birthday (22 February) in 1846. The Liberty Bell used to tour the nation by train as a unifying symbol, a practice halted early in the 20th century to preserve it. Recently moved to a new pavilion on Independence Mall, the bell receives more than 2 million visitors each year, many from nations who do not assume freedom as a birthright. Visitors may brush their fingers lightly on the 2,080lb bell.

Masonic Temple $$ 1 N Broad St; tel: (215) 988-1917; guided tours Tue–Fri 1100, 1400 & 1500; Sat 1000 & 1100; closed Sat Jul & Aug.

Museum of the Pennsylvania Academy of Fine Arts $$ Broad and Cherry Sts; tel: (215) 972-7600; www.pafa.org; open Tue–Sat 1000–1700, Sun 1100–1700.

The Fabric Workshop and Museum 1214 Arch St; tel: (215) 568-1111. Open Mon–Fri 1000–1800, Sat 1200–1600. Museum ($) and retail shop feature outstanding work by contemporary artists.

Masonic Temple

Philadelphia is the mother city of American Free Masonry, and it brethren thought big when constructing this architectural landmark just north of City Hall. Bristling with turrets and spires, the Temple claims to exemplify seven architectural styles, yet retains a resolutely Victorian sensibility. Stunningly excessive interior decoration, using Masonic mystic symbols as recurrent motifs, represents exemplary craftsmanship. All visits are guided, and include viewing of such artefacts as George Washington's Masonic Apron, embroidered by Madame Lafayette.

Museum of the Pennsylvania Academy of Fine Arts

The museum's opulent Victorian Gothic building is a high-water mark in Philadelphia decorative arts. Opened in 1876 as a showpiece for the Centennial International Exposition, the first World Fair, the museum features voluminous, light-filled exhibition spaces, a grand marble stairway and many sensuous marble statues, including a signature angel on the main staircase. Founded in 1805 on the model of Britain's Royal Academy, its collections document three centuries of American art, from Colonial and early Federal portraiture and landscape through late 20th century art. Paintings and sculpture in the 'Grand Manner' – i.e. heroic narrative with classical models dominate the entry hall and balcony galleries of the original building. Although the Academy briefly embraced Modernism in the early 20th century, it became a stalwart defender of realism against the abstract tide. Outstanding works include paintings by Benjamin West, Mary Cassatt, Thomas Eakins and Robert Henri, all at one time associated with Philadelphia. Eakins and Henri also taught at the academy. PAFA gallery space doubled with the opening of the adjacent Samuel M Hamilton building, an 11-storey early 20th-century steel-frame architectural landmark.

Above
The Liberty Bell

Opposite
Philadelphia skyscape

National Constitution Center $$ *Independence Mall, 525 Arch St; tel: (215) 409-6600; www.constitutioncenter.org; open Mon–Fri 0930–1700, Sat 0930–1800, Sun 1200–1700.*

National Museum of American Jewish History $ *5th & Market Sts; tel: (215) 923-3811; www.nmajh.org. Due to open autumn 2010, call for hours.*

Independence Seaport Museum $$ *Penn's Landing at Walnut St; tel: (215) 413-8655; www.phillyseaport.com; open daily 1000–1700.*

Below
Independence Seaport Museum

National Constitution Center

Occupying a dramatic building designed by lead architect Henry Cobb of Pei Cobb Freed & Partners, the National Constitution Center anchors the north end of Independence Mall and looks across to Independence Hall where the Constitution was brought to life. The museum is the first in the US to honour the document and employs interactive displays, performers and exhibits to trace the evolution of the Constitution and its ongoing interpretation over 200-plus years of democracy.

National Museum of American Jewish History

The only museum devoted to three centuries of Jewish experience in the US, this institution is scheduled to open a state-of-the-art facility with five floors of interactive exhibitions on Independence Mall in 2010. The steadily expanding collection includes personal artefacts, documents and photographs of individuals and families who have immigrated to the US. Oral history videos probe Jewish identity.

Penn's Landing

Like many American cities, Philadelphia was cut off from its waterfront by an Interstate highway. Penn's Landing redresses that mistake with a waterfront walkway (popular with joggers and rollerbladers), an amphitheatre and the **Independence Seaport Museum**. The museum relates the history of Philadelphia's seaport 90 miles up the Delaware River from the Atlantic Ocean. The port was a major immigration site throughout the 18th and 19th centuries and became an important industrial port with the discovery of petroleum in Pennsylvania in the 1850s. The walk-through exhibits are rich with artefacts from seafaring days and the museum includes a workshop for wooden boat construction. Visitors can tour the USS *Becuna*, a World War II submarine, and the USS *Olympia*, one of America's first steel ships. During summer visitors can ride a ferry (**$$** *tel: (215) 925-5465; www.riverlinkferry. org*) to Camden, NJ, to tour the battleship *New Jersey* or visit the Adventure Aquarium.

Philadelphia Museum of Art

Ranked among the US's leading art museums, the Philadelphia Museum of Art might be best known for the cameo role played by the long steps of its eastern façade in the melodramatic boxing movie *Rocky*. The great strength of

Above
Philadelphia Museum of Art

🅷 **Philadelphia Museum of Art $$$**
Benjamin Franklin Pkwy at 26th St; tel: (215) 763-8100; www.philamuseum.org; open Tue–Sun 1000–1700, Fri 1000–2045. Fri night 'cabaret' of cocktails, live music and light food is popular with singles.

the collections lies in late 19th-century European painting, including extensive holdings of Cézanne and other Impressionists. Not least among them are the largely sweet canvases of Philadelphia-born Mary Cassatt, who worked primarily in France. The American holdings are likewise strong in local artists, notably the late 19th-century Realist Thomas Eakins. Select exhibits of colonial silver and furniture hint at Philadelphia's erstwhile position as the largest and richest city of young America. The museum's holdings of medieval European art and Asian art are shown to particularly good effect surrounded by period architectural details. The 4-acre Azalea Garden on the west side of the museum bursts into spectacular bloom in late spring and early summer.

Entertainment

🅐 **Mummers Parade**
Tel: (215) 336-3050; www.mummers.com. The New Year's Day folk parade of costumed participants and minstrel string bands on floats is a colourful century-old tradition. Final judging ($$) takes place at Pennsylvania Convention Center (12th and Arch Sts).

Performing arts activities cluster on Broad St, also known as the 'Avenue of the Arts', where more than 20 facilities line a 3-mile stretch.

Academy of Music *Broad and Locust Sts; tel: (215) 893-1999; www.academyofmusic.org.* Serves as home for the Pennsylvania Ballet and Opera Company of Philadelphia.

Kimmel Center for the Performing Arts *Broad and Spruce Sts; tel: (215) 790-5800; www.kimmelcenter.org.* A dramatic new facility with two theatres. Presents the Philadelphia Orchestra and a range of music, dance and theatre.

Merriam Theater *250 S Broad St; tel: (215) 732-5446; www.merriam-theater.com.* Serves as a performance hall for touring Broadway shows and student productions of the University of the Arts.

Wilma Theater *Broad and Spruce Sts; tel. (215) 546-7824; www.wilmatheater. org.* Produces innovative drama and performance art in a 300-seat hall.

World Café Live *3025 Walnut St; tel. (215) 222-1400; www.worldcafelive.com.* Separate upstairs and downstairs rooms serve casual meals, but principally are the venues for live folk, jazz, indie rock and World music.

Shopping

Principal shops in the centre line **Walnut, Chestnut and Market Sts**, with upmarket boutiques located near Rittenhouse Sq. **Jeweller's Row** (bounded by Chestnut, Walnut, 7th and 9th Sts) is the US's oldest diamond district, established in 1851. More than 300 jewellery establishments are located here, most selling to the public at 30–50 per cent off retail prices. Pine St, between 9th and 13th Sts, is **Antiques Row**. Youth-oriented shops, tattoo parlours and counter-culture goods flourish on **South Street** from Front to 10th Sts.

Above
Antiques Row

Philadelphia Flower Show
Tel: (215) 988-8800; www.theflowershow.com. The early Mar displays at Pennsylvania Convention Center (*12th and Arch Sts*) are the oldest and largest in the US.

Accommodation and food

Philadelphia is a major convention city and business centre with a strong selection of chain hotels. Business centre hotels often offer good weekend packages. Chains include Best Western, Comfort Inn, Days Inn, Doubletree, Four Seasons, Hilton, Holiday Inn, Hyatt, Marriott, Omni, Ritz-Carlton, Sheraton and Westin.

Alexander Inn *$$ 12th and Spruce Sts; tel: (877) 253-9466 or (215) 923-3535; www.alexanderinn.com.* The 48 smartly decorated rooms cater to a discriminating straight and gay clientèle. Easy walk to Avenue of the Arts, Independence Mall and Antiques Row.

Penn's View Hotel $$–$$$ *Front and Market Sts; tel: (215) 922-7600 or (800) 331-7634; www.pennsviewhotel.com.* Fronts on the highway at the Market St entrance to **Penn's Landing**. This 38-room hotel offers good value and convenient location. Rates include continental breakfast.

Rittenhouse 1715 $$$ *1715 Rittenhouse Sq; tel: (877) 791-6500 or (215) 546-6500; www.rittenhouse1715.com.* Boutique hotel with 23 rooms, concierge service and luxury amenities in Philadelphia's most desirable central city area.

Philadelphia's traditional markets are attractions as well as ideal places to purchase produce, meats and prepared foods. **Reading Terminal Market** (*Filbert St between 11th and 12th Sts*) closes by late afternoon, but includes many casual eateries, including **Rick's Steaks $. Italian Market** (*9th St between Catherine and Washington Sts*) is a district full of grocers, butchers and greengrocers and is most lively on Saturday morning. **Anthony's Italian Coffee House $** (*903 S 9th St; tel: (215) 627-2586*) is a quiet spot for panini sandwiches and homemade cannoli. At 9th St and Passyhunk Ave is 'Cheesesteak Junction', with **Pat's King of Steaks $** and **Geno's Steaks $** on opposite corners. Both specialise in Italian rolls filled with shaved beef, processed orange cheese and fried onions: the quintessential Philadelphia cheesesteak. Open 24 hours.

You could take every meal at hip New American bistro **Fork $$–$$$** (*306 Market St; tel: (215) 625-9425; open for lunch Mon–Fri, dinner daily, Sun brunch*) or its adjacent storefront Fork Etc, which has breakfast fare, sandwiches and gourmet take-away.

⊙ Welcome America Festival *Tel: (215) 683-2200; www.americasbirthday. com.* A week of events around Independence Day (4 Jul) includes parades, fireworks and sporting events in locations throughout the city.

Upmarket restaurants occupy Walnut St between Broad St and Rittenhouse Sq. One of the best is chef-owner Georges Perrier's very French **Le Bec-Fin $$$** (*1523 Walnut St; tel: (215) 567-1000; open Mon–Sat for lunch and dinner*). A relative bargain is the prix fixe lunch available downstairs in casual but hip **Le Bar Lyonnais $$** (*open Fri & Sat for lunch, Mon–Sat for dinner*).

Suggested walk

Length: about 4 miles.

Duration: 2 full days.

Route: From **Independence Visitor Center ❶**, which introduces you to **INDEPENDENCE NATIONAL HISTORIC PARK**, enter **Independence Mall** to tour **Independence Hall ❷**. Head north to the **Liberty Bell Pavilion ❸**. Visit the **NATIONAL CONSTITUTION CENTER** and then turn right on Arch St, passing the US Mint, the largest in the world.

Above
Italian Market

Betsy Ross House
$ 239 Arch St; tel:
(215) 686-1252; open
Apr–early Sept daily
1000–1700, closed Mon
off-season.

Walk east, pausing at 4th St for the **ARCH ST FRIENDS MEETINGHOUSE** ❹ and at 3rd St for the **Betsy Ross House** ❺, where widow seamstress Elizabeth Ross produced the first official flag of the US. Go one half-block north on 2nd St to pass through **Elfreth's Alley** ❻, a narrow cobbled street of brick town houses continuously occupied from the early 1700s. At Front St walk south to Market St and turn left to cross over to **PENN'S LANDING** ❼. Walk south along the waterfront to Spruce St, using the walkway to resume going south on Front St for two blocks to **South St**, 'the hippest street in town' according to the 1960s pop tune. Stroll west on South St to 9th St.

Detour: Turn left and walk south for three blocks to reach **Italian Market** ❽.

Walk north from South St two blocks to Pine St and turn left. Walk through **Antiques Row** ❾, continuing to Broad St. Turn right and see the theatres and art centres of the **Avenue of the Arts**, ending at **CITY HALL** ❿. Turn right on Market St, then left on 12th St to reach **Reading Terminal Market**.

Also worth exploring

Philadelphia Zoo
$$$ 34th St and
Girard Ave; tel: (215) 243-
1100; www.philadelphiazoo.
org; open daily Mar–Nov
0930–1700; Dec–Feb
0930–1600.

Rodin Museum $
Benjamin Franklin Pkwy;
tel: (215) 763-8100; open
Tue–Sun 1000–1700.

Fairmount Park, the largest landscaped urban park in the US, covers more than 8,000 acres along the Schuylkill River northwest of the city centre. The park is criss-crossed with bicycle, walking and bridle trails. The site of the 1876 Centennial Exposition, the park contains extensive botanical gardens, a 10,000-seat amphitheatre and several colonial mansions open to visitors. Also in the grounds is the **Philadelphia Zoo**, the oldest in the US. The **Rodin Museum** on the Benjamin Franklin Pkwy at the entrance to the park holds 124 original sculptures and casts by Rodin, the largest collection outside Paris.

Right
Independence Hall

Philadelphia

0 ____ 250 metres
0 ____ 250 yards

Valley Forge to Gettysburg

Ratings

Historical sights	●●●●●
Shopping	●●●●○
Gastronomy	●●●○○
Art and museums	●●○○○
Children	●●○○○
Nature	●●○○○
Beaches	●○○○○
Entertainment	●○○○○

This countryside tour begins at the edge of the Philadelphia megalopolis at Valley Forge, the crucible of American military might during the Revolution. It concludes at one of America's most solemn locales, the fields of Gettysburg, where brother met brother during the Civil War in the largest battle ever fought in North America. Between these venerated sites associated with America's two most traumatic wars lie the peaceful farmlands of Pennsylvania Dutch Country, where the pacifist Old Order Amish adhere to their traditional ways, seemingly oblivious to the high-tech, high-pressure rush of the modern world. The drive commences in urban traffic but gives way to uncrowded country roads where drivers might find themselves sharing the right of way with the old-fashioned horse-drawn buggies of the Amish and Old Order Mennonites. The unusual productivity of Amish farmers supports the hearty country cooking featured at almost every restaurant.

GETTYSBURG

ⓘ Gettysburg Convention and Visitors Bureau 8 Lincoln Sq; tel: (717) 334-6274; www.gettysburg.travel. Open Apr–Oct Tue–Sun 1000–1800; Nov–Mar Wed–Sun 1000–1700.

Ⓖ Gettysburg Town Trolley $ Travels between the National Park Visitor Center and Downtown.

Haunted Gettysburg $$ 27 Steinwehr Ave; tel: (717) 334-1200. Walking tours.

During 1–3 July 1863, Gettysburg witnessed the largest conflict ever fought on North American soil when massive Union and Confederate armies inadvertently collided. Even today, the Battle of Gettysburg defines the town, and it is hard to scratch the surface of Civil War commercialism to get at the honest community beneath. Start with the free self-guided walking tour of the town centre, reading the plaques to grasp what the battle meant to the 2,400 horrified residents.

Numerous commercial operations attempt to recreate some aspect of the battle, but few observe the scene on a human scale. At the **Schriver House**, built in the early 1860s and operated as a saloon during the Civil War, costumed guides interpret the life of the family while Confederate sharpshooters occupied the building and during the battle aftermath, when it served as a field hospital.

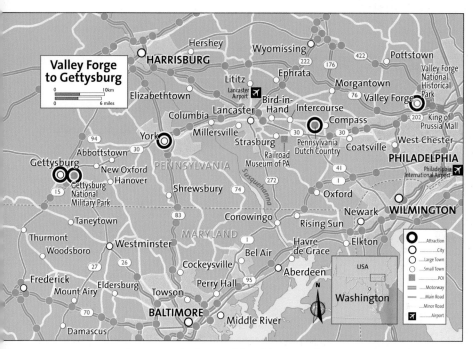

Schriver House $$
309 Baltimore St;
tel: (717) 337-2800; www.
schriverhouse.org; open
Apr–Nov Mon–Sat 1000–
1700, Sun 1200–1700;
Dec & Mar Sat 1200–1700,
Sun 1200–1400.

Gibson's Photographic Gallery 65 Steinwehr Ave;
tel: (717) 337-9393; www.
civilwarphotography.com.
The gallery continues the
wet-plate photographic
tradition of Civil War
portrait photographers.
Call for hours.

The Horse Soldier Old
Gettysburg Village, 777
Baltimore St; tel: (717) 334-
0347. Open Mon, Tue &
Thur–Sat 0900–1700, Sun
1000–1700. A shop that
specialises in high-end Civil
War military antiques.

Accommodation and food in Gettysburg

Artillery Ridge Camping Resort $ 610 Taneytown Rd; tel: (717) 334-1288. The closest site to the attractions.

Econolodge $ 983 York Rd; tel: (717) 334-4208 or (866) 334-6479; www.econolodge.com. Good value, basic lodging on east side of town, about a 10-minute drive from the battlefields of National Military Park.

Lincoln Diner $ 32 Carlisle Ave; tel: (717) 334-3900. Gettysburg's only 24-hour eatery is a classic metal-sheathed, neon-lit diner, where the best bets are breakfast (at all hours), burgers, and an awe-inspiring selection of homemade desserts – most notably, huge slabs of cream pie.

Dobbin House Tavern $–$$ 89 Steinwehr Ave; tel: (717) 334-2100; open daily for lunch and dinner. This historic property features continental fine dining and casual tavern fare.

The Doubleday Inn B&B $$ 104 Doubleday Ave; tel: (717) 334-9119; www.doubledayinn.com. This is an upmarket country inn at Oak Ridge battlefield.

The Gettysburg Hotel $$ One Lincoln Sq; tel: (717) 337-2000; www.gettysburg-hotel.com. A superb historic hotel, built in 1797, offering some rooms with refrigerators.

Memorial Day Parade *Tel: (717) 334-6274.* In a tradition dating from 1867, the parade concludes at Gettysburg National Cemetery where children place flowers on the graves.

Civil War Heritage Days *Tel: (717) 334-6274.* Battle re-enactments and encampment take place in late Jun and early Jul.

Anniversary of Lincoln's Gettysburg Address *Tel: (717) 334-6274.* On 19 Nov services commemorate Lincoln's speech at a cemetery dedication.

Below
Gettysburg battlefield

Abraham Lincoln's Gettysburg address

'Four score and seven years ago our fathers brought forth on this continent a new nation, conceived in liberty and dedicated to the proposition that all men are created equal. Now we are engaged in a great civil war, testing whether that nation or any nation so conceived and so dedicated can long endure. We are met on a great battlefield of that war. We have come to dedicate a portion of that field as a final resting-place for those who here gave their lives that that nation might live. It is altogether fitting and proper that we should do this. But in a larger sense, we cannot dedicate, we cannot consecrate, we cannot hallow this ground. The brave men, living and dead who struggled here have consecrated it far above our poor power to add or detract. The world will little note nor long remember what we say here, but it can never forget what they did here. It is for us the living rather to be dedicated here to the unfinished work which they who fought here have thus far so nobly advanced. It is rather for us to be here dedicated to the great task remaining before us – that from these honored dead we take increased devotion to that cause for which they gave the last full measure of devotion – that we here highly resolve that these dead shall not have died in vain, that this nation under God shall have a new birth of freedom, and that government of the people, by the people, for the people shall not perish from the earth.'

GETTYSBURG NATIONAL MILITARY PARK

Gettysburg Battlefield Audio Tour $$$ Sold at the Park Service Visitor Center.

Licensed Tour Guides $$$ *Park Service Visitor Center; tel: (717) 334-1124.* Guides will drive your vehicle on a tour of Gettysburg battlefield.

National Riding Stable $$$ *610 Taneytown Rd (Rte 134); tel: (717) 334-1288.* Horseback tours through the battlefield.

Museum and Visitor Center at Gettysburg National Military Park *1195 Baltimore Pike; tel: (717) 334-1124; www. nps.gov/gett. Visitor Center open daily Jun–Aug 0800–1800, call for off-season hours; battlefield 0600–2200 and cemetery dawn–dusk.* Museum and film ($$). For security reasons, backpacks, daypacks and large handbags are prohibited in the Visitor Center and Eisenhower Site.

General Lee's Headquarters Museum $ *401 Buford Ave; tel: (717) 334-3141; www. civilwarheadquarters.com; open mid-Mar–Nov 0900–1700.*

Eisenhower National Historic Site $$ *Shuttle from Visitor Center; tel: (717) 338-9114; www. nps.gov/eise; open daily 0900–1600.*

Above
Gettysburg National Cemetery

The Battle of Gettysburg ravaged 25 sq miles of farmland and woods, now preserved by the National Park Service. A new Visitor Center and Museum displays a broad range of Civil War artefacts and provides a cool-headed interpretation that outshines the histrionics of commercial sensationalisers.

A new feature film familiarises visitors with the Union and Confederate strategies and troop movements over 1–3 July 1863. The climactic action of the third day is displayed in Paul Philippoteaux's 1884 painting depicting 'Pickett's Charge'. The painting, which stands 26ft tall and stretches 350ft in circumference, has been installed in the museum following a major restoration.

No amount of interpretation can compare with driving or cycling the battlefield. A free map covers the well-marked 18-mile tour, a trip that can be augmented with an audio cassette or a professional guide. More than 1,300 monuments and markers spell out the action and pay tribute to both armies. The landscape has changed little in 140 years: stone walls and split-log fences mark the farm borders, cannons stand poised along ridges, and massive boulders, chipped by bullets, show where soldiers took refuge. Hiking trails include a 1-mile route through the area depicted in Philippoteaux's painting. On the property of a motel near Seminary Ridge, the stone house that served as the **General Lee's Headquarters** contains a small museum of Civil War artefacts.

The most solemn stop is Gettysburg National Cemetery, where Abraham Lincoln gave his famous speech at the dedication on 19 November 1863. More than 3,000 graves (of 51,000 casualties) fan out in a semicircle from Soldiers National Monument, a plan devised so that all are equal in death.

The Park Service also oversees the **Eisenhower National Historic Site**, the retirement home of the former World War II commander and American president.

PENNSYLVANIA DUTCH COUNTRY

ⓘ Pennsylvania Dutch Convention and Visitors Bureau *501 Greenfield Rd, Lancaster; tel: (800) PA-DUTCH or (717) 299-8901; www. padutchcountry.com. Open Mon–Sat 0900–1800, Sun 0900–1600; extended summer hours.*

ⓒ Mennonite Information Center *2209 Millstream Rd, Lancaster; tel: (717) 299-0954; www. mennoniteinfoctr.com has informative audio-visual presentation (**$$**) and provides a guide to join you in your car for a farm country tour (**$$$**).*

Ed's Buggy Rides $$$ *Rte 896, 1½ miles south of Rte 30, Strasburg; tel: (717) 687-0360; www. edsbuggyrides.com. A 3-mile tour on scenic back roads in an Old Order-style Amish horsedrawn buggy.*

Strasburg Railroad $$$ *Rte 741, 1 mile east of Strasburg; tel: (717) 687-7522; www. strasburgrailroad.com; operates Mar–Dec; call for schedule of trips for children and adults. A 9-mile, 45-min scenic trip.*

ⓗ Heritage Center Museum $$ *5 W King St, Lancaster; tel: (717) 299-6440; www.lancasterheritage.com; open Apr–Dec Mon–Sat 0900–1700. Free.*

Right
Amish farmer

Opposite
Bird-in-Hand craft shop

The second-largest concentration of Mennonite and Amish 'plain folk' in the US live in the rich farmland of Lancaster County. Descended from German religious refugees, many of these Pennsylvania Dutch belong to Old Order Amish and Old Order Mennonite sects that keep their distance from modern culture, eschewing electricity and internal combustion engines and dressing in a distinctive 'plain' style little altered from the 18th century. Black-frocked farmers on horse-drawn buggies share the roads with tourists drawn to the area by Amish and Mennonite crafts and foods.

Lancaster's Central Market dates from the 1730s. Two dynamic museums flank the market complex: the **Heritage Center Museum** which relates local history and culture through furnishings and folk art, and the recently expanded **Lancaster Quilt & Textile Museum**, which displays a priceless collection of Amish quilts. The **Lancaster Museum of Art** shows contemporary art in an 1840 Greek Revival mansion while the **Demuth Foundation** shows the work of Charles Demuth in the artist's home. East of the centre, the **Amish Farm and House** occupies vestigial open farmland.

Further east, the countryside opens into broad farmland, and most attractions are found along Rte 340 (Old Philadelphia Pike) in tiny Bird-in-Hand with its farm-products market and larger Intercourse where a variety of gift and craft shops hint at local customs. Several roadside operators offer horse-and-buggy tours of Amish farmland and the factory tour at **Intercourse Pretzel Factory** hits one of the region's culinary highlights. Many Amish farms and Pennsylvania Dutch crafts shops line the highway to Paradise from Lancaster (Rte 30). More bucolic Rte 896 heads south into the spruced-up village of Strasburg. North of the centre is **Amish Village**.

Lancaster Quilt & Textile Museum $$
37 N Market St, Lancaster; tel: (717) 299-6440; www.lancasterheritage.com; open Apr–Dec Mon–Sat 0900–1700.

Lancaster Museum of Art 135 N Lime St, Lancaster; tel: (717) 394-3497; www.lmapa.org; open Mon–Sat 1000–1600, Sun 1200–1600. Free.

Amish Farm and House $$ 2395 Lincoln Hwy E, Lancaster; tel: (717) 394-6185; www.amishfarmandhouse.com; open Jun–Aug 0830–1800; Apr, May, Sept & Oct 0830–1700; Nov–Mar 0830–1600.

Demuth Foundation $$ 120 E King St, Lancaster; tel: (717) 299-9940; www.demuth.org; open Feb–Dec Tue–Sat 1000–1600, Sun 1300–1600.

Accommodation and food in Pennsylvania Dutch Country

Quiet Haven Motel $ *2556 Siegrist Rd, Ronks; tel: (717) 397-6231.* An older motor hotel surrounded by farmland near Strasburg, Bird-in-Hand and Intercourse. No credit cards.

White Oak Campgrounds $ *White Oak Rd, off May Post Office Rd, Strasburg; tel: (717) 687-6207.* Offers a choice of woodland or meadow camp for tents or RVs.

Amish Country Motel $–$$ *3013 Old Philadelphia Pike (Rte 340), Bird-in-Hand; tel: (800) 538-2535 or (717) 768-8396.* A modest motor inn between Intercourse and Bird-in-Hand, whose rates include a 2-hour tour of Dutch country.

Country Inn of Lancaster $–$$ *2133 Lincoln Hwy E (Rte 30), Lancaster, tel: (877) 393-3413 or (717) 393-3413; www.countryinnoflancaster.com.* A modern motor inn with country décor on the busy section of Rte 30 but minutes from rural attractions.

Limestone Inn Bed and Breakfast $–$$ *33 E Main St, Strasburg; tel: (800) 278-8392 or (717) 687-8392; www.thelimestoneinn.com.* Six guest rooms (five with private bath) in a late 18th-century house in a historic district. With advance reservation, it will arrange an evening meal with an Amish family. No children under 12.

Hotel Brunswick $$ *151 N Queen St, Lancaster; tel: (800) 821-9258 or (717) 397-4800; www.hotelbrunswick.com.* Modern hotel in the town centre well-situated for walking.

Large breakfasts and large midday meals are the rule in Pennsylvania Dutch Country; many restaurants stop serving 1800–2000.

Above
Amish farm

Right
Traditional Amish buggy

Intercourse Pretzel Factory
614 Rte 340, Intercourse; tel: (717) 768-3432; factory hours Apr–mid-Oct Tue–Sat 0930–1500; call for winter hours. Free.

Amish Village $$ Rte 896, Strasburg; tel: (717) 687-8511; open spring–autumn Mon–Sat 0900–1700, Sun 1000–1700.

Railroad Museum of Pennsylvania $$ Rte 741, Strasburg; tel: (717) 687-8628; www.rrmuseumpa.org; open Mon–Sat 0900–1700, Sun 1200–1700; closed Nov–Apr Mon.

Eldreth Pottery
246 N Decatur St (Rte 896), Strasburg; tel: (717) 687-8445; open Jan–Jun Mon–Sat 0900–1700, Sun 1200–1700; Jul–Dec Fri 1000–2000. The pottery features salt-glazed stoneware and Pennsylvania redware.

Old Country Store Rte 340, Intercourse; tel: (717) 768-7101; open Jun–Oct Mon–Sat 0900–1830; Nov–May Mon–Sat 0900–1700. Excellent selection of quilting books, fabrics and quilts.

Outlet centers Rte 30E, near Rte 896, Lancaster. More than 200 shops are housed here.

Cook's Quilts, Crafts and Furniture Rte 741 E, Strasburg; tel: (717) 687-0589; open Mon–Sat 0900–1630. An Amish-operated shop with superb quilts.

above
Amish quilts

Two outstanding markets display local produce, meats, flowers and baked goods – **Bird-in-Hand Farmers' Market** (Rte 340, Bird-in-Hand; tel: (717) 393-9674; open Jul–Oct Wed–Sat 0830–1730; Apr–Jun & Nov Wed, Fri & Sat 0830–1730; Dec–Mar Fri & Sat 0830–1730) and **Central Market** (23 N Market St, Lancaster; tel: (717) 291-4723; open Tue & Fri 0600–1600, Sat 0600–1400).

Dienner's $ 2855 Lincoln Hwy E, Ronks; tel: (717) 687-9571; open Mon–Thur & Sat 0700–1800, Fri 0700–2000. An Amish-run restaurant featuring buffets at all three meals and generous portions of à la carte Dutch country food. A local favourite.

Jennie's Diner $ 2575 Lincoln Hwy E, Ronks; tel: (717) 397-2507. Open 24 hours with low-cost large portions of classic diner food.

Stoltzfus Farm Restaurant $ Rte 772, Intercourse; tel: (717) 768-8156; open Apr–Nov Mon–Sat for lunch and dinner. Traditional fare served family-style in Amish homestead.

Carr's Restaurant $$$ 50 W Grant St, Lancaster; tel: (717) 299-7090; open Tue–Sat for lunch and dinner, Sun for brunch. Stylish dining room near Central Market serves updated American fare.

VALLEY FORGE

ⓘ Valley Forge Convention and Visitors Bureau *1000 First Ave, Suite 101, King of Prussia; tel: (800) 441-3549 or (610) 834-1550; www.valleyforge.org; open Mon–Fri 0900–1700.*

ⓗ Valley Forge National Historical Park *Rte 23 and N Gulph Rd, Valley Forge; tel: (610) 783-1077; www.nps.gov/vafo. Park free. Washington's Headquarters $. Welcome center open daily 0900–1700; park daily 0600–2200; enquire for Washington's Headquarters hours. Trolley tour mid Jun–early Sept $$$.*

Washington Memorial Chapel *Rte 23 in National Historical Park; tel: (610) 783-0120; www.washington memorialchapel.org; open daily 0930–1700. Carillon concerts Jun–Sept Sun & Jul–Aug Wed; call for hours.*

Mill Grove *$ Audubon and Pawlings Rds, Audubon, Pennsylvania (adjacent to National Historical Park); tel: (610) 666-5593; http://pa.audubon.org. Museum open Tue–Sat 1000–1600, Sun 1300–1600; grounds Tue–Sun 0700–dusk.*

George Washington's 12,000-man Continental Army marched into camp at Valley Forge on 19 December 1777 after failing to save Philadelphia from British occupation. Undernourished and poorly clothed, 2,000 soldiers died that winter and thousands more became unfit for duty. But thanks to the discipline of Prussian drillmaster Baron Friedrich Wilhelm von Steuben, they marched out on 19 June 1778 as a highly trained force that saved New York City by defeating the British at the Battle of Monmouth. The rolling landscape is now **Valley Forge National Historical Park**, a symbol of patriotic triumph over hardship. The newly renovated Welcome Center shows a moving 18-minute orientation film and displays rare uniforms, weapons, documents and other artefacts. A driving tour passes forts and earthworks, the artillery park, the parade ground where von Steuben rebuilt the army and Washington's headquarters. The local community takes full advantage of the park's recreational amenities, including three picnic areas, 10 miles of bridle paths and a 6-mile bicycle/foot path. The Schuylkill River Trail begins in the park and connects to an 18-mile bikeway that follows an abandoned railroad bed to Philadelphia.

Privately owned attractions within the historical park include the richly ornamented **Washington Memorial Chapel**, which is known for its carillon concerts.

The 175-acre **Mill Grove** was John James Audubon's first home in America and his introduction to American birds and wildlife. The mansion displays Audubon paintings and illustrations and the artist's studio and taxidermy room are recreated in the attic. Miles of trails wind through the sanctuary, where more than 175 species of birds and 400 species of flowering plants have been identified.

Accommodation and food in Valley Forge

Most lodging lies 10 miles east near King of Prussia Mall on Rte 202, where major chains are represented.

King of Prussia Mall *Rte 202, King of Prussia; www. kingofprussiamall.com; open Mon–Sat 1000–2130, Sun 1000–1830.* Two food courts with over 20 vendors and more than 15 restaurants. The mall bills itself as the largest shopping centre on the US east coast, with 365 speciality shops and seven major department stores including Lord & Taylor, Bloomingdale's, Macy's, Nieman-Marcus and Nordstrom.

Lodge Restaurant *$ 1371 Valley Forge Rd – 2 miles west of the park on Rte 23; tel: (610) 933-1646; open Mon–Fri 0600–1430, Sat & Sun 0700–1400.* Does good home-made soups and daily specials for breakfast and lunch.

Opposite
Valley Forge

HEADQUARTERS COMPLEX

THE HEADQUARTERS HOUSE, OVERLOOKING THE CONFLUENCE OF VALLEY CREEK AND THE SCHUYLKILL RIVER, WAS THE HUB OF MILITARY ACTIVITY. IT WAS FROM HERE THAT GENERAL WASHINGTON, WITH THE ASSISTANCE OF HIS STAFF, CONDUCTED THE DAILY ROUTINE OF THE ARMY. OFTEN THERE WERE MORE THAN TWENTY OFFICERS AND AIDES PRESENT TO ASSIST THE COMMANDER-IN-CHIEF IN HIS DUTIES.

YORK

York County Convention and Visitors Bureau *155 W Market St; tel: (888) 858-YORK or (717) 852-YORK; www.yorkpa.org; open daily 0930–1600.*

Colonial Complex **$$** *Market St and Pershing Ave; tel: (717) 846-6452; open mid-Apr–mid-Dec Tue–Sat; tours 1000–1600.*

Historical Society of York County Museum **$$** *250 E Market St; tel: (717) 848-1587; www.yorkheritage.org; open Tue–Sat 1000–1600.*

Harley-Davidson Motorcycle Company *1425 Eden Rd; tel: (877) 883-1450; www.harley-davidson.com. Tours Mon–Fri 0900–1400. Free. Close-toed shoes required. Packages prohibited. Tours open to age 12 and up. Visitors under 18 must be accompanied by an adult.*

Factory Tours *More than a dozen factories offer guided tours; some have outlet stores.*

York Fair *Tel: (717) 848-2596; www.yorkfair.org. This September funfair dates from 1765.*

Located midway between Gettysburg and Lancaster in the Susquehanna River valley, York was settled in 1749. More than half the downtown buildings are enrolled on the National Register of Historic Places, with the 1888 Central Market House the principal attraction. York was the American capital from 30 Sept 1777 until 27 June 1778, while Philadelphia was under British occupation. The Continental Congress met in the **York County Colonial Courthouse** (now reconstructed) to adopt the Articles of Confederation and issue the first National Thanksgiving Proclamation. The 20-mile York County Heritage Rail Trail begins behind the courthouse.

The Courthouse is part of the **Colonial Complex** which traces the city's growth. The Golden Plough Tavern, circa 1741, is York's oldest surviving structure. The General Horatio Gates House, circa 1751, is an English-style stone house. American Revolutionary War hero Gates lived here while attending the Continental Congress. The Bobb Log House, circa 1812, represents a sturdy country home of the early 19th century. The same ticket includes the **Historical Society of York County Museum** with exhibits on York's role as a centre for early automotive manufacturing.

The **Harley-Davidson Motorcycle Company** has built two-wheelers here since 1903. The plant tour shows the assembly process and the museum displays every model produced since 1906.

Accommodation and food in York

Central Market House *W Philadelphia and N Beaver Sts; tel: (717) 848-2243; open Tue, Thur & Sat 0600–1400.* A good place to stock up on produce and baked goods as well as meats, cheeses and sausages. Local specialities include hotdog cooked in pretzel dough, pickled vegetables and 'wet-bottom' shoo-fly pie.

White Rose Bar and Grill $–$$ *48 N Beaver St; tel: (717) 848-5369.* Has a café and tavern specialising in open-pit barbecued meats.

The Yorktowne Hotel $$ *48 E Market St; tel: (800) 233-9324 or (717) 848-1111; www.yorktowne.com.* A classic business hotel, built in 1925 and completely renovated.

Above
White Rose bar and grill

Opposite
York County Colonial Courthouse

Suggested tour

March-in Program
Tel: (610) 783-1077.
Activities on 19 Dec
commemorate
Washington's troops
entering Valley Forge.

Length: 108 miles, 138 miles with detour.

Time: 6 driving hours, 3 days with stops; add 1 hour driving time for detour.

Links: Area connects to Philadelphia (*see pages 252–65*) on the east, to Frederick, Maryland (*see page 193*), on the south. Rte 15 south connects to Frederick, Maryland, in 34 miles.

Route: From **VALLEY FORGE** ❶, follow Rte 202 west for 11 miles to Rte 30, continuing 18 miles through several small towns to Rte 10. Turn right to go north 3 miles to Compass. Turn left on Rte 340 through **PENNSYLVANIA DUTCH COUNTRY** ❷, going 9 miles to Intercourse and another 4 miles to Bird-in-Hand.

Detour: Shortly after Bird-in-Hand, turn left on Rte 896 through Amish farmland 3½ miles to Strasburg. Turn left on Rte 741 to drive 4 miles east, then 1½ miles north to Rte 30. Turn left on Rte 30 to enter Lancaster 7 miles west via shopping malls. To resume the route continue west on Rte 340 for 3 miles into Lancaster.

Continue west on Rte 30 for 21 miles to pick up Rte 462 for 6 miles through the centre of **YORK** ❸. Resume westward travel on Rte 30 for 15 miles to **New Oxford**, self-proclaimed 'Antiques Capital of South Central Pennsylvania' with 40 shops, some representing the wares of as many as 60 dealers. Rte 30 continues west another 10 miles to **GETTYSBURG** ❹.

Also worth exploring

Redolent with the smell of chocolate, **Hershey**, **Pennsylvania**, can be reached from Lancaster by driving 16 miles west on Rte 283, then 1 miles north on Rte 743. Top attraction is a tour of **Hershey' Chocolate World** to see how chocolate is made.

Opposite
Hershey's Chocolate World

Photography in Amish country

Visitors often find the Amish lifestyle irresistibly picturesque, but the Amish themselves believe that photographs in which they can be recognised violate the Biblical injunction against making graven images. Moreover, they consider that agreeing to pose for a photograph constitutes the sin of pride. Officially, visitors are discouraged from making photographs or video images of the Amish. Unofficially, casual photography is tolerated if the image does not show a person's face and if the photographer shows discretion and respect.

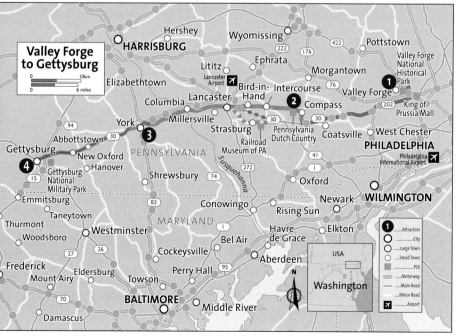

Capital speak

While the official language is English, Capital Region residents speak a peculiar blend of American, Southern and Political English, sometimes bearing only a confusing resemblance to the Queen's English.

DC-specific

Beltway insider (or *Inside the Beltway*) Someone inside Washington political circles.

-gate Washington reporters and politicians routinely add '-gate' to the name of a principal feature in the scandal of the moment. It comes from the Watergate Hotel, where Richard Nixon's operatives bungled a burglary and brought down his presidency.

Governmentality This approach to business emphasises paperwork over progress.

Spin doctor A political operative who informs others how to interpret the news in the best possible light for the politician who employs the spin doctor.

The Spur The northeast corner of the Beltway, also known as *The Spur Parking Lot* during commuting hours (0800–1000 and 1600–1900).

Wore-shing-tun Local pronunciation of the capital city of the US.

General

Alternate is an Americanism indicating not 'every other' but an 'alternative' – as in 'alternate route' or 'alternate service' (as on an American timetable). *Alternative* is usually associated with *lifestyle*, connoting a sexual preference of which the speaker disapproves.

Bed and Breakfast (or *B&B*) Overnight accommodation in a private home or small inn, with or without rooms en suite.

Holiday Not a private holiday (which is called a vacation) but a public holiday such as Independence Day (4 July) or Labor Day (first Monday in September).

Lodging Generic term for all variety of accommodation.

Outlet shopping Shopping at large stores specialising in factory over-runs, returned goods and imperfect goods at reduced prices. 'Factory stores' are often cut-rate retail shops selling a special line of goods direct from the factory.

Food

Barbecue (variously spelled BBQ, barbeque or *bar-b-que*) Sliced, chopped or shredded beef or pork served with a tangy tomato-based sauce. Also beef or pork ribs basted with a similar sauce and cooked over charcoal or wood fire. *Pulled pork* is shredded roasted pork, often doused with a sweetened vinegar sauce.

Brewpub A tavern that brews its own beer. Contrast with *microbrewery*, which is a small brewery that produces high-quality beer or ale for local consumption.

Chips Crisps, usually made from potatoes, sometimes from corn (maize).

Crab The region's favourite crustacean can be served boiled or breaded and fried, but is often presented whole and steamed, leaving the diner to crack and dismantle it at the table. *Crab cakes* are usually a breaded blend of crab meat, onions, breadcrumbs and a binder, fried and served with a mayonnaise-based sauce. *Soft shell crabs* are those that have recently shed their shells. The new shell is tender and edible and considered a delicacy. The whole soft shell crab is usually battered and fried and often served in a sandwich.

Raw bar A section of some restaurants filled with uncooked seafood, especially raw oysters on the half shell. Many raw bars also have other seafood 'cooked' by being marinated in vinegar or citrus juices.

Rockfish A striped bass harvested wild from the Chesapeake Bay and its tributaries.

Index

A

Accident, MD 207
Accidents 22
Accommodation 7, 12
Airports 12, 28
Alexandria 60, 63, 64–5
American Revolution 34
Amish community 205, 270–3, 278
Amish Village 270
Annapolis 170–79
Annmarie Garden 214
Antietam National Battlefield 204
Antiques shop-hopping 71
Appalachian Mountains 76
Appalachian Trail 82
Appomattox 88, 90, 91
Appomattox Court House National Historical Park 88, 90
Arlington 60
Arlington National Cemetery 60
Assateague Island 187, 226, 228
Assateague Island State Park 226
Assawoman Wildlife Area 230

B

Back Bay Natural Wildlife Refuge 152
Baltimore 156–69
Bath County 76, 78
Battery Park, Delaware City 247
Battle Creek Cypress Swamp Sanctuary 213
Bayshore Northern Neck 128, 130
Bedford 90–1
Belle Island, Richmond 110
Belle Isle State Park, Tidewater 134
Berlin 226, 228
Bethany Beach 230
Big Elk Creek 224
Blackwater National Wildlife Refuge 182
Blue Ridge Mountains 76, 82
Bombay Hook National Wildlife Refuge 229
Brandywine Battlefield Historic Park 244
Brandywine Creek State Park 243
Brandywine Park, Wilmington 237
Brandywine Valley 244–51
Brandywine Zoo 237
Breakdowns 22
Breezy Point Beach 208
Brown's Island 110
Bryce Resort 78
Busch Gardens 136
Buses 18, 29

C

C&D Canal 247
C&D Canal Wildlife Area 247
C&O Canal 47
C&O Canal National Historic Park 194
Caledon Natural Area 132
Calvert Cliffs State Park 213
Cambridge 180, 182
Camper vans 22
Cape Henlopen State Park 232
Cape May 234
Capitol Building 43
Capitol Hill 43

Car hire 22–3
Caravans 22
Cass 86
Catoctin Mountain 190, 192
Catoctin Wildlife Preserve and Zoo 190, 192
Centreville 250
Chadds Ford 244, 246
Chancellorsville Battlefield 125
Charlottesville 91–3
Chesapeake Beach 208, 210
Chesapeake City 218, 220
Chestertown 220–1
Children 12–13
Chimborazo Hill 117–18
Chincoteague Island 187
Chincoteague National Wildlife Refuge 187
Civil War 36
Climate 13
Clothing 18
Crisfield 188
Culpeper 74
Culture 36–7
Cumberland 198–200
Cunningham Falls State Park 190
Currency 13–14
Customs regulations 14

D

Dark Hollow Falls 82
Dayton 86
Deep Creek 201
Delaware 229–30, 232–44, 247, 248–9
Delaware City 247, 250
Delmarva Peninsula 180–89
Disabilities, travellers with 20
Documents 13, 22
Dover 229
Drinking and driving 14–15, 23
Driving 22–7
Du Pont family 236, 239

E

Easton 183
Eating out 15
Electricity 13
Elk Neck State Park 223
Endless Caverns 80
Entry formalities 13

F

Fair Hill 224
Fairmount Park 264
False Cape State Park 152
Fenwick Island 230
Ferry 143
Festivals 15–16
First Landing/Seashore State Park 152
Food 7, 16, 280
Fort Delaware State Park 247
Franklin, Benjamin 256, 257
Frederick 193
Fredericksburg 120, 122–4
Fredericksburg area 120–7
Fredericksburg Battlefield 125

Fredericksburg and Spotsylvania National Military Park 125
Front Royal 74
Frostburg 207

G
Geography 30–31
George Washington Birthplace National Monument 132
George Washington National Forest 86
Georgetown 46–7
Gettysburg 266–8
Gettysburg Address 268
Gettysburg National Military Park 269
Gloucester 131
Government 54
Grand Caverns 80
Great Dismal Swamp National Wildlife Refuge 154
Great Falls 194
Gunston Hall 62

H
Hagerstown 202–3
Hampton 146–7
Hampton Roads 146–55
Hancock 207
Harpers Ferry 203–5
Harrisonburg 86
Havre de Grace 221–2
Health 15, 16
Hershey 278
Highland County 76, 78
History 31–6
Hopewell 112, 114
Hotels 12

I
Independence National Historical Park 257–8
Information 14, 24
Insurance 15, 25
Itineraries 38–9
Iwo Jima Memorial 62

J
Jamestown 136–8
Janes Island State Park 188
Jefferson Patterson Park and Museum 213

K
Kanawha Canal Locks 109
Kent Island 222–3
Key, Francis Scott 161
Kilmarnock 134

L
Lake Anna State Park 126
Lancaster, PA 270
Lancaster, VA 134
Lee, Robert E. 64
Leonardtown 216
Lewes 232
Lexington 79
Liberty Bell 257–8
Library of Congress 43
Lilypons Water Gardens 195
Lincoln, Abraham 45, 268
Lincoln Memorial 49
Longwood Gardens, Pennsylvania 247–8
Luray Caverns 80
Lynchburg 93–4

M
Malvern Hill 118
Manassas Battlefield 68
Maps 16
Maryland 156–225
Maryland Zoo in Baltimore 161
Meem's Bottom Bridge 86
Mennonite community 270, 272–3
Middle Peninsula 131
Middleburg 74
Mill Grove 274
Monocacy National Battlefield 193
Monongahela National Forest 86
Motels 12
Mount Vernon 62
Museums 16–17

N
Nassawango Creek Cypress Swamp Preserve 185
National D-Day Memorial 90–1
National holidays 15
National parks 17
National Zoo 50–51
Native Americans 31–2
Natural Bridge 80
New Castle 248–9
New Market Battlefield 81
New Oxford, PA 278
Newlyn Grist Mill, Pennsylvania 249
Newport News 148–9
Newport News Park 148, 154
Norfolk 149–50
North Chesapeake Bay 218–25
North East 223
Notes 285–6

O
Oakland 205–6
Ocean City 231
Opening times 17
Orkney Springs 78
Oxford 183

P
Packing 17
Pamplin Historical Park 114
Parking 25
Passports 13
Pea Patch Island 247
Pemberton Historic Park 184
Pennsylvania 244, 246, 247–48, 249–50, 252–79
Pennsylvania Dutch Country 270–73
Pentagon, The 65
Petersburg 115
Petersburg National Battlefield Park 116
Petrol 24
Philadelphia 252–65
Philadelphia Zoo 264
Photography 278
Piedmont 88–99
Pocomoke River State Park 185
Point Lookout 211
Police 26
Poolesville 196
Port Tobacco 212
Portsmouth 151
Post 17
Prince Frederick 213

Public holidays 17–18
Public transport 18, 29, 143

R
Reading 18
Reedville 134
Reflecting Pool 49
Rehoboth Beach 232
Richmond 100–111
Richmond battlefields Park 112–19
Richmond National Battlefield Park 116–17
Road signs 26–7
Roanoke 95–6
Rock Creek Park 50–51
Rockville 194
Rocky Gap State Park 199
Roddy Road Covered Bridge 192
Roosevelt Island 65

S
Safety and security 17, 20, 23, 26
Salisbury 184
Salisbury Zoo 184
Sandy Point State Park 174
Scottsville 98
Seasons 13
Seat belts 26
Seneca Rocks 86
Shenandoah 76–87
Shenandoah Caverns 80
Shenandoah National Park 82
Sherwood Forest 110
Shopping 18–19, 71
Sideling Cut 207
Signers of Declaration of Independence 173
Sky Meadows State Park 70
Smith Island 188
Smithfield 154
Smithsonian Institution 44, 46
Snow Hill 185
Snowshoe 86
Solomons Island 214
Spas 76–7
Speed limits 26
Sperryville 71–2
Sport 16
Spotsylvania Court House Battlefield 125
Spruce Knob 86
St Mary's City 215
St Michaels 186
Star-Spangled Banner 161
Staunton 84–5
Stephen Decatur Memorial Park 228
Stevensville 222
Stony Man Mountain 82
Strasburg 74
Sugarloaf Mountain 195
Surry County 143
Swallow Falls 201

T
Tangier Island 134, 188
Tappahannock 131, 134
Tawes Drive Covered Bridge 224

Tax 18
Telephones 17, 19
Terrapin Nature Park 222
Tidewater 128–35
Tilghman Island 186
Time 20
Tipping 18
Toilets 19
Tolls 26
Trains 18, 29
Travellers with disabilities 20

U
Uniontown 196
Upper Northern Neck 132–3
Urbanna 131
US Supreme Court 43

V
Valley Forge 274–5
Valley Forge National Historical Park 274
Vietnam Veterans Memorial 49
Virginia 60–155, 187, 226, 228, 231
Virginia Beach 152–3
Virginia Living Museum 148–9
Virginia Zoological Park 149
Visas 13

W
Warrenton 70–71
Washington, DC 10–11, 40–59
Washington, George 64
Washington, Little 71–2
Washington Monument, Baltimore 164
Washington Monument, Washington 49
Water Country USA 140
West Chester 250
West Virginia 86
Westminster 196
Westmoreland State Park 132
White House, The 52
White's Ferry 196
Wilderness Battlefield 125
Wildlife 82
Williamsburg 140–42
Wilmington 236–43
Wilson Bridge 207
Winchester 72–3
Wineries 74, 96
Wye Mills 222–3
Wyeth family 246

Y
York 276–7
Yorktown 137–8
Yorktown Battlefield 137

Acknowledgements

Project management: Cambridge Publishing Management Limited
Project editor: Karen Beaulah
Series design: Fox Design
Cover design: Liz Lyons Design
Layout: Cambridge Publishing Management Limited
Mapwork: PCGraphics (UK) Ltd
Repro and image setting: PDQ Digital Media Solutions Ltd and Cambridge Publishing Management Limited
Printed and bound in India by: Ajanta Offset & Packaging Ltd

We would like to thank Ethel Davies for the photographs used in this book, to whom the copyright belongs, with the exception of the following:

Tom Bross (pages 11, 112, 114, 120, 122, 123, 136 and 146)

Bryce Resort (page 78)

Delaware Art Museum (pages 18 and 239)

Dreamstime (pages 52 (Timehacker) and 159 (Gian Marco Valente))

Pat Harris (pages 239 and 266)

David Lyon (pages 236, 242, 250, 258, 272A, 272B, 275 and 276)

Mauritius World Pictures/Photoshot (page 148)

Pictures Colour Library (pages 38 and 56)

Stillman Rogers (pages 23, 30, 174, 176, 190, 192, 194, 195, 198, 200, 201, 202, 204, 205, 206, 211, 212, 213, 215, 222 and 223).

Virginia Tourism Corporation (pages 100B (Douglas Peebles), 107 (Richard T. Nowitz), 110 (Keith Lanpher), 133 (Tidewater Colonial Historic National Park) and 150).

Wikimedia Commons (page 199 (Sallicio))

World Pictures/Photoshot (pages 21, 24, 32, 92, 93, 102, 108, 141, 162 and 264)

York County Convention & Visitors Bureau (page 277)

Feedback form

We're committed to providing the very best up-to-date information in our travel guides and constantly strive to make them as useful as they can be. You can help us to improve future editions by letting us have your feedback. Just take a few minutes to complete and return this form to us.

When did you buy this book? ....

....

Where did you buy it? (Please give town/city and, if possible, name of retailer)

....

....

When did you/do you intend to travel to Washington DC? ....

....

For how long (approx)? ....

How many people in your party? ....

Which cities, national parks and other locations did you/do you intend mainly to visit?

....

....

....

....

Did you/will you:
❑ Make all your travel arrangements independently?
❑ Travel on a fly-drive package?
Please give brief details: ....

....

Did you/do you intend to use this book:
❑ For planning your trip?   ❑ Both?
❑ During the trip itself?

Did you/do you intend also to purchase any of the following travel publications for your trip?
A road map/atlas (please specify) ....
Other guidebooks (please specify) ....

Have you used any other Thomas Cook guidebooks in the past? If so, which?

....

....

Please rate the following features of *driving guides Washington DC* for their value to you (Circle VU for 'very useful', U for 'useful', NU for 'little or no use'):

The *Travel facts* section on pages 12–21	VU	U	NU
The *Driver's guide* section on pages 22–27	VU	U	NU
The recommended driving routes throughout the book	VU	U	NU
Information on towns and cities, National Parks, etc	VU	U	NU
The maps of towns and cities, parks, etc	VU	U	NU

Please use this space to tell us about any features that in your opinion could be changed, improved, or added in future editions of the book, or any other comments you would like to make concerning the book:

....

....

....

....

....

....

....

....

....

Your age category: ❏ 21–30   ❏ 31–40   ❏ 41–50   ❏ over 50

Your name: Mr/Mrs/Miss/Ms ....

(First name or initials) ....

(Last name) ....

Your full address: (Please include postal or zip code)

....

....

....

....

....

Your daytime telephone number: ....

Please detach this page and send it to: driving guides Series Editor, Thomas Cook Publishing, PO Box 227, Coningsby Road, Peterborough PE3 8SB.

Alternatively, you can e-mail us at: *books@thomascook.com*